# The Insiders' Guide to Self-Help Groups in Illinois

**Daryl Holtz Isenberg, PhD**

## Illinois Self-Help Coalition

# The Insiders' Guide to Self-Help Groups in Illinois

Published by
**Illinois Self-Help Coalition**
Wright College South
3400 North Austin Avenue
Chicago, Illinois 60634
Phone: 773/481-8837  Fax: 773/481-8917
www.selfhelp-illinois.org

For information on ordering copies of the *Insiders' Guide to Self-Help Groups in Illinois*, contact the Illinois Self-Help Coalition at 773/481-8837. Cost is $20.00 per book, $5.00 shipping and handling.

# Table of Contents

# SECTION II: REGISTER OF SELF-HELP GROUPS IN ILLINOIS

# How the *Insiders' Guide* Can Help You

Since 1978 the Illinois Self-Help Coalition has published directories to help connect individuals to self-help groups. The new *Insiders' Guide* is designed to provide an even more comprehensive introduction to the self-help community. Learn the first steps to take to put yourself in the caring hands of self-help groups, the different ways in which these groups operate (from providing education and advocacy to creating a deep bonding), and how to get the most out of your participation. The *Insiders' Guide* introduces you to some extraordinary people involved in self-help groups, people who are willing to share their stories so that you may begin to realize that even with a life-threatening condition, you, too, can "stop and smell the roses." We hope their stories will motivate you to use the information provided on Illinois self-help organizations as a pathway to supportive new friends and reliable answers.

The *Insiders' Guide* shows you how to optimize your experience in a self-help group, which can help you achieve new possibilities in your life and health. The *Insiders' Guide*:

- Directs you to health information and support for nearly 500 problems via 2500 self-help groups, health organizations, alliances, and clearinghouses, including Internet resources.

- Provides encouragement for newcomers who had never thought of joining a self-help group.

- Assists those who are seeking help for family and friends.

- Educates professionals and self-help providers about the roles and responsibilities in self-help groups.

- Describes how to recognize successful group leadership and to get what you need during the group meeting, so you can get comfortable in a self-help group.

- Offers advice about how to "shop" for a group that meets your particular needs.

## The People Behind the *Insiders' Guide*

Members of the Illinois Self-Help Coalition have a long history of creating state and national databases of group information, publishing directories, and assisting in the development of groups. Self-helpers volunteering with the Coalition worked closely for two decades with Len Borman, PhD, founder of the Self-Help Center in Evanston. In the early 1970s, Len was one of the first researchers to bring attention to self-help as a national resource that could be better organized to address health and life needs that were not being adequately met by existing professional health and human services. Although people may generally be aware of the thousands of groups for hundreds of different problems, only members of those groups are likely to know the extent to which group members help one another resolve common and individual problems. As the benefits of groups become more widely known, perhaps they will be more effectively used to bring a humanizing element to an increasingly dehumanizing health care system.

Coalition members have been central to state and national developments in self-help. Realizing the need for recognizing the contributions of self-help to the health of American citizens, we sought the assistance of Surgeon General C. Everett Koop, MD, in conducting a national workshop on self-help and public health, followed by a book of recommendations and meetings on similar topics. Increased awareness among health and public service professionals was accomplished through inclusion of self-help group objectives in publications related to *Healthy People 2000* and *Healthy People 2010*, self-help tracks in dozens of national meetings on topics ranging from the benefits of self-help groups in reversing heart disease to their role in care at the end of life, and consumer involvement in testimony, contracts, and grants related to 13 federal agencies.

The primary focus of the Coalition is to bring self-help peer leaders and supporters together. Through our Internet Web site, we provide information and offer courses on self-help leadership. In addition, we are bringing to Illinois a unique self-help program for student athletes at www.athletenetwork.com. Through the Coalition members' participation in national conferences and a research study, we have a strong commitment to improving the ability of self-help groups to provide support at the end-of-life.

## Resources

- If you are interested in beginning a group or want to attend networking programs contact us at:
Illinois Self-Help Coalition, Wright College, 3400 N Austin Ave, Chicago, IL 60634
773/481-8837  Fax 773/481-8917  Email: selfhelp@enteract.com  Web site: www.selfhelp-illinois.org

- To find related services or groups not listed in the *Insiders' Guide*, call Connections: 847/689-1080.

- For additional groups in central Illinois, contact the Family Services/Self-Help Center at:
405 S State St, Champaign, IL 61820  217/352-0099  Fax 217/352-9512  TDD 217/352-0160
Web site: www.prairienet.org/selfhelp

- To order *The Self-Help Sourcebook* or to register national groups, contact the American Self-Help Clearinghouse, Northwest Covenant Medical Center, 25 Pocano Rd, Denville, NJ 07834
973/625-3037  Fax 973/635-9053  Web site: www.cmhc.com/selfhelp

## Acknowledgments

This book is dedicated to the true heroes and "trusted servants" in self-help groups. Quietly, in many cases after work and family caregiving responsibilities, these volunteers respond with compassion to their Illinois neighbors whose lives or health are in jeopardy.

We present their story in a new format, a departure from our first nine editions, which began in 1978 with just 200 listings. We are immensely grateful to the many people who contributed their expertise in developing the database or in preparing the articles for this edition. No service or product of the Illinois Self-Help Coalition has been produced without the motivation and hands-on support of Maurine Pyle. For 15 years, our published documents and proposals have reflected Hannah Hedrick's writing and editing skills. I will be forever grateful for the countless hours she contributed in producing the *Guide*. For 10 years, Burt Friedman, our beloved volunteer and database magician, has also desktop-published the entire directory database. Len Jason has made numerous suggestions for this book and solicited volunteers to help organize it. Shirley Sachs, Barbara Giloth, Therese and John Goodrich, Ed Zaleski, Norm Kellerman, and Ellen Pesch responded quickly to requests for articles, advice, and expertise for this project. The remarkable staff at Wright College inspired us to keep going when times were hard. And I want to give special thanks to my son, Marc Isenberg, for sharing his writing skills in our first chapter.

We are, as always, profoundly indebted to Ed Madara of the American Self-Help Clearinghouse and to Sharon Dorsey of the Champaign, Illinois Family Services/Self-Help Center for sending self-help group information and articles to us. Librarian Laura Sklansky offered helpful ideas for the Internet section. Volunteers Esther Mann, Burt Batchco, and Virginia Gordon edited updated self-help group information. LeRoy Murphy heroically organized the database, and our dedicated staff, Jonelle Medina and Maria Navarro pulled the database work together. Julie Rosenbaum brought order out of chaos by organizing the categories for the group listings. Mary-Ann Lupa of Lupa Productions contributed the cover. Without the timely editing and desktop publishing of Mary O'Leary of MouseWerks, we would still be going round in a maze.

And my life companion, Steve, has my gratitude for his insightful advice, as a true self-helper, on all aspects of this project; for critiquing each section of the book; and for his support (including doing the laundry alone) for the months when my primary relationship has been with my computer.

***This edition was made possible by generous support from the MR Bauer Foundation, the Barr Fund, and Alfred and Sylvia Holtz.***

# SECTION I:

# THE POWER
# OF SELF-HELP

# You Are Not Alone

*In every community, whether one has lost a child or had heart surgery, there are people who weathered that storm and are reaching out to help others.*

**Researcher Brian O'Connell in**
***Voices from the Heart*, Jossey Bass, 1998**

## The Editor's Journey

When my cousin was diagnosed with a rare neck cancer, I found myself absorbed in her experience. I searched to learn how to still her nighttime anxieties and help her get through the daily terrors—alarming symptoms and the daunting health care system—of those first years as a cancer patient. I joined organizations initiated by cancer patients: Make-Today-Count, Cancer Contact (the first peer run phone support for cancer patients), and the Center for Attitudinal Healing in Tiburon, California. I found that people got more help from each other than from professionals or hospitals.

In these groups, I learned that individuals whose lives were threatened could move from immaturity to wisdom at any age. I was baffled when young children appeared to accept their death with serenity rather than fear. This transformational process taught me how to use a life-threatening illness to put everything in perspective. After receiving the diagnosis and dealing with the immediate medical crisis, many people in self-help groups are able to learn from peers to attach less importance to their other problems and to go right to the heart of living each moment.

To this day, I continue to be moved by the generous people who actively participate in groups. They teach us so much about our capacity to love and to heal emotional wounds. As a mother of a child with a brain tumor observed recently, "Being in a self-help group like this really strips us down to our common humanity. Families worried about a child with cancer are alike, no matter where they come from or what they do for a living."

My continued ties with cancer groups have helped me cope with the deaths of loved ones and learn how to grieve and let go. My positive experiences are echoed in thousands of persuasive personal stories exchanged at self-help group meetings and elsewhere, as members help one another sort out difficult relationships, parenting struggles, coping with a new diagnosis, surviving a serious illness, and even experiencing death and loss. While professionals can diagnose and prescribe, self-helpers closer to the problem work together to address the larger issues, including excuses and denial, that keep them from enjoying the highest possible quality of life.

I've since been involved in other self-help groups, for other reasons. I have learned what I can do to control my asthma, take charge of crises, get support and guidance on parenting issues, and receive help with my most recent concern, aging parents. Professionally, I have worked with hundreds of other groups and have witnessed each of them help members overcome feelings of victimization, helplessness, and despair.

Groups offer practical knowledge and give support specific to each crisis that is not available from any other source. In a group conducted according to self-help principles, no one leaves feeling discounted, unheard, or more confused than when they came. This is not always the case when people leave a rushed professional encounter during which only the bare medical necessities are addressed.

## Discover Others like You

People in groups commonly say, "My group got me through the loss of my child, . . . my cancer treatments, . . . my divorce." They even say, "My self-help group saved my life by helping me learn how to express anger without hurting anyone, . . . by getting me off drugs, . . . by helping me learn how to live with diabetes, . . . by making me feel that I am never alone." A cancer survivor who used to be a too-busy professional says, "I learned to smell the roses." A widow says, "My family has been great, but they get tired of hearing about my grief. Friends in our widowers' group go for walks and to movies, help me live in my empty house, and advise me about money."

Why have we turned to each other for help? Only 50 years ago we had the support of friends and family in times of crisis. Today, our increasingly mobile society continues to reduce that tradition of help. Managed care attempts to counteract runaway health care costs have resulted in reduced services and less time for personal interactions. As a result, people with life-disrupting problems feel even more isolated and alone.

To counter this, more and more people are turning to each other. A recently released 10-year study of 8,000 Americans by the MacArthur Foundation Research Network on Successful Midlife Development found that 18.8% of respondents have attended a self-help group, a 67% increase over 1970. This growth, researchers suggest, probably reflects increasingly restricted access to health care and the desire of many Americans to play an active role in their own treatment. Today an estimated 15,000,000 Americans are coming together with others who share similar difficult circumstances or health problems.

## Listen to Their Stories

Who are these people? They are just like you and me, regular people dealing with life-disrupting problems. We can recognize ourselves in the stories shared at group meetings. In self-help groups, such stories are the communication medium. The storyteller describes his or her perception of a challenging event or crisis and shares strategies for coping. These tales allow listeners to assimilate and apply these remedies in their own lives. Inspired and motivated, listeners are persuaded that they too can get through this ordeal. The members are willing to entrust the group with their highly personal stories because of the absolute confidentiality that is intrinsic to self-help groups.

The following stories are a sampling of many collected by the author from individuals during hundreds of group meetings, presentations, summaries of writings and commentary, and interviews. In most cases, storytellers requested anonymity. In some instances, the story reflects several stories woven together to convey a broader scope of the topic.

Perhaps these stories will strike a familiar chord within you.

## Alcoholics Anonymous (AA)

*Story One*

"I would have continued to drink or use more drugs if not for a man I was doing some work for, who broke his anonymity and invited me to a Narcotics Anonymous convention. If you can imagine a convention with thousands of people in recovery, you would know that it could change your life. When I accepted the invitation, I realized that I was tired of where I was in my life—wrecking cars, afraid, bankrupt, and desolate.

"I didn't make friends easily then. I preferred to solve my own problems. Most people coming to the first AA meetings don't want to be there. They come because a wife or a girlfriend threatens to leave, or the court mandates attendance for a Driving Under the Influence (DUI) charge or for domestic violence. At first, I didn't want to change my life. I didn't want to focus on my character defects of overspending or lying so people won't know who I am. I didn't like some of the people in the group. I had a problem with the idea of "God." I just wanted to stop drinking. Seven of ten people don't stay clean and some might die.

"When this first guy talked about his problem with drugs, and I heard others in every meeting talk about who they are, what they learned, where they're going, I was attracted to that possibility. People were genuine. When they tell us about their life, it gives us freedom to be just as honest. I don't forget the first or last time I was drunk. The 12 steps of AA make it easier to focus on character defects and changes in our lives, one step at a time. I learned to be honest, open-minded, willing. AA taught me to see in the people I disliked the same behaviors that I didn't like in myself. Then, I could have compassion. I learned that the newcomer is the most important person at the meeting because when someone comes from a binge, they are the most real. I feel it and get emotional every time. I hear myself in that newcomer and I don't forget where I came from. I learned the language of recovery. This language gives me a daily reprieve of my sentence. For instance, I learned that I had to focus on something to gain faith if I rejected God and higher power. At first, I focused on the faces of the people in AA that I admire. I substitute Good Orderly Direction for the name of God.

"For people thinking about joining a 12-step group in Illinois, hotlines at AA's central offices are listed in every phonebook in the state and country. Everyone who answers those phones is in recovery. You can tell them you're new in town or that you're having a problem. They are truly helpful people. They will send you information and you can ask them about meetings that you will be comfortable in.

"It is easiest to begin attending meetings at a clubhouse. Clubhouses host many 12-step group meetings all day and night long. At each meeting, the chair asks if anyone is from out of town, new to this group, or if this is a first meeting for anyone. Members will come up after the meeting and will welcome and orient newcomers.

"You will observe something that you admire in some of the people at the meetings. As soon as you're ready, you can approach someone to become your sponsor. Choosing a sponsor isn't forever. You can choose someone else with different qualities later. But you will want a sponsor that has had at least a year in the program and it is important that your sponsor is the same sex as you to keep the relationship uncomplicated."

*Story Two*

"Prior to going to AA, I was hopeless and helpless. I found myself on skid row. I never knew what it was like to not drink and drug on a daily basis. When I got to the first meeting, a recovering alcoholic told me, 'If we can't relate to being an alcoholic, we can relate to being negative.' I could definitely relate to being negative. And he said, 'Try to find something positive from the meeting to focus on.' You can't stay in treatment forever. But you can stay in AA one day at a time. We are recovering from a seemingly hopeless condition. It's been a treat to see God use me to help others."

## Alzheimer's Association

*The following address was presented at a seminar for professionals and families of Alzheimer's patients.*

"I was asked to talk about being a caregiver. I do not consider myself a 'caregiver.' I am a wife whose husband has a combination of terrible diseases, and so I am a helper or facilitator.

"My husband does not need me to physically take care of him. My big challenge is to help him make his life easier, to keep things calm and normal, to help him structure his days so that he has interesting activities, but does not get overtired . . . and to drive him wherever he wants or needs to go.

"I must do all of this while keeping calm and pleasant. I must try not to react to his constant verbal abuse! Enormous task! How well do I succeed? I keep trying, and learning. I cannot tell you that I have solved the problems, or that life is beautiful and fun (we do still have some good hours and even days), but I will share with you some of the ways that seem to make life a little better for both of us.

"I learned the hard way that one of the most important ways that I can help him is to take care of myself. When I am sick, he falls apart. He needs me to be strong for our situation to remain stable. If I am tired or achy or in any way incapacitated, he becomes more irritable and irrational. If I can maintain a calm, orderly, stress-free environment for him, he functions better. And, if I get sick, who will be there to help him?

"I prepared myself when I began to notice some early signs that all was not well, which happened most often when he was in a stressful situation. He drove erratically. He began to lose his sense of direction. I lost him in airports, large malls, and unfamiliar or crowded places. His behavior became increasingly impulsive and irritable; he began to have some memory loss. Although these behaviors occasionally may seem part of normal aging, they became more frequent and soon established a pattern.

"I began to make and implement long-range plans. I took on some of his tasks to help make life more stress-free for him. I was already taking care of the mail and writing all of the checks. I began to do the small errands, such as taking the car in for servicing. We both took out long-term care insurance policies.

"I had already quit my job to computerize his office, and I chose not to do the consulting that I had planned to do. I realized that I could not take on any regular volunteer jobs. I began to plan some at-home activities for myself that would keep me available to him but interested and still living my own life as much as possible. I maintain a regular exercise schedule for myself. I enrolled in a writing workshop, and even splurged and bought myself a new computer!

"When he was diagnosed and had to stop working, I called the Alzheimer Help Line to find an appropriate support group. When I began to go to meetings, the other spouses were much further along in the disease. It is frightening to hear what I have to look forward to, but knowledge is power. I can prepare myself and won't be as surprised and shocked if my husband begins to exhibit these symptoms. The group helps me with problem solving both directly, by addressing my concerns, and indirectly, by giving me ideas while discussing theirs. For example, my husband has had to stop driving, and refused to let me hire a driver for him. At a support session, one of the women told us that her husband accepted a housekeeper's help but would not have a home health aide in the house. When I got home, I told my husband that I needed our cleaning woman more frequently, and that she could drive him wherever he wanted to go when she was there. He agreed!

"I find great comfort in the compassion, warmth, and goodwill of my fellow spouses, vital to my current emotional well being. Most important is the setting in which I can share my feelings, fears, and successes. Because I feel that I have to protect my husband and his privacy, I do not discuss his strange behavior in more public settings, but I can and do among the people who understand, my support group.

"I try to keep my sense of humor, wonder at the beauty of the world, and, most of all, my own identity. I am mother, grandmother, daughter, retired human services worker AND wife of a wonderful man who is terribly sick. Caregiver? Not part of my self-image!

## Attention Deficit Disorder (ADD)

"I never really understood the value of self-help peer support until my son began having problems in school at the age of 4. After 4 years of misdiagnosis, failed treatment and much blaming, frustration, and disappointment, one of my professional peer/friends suggested that my son might have ADD. I finally had his diagnosis confirmed by a neurologist. Not knowing anything about ADD, I looked for other parents who were dealing with children with ADD. I desperately needed compassion, empathy, knowledge, understanding, people to share with, solutions to problems, and proven resources. I looked in a directory of self-help groups, but there were no groups for ADD. I felt very alone—a helping professional who was helpless.

"It wasn't until several years later that I read about two women who had started an ADD parent support group. I immediately contacted them. I got involved in the organization, serving as secretary, and the healing began. Fifteen years later, I am thrilled to be able to say that my son is an independent, successful, self-supporting college graduate.

"Since then, the first thing I have done in my life every time I've faced a new problem is to seek a self-help group. When there hasn't been one, I started one!"

## Bereaved Parents, USA

### Therese Goodrich

"In 1971 our 15 year-old daughter, Paula, was struck by a car and died instantly. We were overwhelmed with our new experience of parental grief. We had no one to say 'It's all right if you're up all night and you think you're going crazy.' No one told us that the anger and guilt, the feelings of loneliness and sadness that came over us in waves, were normal.

"We had feelings we didn't understand. I had moments of panic when I thought that if we could just get our other children past 15—when our daughter died—if they can just get past 15. The youngest one, who looks the most like Paula, said, 'Mom, I'll be Paula for you.' I told her, 'You be Roseanne. That's enough of a job for you.' Later, the other children were able to tell us that they felt neglected and thought that Paula was more special to us.

"We found that women grieve differently than men. Fathers tend to look into the future; when a child dies, that future is taken away. Women, the nurturers, carry the child in the womb; the loss of today, of shared routines and responsibilities, is hardest for mothers. We talk about these and other things in our group."

## Cancer Wellness Center

"Upon my diagnosis of rectal cancer, my wife and I were stunned. We had friends and family for immediate support and they were of great help. But we had no one to help us in terms of coping with the suddenness of the onset of the cancer and the emotions of having cancer. A physician gave us the telephone number of a group that was just forming. It's been 8 ¾ years since my diagnosis and I've been with the Cancer Wellness Center for 8 ½ years. It has given me tremendous benefit in terms of releasing the emotions of the fears of cancer and it's given me camaraderie with others who have had quite long survivals."

## Chronic Fatigue Syndrome

**Carole Howard,** Chicago Chronic Fatigue Syndrome Association

"For the newcomer to the support group, one of the first comments is that it's a great relief that here at last are people just like me. I thought I was the only one. I can't believe that I just found people who understand my problems, the brain fog and all the rest. I thought I was going crazy!

"Because of the nature of this illness, many people who meet become phone friends and resources for each other. It's truly wonderful to know others who really understand. My husband and family think I'm lazy. They just don't believe me. They say I don't look sick."

## Debtor's Anonymous (DA)

"I initially joined Debtor's Anonymous because I found myself in terrible straits, after struggling with debt and personal financial goals all my life. I was jeopardizing my own, and even my company's, credit, as well as my relationship with my wife. The phone rang constantly and my children made excuses for me. When creditors called my employers, I found myself being dunned for bills. I had bottomed out.

"Now, my phone has stopped ringing. For the first time, I have been able to put a financial plan together through guidelines in DA's program. At work, I sat down with my supervisor and told him that I had gotten myself into a self-help group and am working on straightening my finances out with the help of DA. He has been very encouraging."

## Divorce Anonymous (DA)

"I joined Divorce Anonymous because I had low self-esteem. My emotions were topsy-turvy. I was seeing a therapist but I found that I needed a little more. The first meeting is the hardest, but by the end I felt so relaxed. DA has given me a full range of emotions; it's given me friends and I've become a full person."

## Manic-Depressive and Depressive Association

**Rose Kurland,** Manic-Depressive and Depressive Association of Chicago

"It was a long time before I was correctly diagnosed with manic-depressive illness. Five years later, I still had not spoken to anyone who had manic-depression outside of the hospital. When a friend's sister asked if I knew of any group specifically for persons with bipolar affective disorders, I didn't know why she would want to go to one. Without any idea of what I would get from a support group, I decided to help start one. At first, I read all I could at medical libraries and spoke with individuals who had started other support groups. We arranged for a noted psychiatrist to give a presentation at a library. I doubted if more than a handful of people would attend, but 120 showed up. We all lived with so many stigmas. Families didn't want to discuss mental illness with outsiders. Then, professionals knew very little about the disease. No one seemed to know how to help us return to a normal life.

"Second only to raising my children, the years I spent in the Manic-Depressive and Depressive Association were the most valuable years of my life. Through our organization, I became friendly with the most interesting, knowledgeable and kind people. I learned from the best scientific authorities and from fellow self help members to understand manic-depression, and how to cope and get on with my life. In all that I learned in a self-help group, I appreciate most what I learned about compassion. The homeless person walking down the street could have been me."

## Men Overcoming Violence

"Our self-help group of men talk together about violence toward women, children, and other men. We come from several sources: a girlfriend says she is leaving if he does not get help; the court orders him to the group; he is afraid his wife will ask for a divorce. The first step is becoming aware of what we do when we're stressed or hurt and talking about the violence each of us caused. The second step is learning how to end the violence. Some of the men have been in the group for months and even years. Taking personal responsibility for violence and asking for help brings a change for those who stay connected to the group. Some men do not change. In our group, men forge ahead learning how anger explodes and support each other to let it fade away. Sadly, the damage to others cannot be reversed. Thankfully, we found that we can live our lives another way."

## Multiple Sclerosis (MS)

"I was diagnosed with MS in my late 20's. After I had three children and was in my late 30's, I developed fatigue and poor balance. I was afraid and alone until the MS Society suggested that I attend a self-help group. For the first time I was able to talk to people with MS about parenting, fatigue, and the uncertainty of MS symptoms. I learned to manage the fatigue by taking naps, cooling my wrists with cold compresses, and worst of all, accepting that I needed to use a wheel chair. After getting my new wheels I was able to attend my children's school programs and had energy to go Disney World.

"Before the group, I sat back and assumed there was nothing that could be done for MS. Therefore, I never looked into or discussed my treatment options with my doctor. The group gave me information and courage to ask my physician topics I had on my mind concerning sexuality and new treatments. With the help of my doctor, I tried new medications. Some helped reduce fatigue and others didn't help at all. But now I am a partner with my physician and feel more in charge of my health treatment."

## Lung Transplant Support Group

**Carole Rothman**

"Before I had lung transplant surgery, we had a consultation with the transplantation staff. They told me I would be in the intensive care unit for 3 days and I might be back at work in 3 months. When I was still in the hospital 3 months later, I wondered what was wrong with me. I first went to the support group, because I needed to find out if something was wrong. I learned with a transplant it is normal to have so many complications. Many things can go wrong because of medication reactions, transplant rejection, and a suppressed immune system. No matter what the hospital staff might say, I needed to see others who made it before I could accept that when I have a setback I won't die.

"Some people in our group have been on the organ donation waiting list for 2 years and they attend every meeting. I think the group is really helpful to them. Not only do they learn first hand about these complications, they also see there are so many of us

alive and breathing. Had I gone to the group earlier, I know that I would have avoided much of my anguish.

"After a presentation at our support group from the regional organ bank, I became a volunteer to raise awareness about organ donation. On my one-year anniversary, I sent a letter to the family of my donor through the organ bank. In her letter to me, the donor's mother let me know how happy she is to learn that I am doing well."

## Parents Anonymous (PA)

**Susan**, Parent Leader
From the Winter 1994 edition of *Statewide News from Parents Anonymous (Illinois)*; reprinted by permission of the author.

"Ask for help. If you are losing control with your kids, please ask for help. Terrified of what I might do, I finally told a counselor what was happening with my son and me. The counselor told me that I just needed more time to myself. More desperate than before, I left the office thinking the counselor had told me that the cure for my lifetime of abuse was to go home and take a hot bath.

"When I told my spouse what I understood, he said it sounded like I should talk more to my counselor about this. Asking for help once was hard enough…. I soon began to scream for help. One day, I panicked and then decided to call the Department of Children and Family Services (DCFS) on myself. DCFS interviewed me and recommended some respite daycare over the next 12 weeks. It took me 7 weeks to find a licensed provider who would take my kids, which left me with 5 weeks of care.

"When the period of daycare was about to end, I became very anxious. What would I do now? I remember lying in bed at night and begging God, 'Please don't let me do this anymore. Don't let me scream at or hit my son.'

"Then a social worker who happened to do childcare for Parents Anonymous (PA) in my town suggested I try PA. At that point I was willing to try anything. My first meeting replaced despair with hope. My second meeting replaced helplessness with new ideas. It's now been 3 years and I am the parent leader of my group. Just taking home even one small bit of information once a week has given me an entire treasure chest full of new skills, friends, and hope to turn to when times are stressful.

"A great load lifted from my shoulders just knowing I was not alone. I came to realize that I am in control of my life; I am the one who makes the changes in my life. My journey with PA gave rewards that are not measurable. We can never do it alone. Parents coming together are what make it happen. Three years ago, I never would have dreamed that I could be the person that Parents Anonymous has helped me become."

## Sarcoidosis

Self-Help Group (Online), *Sarcoidosis Community Web site, December 1, 1998*

"Hello everyone. I just found this site. I don't know how I missed it when I first began my search on this disease in March of this year. I began to print out the November entries, thinking I could respond to each individual but then I saw it would be a 40 page printout and wised up. So here's my advice based on my own experience: I went the Western medicine route but also used supplemental therapies. My parotid glands swelled up like two balloons on either side of my head. I hadn't been feeling well for several months and it was the parotid swelling that began the long torturous road to diagnosis.

"I began treatment with an acupuncturist and, after a month of the swelling, the glands went down within a week of the treatment. Now, maybe it was just good timing but she also diagnosed liver involvement a full 4 months before I finally got the right doctors to diagnose it and the right medical treatment. Nutrition is also a must. If your doctor is dismissive of your pain, unsympathetic, or says, 'this disease can do anything,' as if you're supposed to just grin and bear it, then GET A NEW DOCTOR! Don't be polite; don't worry about it—if you have the freedom to choose, then get the heck out.

"When I had to choose a new doctor, I went to a friend of mine who has a chronic health problem. It is not at all like sarcoidosis but it requires the response of a sensitive, intelligent physician who stays current. My friend was very happy with his physician and I found that when I began with him, he was current on sarcoidosis and the uses of prednisone. Keep a journal of your symptoms. Monitor yourself. Listen to your body. Go into the doctor with a list of questions along with your journal. We all know that prednisone can

make you pretty loopy so it is important when managing the disease to find ways to stay focused and be able to articulate our needs.

"Spirituality—I wouldn't have made it through this illness (and thank God the symptoms have been steadily remitting) without a strong sense of my place in the Universe and my relationship with the force of love generally known as God. Even if you are an atheist, it is possible to take a spiritual approach to illness. Sounds kind of wacky, doesn't it? Well, I have tried to see sarcoidosis as my teacher. It hasn't always worked, believe me. I have had moments of terror and despair. But, all in all, I am grateful for the person this disease is making me. I feel I have more compassion for others and a much deeper understanding of what it means to need help. I had always been very independent. I had always been a professional helper (I'm a social worker). Now I am the one who has required help. It was a humbling, life transforming experience.

"I feel that, in framing this positively, it has helped speed the healing. There is no magic bullet but the mind is a powerful thing. I think of myself in terms of being a soul connected to others and to the Godforce but, again, that was my path. If it is one you feel comfortable with, I know it will help tremendously. If a spiritual/religious approach doesn't work for you, you still will benefit from considering the power of your mind. The mind exists not just in the brain, but throughout the body (there is recent scientific evidence for this, by the way) so get busy and start manufacturing those healing chemicals.

"Well, I have rambled on enough. Thank you all for sharing your experiences. I remember, when things were much worse, how terribly alone I felt. Even with a loving and supportive family (without them I don't know where I'd be), I felt very alone. While I don't wish this experience on anyone else, it is good to know you are out there. Anyone is welcome to contact me via email and if there are any Bostonians out there, let's get together! Wishing you healing and peace."

## Spinal Cord Injury

"At 20 years old, I was shot in the back during a robbery. I was angry, wanted revenge, and isolated myself at home. I was too angry to get involved at the hospital when I went to my first support group meeting. I didn't feel that I fit in, I was quiet, didn't speak up, and thought I didn't relate to any of these people. Later, a person from the group encouraged me to come to another meeting. The topic at this meeting was relaxation and imagery. During this exercise, I was able to fantasize my revenge. After we discussed the fantasy I had, I was no longer consumed with rage. After that day, I continued to attend the group meetings. I was never interested in finishing school, never believed I could make anything of myself. With the encouragement of the group, I completed my GED and enrolled in college. Now, I am studying psychology and am a peer counselor."

## Test Positive Aware Network (TPAN)

"Early last year I came to Test Positive Aware Network looking for understanding and some answers. I had recently become sober and realized that many areas of my life were in chaos due to HIV and substance abuse. I was terribly confused by the enormous volume of medical information about HIV available to me. Should I start therapy now? If so which therapy should I start? More upsetting, I had alienated myself from friends and family before dealing with my substance abuse. I worried that if they knew I was HIV positive, they would stay away permanently. The more I thought about my lonely existence, the more hopeless I became. I was increasingly unable to cope with my disease. A friend suggested I stop by TPAN's offices to talk to someone who was also positive and going through the same 'thing' I was going through.

"I was extremely nervous walking into the building that first time. Although I had been told that TPAN was a great place to get support and information, I was skeptical. During my yearlong struggle to become sober, I had not met another person with HIV in any of my support groups. Imagine how relieved I was to finally find a safe space with a sympathetic ear to allay many of my fears. I didn't feel so isolated anymore. I signed up with an HIV+ buddy who could help me work through some of the medical and personal dilemmas. I also became a regular participant in the Newly Diagnosed support group, where I learned about self-empowerment and how to make better health choices.

"I had been out of work for 2 years. With the help of TPAN's Positive Vocational Network, I am now working full-time. Although I sometimes struggle keeping on my medication regimen and dealing with recovery, I am committed to living. I know TPAN is always a safe place I can come to when life becomes overwhelming."

# Taking Charge

*"When is a crisis reached?
When questions arise that can't be answered."*
**Ryszard Kapuscinski**, Polish journalist, *A Warsaw Diary*
(published in *Granta*, no. 15, Cambridge, England 1985)

You have seen people who seem to manage their condition and live as normal a life as possible. With support provided by self-help groups, which are low-cost or free and are run by peers, you too can learn to keep your problem or illness from dominating your life.

Self-help groups are an important source of help for 15 million people coping with a serious physical illness or emotional or mental distress. In 1999, a MacArthur Foundation study of midlife reported that nearly 19% of Americans have attended a support group. The study defined a self-help group as "groups organized and run by people who get together on the basis of a common experience or goal to mutually help or support one another." Support is available worldwide in neighborhood small group meetings such as Alcoholics Anonymous and its offshoots, 12-step groups, and groups for every imaginable condition. Some groups that have grown into national advocacy or health organizations but others are unique or have a few chapters. And this informal help is typical in local, one-of-a-kind health and disability groups.

Groups benefit more than just their members in self-help groups. Participants become empowered, aware of what works and how to take responsibility for helping themselves and others. Medical care providers find self-help groups to be valuable support resources to enhance and supplement knowledge required by their patients and themselves. The payor, understand-ably concerned about runaway health care costs, realizes that the kinds of assistance provided by self-help groups can help patients use professional health care resources wisely.

## Receive the Latest Health Research and Information

Each group has a set of beliefs about how to deal with the illness, how to run the meetings, and how to work with those who relapse. Whether connected to a national health society existing as a local independent group, an established group develops or collects distilled trustworthy health information. This information ranges from simply sharing reprinted articles and other helpful handouts to distributing packets of information, pamphlets on how to organize new groups, and primers describing the problem or symptoms and treatment for orphan diseases.

The members of the group will provide practical information about and support for your problem, as well as help you to decide if you are getting the best possible medical care. If your condition becomes so severe that you cannot work, chances are someone in the group knows how to handle insurance coverage or find other ways to handle the medical bills. But what if you need help with your children's reaction to your problem or your spouse needs assistance in figuring out how to deal with your condition? Or maybe you live alone and don't have anyone to help take care of you. Again, groups have multiple mechanisms to help you cope with fear and anxiety-producing situations that accompany life-disrupting problems.

If you want to know what the group is like, find out what leaders believe are the group's primary goals, how they accomplish these goals, and what goes on at meetings.

## Bond with Other Members

Self-help groups connect people who share a common condition, problem, or experience and they are organized to help people cope with whatever comes up. Self-help groups give compassionate support coupled with practical experience and knowledge. They enable you to talk directly to other people in a similar situation until you eventually have enough confidence to share your views to help less experienced members. Help from family members and professionals with expertise in your problem may also be available through the group. Imagine being with ten people sharing their experiences with similar symptoms, medications, and other treatments. What a relief to be able to compare notes and to share your own negative and positive experiences. In many groups, the generous sharing results in trust, friendships, and bonding.

Participants help each other by tapping into their collective resources, the "wisdom" of the members. Sometimes it's help dealing with the bureaucracy of insurance companies. Or it might be locating the right doctors or other professionals. Members make decisions by consensus, and take responsibility for the group. Professionals may make important contributions, but they respect members' preferences and agendas and are careful not to control or interfere with the group.

## Tell Your Story, Hear How Others Cope, Find Hope

When we don't take charge, our stress escalates. With avoidance, what began as merely a difficult or painful event turns into a crisis. In a self-help group meeting the focus is on our daily experiences and how we are solving the problem. These common experiences predispose self-help group members to want to listen intently to each other. Visit any support group and there will be stories. Even if the meeting is packed with lectures and business, members will find each other over refreshments or go out after the meeting for a cup of tea and tell stories about what has happened.

In a parents' group for children with asthma, a very agitated new member said, "My 4-year-old child was diagnosed with asthma last month. When I took her to the doctor for a bad cold and cough, I was devastated when he prescribed antibiotics and prednisone. I thought all those medications were for serious conditions. And the antibiotics were so expensive. I don't want to give her these medications every time she becomes sick." This new member learned from

other parents that asthma is a chronic illness and complications can become serious, even life threatening. And she heard what other moms do to prevent complications.

When members tell stories about a shared problem, even very anxious members begin to pay attention to the conversation. Soon, the genuine emotions in these stories fully engross us in their drama. As the group's stories unfold, we find words for our own fears and concerns or we let go of the fear and agitation we brought with us. When we allow ourselves to listen with full involvement and to speak from our deeply felt experience, we become calm. This is a rare opportunity to really listen and hear new perspectives in others' stories. At times, we can find in these stories new options and new hope we have never considered for ourselves. As the group zeros in on the pain of a father or husband in our group, we realize his behavior is similar to our harsh words when we are upset with our child or spouse.

In self-help groups, we constantly learn about the problems we face and about ourselves. If you attend a group for the first time with a new diagnosis of breast cancer, for example, members will ask about what has happened recently during your radiation treatment and how you are dealing with specific issues that they know you must cope with. Other members share their stories from the same time frame, when they too were receiving radiation. They will discuss their increasing fatigue several weeks into the treatment, how they limited their responsibilities at this point, and how they learned to ask for help. As a dividend, reduced stress for health care users improves cooperation with our professional caregivers.

## Receive Help from Veterans

Veteran self-help group members who provide help to others were once newcomers seeking help. These veterans know from what people say or don't say how they might be masking their pain and shame, how they might be covering up negative thoughts and abusive behavior. As the veterans tell their stories, they give the newcomers confidence to share their deepest fears and concerns, which is frequently as beneficial as any practical advice they might receive from the group.

Art's story is typical of veteran self-helpers. "After getting injured on the job, I suffered for 25 years with debilitating pain. I thought I was the only person on earth dealing with this type of pain." After joining a chronic pain self-help group, Art said, "I was swept away by the breadth and depth of the knowledge of members in my group, and their eagerness to share it. I was also impressed with the members' ability to describe their experiences and beliefs with drama and humor. One of the best outcomes is something I never expected—while I am helping someone, I forget about my own pain."

The veterans know, as Art reported, that helping others is the best way for them to help themselves. The benefits of helping other people flow back to the helper because that act reinforces new skills and instills compassion. Through involvement in a self-help group, the problem they saw only as a liability (such as epilepsy or depression) becomes an asset because the experience enables them to empathize with and guide others.

## Create a New Norm

Because people feel so alone in their experience, they welcome the opportunity to interact with people like themselves. They usually feel that they are the only ones reacting as they do to their problem—with fear, for example, that they might die or that they are incompetent. Or they feel guilty for giving their child the wrong food or not going to the doctor soon enough. Or they are concerned over the way their family, physician, or insurance company is responding to their needs and requests. It is critical that people experiencing a very personal and emotional reaction hear that others feel the exact same way. Here's what a group can do when a cancer patient feels self-conscious about the removal of her breast. Rather than discussing the medical aspects as a nurse, the co-leader asks other group members to relate their specific connections to this problem. When another member frets about the odds of her daughter also having breast cancer, a wise group facilitator turns to the other members and asks if they have daughters and if they have had a similar conversation with them about cancer risk. Invariably, members assure each other that these feelings and fears are common for all members in the group. What a relief when a newcomer begins to feel "normal"!

## Communicate Openly

Group members will help each other see the possible good that can come from the shared condition. Even if the feedback painfully confirms losses, the heartfelt sharing connects those surviving the same experiences. For Anita, a member of Make Today Count, being helped and being able to help others by talking openly changed her attitude from negative to positive. "It is through honest communication that the quality of life—anyone's life—improves." A negative event provides many opportunities to nourish the emotions. My "cancer friends . . . have accomplished this for me. I have learned with them how to cope one day at a time. One of the best ways I find of coping with cancer is with honesty—facing it openly and realistically." Because members willingly, often courageously, talk openly about personal matters in their groups, other members receive help to redefine painful experiences or find solutions.

As the members remain in the group long enough to trust each other and themselves, they also become more open and honest in confronting and challenging others. They learn to be direct in asking for help and to give sensitive feedback to other members.

## Prepare for the Unknown

Self-help groups usually provide opportunity to listen to members in different stages of their experience. Although it may be difficult, listening respectfully to people describe how they are experiencing a metastasized cancer or an amputated limb is a healing experience for the storyteller and the listener, even if the listener's condition does not take the same route. Being able to comfort others in their time of need is very gratifying for many members. And those who find themselves uncomfortable with this glimpse into their possible future can put it out of their minds and recall it if they ever need it. If you are ever in a similar situation, your unconscious mind will bring back the storytellers' acceptance of their fears of immobility and how they nonetheless made new friends, committed to making each day count, and found treatments that helped.

This anticipatory preparation is useful when no other medical treatment is available and the focus is on quality of life rather than life-extending treatment. Physicians and other health workers may not be as directly involved in your care as in the past. As Anita once said of her physicians, "At first, they were delighted to be part of my medical case. I was a success to them—I was a success to myself! Now I think I've become a reminder of their failure. It isn't so easy for any of us anymore. In fact, this is one difficult set of circumstances I'm in." When self-help group researcher Len Borman was dying, his primary physician went on vacation. We found ourselves in a desperate conflict with intensive care staff over their inappropriate life-extending treatment for a person with a late stage of leukemia and in a coma. It was impossible for us to sort out what was actually happening until we called another member who reminded us of Anita's lesson from our cancer support group. It provided a small comfort to recognize in this attending physician his reminder of failure.

# Group Structure

## Educational Goals

The major goal for both professionally sponsored support groups and peer initiated self-help groups is to educate their members about their condition. And the benefits of groups go beyond management and coping with disease. Group members can actually participate in transforming themselves, fellow sufferers, and society. Many groups focus on personal growth, while others emphasize social change.

*Medical groups* are sponsored by hospitals, health organizations, and physicians. These groups hold educational programs fostering discussions on aspects of the disease, stages, and treatment options. This forum brings people together to talk about their common illness.

Many peer initiated groups have a *therapeutic* focus and they consist of people with mental or physical illness, or those dealing with *life and family transitions* such as divorce or death. Here the group provides peer therapy, helping members reframe painful experiences or hurtful responses to the way they see their problem. Therapeutic goals also underlie *mental and emotional groups* for addictive problems including those in Alcoholics Anonymous or Debtors Anonymous, disease groups for chronic and life-threatening illnesses, and emotional illness groups including obsessive-compulsive disorder and schizophrenia.

Peer initiated groups focusing on *social advocacy* aim to change attitudes by trying to address problems that are endemic in society. For populations not receiving services and those living outside social norms, the self-help movement has promoted acceptance of diversity. First to work on social change were families with disabled children. With the groundbreaking work of the Alliance for the Mentally Ill, families of persons with mental illness have influenced awareness of stigma and dramatically improved attitudes toward and options for mental health consumers. In many areas, alliances of self-help groups effectively organize to advocate for additional research related to the problem or disease and the need for services. With the help of the Internet, organizing is much more effective. AIDS groups were able to accomplished goals to increase the research budget and national awareness in just a few years that previously would have taken decades.

In the last several years, more advocacy groups have incorporated a therapeutic focus into their groups. The Older Women's League and the Alliance for the Mentally Ill blend advocacy with support strategies. One example of these different strategies stands out. Years ago, Therese Goodrich, founder of Bereaved Parents, USA, was on a panel with a presenter from Mothers Against Drunk Driving (MADD). Both speakers had lost children. As advocates for safe drivers, the MADD presenter described how members spend countless hours working to identify traffic deaths caused by drunk drivers and decrease the legal alcohol limit in drivers. Therese told how in the Bereaved Parents group, members discuss the tragic loss of a child, ways of handling grief, and how they acknowledge the life of their deceased child in their family.

The panelists began to discuss why MADD works so hard to never let other children die at the hand of a drunk drivers and how their group's mission desperately serves to displace their tragic loss. Finally, the presenters agreed it was difficult and dangerous to the family to work so hard for this cause without having a place to deal with their profound grief. Now, in addition to their successful advocacy activities, MADD also offers support groups to address the emotional needs of its members.

## Meeting Format

Successful groups offer many strategies that help members become involved, active participants. Even groups dedicated to advocacy want to meet the personal needs of their members. The reason groups spend time thinking about their meeting formats and group guidelines is because the meeting format sets the stage so members can spend quality time sharing one another's experiences. A simple meeting plan with a consistent, predetermined format becomes a ritual that can help members know what to expect. A good plan assures everyone quality time to listen to others and tell their stories. Set time allowances are often helpful, because they help members stay within a time frame that allows others to share.

The elements of the meeting structure differ with each group. Some organizations emphasize a formal educational format. Here, members of the group select topics and either a member or a professional solicits presenters. Members of other groups expect to interact informally during the entire time the group meets. Many groups prefer to have a format that includes both education and group discussion, while others alternate educational meetings and group discussion meetings. Frequently groups offer a presentation during half of the meeting, followed by group discussion. A group's format may be very informal and interactive or it may be very structured, with pre-selected discussion from the organization's text, panelists, or invited presenters.

## Format Fits Group's Purpose

There is no one way to organize a group. During the meeting itself, the process should support member interactions that allow common experiences to surface. To get the most from the time spent together, groups need an organized meeting format. Some groups will inherit a very well-defined structure, such as AA and recovery groups, the more than 100 groups that have adapted AA's 12 steps, called 12-step groups, and weight control groups such as TOPS (Taking Off Pounds Sensibly) and Overeaters Anonymous.

Newer groups plan a format that accomplishes their unique goals. Tough Love for parents of troubled teenagers developed a process for educating members. Following their training programs, members support each other to maintain limits and link to other groups across the country to retrieve their children when they run away. In People First, young adults with develop-mental disabilities learn about their rights and responsibilities and select their own community sponsors and group activities.

While members need specific and immediate information to deal with complicated problems, outside presenters may impinge on members' interaction time. The same holds true for a group that dedicates its time to changing laws or improving services. They feel the best approach is to discover cures for these horrible diseases, deliver equitable health and human services, get people who are sleep-deprived or use mind-altering substances off the road, etc. If the group mainly hosts educational meetings or organizes rallies, the bonding experience may not permeate the membership and members may not get the personal support that comes from sharing each other's stories. For groups committed to advocacy there will always be tension between members wanting to change society's stigma or find a cure, and those needing emotional support. If the group makes decisions based on consensus, the group format will addresses these problems based on its collective understandings.

## Recovery, Inc.—A Structured Group Format

Recovery, Inc. is a 55-year-old national self-help organization entirely operated and supported by the people it serves, people with emotional and nervous disorders. Who are these participants? People like Anne, whose paralyzing anxiety had made her unable to participate in and get pleasure from many ordinary aspects of life. And Betty, who lived an active and fulfilling life until her depression affected her job. "I was demoted. I found myself lying in bed all day watching the clock go round and hating myself for it. You feel worse than a worm on those days, covering up for your actions." And Barbara, who suffered from an abnormal fear of public places (agoraphobia) complicated by depression, which compelled her to quit her job and stay at home.

A Chicago psychiatrist, Abraham A. Low, MD, began Recovery, Inc. to help chronically nervous people get well and help former mental patients stay well. Recovery Inc. has expanded internationally to 700 groups, which serves hundreds of thousands of people who want to improve their emotional well being. Participants include ordinary people whose lives are impaired by anxiety, depression, panic attacks, excessive stress and nervousness who may never have consulted a mental health professional, as well as patients currently or formerly in treatment for serious emotional problems.

Through a consistent format, Recovery, Inc. meetings help people identify their self-defeating and illness-promoting thoughts and impulses and replace them with self-endorsing thoughts and wellness-promoting actions. Participants might learn, for example, "how not to repeatedly relive upsetting events in our minds, which only causes us to stay upset," Barbara explained. "The Recovery method relies on taking action to help oneself," she said. At the core of the Recovery Method is the self-help technique called spotting, in which members recognize an emotional disturbance when it occurs or is about to occur, give it a name, and identify the factors precipitating the dysfunctional response. Other techniques involve will-training and commanding one's muscle to act in ways that prevent the disturbance from disrupting one's life.

The Recovery, Inc. method involves reading the books by Dr. Low, attending weekly meetings, and practicing the principles in everyday life. The 2-hour meeting begins by listening to a taped lecture by Dr. Low or reading aloud from one of Recovery's authorized books. Four or five members of the group present examples of troubling events in their daily lives and describe how they applied Recovery techniques in these situations. Each example follows an outline for the sequence of events and is completed in 5 minutes, with 10 more minutes used for comments by those familiar with the Recovery method (the spotting technique). At the end of the session, members have an opportunity to provide mutual support, do further spotting on the example, and attendees are encouraged to give themselves credit for their efforts.

Barbara tells us, "With the encouragement and help of group members, we do things to get well. We don't wait to get well to do things." For example, for a woman who panics at the thought of taking on a new responsibility at work, the group helps her divide the demands into small tasks. She gets help to organize the task, an office party. Group members coach her to start well in advance and do one thing at a time (invite people, plan the menu, find the recipes, organize the activities for the party, and so forth) and each task is, in turn, broken into small units.

For a more serious problem, such as the undiagnosed panic attacks Anne realized she had been suffering since childhood, participants learn what sets off their panic reactions—pounding heart, cold sweat, chest pains, etc.—and how their emotional response to the

symptoms sets up a vicious cycle. As Anne described it, "Fear feeds the symptoms and the symptoms feed the fear." Recovery Inc. is not, however, intended to replace psychotherapy or medication for serious problems. Not everyone who suffers from panic attacks, for instance, would find the group's meetings alone enough to solve their problems, and when a problem is severe, group members will suggest other forms of help.

## Facilitation

People who organize the group and conduct the meetings are called group facilitators or leaders. There are many styles of group facilitation, depending upon the group's goals and structure. Imagine you had the authority to address the group from the front of the room. Would you feel like you were the center of attention from this position? What would be your effect if you stood in the back of the group? While some facilitators seem to enjoy speaking from the middle of the room, the best facilitators are able to stay in the background observing not just what people say but also how they communicate, and noticing who hasn't spoken and what their body language expresses.

Facilitators are most effective when they or a family member share the same condition as the group members. Similarly, social workers, nurses, or physicians are often effective facilitators when they share a professional relationship with the members and they expressly request this task. Effective facilitators will have experience or training in how groups develop; an understanding of running meetings and group process; personal qualities, including self-awareness, respect, empathy, warmth; and a willingness to demonstrate and encourage honest and direct communication in the group. The ability to facilitate groups can be a natural or a trained skill You will notice that everyone in the group has some of these skills, especially when the meeting goes well.

Some skills include:

**Active listening**: Hearing and understanding direct and subtle messages.

**Reflecting**: Repeating what a member says.

**Linking**: Relating questions or comments to the concerns of other members.

**Clarifying**: Helping members understand underlying issues and conflicting feelings.

**Blocking**: Stopping gossip, intellectualizing, and side conversations without attacking.

**Confronting**: Effectively getting the person to look at the behavior in a non-defensive manner.

**Empathizing**: Intuitively understanding what members are experiencing.

**Supporting**: Discerning when and how to support.

**Summarizing**: Presenting the key elements of the meeting in a summary.

Adapted from Gary Lawson, et al., 1996

## Successful Formats and Exceptions

The group will offer help based on the way they interpret the members' needs. When decisions are determined by consensus, the outcome is always positive for those who participate in the group. Underlying the group's goals will be a stated or unstated framework of education, therapy, social, advocacy, or some combination as described previously in "Group Structure: Educational Goals". When leaders are clear about the goals and purpose of the group, they can monitor when their members' needs shift. Often, they will notice that newer members are not returning. While some members may drift into cliques or lose interest in reaching out to new members, the group as a whole can usually help design meeting formats to meet the needs of new and continuing members. Some groups hold a general meeting and break out into smaller groups for members with similar concerns or stages. Others simply keep the focus on the new member and ask "graduates" to play roles in business meetings or boards. An article in the upcoming chapter "Supporting Vulnerable Members" suggests additional ways groups can respond.

We have found the following characteristics useful in recognizing successful formats.

• The group has articulated its goals to members.

• Members have input into how the group/meeting operates.

• Many members have leadership roles.

• The format optimizes time for personal support.

We don't mean to suggest that all successful groups look the same. Every instance of group format and leadership is subject to an exception. For example, you will never find two AA meetings, the most structured organization, which are identical. Nor will you find any two groups operating entirely the same. Each group adapts to the unique character of the needs, culture, members' personalities, and leadership styles.

What happens when the group's entire leadership is seriously ill? Or what keeps the group together when the group is comprised of people who have recently received an organ transplant? An organ transplant support group nurse or social worker organizes the group, yet conveys responsibility during the meeting to the group by turning the questions asked back to the members and by encouraging members to plan social activities. This is one way professionals can provide the group's continuity and history at the same time that they maintain self-help principles and nurture leaders from within the membership.

Does this example support the premise that you can stretch self-help principles? In the example of a hospital organized group where attendance of seriously ill members is sporadic, the professional plays a delicate balance between supporting and compromising the autonomy members need to accept ownership.

The bottom-line test of a self-help group is its autonomy. What would happen if the group wants to communicate with ill or hospitalized members and the staff refuses? A group dominated by a professional would accept this refusal. In contrast, an empowered group would insist on sitting down with the administration to work out an agreeable solution. When professionals see their role as conservators rather than empowerment consultants, the latter rarely happens.

## Accommodating Members in Different Stages

Many groups are less structured than Recovery, Inc. and AA, and must develop ways to embrace both newcomers and people who have been in the group a long time. People currently dealing with a serious situation say they are concerned at first with handling the immediate crisis phase or the medical decisions they must make. Soon, they find that they are equally concerned with how their situation has changed the quality of their lives. And years later, these same people have new issues as survivors or their children with Down's Syndrome have become teen-agers and young adults. This can be a critical point for groups if their focus becomes diluted and members splinter. Although one volunteer group can't be all things to all people, hopefully it will have some creative strategies to meet the needs of members at various stages.

Whatever the structure, new members are usually informed of how the meeting will operate at the outset of each meeting and in materials sent through the mail. Reading the group's guidelines aloud at each meeting and sending them to newcomers gives a clear message that the group collectively supports these principles and rules. Many groups supplement these orientation materials with a contact person or "buddy" who is available to answer specific questions, talk on the phone, and make new members comfortable during meetings.

## Shared Leadership

The strength of a support group can be measured by the number of people involved in developing and maintaining the group. Maintaining shared leadership is a challenge, sometimes even a struggle, for self-help groups. When the founder and early leaders leave, who will replace them? How can a group get members to assume roles and responsibilities that require high level skills and time-consuming commitments? Leaders constantly search for ways to strengthen the group and, at the same time, distribute some of the responsibilities.

Involvement is not only for the benefit of the group. Research on self-help groups such as Mended Hearts, Grow in Illinois, and Depressive and Manic Depression Association typically finds that the quality of life improves most for those most involved.

## Participation Opportunities and Benefits

Self-help is peer run, which means that the leaders come from the membership. Ideally, self-help groups involve many members in leadership and other responsibilities. As we worked with Illinois Parents Anonymous, PA's board of directors came to realize

how important it is that all facilitators understand the PA model. When everyone in the organization clarified how a self-help model operates, it became easier to attract parent leaders who would take responsibility.

Members in all stages have opportunities to participate at their level of comfort:

- respond to inquiries
- greet newcomers
- bring snacks, set up, and close the meeting space
- organize activities
- visit and stay in touch with members
- solicit new members
- cultivate new leaders
- plan the organization's development
- handle finances or fundraising

Facilitators may agree to share responsibilities for various functions for a period of time, after which the duties are rotated to new facilitators. Typical functions include:

- greeting members and coordinating hospitality
- monitoring time allotted for different meeting segments
- monitoring interruptions or negativity
- choosing the agenda
- keeping the group on track while responding to members' needs as they emerge
- organizing social functions during or outside the meeting

Participation provides an opportunity to discover and develop talents that members were not aware they had. Newcomers getting connected to the group might be encouraged to discuss how they think their experiences and talents could benefit the group. Usually, a long-standing group has leaders who have learned to recognize the strength of its members and involve the newcomers in helping with the needs of the group.

Through her participation in her overeating group, a shy homemaker developed confidence. Taking over small tasks at first, she grew into a dependable and inspiring leader. She understands the need to identify group needs, and she is not shy about asking a likely member to take over this responsibility. This not only accommodates her shyness by allowing her to avoid public roles, but also lets other members know that the group's survival and success depend on shared leadership. Often, leadership opportunities blossom with assistance from professionals. In Florida, a self-helper with breast cancer writes a newsletter for breast cancer patients that, with a social worker's help, boasts four hundred paid subscribers in its first year and has sponsors underwriting costs.

# Recognizing a Safe Environment

Would you go to a meeting if you didn't feel safe revealing your deepest concerns or walking or parking on the street? Members feel safe emotionally when they are free to disclose personal information without other members responding judgmentally. The group rules listed below for handling conflict further assure members that they feel emotionally secure at meetings.

Since many groups are held in the evenings, what can members do to assure that the meeting place is secure, comfortable, and accessible to members? The site should be close to public transportation and/or parking. Members can contribute to safety features by making provisions for each other's security.

## Confidentiality

Everything said in the group must be treated as completely confidential, and the facilitator should mention this at every meeting. People are concerned about whether or not what they say in self-help meetings will be talked about outside, and they need reassurance that even if other members do not consider something as being particularly private, they will keep all sharing confidential.

## Group and Personal Limits

There are limits in the assistance that a self-help group can provide. While members can give various kinds of support, each person remains responsible for getting necessary therapy or medical care and arranging for most of the activities of daily living.

Groups usually provide some guidance on respecting personal limits, but you may need to set additional limits of your own. One member may tell another to call "anytime" he or she needs someone to talk to. But

"anytime" can turn out to be when the contacted member is fatigued, overwhelmed with work or family responsibilities or his or her own condition, or just asleep in bed! Providing qualifications about one's availability and indicating realistic limits at the beginning demonstrates respect for oneself and other members and can prevent misunderstandings stemming from unmet expectations.

## Group Rules and Guidelines

Conflicts among members or other inappropriate behavior sometimes occur during meetings, but they can be minimized when the group follows a clear set of guidelines for behavior during and outside group meetings. Rules that do not allow interruptions or negative comments and insist on courtesy ensure that members understand and respect each other's right to speak. The discussion may continue from person to person around the room (anyone can decline or ask to talk later), or the group may borrow the Native Indian ritual of passing an object (a talking stick, feather, or other symbol), signifying when it is the next person's turn to talk. Most groups permit a number of individuals to assume responsibility for meetings.

Periodically, members will want to review the rules to see how well they are working. It is wise to adapt the rules to account for everyone's concerns and ideas, thus inviting all members to accept responsibility for speaking up at meetings or afterwards to clarify the group rules, especially those related to disruptive behavior.

In addition to the previous rules, a group may also want to distribute or discuss the following:

- We are a group of people with a common bond, sharing our troubles, understanding, and wisdom.

- We listen, explore options, and express our feelings. We do not prescribe, diagnose, or judge.

- We talk about what has worked for us; we do not say, "I think you should…."

- We know what we share is confidential and we have the right to remain anonymous if we choose.

- We have the right to decide whether or not to take part in any discussion. But we actively listen when someone is talking and avoid side conversations.

- We encourage "I" statements, so that everyone speaks for her or himself.

- Having benefited from the help of others, we recognize the need for offering our help to others in our group.

- We each share the responsibility for making our group work.

- We encourage members to share their strengths, skills, insights, successes (however small), and their hopes.

(Guidelines adapted from *The Sharing Network: A Handbook on Self-Help Programs for People with Multiple Sclerosis and Their Families*, published by the Multiple Sclerosis Society of Canada, 250 Bloor Street E, Toronto, Ontario M4W 3P9  416/922-6065)

Lawson, G. *Essentials of Chemical Dependency Counseling, 2E,* Aspen Publishers, Inc. 1996

Yalom, ID. *The Theory and Practice of Group Psychotherapy.* New York, Basic Books; 1980

With the structure of meeting formats and guidelines in place, a group can focus on supporting its members, both by dealing with the specific condition that brought them together and by promoting healthy lifestyles in general. The following article discusses the encouragement and support that self-help groups provide to help members adopt healthy behaviors.

# Groups Support Behavior Change

Hannah L. Hedrick, PhD

*Company is better than will power when you are trying to change behavior.*
**Amrit Desai**

One of the ways that groups help members take charge is by supporting their efforts to be as healthy as possible throughout their recovery or illness. The same techniques used to help members cope with the common condition that drew them together—sharing stories, offering constructive advice, and mentoring—may be used to promote healthy behaviors in general.

Recovery (12 step) groups are known for their success in using a sponsor system to help members stop drinking or drugging. Some groups, such as Parents Anonymous (PA), focus primarily on presenting very specific techniques parents can use to replace their abusive behavior. PA has a long history of testimony and research about how it has reduced risks related to domestic violence and how it has been effective in educating the public as well as members. The National Committee for Prevention of Child Abuse is among the national organizations that have praised PA for its role in reducing the propensity for future abuse.

Almost all groups offer some techniques for helping members with changes related to the specific condition that drew them to the group. But the kind of help provided in self-help groups goes far beyond

stopping harmful or unhealthy behavior. If you talk to people associated with the wide range of groups listed in the *Register* (Section II), you will find many who report that for the first time in their lives, they were able to stick with lifestyle changes.

Groups for stroke and diabetes are known for their disease prevention activities, both for their members and for people unaffected by either condition. Many groups not as well-known for their self-care activities also sponsor presentations, demonstrations, and even ongoing programs on movement techniques, food choices, and other self-care techniques that can improve general health. Groups may devote a section of their newsletter or even a special issue to complementary therapies (see list in the "Supporting Vulnerable Members" chapter).

In true self-help fashion, relatively new groups, such as those formed to help people impacted by HIV/AIDS, have picked up on the self-care benefits derived from group participation. These groups were recognized by the prestigious *Population Reports* (September 1989) as providing the "knowledge, emotions, and skills [that] reinforce healthful changes." The information, services, and support they provide were praised for persuading "people to change their behavior and to maintain new behavior."

Groups have several mechanisms for encouraging members to assume responsibility for retaining and maintaining as healthy a lifestyle as possible, whether at home or in the hospital. Just as groups form buddy systems to make new members feel comfortable, they also encourage members to pair up to help each other give up that pint of Haagen-Dazs at bedtime, to dance around the room or do deep breathing when they feel like having a cigarette, or to shop and cook together to pool their knowledge about nutrition. The intimacy developed during these shared activities contributes to the healthy benefits of belonging to a self-help group.

## Special "Caring" in Groups Promotes Self-Care

How can participating in a self-help group bring about changes that all the nagging in the world from loving family and friends cannot accomplish? Maybe its because your sponsor or buddy knows exactly how difficult it is to "just say no," to drag yourself out of bed to go for a walk, or to get up the courage to leave the house or even your bedroom. Maybe having someone there to hold your hand (literally) or to listen to you cry at 2:00 a.m. also helps. Maybe hearing all the stories of struggle and success convinces you that you, too, can improve the quality of your life by making better choices and acting on them.

## The "Helper-Therapy" Principle

The encouragement and company of someone who has "been there" is no doubt highly motivational. But another attribute of self-help groups also contributes to long-term behavior change. Having opportunities to use your experience to help others, as discussed previously, is one of the major benefits provided by groups. And one way to help is to keep someone company in a healthy activity.

You are less likely to sit in front of the TV and reach for another beer or pretzel when you have promised a self-help group friend that you would do t'ai chi or yoga together or take them to your massage therapist for their first massage. Thousands of studies have been done on how the benefits of altruism accrue to the giver as well as the receiver. The great personal inconvenience members sometimes endure, whether helping with the condition that draws members

together or helping members assume more control over all aspects of their lives, is a prime example of altruism. In fact, even if your altruistic efforts to help someone fail, you usually benefit anyway.

*"Love is literally a life-giving force.... Altruistic people have on the average a far greater duration of life than egotistic persons. Love annuls loneliness and is the best antidote to suicidal and morbid tendencies. Love...beautifies anything that it touches.... Love is...the best remedy for any fear.... It is the best therapy against hate, insanity, misery, death, and destruction. Finally, it is the only means of transcending the narrow limits of Lilliputian egos and of making our true self co-existent with the richest manifold infinity."* **Altruistic Love, 1950, pp. v-vi**

## How You Can Benefit and Help

Groups are pretty much on their own when figuring out how to support self-care and health promotion activities (although the International Information Centre on Self-Help and Health pointed out a decade ago that the health care system should provide support for groups ready to undertake these roles). They can use this *Guide* and the Illinois Self-Help Coalition as resources, but member participation is essential for the success of any self-care program designed to support behavior change.

# Is This Group for Me?

*Although the world is full of suffering
it is also full of overcoming it.*
**Hellen Keller**

Groucho Marx once quipped, "Any club that would have me for a member, I wouldn't join." Although self-help groups are generally open to everyone, thinking about joining a group can provoke reasonable questions amidst excuses, assumptions, and myths. What motivates people to go out into a stormy night to attend a self-help meeting?

If you can get beyond your initial resistance to joining a room full of strangers, you will see and perhaps experience the benefits of asking questions and finding answers from people in the same boat. These "strangers" become mentors and models for how you can get through similar challenges. Joining a self-help group is an empowering step. With additional health information and support from the group, you will soon take an active role in all aspects of your life and feel more in charge of your destiny!

## Who Goes to Groups?

Nancy was awakened at 2:00 one afternoon when the Department of Children and Family Services worker rang her bell. Nancy awoke to learn that the state could take her son away. Why? She didn't believe she had a problem with alcohol. She insisted she could stop drinking whenever she wanted to.

George and Lila had two grown children and were preparing for retirement when their 33-year-old son, John, was diagnosed with a brain tumor and returned home. They each held demanding jobs and began to juggle responsibilities so their lives could revolve around the medical care their son required. After each surgery, their hopes for John's full recovery diminished. Five years later, they slowly recognized that John was increasingly incapacitated and might die.

Nancy joined Alcoholics Anonymous and, later, Parents Anonymous to learn better parenting skills

and to control her anger. Soon after their son was diagnosed, George and Lila went to their first family cancer group. With every ounce of their energy, George and Lila wanted to spare their son pain and hold onto their dream for his future, and finding others in the group who shared their hopes and grief comforted them.

Over a period of time, Nancy, George, and Lila found themselves immersed in the lives they now share with what were once perfect strangers. They have a place to discuss challenges with bureaucracies, such as government services, the medical system, and other professionals. In fact, George and Lila attend both a brain tumor support group, which focuses mainly on education (lectures on brain tumors), and a more informal group, which they call their "family," that allows time for more interaction and discussion. They can discuss problems in minute detail and everyone understands.

## Belonging

**Maurine Pyle, MS**

*Editor's note: Groups differ in their use of old fashioned language, customs, and rituals. In spite of these differences, the language and rituals are usually intended to establish a safe environment for expressing genuine caring, which people tend to respond to first when in crisis.*

Rosetta had never attended a self-help group before. She wasn't sure what to expect. Her counselor had urged her to go many times, yet she never could gather enough courage to risk it. Now her feelings of desperation were pushing her to take this step. She was hopeful that maybe a self-help group could fill in the gaps that she was unable to fill by herself. Grasping the doorknob and taking a deep breath, she entered the room.

First encounters tend to be the hardest. As this scenario indicates, making an entrance into a group of strangers, even friendly ones, is never easy. Extroverts as well as introverts struggle in the role of newcomer coming into an established group. Likewise, the group members may have difficulty accepting the new-comer. There is often discomfort on both sides of the equation. The question we pose here is how do we help new members feel accepted in a self-help group.

I recently attended a self-help group as a first-timer and found I felt completely at ease. Something had happened to help me and the group overcome the shyness of a first encounter. That group exemplified a style of leadership that I call *leading with spirit.* An old Quaker expression sums it up: "walking cheerfully over the earth, answering that of God in everyone." In other words, recognizing and rejoicing in the spiritual connection of our human personalities. The Hindus say "Namaskar," which means "my spirit salutes your spirit."

This spirit-centered method of leadership could be observed in the functioning of the self-help group I just experienced. The first quality of the group I noticed was kindness. Beyond the exchange of the usual *polite* greetings, I felt genuinely welcomed. Immediately I felt their warmth and concern for me as a newcomer. The group leader made sure I understood the process they would be following, and people gave me reading materials. By sharing the rules of the road and giving me an opportunity to speak early in the meeting, I was made to feel a part of the group. By giving me the chance either to participate or to pass, they relieved my fears of being excluded or put on the spot to perform. Some of the initial questions that arise early in the process of joining a group were answered by their actions. Am I welcome here? Who is the leader? How does the process work? What are the boundaries? Can I remain anonymous if I choose?

I also noted that the group leader was acting as the facilitator of group wisdom. She guided with a gentle hand, acknowledging each member as a contributor to the process, yet keeping everyone on task. I was reminded of the traditional medicine circle of the Native Americans who drew upon the collective wisdom of the group as they passed the talking stick.

Here the method of communication was people reading aloud from a book and sharing stories of how they were implementing self-help principles in their

daily lives. The leader provided the necessary structure to facilitate effective group action.

Leadership of a self-help group depends upon achieving a balance between the needs of the regulars and the needs of newcomers. The elders who have made a commitment to the group see themselves as the keepers of the flame, the guardians of tribal wisdom. It is their strong desire to share the secrets of self-help with initiates. To achieve balance between maintaining the tradition and risking stagnation is to keep the door open for newcomers while upholding the acquired wisdom of the group.

Sojourners, who have come for a short stay, can refresh the group if they find acceptance. They offer a fresh perspective, the aspect of a learner, which challenges the elders to teach what they know to be true. Without new members, groups become frozen and eventually die. Both the old and the new are essential components to the life of any group.

Spirit-filled leadership is open, intuitive, and accepting. It is exemplified by the willingness to take risks, to be moved, and to adapt to the new. It encourages, nurtures, supports, educates, and builds. It facilitates, mediates, and heals. We are all capable of leading with spirit because we are all inheritors of the original spirit-wisdom.

The meeting closed with an ancient prayer of the Navajo:

*With these before you, happily may they come*
  *with you,*
*With these behind, below, above, around you,*
  *happily may they come with you,*
*Thus you accomplish your tasks.*
*Happily, the old men will regard you,*
*Happily, the old women will regard you,*
*The young men and the young women will*
  *regard you,*
*The children will regard you,*
*The chiefs will regard you,*
*Happily, as they scatter in all directions they*
  *will regard you,*
*Happily, as they approach their homes they will*
  *regard you,*
*May their roads home be on the trail of peace.*

# Intimacy in a Self-Help Group

*Insiders' Guide* asked psychologist **Monique Savlin, PhD**, what we need to know about intimacy when we are joining a self-help group. She has written and lectured about intimacy for many years.

**IG**: How is joining a group similar to having intimate relationships?

**MS**: The challenge intimacy gives us is that our longing to share our life with another human being and grow in a relationship conflicts with our fear of being overwhelmed and controlled by that person. On one hand we need closeness, and on the other we resent losing too much autonomy. Without relationships we become isolated and this creates anxiety.

**IG**: How do you know if you "belong" in a particular group?

**MS**: Intimacy is simply self-revelation; people talk about who they are, their hopes, dreams, worries, and fears. If you are able to be yourself, you're comfortable and the group feels comfortable. Sometimes you're with people and become tired. If someone is pretending, phony, you sense that and, in turn, you're not real. That's why you feel tired. You repress, hold back parts of yourself, and holding back takes energy. If people appear phony and stay on a superficial level in their conversation, the message is that the group is not ready to move to deeper levels of self-revelation.

If things don't work out it could be a matter of timing. Your attempts at intimacy may have come too soon. People need time before they reveal a deeper level of themselves. Or on that evening, the group may not have helped bring up topics that would let you know that you have common experiences. The leader ordinarily invites people leaving under these circumstances to come back and give the group another chance.

**IG**: What are the signs that it is safe for you to reveal personal information to the group?

**MS**: The first time you attend a group, you reveal why you came and describe your situation. You are gathering information at a superficial level. The more you know about the group, the safer you will feel.

However, if people ridicule, don't listen to each other, or give inappropriate advice, the message is they are not ready to move to a deeper level of self-revelation. If you are in a crisis, it is important that the leader or group leadership knows how to contain what is going on. You should be given an introduction that includes what the group is about, guidelines, confidentiality, and a request that anyone in crisis listen for awhile and later make a brief statement about their situation. If you reveal too much to soon, other group members might become frightened by your painful emotions.

**IG**: In self-help groups, members share the responsibility for how the group operates, including the group meeting. Is there special caution or expectation in these groups that new members should be aware of?

**MS**: If you are uncomfortable talking at first, it should be clear from the group that it is fine to remain silent. But the leaders should be able to develop empathic responses at just the appropriate level, such as "Does anyone else have that experience or reaction?" The leaders will draw out our ability to express our fears and our love. If you are a new member, you should pace your level of emotional control and determine when you are ready to talk about your experiences. Then, you can express yourself, open up, listen to others, let yourself be vulnerable, take a chance, and risk it!

# Why Come Back?

The person joining the group must acknowledge characteristics he has in common with the group. Belonging includes friendship, mutual aid, and intimacy. You can learn valuable lessons in every group and the first lesson all groups emphasize is that you are not alone. When you ask, "Is this group for me?" you also wonder if the group beliefs embrace the possibilities you hope for yourself.

## You Share the Group's Beliefs

The process of becoming a "believer" flows easily when you can accept the group's authority to define what recovery or coping is and the responsibilities you will take if you are to succeed in getting through your crisis. After observing people in hundreds of groups, it appears to me that the key to any successful value system is simply to fully believe that what you do will make a difference. In some ways, no matter what you believe will work. Mostly, people just want to get through this crisis and members who discuss the group's beliefs in terms of their own experiences offer hopeful strategies .

## You Are Empowered

We sometimes see equal success in very different approaches. In a Grow in Illinois group, a veteran member with a history of mental illness discusses with a newcomer her work environment where she had struggled with a critical manager. The strategies she employed to handle this conflict reflect the group's therapeutic belief system. A disability group organized as an advocacy model might take an entirely different approach, one that strongly advocates for accommodation. Either way, the group empowers you to take a stand.

## You Feel Hope

What if you believe you can recover and group members claim that you will always be "in recovery" from an addiction? What if group members claim that you will always need to take medication to control mental illness, asthma, and diabetes? Empowerment means different things at different times in this journey from crisis to getting your life back. You will want to understand what is possible and evaluate whether the group's beliefs can help you achieve empowerment. If, for example, you have a spinal cord injury and you find hope in believing that you will walk one day, a group that rejects the belief that technology will eventually stimulate nerve fiber to regenerate will dash your hopes. It is difficult when the group beliefs differs from your beliefs..

## You Have Options

Some people who balk at AA's core belief that you are powerless to control drinking choose to explore empowering beliefs in Rational Recovery or, if alcoholism isn't an issue, in an alcohol moderation management group.

Some groups for people suffering from mental illness help members cooperate with psychiatrists and comply with medication. Other groups contend that members alone are responsible for their destiny. One exciting new direction in Illinois' Department of Health and Human Services is a group developed with the help of mental health consumer advocates. This group focuses on managing responsibilities, and members determine what success means to them. In

this way, the group builds its own meaning for empowerment.

If you want to learn quickly if the group beliefs and methods seem appropriate for you, identify them from what people say in the group. Are they pro-conventional medicine all the time, or is it fine to have conversations about echinacea or other herbs? Does the group work to manage your medication or help you choose what responsibilities you want to manage? You can read the group's literature to discover its beliefs and you can listen to what members say about how they recover and sustain. It is fun to learn from different groups. If you find that you are not making progress or do not feel at home in a group, try attending, calling, or going online with another one. But don't give up hope. Grow in Illinois tells us, "there is no such thing as a no-hoper."

# First Meeting Tips

Going to a new self-help or support group holds an unknown emotional element, because even at your first meeting, the stress of a life or health crisis might surface. You gather all your courage, get to the door, and no one greets you or helps you feel comfortable. In a group just starting out or one where people have trouble getting to meetings, as do caregivers or people with panic attacks, a small turnout does not mean that the group is not functioning successfully. Even three or four people can help one another in very meaningful ways.

At first, you may wish to refrain from responding to deeper, probing questions. The group may not know how to rescue you from a year's worth of stored up emotions. But if such emotions do erupt, the group will be there for you. Members in "successful" groups sense one another's zone of comfort and rarely probe into deeper emotional issues. Groups in which deep emotions frequently surface sometimes have professional therapists co-facilitate the meeting with a peer member.

Becoming part of a group may feel complicated. Sometimes, the group beliefs or the jargon may unintentionally undermine a positive experience for you. Newcomers to AA frequently resist the words "higher power." Perhaps, on the night you come, the leader familiar with handling conflict is on vacation. A very anxious member talks for most of the meeting and you wonder why you ever came. Remind yourself that first impressions are not always accurate. If you do go to your first group meeting, will you return a few times to understand how the group operates and how you can get help?

## Group Autonomy

Remember, members *are* the group. The group meets when it is convenient for the members. Members decide the course of the meetings: what presenters they want to invite, the format of the meeting, what will be discussed.

## Essential Qualities

Some qualities essential to achieving the fundamental bonding and support in a successful self-help group are:

- unconditional acceptance
- caring
- respect
- safety

## When Expectations Are Not Met

We should have expectations for our group, but remember to ask yourself if it is possible that you are using some expectations as if they were obstacles rather than as hurdles.

So many things can go wrong. The meeting might be held in a neighborhood where you do not feel safe. You may have suffered through a meeting where one of the members wore heavy perfume, or smokers congregated just outside of the meeting room. The memory of a negative impression may outweigh a positive one and, after just one or two meetings, you might be ready to bolt.

Some features of self-help groups are not negotiable. The group's beliefs may be too spiritual or not spiritual enough for you. Issues of concern to minorities may not be represented in the group as much as you would like. In this case, find another group or start your own chapter emphasizing these beliefs or populations. You might test the water by asking if there is a meeting geared to a different approach. Other people may also feel the way you do.

Think of yourself as a stakeholder in this under-budgeted or no-budget venture. After a few meetings, assess your experience. Don't take the group's failures personally. If you don't think the group is operating

with self-help principles or the group doesn't seem right for you, you can discuss issues with group leaders or other members and explore your many options:

- Leave without a sense of rejection or anger and try out other groups. You can always go back. Try one or two other groups and at least one with different formats. You will learn from any group experience, even if you can't find a nearby group for the same problem.

- Leave and find another group, if there are several groups serving the problem you have. Look in the *Register* (Section II of this *Guide*) for listings of groups with similar problems.

- Become part of the solution. Decide if you have enough patience to make a difference for the next people that will need this group. You might suggest ways to improve future meetings. One easy way that isn't confrontational is to copy some of the articles in this book and give them to the group's leaders, or recommend that they get a complete copy of the *Insiders' Guide* for themselves.

- Start your own group. Check other groups and models to get ideas. Find another person to share the responsibilities and create a group to meet your needs.

# How to Recognize a Group that's Right for You

Any time we enter a totally new situation, like a support group meeting, it helps to know what to expect from that experience. Your goal is to understand what you need and see if you can get it from that particular group. The following checklist will help you determine if the group is right for you.

1. Consider some of the ways mentioned previously in which successful groups reach out to newcomers.

2. Think about and write down what you really want the group to address.

3. If you can reach a contact person before you go to the meeting, briefly discuss who attends meetings (the person with the problem or disease or family member, their age and cultural background, if that information is important to you), and how your

concerns will be addressed in the group. Request material about the group.

4. At the first few meetings, observe what the group actually does and how it could meet your needs.

5. How caring is the group? Are you greeted when you come to the group meeting? Do members welcome you, invite you to be seated, and walk up to you before the meeting even starts?

6. Do you have ample opportunity as a member of this group to learn how people in your situation have coped and taken charge of their problems? Potential learning opportunities include:

   • the meeting itself, where you will hear individuals telling their stories

   • educational programs and presentations, and informal time before and after meetings when members approach newcomers

   • members who network you to individuals with very similar conditions or to community resources

   • current informational material available at the meeting or mailed to newcomers

   • the group's Internet online self-help communities, if there is an Internet presence available

7. How comfortable are you with the group's format? Have you heard explained or seen material about the group's purpose and guidelines? Is there a clear agenda and are meetings regularly scheduled?

8. Can you accept the beliefs of the group? Do you want more or less formal structure, rituals, interaction, or member interaction?

9. Does the group demonstrate that it invites everyone's participation, is non-judgmental, and keeps interactions emotionally safe and comfortable? New members should not feel that they are probed to reveal more than they want to.

10. Does the leadership of the group demonstrate that it knows how to involve everyone and manage strong personalities and conflict?

11. Do many members play a role in planning and maintaining the group or is one person responsible for everything? Do you see new people stepping forward or are the same one or two people in control? Groups work best if there is a strong infrastructure of members who share responsibilities for the group. With this open structure, you might see how you are needed in the group.

12. If this group doesn't meet your expectations, consider ways you can get what you need from individual members or by discussing the group's structure with a leader.

13. Just seeing two, three, or a roomful of other people with the same condition relieves the immense sense that you are the only one with these feelings and experiences. If you feel that way, the meeting has accomplished an important need.

14. Breaking through from a newcomer to an "insider" takes a few meetings. It is difficult for these group members to handle many of the concerns and problems you have in addition to trying to help others and maintain this group.

15. You can do your part to make this transition by anticipating that you might cut off the real opportunity too soon. Try to remain open to the possibility that there may be something there that will benefit you and give this experience a few meetings before you decide to commit or to leave the group.

16. Do you expect the group to answer needs beyond what it is set up to do—give information about your common problem, share experiences, and offer friendship? Ask the group to help you meet additional needs through community agencies and professional counseling.

# Supporting Vulnerable Members

*If we don't have peace, it is because
we have forgotten that we all belong to each other.*

**Mother Theresa**

Self-help groups frequently focus on humanistic activities that emphasize the values, capacities, and worth of their members. They incorporate positive findings from research on the mind-body connection. In this chapter, we highlight body/mind activities to help members deal with the physical and emotional challenges of an illness, including at the end of life.

We know from the widely published works of researchers Dean Ornish and Meyer Friedman that the mind can modify behavior, altering the course of heart disease. Mental interventions appear to be more potent than any diet, drug, or exercise. Ornish gives credit to the positive effect of support group training demonstrated in his study. Lawrence LeShan gets similarly impressive improvements from helping cancer patients access repressed negative emotions.

Neuroscientist Candace Pert has helped us understand the roles of neuropeptides and how emotions and health are connected at the molecular level: "Emotions are a key element in self-care because they allow us to enter into the body-mind conversation and direct them through the psychosomatic network." (1997, p. 283). Elmer Green, a scientist who quantifies the practical value of meditative states, provides a measurable technology, biofeedback, for accessing an inner intelligence: "We have been inhibited, repressed, and hypnotized by our cultural conditioning and education to see ourselves as powerless to control or change events in our bodies and lives. We have not been informed that our bodies tend to do what they are told to do if we know how to tell them. Only when we do not accept this limiting image of ourselves can we break the thralldom and begin to operate as free beings, capable of influencing to a significant extent the course of our lives" (from conversation cited in Schwartz, 1995, pp. 117-118).

The unconditional support and nurturing environment created by stable self-help groups are very conducive to these kinds of humanistic interventions, especially in reducing stress and replacing destructive behaviors with healthier choices. Most self-help groups seem to be able to use these interventions constructively without falling into the trap of implying that members are in some way to blame for their condition or disease. With their spontaneous and adaptive responses to human needs, self-help groups frequently use body/mind interventions to accomplish their goal of empowering people to take charge of their lives. These interventions can occur through a number of avenues:

- Members inevitably informally link each other to complementary and alternative health care services and other sources of support for positive behaviors.

- Self-help groups increasingly incorporate health-inducing activities, such as t'ai chi, art therapy, massage, journaling, meditation, guided imagery, nutrition, and pet therapy, as well as support for member's spiritual development.

- Instead of conducting ongoing programs, the group may sponsor presenters to facilitate acquiring the benefits of body-mind activities.

- Professionals can incorporate peer or professionally co-facilitated body/mind interventions among peers. The founder of AA is well known; other innovators include Jerry Jampolsky, MD, Center for Attitudinal Healing; Bernie Siegel, MD, the Exceptional Cancer Patient; Dean Ornish, MD, heart support programs; Simon Stephens, MDiv, bereaved parents program, The Compassionate Friends; Con Keogh, MDiv, Grow, International, for people affected by chronic mental illness; and other professional founders of groups mentioned elsewhere in this book.

The following two articles extend the benefits of these body/mind interventions and other humanistic care techniques to vulnerable group members.

# Group Roles in Life-Threatening Illness

Daryl Holtz Isenberg, PhD

Hundreds of studies, especially on the elderly, have found that social support contributes significantly to recovering from illness and loss. In his 1989 study, psychiatrist David Spiegel reports the difference in survival rates of two groups of women, those who attended a weekly group session with other metastatic breast cancer patients and those who did not. The women who participated in weekly sessions lived an average of twice as long as those who did not, 36.6 months versus 18 months.

While studies of other groups have not found such dramatically increased survival rates, there is no doubt that the positive attitudes and coping strategies learned in peer support groups improve the quality of members' lives and can sustain them at the end of life. However, we could not find specific studies describing the way self-help groups are organized to specifically address emotional or physical challenges at the end of life.

To begin to understand the roles of self-help groups providing support to members who are dying, I asked leaders from groups for cancer, breast cancer, Huntington's disease, scleroderma, heart disease, chronic fatigue syndrome, manic depression, colitis and ileitis, ostomy, sarcoidosis, and multiple sclerosis how they handle end-of-life issues.

Support for dying members was again discussed in a panel we organized for a 1997 symposium on "The Other 74%: Non-Cancer Life-Threatening Diseases and Their End-of-Life Components." The panel consisted of the executive director of the National Self-Help Clearinghouse, Audrey Gardner, PhD; the founder of Disability Online, Arlette Lefebreve, MD; past board vice president and area leader of Recovery, Inc., Delores Gregory; and founder, National Sarcoidosis Resource Center, Sandra Conroy. They all reported that the potential for members to be helped in self-help groups is profound. They described the existing structure of their group, indicating that self-

help groups support members in many ways at all stages of a life-threatening illness, including the end of life. However, the panel reported that their groups did not have specific guidelines for helping members during that process.

We have now initiated a program of positive interventions to help self-help groups develop structures to more clearly understand and meet the needs of members and families preceding and following a death.

## Joining a Life-Threatening Illness Group

Typically, self-help groups do a tremendous job of meeting the needs of newly diagnosed members, when the family has just weathered the initial crisis of learning of an illness. Groups help new members by providing information and strategies for coping with the full scope of problems related to their illness. Members require an orientation to the culture of this specific illness. They come desperate to:

- learn how to negotiate the health care and other bureaucratic systems
- understand their illness and treatment
- receive support in making medical choices
- evaluate the effects of medications and treatment
- accept the impact of their illness
- shift to a different self-concept and identity
- relate to family, friends, and employment

Self-help groups are responsive to the needs of both veteran and new members as the condition either improves or becomes more serious. Wherever they are in the spectrum of their condition, members are looking for the intimacy and immediate understanding offered by others in similar stages. Self-help group members become resources to each other through their openness, shared experiences, mutual problem solving, and networking. With the added emotional impact of a pending death, family members must handle their own challenges while helping to make decisions for a loved one.

While families and professionals may be tempted to act expediently, it is critical for the ill person at the end of life to feel in charge. Through involvement in a self-help group, members get the experience and support they need to feel that they are in charge of major decisions related to their disease and their lives, and to prepare for the possibility of their death.

## Group Assistance for Multiple End-of-Life Issues

Life-threatening illnesses require a response to loss, grief, and the meaning of existence. Serious illnesses demand an adaptation in roles as women or men, family members, employees, and friends. An essential characteristic of self-help groups is their capacity to support change during these periods of transition and to assist in shifting the individual's attitude from fear, anger, and resentment to the concrete joys of the present moment.

Despite their diversity, most self-help groups share the common characteristics identified by Borman (1990):

- Members share a common condition, problem, symptom, and experience. These bonds create a climate of acceptance of other members.

- Members govern themselves. They are not hierarchical; decisions are made by consensus. Members recognize that they are included and that their votes count.

- The group has a set of beliefs about how to deal with the illness, run meetings, and deal with people who backslide in the program. When connected to a national health or self-help organization, the group develops or receives distilled, trustworthy health information packets. This material guides the organization of new groups, describes the illness and common issues, and is updated and distributed frequently when new health information is available.

- Groups advocate self-reliance and commit to self-responsibility and therefore retain the locus of control in their lives. When members experience an existential conflict upon learning of a relapse,

the task is to encourage members to evaluate their lives in relation to the fulfillment of expectations, responsibilities, and emotional satisfaction with significant relationships.

- Groups advocate helping each other. The "helper therapy principle" observed by Reissman (1984) states that the person helping benefits even more than the person helped. This occurs when the act of helping reinforces new skills. Helping a peer tends to opens one's heart in compassion. It was easy to engage a resistant teenager with lymphoma to attend a meeting when asked if he would be willing to help a newly diagnosed child. In the meeting, this veteran reinforced taking medication and gave ideas about how to swallow large pills.

- Groups offer hope through others who have sustained similar diagnoses, treatments, and experiences, and act as role models. Seeing a 10-year-old child who was active and happy at a meeting shifted the gloom of parents of a 5-year-old who was newly diagnosed with acute lymphoblastic leukemia.

- Self-help groups charge little or no fees and operate outside institutional sanctions. When professional services are insufficient or are not available, self-help groups pave the way for new treatments and services. They often choose to struggle and retain their autonomy rather than to be absorbed by a bureaucratic organization. However, groups welcome cooperative relations with professionals.

## Principles Valid with Later Stage Illnesses

The basic principles in these characteristics are valid at the end of life, even if there are no specific group guidelines for meeting the needs of members when they have relapsed or are dying. For group participants who have an ongoing relationship in a group, the family often makes it a point to communicate to the group how meaningful their phone calls, visits, balloons, and cards were right up until their loved one's last days.

Unfortunately, most group members are better prepared to help each other accept and cope with their illness than deal with its terminal phase. Given the increasing attention to improving the quality of care at the end of life, self-help groups have a tremendous opportunity to codify the various ways they do and could support members throughout the dying process. This new emphasis for self-help groups is particularly important because of the support it gives to the efforts of health professionals who are also struggling to provide better care for their dying patients.

## Trauma/Crisis at End of Life

The diagnosis of a relapse or terminal stage abruptly disrupts the patient's hopes and dreams of having succeeded in "beating" the initial diagnosis. Patients may experience despair when they perceive their laboratory report as diminished fortune or odds. Feelings of loss of control and death ideation may follow. During interactions with family and professionals, patients may sense other people's disbelief, shock, or revulsion in the reality of their potential death. With this scenario, patients may become disoriented or isolated and experience mood swings. And stigmas about the specific illness and the concept of death increase the patient's and family's feelings of alienation and fear.

Add to this scenario the desperation to find the very best traditional and/or alternative treatment options available. It is no surprise that at the end of life of a child, parent, or sibling, the entire family risks depleting its financial resources and the caregiver's health to locate and provide heroic life-saving treatments.

There may also be a shift in the relationship with medical staff. At the earlier stages of illness, physicians were happy to guide medical decisions, but they have not yet been prepared to deal with the issues that arise when remission is no longer possible. Moreover, medical staff may have different values than the patient or family regarding the use of high or low technology at the end of life. Physicians may perceive that the family is unrealistic in its expectations about the benefits of life-extending measures, yet they do not have the training or time to gently explore the psychological issues the end of life evokes. If the patient is hospitalized with an end stage illness, miscommunications between the medical staff can leave family members feeling helpless to protect the wishes of the patient.

With modest support, self-help groups could provide families facing the death of a member with information and comfort to support them through the various stages of illness. These groups could be invaluable conduits for distributing consumer health education and actual assistance during the dying process. The burgeoning online support available on the Internet is particularly helpful when mobility is difficult and when needing immediate communication from peers or professionals about whatever issues arise during the end of life, especially dealing with symptoms other than pain.

## Group Healing Methods at Later Stage Illnesses

Group members continue to stay in touch informally with members at this stage. Two important mechanisms play a growing role for members in later stages:

- Members learn to anticipate possible future scenarios of relapse and terminal stages when they observe role models in later stages of illness; they can rehearse their own capacities at later stages of illness. A newly diagnosed young woman with chronic myocitic leukemia attended a group quite a while before her illness became acute. She said she learned how to handle her situation during the previous 2 years of involvement in the group.

- Group members visit informally or, as a group, meet phone-to-phone or via the Internet.

## Physical, Behavioral, Psychological, and Social Help

Patricia Fennell's Four-Phase Method for treating chronic and trauma syndromes provides a useful model for self-help groups serving members at the end of life. It is geared to help people come to terms with the impact of physical, behavioral, psychological, social, and interactive forces. Fennel's four phases of chronic illness include: 1) trauma/crisis, 2) stabilization/normalization failure, 3) existential conflict, and 4) integration. Like all stage models, including Elizabeth Kubler Ross' Stages of Dying or Lawrence Kohlberg's Stages of Moral Development, Fennell's approach is not sequential; phases may occur out of sequence and be repeated. For instance, a relapse can trigger the return of issues in the crisis phase. If the initial crisis was successfully handled, these competencies return and the depth of suffering is less extensive.

Self-help groups are uniquely positioned to acquire and use these tools to expand their outreach and better serve members at the end of life. Groups could seek external funding to conduct workshops geared to sensitize members about the need to provide support at the end of life and to learn how to apply the Four Phase Method.

Self-help groups offer a laboratory for observing and learning about effective strategies for providing peer support at the end of life. Depending on the group, there are a number of options to serve members at the end of life. Groups would need to understand who attends their meetings, the needs of current members, and the needs of people who contact the group but decide the group doesn't meet their needs. By better understanding these constituencies, group members could then address various options for meeting unmet needs for the goals they target.

Some possibilities to explore with life-threatening illness groups include models offering:

- *Homogeneous groups for later stages of these illnesses.* Groups for AIDS and cancer may offer special meetings. Test Positive Aware Network offers daytime meetings for late stage AIDS members, distinguished as "day-timers" because they are too ill to work. Y-Me for breast cancer and the Cancer Wellness Center also regularly provide separate sessions for members in advanced stages.

- *Integrated groups within part of the regular structure, with members meeting together for educational programs responding to the needs of all members.* This scenario would also require that the entire group be assisted in learning to handle emotional conflict, grief, and loss. Professional collaborations would enhance this structure.

- *A subset of groups focusing on issues important to members, including the end of life.* Following meetings of the entire group, members would select break-out groups for relevant topics.

- *Outreach activities serving members at the end of life.* Self-help groups would create opportunities for online communication and visiting programs, would be available during critical events pre-selected by the terminally ill member, and would assist in connecting families to hospice- and institution-based programs.

We need answers to questions that will help us understand the risks and benefits of exposing self-help group members to end-of-life issues, how best to structure groups, and when it would be beneficial to bring together members at all stages of the disease. We know that as self-help groups become stable and funded, they will respond to the challenges presented when members face the end of life. And, importantly, we hope to learn to assist self-help groups in developing and coordinating end of life programs.

## References

Borman, LD, Self Help/Mutual Aid Groups in Strategies for Health, in *Self-Help Concepts and Applications* edited by A Katz, H Hedrick, et al. Philadelphia: Charles Press, 1992.

Galanter, M. Zealous Self-Help Groups as Adjuncts to Psychiatric Treatment: A Study of Recovery, Inc. *American Journal of Psychiatry* 145(10): 1248-1253, 1988.

Isenberg, DH. *Coping with Cancer, Belief Systems and Support in Cancer Self-Help Groups.* Doctoral Dissertation, Northwestern University, 1981.

Katz, A and Bender, E, Toward Definitions and Classifications of Self-Help Groups, in *Helping One Another: Self-Help Groups in a Changing World*, Oakland, California: Third Party Publishing, 1990.

Fennell, Patricia, in Jason, Leonard A, Afterward: An Eco-Transformational Application: Bridging the Macro to the Micro. *Community Building, Values for a Sustainable Future.* Westport, Connecticut, 1997, 111-114.

Kurtz, LF. Mutual Aid for Affective Disorders: The Manic Depressive and Depressive Association. *American Journal of Orthopsychiatry* 58(1): 152-155, 1988.

Lieberman, MA and Borman, LD. *Self-Help Groups for Coping with Crisis*, San Francisco: Jossey Bass, 1983.

Pert, C. *Molecules of Emotion*, New York, Simon & Schuster, 1997.

Raiff, NR, Some Health Related Outcomes of Self-Help Participation. Chapter 14 in *The Self-Help Revolution*, edited by Alan Gartner and Frank Riessman. New York: Human Sciences Press, 1988.

Schwartz, T. *What Really Matters, Searching for Wisdom in America*, New York: Bantam Books, 1995.

Spiegel, D, Bloom, JR, Kraemer, HC and Bottheil, E. The Effect of Psychosocial Treatment on Survival of Patients with Metastatic Breast Cancer, *Lancet*, 1989; 2:888-891.

*Surgeon General's Workshop on Self-Help and Public Health.* US Department of Health & Human Services, Public Health Service, Health Resources and Services Administration, 1987.

# Self-Help Groups and Compassionate Dying

Hannah L. Hedrick, PhD

Self-help groups for life-threatening illness are filling a major gap in health and human services, which generally have no provisions for helping people die. Even if hospice care were available to everyone who wanted it, self-help group members would still be more appropriate in participating with families in the simple but potent activity of coordinating a compassionate and respectful death. Centuries-old techniques can be successfully adapted by self-help groups to prepare families and group members with new skills that benefit and nurture everyone involved.

The simple techniques I use to orchestrate a compassionate, respectful death bring to the final moments of life principles learned from many years as a student and teacher of yoga and t'ai chi chih. Texts from various traditions present the moment a dying person enters the "sacred doorway" as an opportunity for creating a spacious, loving presence that facilitates spiritual growth.

These techniques can be used by anyone wanting to experience the deep sense of intimacy and spiritual growth that can occur during the transition from life to death. The breathing meditation and other activities can be practiced to improve the quality of life for the ill person and the family in the years, months, weeks, or days preceding death.

## Creating a Peaceful Environment

Everyone involved in orchestrating a conscious death should keep the focus on the dying person so the supporters can intuitively respond and enter fully into the dying process.

*Sound:* Sound and music special to the individual, including singing, chanting, toning, and repeating a mantra, can be used to improve the quality of life as well as to bring comfort during the dying moments. On many occasions, tapes I used as background music when doing bodywork on ill friends have been requested for their final moments and their memorial service.

*Scent*: Although aromatherapy is sometimes ridiculed by skeptics attempting to discount the benefits of

complementary health practices, people with an illness are frequently comforted by smells they associate with pleasant memories, from cooking smells to baby powder or a favorite perfume.

*Ritual:* Prayer, meditation, or other spiritual techniques and rituals appropriate for the individual and family can enhance health and provide comfort in preparation for death and at the moment of death. Family rituals that invite others to enter a space of silence and stillness can be reviewed and repeated.

*Unfinished business and messages*: If there is time and if unfinished business (such as expressing gratitude, saying good-bye, or recording a video, audio, or written life review) has not been resolved, the guide can help identify tasks and facilitate their accomplishment. If time is short, the guide can share spoken or unspoken messages. It still seems very strange to me that when I am privileged to orchestrate a death, I feel moved to say things that are very meaningful to a friend or family member, although I am unaware of that meaning. If a dying person appears to be struggling to wait for someone's arrival, assure the dying person that he or she can communicate directly with that person "from the heart" and that you will also deliver a loving message.

## Breathing Meditation Traditions

The well-established benefits of meditation have been reported in scientific peer-review journals in recent years by physicians such as Herbert Benson, Dean Ornish, and Andrew Weil. Release of tension through moving or seated meditation, both involving breath awareness, can diminish physical pain, nausea, and shortness of breath and alleviate anxiety, anger, fear, and sleeplessness. Cross breathing or co-meditation, in which one person helps another person to relax by breathing audibly, has been practiced for an estimated three thousand years. Richard Boerstler and Hulen Kornfeld have worked since 1979 to bring a modified co-meditation process into widespread practice. Their technique includes progressive muscle relaxation; a body scan; a sound sequence based on repeating "ahhhhh" together and then by the facilitator alone; counting from one to ten for 5 minutes to the rhythm of the recipient's breath; repeating a word, words, or prayer chosen by the recipient; and concluding the session, which may include verbal cues for reducing tension.

## Peer Breathing Meditation— "Release to Peace"

About 15 years ago, I began to attend Daryl Isenberg's Family Cancer Support Network and soon found myself at the bedsides of people who had attended the Network's yoga, t'ai chi chih, and meditation sessions. Being with fellow practitioners of these techniques at the moment of death was a natural progression of our shared meditative states. Twelve years ago, I began to teach two nights a week at an HIV/AIDS group. Many participants became regular meditators, and on several occasions, with no previous experience with a dying person, were perfectly comfortable participating in a "release-to-peace" group meditation. The power of this group process provides a cushion of comfort to family members and friends, who appreciate guidance in actively supporting the dying process of a loved one.

The processes vary tremendously, depending on the environment (intensive care, intermediate care, long-term care institution, home with hospice, home without hospice, nursing home hospice, institutional hospice) and the mental and physical state of the individual. However, some elements are fairly constant: supportive physical position, sustained focus, gentle touch, following the breath, body/mind/spirit connection, and asking for help and receiving guidance. Beyond that, various scenarios call for different accommodations.

*Supportive physical position*:  After doing what can be done to establish a peaceful environment, the guide or healing team members approach the dying person with respect and silently request permission to enter that person's space to support the dying process. Usually people will move intuitively to a supportive position. I sometimes position myself at the feet, move during the process to points higher on the body, and find myself around the head during the last breath.

*Sustained focus*:  The guide reminds supporters that if their focus shifts to their sense of loss or other issues, they should gently withdraw from close proximity until they can regain a meditative focus.

*Gentle touch*:  Depending on the mental and physical state of the person who is dying, and where they are in the dying process, the guide and other members of the healing team can do gentle "comfort" touching, staying in a state of absolute reverence and respect and being careful not to distract the focus of the dying person. Sometimes the dying person is connected to so much technical death-delaying equipment that the feet and the head are the only parts of the body that can be touched. As the dying process continues, the guide and healing team members generally hover their hands above the body to reduce the possibility of influencing the dying person's process.

*Following the breath*:  As soon as I enter the presence of the dying person, I listen and look for the breath in order to let it guide mine. Instead of following any specific technique, I tune in as deeply as possible to the person's breathing pattern and sound.

*Body/mind/spirit connection*:  The intense joint meditative state created by the above steps involves a body/mind/spirit connection of all involved. An experienced facilitator can coach others in entering the space of the dying person instead of requiring that person to be responsive to external stimulation. Distressed loved ones are taken aside and comforted by members of the team. Even if they are too fragile to participate, they feel comforted by the healing process taking place.

*Asking for help*:  Once our breathing is synchronized and the connection with the dying person is established, I simply ask sincerely for help in where to be, what to say, and what to do to support the dying person and in keeping my own opinions, ego, personality, and preferences from intruding. This state of receiving guidance continues throughout the dying process. Frequently, I end up positioned above the crown center at the top of the head during the final breath, feeling as if the person has given birth to his or her soul into my hands.

*Accommodations for varied scenarios*:  Sometimes just entering a state of respectful communication and support with the dying person can visibly reduce agitation and distress. Sitting or kneeling by the bedside in absolute silence and stillness, with your outside hand holding the dying person's hand and your hand lightly on the upper abdomen or heart center, can produce additional signs of relaxation. If a healing team is present, I am alert to excessive stimulation that can distract the dying person. If active aspiration feels appropriate to diminish signs of physical and emotional agitation, it is done by one person. Healing team members are supportively positioned around the dying person. If the process is prolonged and tiring, I will sit in bed behind the dying person, cradling his or her body with my arms and legs. In this position I can actively feel the breath and use my own to model softness.

Self-Help groups wanting a presentation on this process should contact the Illinois Self-Help Coalition, Wright College, 3400 N Austin Avenue, Chicago, Illinois 60634, phone 773/481-8837, email: selfhelp@enteract.com.

## References

1.  Katz, Alfred H; Hedrick, Hannah L; Isenberg, Daryl H; Thompson, Leslie M; Goodrich, Therese; and Kutscher, Austin H. *Self-Help: Concepts and Applications*. Philadelphia: The Charles Press, 1992.

2.  Boerstler, Richard and Kornfeld, Hulen. *Life to Death: Harmonizing the Transition*. Rochester, Vermont: Healing Arts Press, 1995.

3.  Levine, Stephen. *Healing into Life and Death*. New York: Anchor Books/Doubleday, 1987.

4.  Rinpoche, Sogyal. *The Tibetan Book of Living and Dying*. San Francisco: Harper San Francisco, 1992.

# Complementary and Alternative Health Practices

*Alternative medicine is here to stay.*
*It is no longer an option to ignore it or treat it as*
*something outside the normal processes of science and medicine.*

**Wayne Jonas, MD**
In Alternative Medicine: Learning from the Past, Advancing to the Future.
***Journal of the American Medical Association,***
***November 1998***

Hannah Hedrick, PhD

The topics of self-care and behavioral change in self-help groups almost invariably bring up the topic of complementary and alternative health care practices. (The terms "complementary" and "alternative" refer to interventions for improving, maintaining, and promoting health and well-being, preventing disease, or treating illness that are not part of a standard North American biomedical regimen of health care or disease prevention.) In fact, a component on "self-help groups" frequently appears in the comprehensive manuals and encyclopedias on "alternative medicine" published during the second half of the 1990s. Self-help groups are praised by the leading physician practitioners and advocates. But when you put these two elements together—self-help groups and complementary/alternative health practices—old fears arise. A decade ago, professional medical publications reported the opinion of physicians that "these lay-led organizations" disseminated only information that would be "anti-medical and even injurious." Physicians in general, excluding those practicing or receiving the techniques themselves, were described as "suspect of the movement."

Research results on the safety and efficacy of some self-help groups and some complementary and alternative health care practices have partially alleviated those fears and suspicions. Because self-help groups now have access to much of the information available to health and human service providers, they can assess the safety and efficacy of modalities reported to be beneficial to self-care and behavioral change.

## The Filter of the "Wisdom of the Group"

New members may come to the group with a lot of experience in self-care and interest in and knowledge about complementary and alternative health practices. At first, they may feel they can make a greater contribution sharing information about these topics than about their problems. Other new or experienced members may have healthy skepticism about some of these techniques. Most groups can accommodate both attitudes, but people at the opposite ends of the spectrum might be more comfortable in groups with the same orientation.

Groups, in general, have mechanisms to avoid undue influence on members to use "unproven" and perhaps even "unsafe" practices. Even groups that regularly present information about a wide variety of self-care and complementary modalities rarely give blanket approval if there are any questions at all about the efficacy and safety of the approach.

In addition to hearing from the experts (and frequently advocates), groups usually invite members to share their opinions and experiences. This "wisdom of the group" provides a unique filter of personal testimony that assists members in deciding for themselves whether or not to try a general or specific remedy.

# Little Evidence of Harm

Just as there is little evidence that autonomous, grassroots, peer-led self-help groups harm members in any way, most complementary and alternative health care practices are noninvasive and therefore relatively safe. Feel free to share the following list of Selected Complementary and Alternative Health Care Systems and Practices with your self-help group. If you would like additional information, contact the author through the Illinois Self-Help Coalition.

## Check It Out

If you are considering going to a group meeting for the first time, you might want to check out where the group stands on issues such as self-care, support for behavior change, and presentation of complementary and alternative health practices.

# Selected Complementary and Alternative Health Care Systems and Practices

## Mind/Body Interventions

Aromatherapy
Art therapy
Biofeedback
Dance and movement therapy
Hypnosis
Imagery
Meditation
Music therapy
Prayer and mental healing
Self-help and support groups
Qigong (including T'ai chi)
Yoga

## Non-Biomedical Systems

Acupuncture
Anthroposophic medicine
Ayurveda
Latin American community health care
Native American healthcare
Homeopathy
Naturopathy
Traditional Oriental/Chinese medicine

## Diet and Nutrition

Cultural diets
Macrobiotic
Mediterranean
Traditional Native American
Diet modification regimens
Supplemental therapies
Amino Acids
Minerals
Vitamins (e.g., antioxidants)
Enzymes

## Bioelectromagnetic Applications

Electroacupuncture
Neuromagnetic stimulation
Transcranial electrostimulation

## Manual Healing Techniques

Biofield therapeutics
Healing touch
Polarity therapy
Reiki
SHEN physioemotional release therapy
Therapeutic touch
Chiropractic
Massage and related techniques
Deep tissue massage
Manual lymph drainage
Neuromuscular massage
Postural reeducation therapies
Alexander technique
Feldenkrais method
Pressure point therapies
Trager psychophysical integration
Sports massage

## Herbal Medicines and Remedies

European botanical medicines
Latin American herbal remedies
Native American herbal agents
Oriental herbal agents
Chinese
Japanese-Kampo

## Pharmacologic and Biologic Treatment Agents

Antineoplastons
Bee venom
Cartilage products

Ethylene diamine tetraacetic acid (EDTA) chelation therapy
Hoxsey method
Immunoaugmentive therapy
Ozone therapy

# Selected Complementary and Alternative Health Care Practitioners Describe Their Approaches

Illinois has thousands of practitioners. The following descriptions reflect some of the attributes and approaches self-help group members might encounter when they begin to explore complementary and alternative health care.

## Mira Didinsky, ND, CNC, PhD

Relaxo-Therapy Center
1050 North State Street, Chicago, IL 60611
312/951-7418

*Came to the United States after 25 years of study and practice in Russia, in an atmosphere where treating the whole person, not the problem or symptom, was the norm. Has nutrition degree and PhD in botany; packages own herbal products.*

"Physicians in this country have so much technology to use. They are able to pinpoint problems with technology and treat disease very powerfully. But the current health care system limits the time available for helping the patient enjoy life and shift the way he sees his disease. I studied with famous Russian, Japanese, Tibetan, and Chinese shamans, physicians, and health practitioners and learned techniques that have helped millions of people for centuries. If we reduce stress, we can reduce the symptoms of many diseases.

"We return to a more healthy state when we give attention to both the emotional level and the physical level. It helps to imagine love as a symbol of emotional health. To learn to love yourself, you can look in the mirror each day and tell yourself, You are loveable, you are wonderful. With one client, we have worked to peel away each resentment and anger so she can do something to resolve them.

"To detoxify the body for conditions such as colitis and chronic diarrhea, I use diet, herbs, juice, water, and fasting for 24 hours. One client had followed both conventional and alternative medical treatments. She had completely restricted her diet, but she was still suffering. I changed her diet and put her on a simple regimen to detoxify her system. Since her first session, she has had no diarrhea and has been able to add more foods. For patients with asthma, the cornerstone of treatment is hot water compress, reflexology, and therapeutic massage.

"And the client must do his part. He can do t'ai chi or yoga to increase his energy or he can dance and listen to music. He can go to self-help groups. His job is to lighten up, let go, and laugh. I like self-help groups because they give people an opportunity to feel loveable when they help each other solve their problems. It is surprising how simple it really is to be happy and to love when surrounded by supportive people in self-help groups!"

## Martha Howard, MD

Wellness Associates of Chicago
706 West Junior Terrace, Chicago, IL 60613
773/935-6377

*Received Master's degree from Harvard in Oriental Studies prior to receiving an MD from Loyola University Stritch School of Medicine. Teaches Qi Gong, studies t'ai chi and is a frequent presenter at national conferences on integrative health. Wellness Associates employs four additional practitioners who offer Chinese and indigenous herbs, acupuncture, chiropractic, naprapathy, and massage.*

"With 43% of people using integrative health services, conventional physicians must go beyond their current knowledge and look up the alternative products patients are using. Patients should interview their physician and look for one with compassion and a broad base of knowledge. They are entitled not only to doctors who listen and are kind, but who also will guide them to treat their diseases preventively. Doctors must not only prescribe medication, they must advise patients how to live well with diabetes and arthritis by reducing sugar and stress.

"In Wellness Associates, we start with the patient's problem and offer modalities that we believe will prevent unnecessary surgeries and harm to vital organs. I have a patient who had terrible psoriasis. She used one topical application after another and was about to enter an experimental study. We tested her for food allergies and found that she was allergic to milk and eggs. Other modalities we offer in our office include diet, acupuncture, naprapathy, chiropractic, and massage. We suggest changes in diet, attitude, and stress. We offer homeopathy, herbal, and Chinese medicine to boost the immune system."

## Virginia Gordon, LCSW

Private practice on Chicago's Northshore
847/433-5133
*Psychiatric social worker with 18 years of experience working with individuals, couples, and families in a variety of clinical settings. Contributes articles to the Wall Street Journal NBEW and other national publications. Currently offers a group to heighten participants' awareness of their reactions to stress and learn how to counter negative responses.*

## Anti-Stress Practices

"We all have a source of power within us that can bring us fulfillment. Too often, it goes underground when our lives are demanding and stressful. What can we do to begin to reawaken this life-giving balance and humanity? These simple though challenging practices can be done either on your own or shared with others in your self-help group.

1.  Pay attention to your breathing. When you notice your breath is shallow, short, and in the upper part of your lungs, plan to draw the next breath deeper to the lower part of your lungs, gently expanding your ribs and stomach.

2.  When you find yourself rushing, slow down to a pace ½ as fast and then perhaps ½ as fast as that.

3.  When you become aware that your thoughts are wandering to future or past events, other than to do necessary planning, refocus your mind in the present. Note what you hear, see, and feel. Each time your mind wanders backward or forward, gently bring it back to the here and now.

4.  Avoid negative, over-stimulating input such as the chatter and aggressiveness of TV programs, music that is not calming, unnecessary conflicts with others, and other interactions or experiences that agitate and wear you out.

5.  Set appropriate limits for what you can and cannot do and state these limits clearly to others.

6.  Skip the guilt.

7.  Ask questions about what you need to know and what you don't understand.

8.  Take care of yourself—get as much sleep, love, and nutritious food as you need.

9.  Eat healthy. Avoid sugar, caffeine, alcohol, and any foods that rev you up.

10. Find a self-help group, one or a few good friends, or a professional, who will let you talk about anything on your mind or in your heart and will listen without judgment.

11. Keep the feeling of loving vibrant daily.

Good luck in the journey ahead. May these suggestions ease your way."

# Information Age Self-Care

*Seventy to ninety percent of doctor visits are in the mind/body,
stress-related realm that is poorly served by drugs or surgery.*

**Herbert Benson, MD, Harvard Medical School**

## Peers Help in Communication Technologies

Over the past 30 years, the self-help group movement has stepped up to the plate to fill in when over-committed and financially burdened families could not cope. Each year, extraordinary citizens of all ages, searching for help and information for their own problems, reach out to newcomers in their groups or begin a new group or chapter. This grassroots explosion of voluntary leadership enriches our communities and our world.

The revolution in communication technology, primarily the Internet, is now expanding the capabilities of self-help groups, making it possible for people to reach around the world to help each other in ways unimagined just a few years ago. As many as 60 million adults used the World Wide Web in 1998 to find information about health care, according to a poll by Louis Harris & Associates. Many segments of the Internet operate like one big self-help group. No longer are we constrained by small networks of friends, family, and local self-help groups. You can turn on your computer or Web TV, day or night, and enjoy, learn from, and help people all over the world. Many people on online health forums—message boards, newsgroups, mailing lists, chat groups, and community run Web sites—are linked to or represent face-to-face self-help organizations. And, as the section on Self-Help and the Media in this chapter suggests, there are additional opportunities for self-help groups to further influence media communication. Technology can link populations through voice messages, teleconference, radio, and television.

The benefits that this technology provides are immeasurable—people and information that can help, are easily accessible, all of the time. Jerry looked on the Internet and found a new treatment his health facility didn't offer for his newly diagnosed prostate cancer. Sandra's diabetes complications presented daily obstacles. She initiated a Web site for people with chronic illnesses, helping people advocate for the best medical decisions and solve work and family problems.

Once patients were not aware that they could participate with their physician to better treat their health conditions, or did not know where to turn to find current information to guide them through the maze of health decisions. Thankfully, that has changed. Like a great many Internet users today, Jerry and Sandra wanted the latest health information, even more current than that found in consumer books and articles. And after getting the help they needed, in true self-help fashion, they remained online to help others avoid the obstacles they had once faced.

Self-helpers now have a variety of ways to communicate online:

- Email—private online mail sent between two or more individuals

- Mail lists—mail broadcast to everyone on a list

- Chat groups—online meetings with numerous people signing on at the same time

- Web sites with professional and consumer produced health information

- Hyperlinks that transfer from the site in use to other sites with additional health information

- Identifying, planning, or initiating local face-to-face self-help groups

## Managing Our Health

Today, people needing answers to health questions in a rapidly changing health care industry are offered a beacon of hope by online health information and computer-assisted programs. These programs supporting disease prevention and management, as well as patient education. Disease prevention assistance is particularly helpful, as this area is seriously neglected by managed care organizations. Their "prevention" interventions appear to be focused on managing such conditions as mental illness, health problems of older citizens, diabetes, HIV, and cancer.

The Internet now offers health information and support without a profit motive, bringing self-care and peer support right to the vast wasteland of people overwhelmed by illness and confused about how to be happy and healthy. In his book, *Health Online* (1996), Tom Ferguson, MD introduces us to information age health care. Ferguson describes opportunities for an empowered health care consumer in the 21st century, existing in a peer support environment. Ferguson communicates a respect for consumers like Jerry and Sandra, who produce their own information as they reach out to help each other on online message boards, mailing lists, self-help groups, and information forums and services. The Internet is a great equalizer. It gives the 100- pound person with a Web site the communication power of a 10-ton telecommunications Goliath.

While the Internet is vital for the self-help community to share information on every topic imaginable, today's online health environment also benefits from fare offered by professionals. Health organizations, libraries, public health services, hospitals, and universities have plunged into consumer health programming. Their products are intended to help health care consumers manage their health with varying degrees of personalized, tailored services.

These health information technology services and products can be categorized as "clinical tools" or "community health information services."

## Clinical Tools

Medical information technology consists of medical self-care computer programs and interactive software intended to augment professional care. Examples of medical self-care projects are home health work-stations, medical decision support, diagnostic spreadsheets, and short-term therapy. Right now, in selected communities, voice mail message services are available to the homeless, modem connected message boards to Alzheimer's caregivers, and self-care computer programs to HIV and breast cancer patients.

Physicians are answering patient questions through email. Thousands of people are pilot testing health forums on interactive television.

## Community Health Information Services

People have unanswered questions about their diseases, and individuals, health organizations, universities, and medical libraries bring their expertise to provide answers and support. They offer voluntary or professional online resources, computerized information, and phone services. In the not too distant future (when technology becomes invisible through phone lines, satellites, and cable), self-care, support groups, and health information will be a huge industry.

Until 8 years ago, most health information was available only on text-based databases. Health information technology is getting more and more convenient. Rather than searching through the entire Web, health information is pre-packaged for health consumers by the online commercial service providers America Online, Prodigy, and CompuServe. They offer comprehensive one-stop Web sites with fanciful bells and whistles. Along with online commercial services telecommunication giants, AT&T and IBM offer health villages, health malls, health worlds that are available via phone, and cable. With all this multimedia entertainment, why did we think researching health information questions was tedious?

Medical Library Association president, Carla Funk, feels that the emphasis on costly entertainment value employed by such high-tech organizations as AT&T and IBM is a waste. She reminds us that "people become engaged when their health is on the line," not because they are attracted by expensive entertainment packaging. Library programs may not have any frills, but they offer rich data links to community groups and splendid health information online. (See National Library of Medicine listing in "Internet Terms and Web Sites" section.)

# What Online Health Consumers Value

Want to know what people online are interested in learning about their health problems? According to Dr. Ferguson, nine times more than other online activities, the first interest of people with chronic problems is to communicate with someone authoritative (someone with their same experience, family members, or professionals). They also want answers to their own questions, answers to questions others ask, and results of information searches. What they want least is patient education text, what self-helpers call shovelware. It is of least interest to online health consumers. At a conference in 1998 on the Emerging Health Information Infrastructure, Secretary of Health Donna Shallah said, "I never saw an American teenager that ever read a brochure."

Whether you are trying to understand what your disease is or what your options for treatment are, you can search the Web sites and gateway sites, which connect you to other sites through links. You can also venture out to find specific types of newsgroups, mailing lists, medication and treatment information, organizations, bulletin boards, and chat groups.

For example, your online access service usually is equipped with a newsreader allowing you to subscribe to online "messageboards" called newsgroups. These newsgroups are downloaded whenever you want to read them. If you are first learning about newsgroups, and you want to know about diabetes, look for a diabetes newsgroup and read the Frequently Asked Questions (FAQ). Then read the conversations (called articles) and responses (called message threads). You add your question to these message threads, which can be read by everyone on the newsgroup. You may also choose to enter a chat group.

Chat groups can be intimidating to newcomers. Chat sessions consist of multiple conversations. Questions are asked in quick succession and to survive the experience you may find yourself focusing on just the screen names (that automatically pop up when you send a message) of the people whose questions and answers you are interested in. In a chat session, people inquire about new members online, discuss medical questions, give support and encouragement, advice, and gripe and whine in safety. Facilitators are mainly traffic cops; members ask and answer questions. On some well-organized chat groups, following the online chat, you will receive an email primer lovingly compiled by someone in the group that is packed with information about the topic condition and at times a summary of the chat session.

A mailing list is email sent to the entire group. Mailing list members subscribe to the group and read what everyone else posts. The list culture and rules are explained when you subscribe. There are unmoderated

lists, which post all messages, and moderated ones, with a host who screens inappropriate mail. Mailing lists are often the most civilized of all online interactive communications, because personal expression is exchanged democratically and non-judgmentally. The quality of understanding, compassion, and help these mailing list exchanges provide is unmatched.

---

**HUNTINGTON DISEASE MAILING LIST**

>*How do you cope with anger? Part of my husband's response to HD is that he has lost his ability to control his emotions, in particular anger.... any attempt on my part to calm him generally causes him to focus his anger on me as the cause<*

Sue, I think anger is often a byproduct of any illness that takes away a person's independence and an ability to do those things they consider to be most important to them. Mary certainly was often angry, as is a neighbor who has MS. It is a way or releasing frustration. I know when I tried to calm Mary down by trying to show her it was not really a big deal, it only intensified the anger because it seemed to be just another indication of something she could not do. I tended to back right off, agree with her and ask her what she thought we should do about the situation. Even though it was often not possible to implement her solution, it gave us an opportunity to talk it out, rather than be a confrontation.

---

At a Web page with a message board, another option promoting interaction, you can read other people's messages and ask your own; you can also write personal emails in response to a question.

# "Virtual" and "Real" Groups— Same Goal, Different Method

Many features of online and face-to-face groups are similar. They each distill, organize, and share information, and offer their personal experience in the form of a story to make it authoritative and non-judgmental. They differ, however, in scope of outreach and type of interaction.

The Ostomy Association understands that it isn't getting to the person in a rural area with an ostomy. The Internet and other electronic formats make it possible to connect new people the group simply can't reach in person. A great many people are too burdened with care-giving responsibilities, are too ill, or prefer not to join a face-to-face group. Others just want more contact and can turn on the computer after a bad day. For many people who are chronically ill, cannot leave home, or live in a rural area, the Internet is the most viable option.

On the other hand, some people still prefer the healthy human interactions you can only get in face-to-face groups: the hugs, seeing someone's eyes well up, reading their body language, learning about local meetings and networks, and gaining friendships, sharing books, equipment, and difficult appointments or hospital visits

## Where to Look

By going online, you can get expert or consumer disease information, treatment, directories, or decision support. You can get immediate answers by phone or the Web site of the National Library of Medicine (see below).

If you prefer to interact online, you can email, join newsgroups, mailing lists and list-serves, or chat rooms. (It will help if you read the Frequently Asked Questions.) It will also help to learn to define search criteria to better locate information from health databases and institutions. Instructions for searching at each site are usually linked near the search dialogue box. A very handy Web site, Deja News (http://dejanews.com) archives directories of mailing lists. You can read anything anyone has posted in a newsgroup because it is all stored and indexed.

You can now access the Internet easily, even without a computer, by using WebTV. If you own a television set, you can be connected and receive packaged services with most of the features of the Internet for about $100, and without any knowledge of computers at all. WebTV can be purchased online, of course, or through stores that sell electronics. If you do have a computer, consider a commercial service such as America Online (AOL) or Prodigy. They are easy to use—you just insert a floppy disk, call an 800-number, and take a tour. In minutes, you will learn how to connect to interesting features. Many such commercial services give a number of free online hours so you can try them out, and comparison shop. An Internet user's monthly email account ranges from $4.95 for unlimited use of most Internet access providers (direct Internet access and email capability only) to commercial services, such as AOL and Prodigy, for up to $21.95.

Formal health services often keep people from asking their questions. However, the Internet rewards informality. Here's how one incredible woman made her last days count.

In AOL's cancer section, KEYWORD: GLENNA, a message posted 4/11/97 reads:

---

***On the Importance of Community Support***

*>Hold on to one another, help each other, give hope and love to all you meet here. Above all, be prepared to welcome others into your world of grief and mourning.*

*Never believe that you are alone. Do not focus on what you have lost, but look always at what you have left. You are surrounded by people that love and care about you.*

*Live with them, love with them and laugh with them.<*

---

## What Questions Remain?

The voluminous information from so many sources can be more overwhelming than helpful. How can people evaluate the quality of information they receive from various sources, including the information from self-help groups?

Will online technologies, including those offered by self-help groups, assist people in making healthier choices when other media efforts have failed? And how can we determine if these efforts are having a beneficial impact?

On the Internet, you will learn whatever you have time to research. But how will you use this information? Physicians already strapped for time may not appreciate using their time explaining when specific treatments and medications are really inappropriate.

You can help to reduce this sort of confusion and be confident that the information is reliable when you verify the source of the information. Here are some guidelines to help you help yourself.

- Look for answers based on personal experiences.

- See whether the information comes from a credible source such as a medical society, university, or "brand name" recognizable health organization or patient advocacy group. See if that information comes up several times.

- Look for informative Web sites mentioned in message boards, newsgroups and chat groups.

- Stick with mailing lists and newsgroups until you feel ready for "real time" chats. If you feel

vulnerable, don't join a chat group that doesn't have a host monitoring the discussion.

- If anonymity is an issue, use a pseudonym or different screen name for chat rooms or have an anonymous header on your newsgroup posting.

# Self-Help in the Media

Leonard A. Jason, Susan C. Jahn, and Meredith Miller
DePaul University

Is it possible for those with interests in the self-help movement to work in a more positive way with the media? Rather than just witnessing the abuses perpetuated on the TV and internet screens, we might be able to work with the media on initiating and implementing large-scale, self-help interventions (Jason & Hanaway, 1997). For example, there are now radio programs that help listeners understand the self-help process (WBEZ has a show on addictions on Sunday mornings). In addition, cable stations are becoming more interested in self-help topics, and there are also dozens of sites on the Internet that also provide millions of people an inside look at the self-help process. Self-help groups could contribute ideas to these venues as well as actual groups and personal experiences could be broadcast through the media.

How does one get involved in these types of innovative self-help programs? We would like to provide a few general guidelines. No large-scale, self-help intervention can be implemented by one person (Jason & Salina, 1993). As a first step in designing a program, a group of interested sponsors could be invited to an organizational meeting. Sponsors could be executives at a TV station that might be interested in increasing viewers, not-for-profit health care organizations (the lung association would be a likely sponsor for a smoking cessation group), and for-profit agencies that might serve as a vehicle for distributing materials to the public (Tru-Value hardware stores, as an example, paid for one large project that involved having the public come into their stores to pick up self-help materials). At such a meeting, it is also important to encourage all invited guests to participate in brainstorming and problem-solving sessions to better meet the problem. Programs could be organized around

losing weight and better nutrition, overcoming alcohol and drug addictions, etc. The key issue is that all parties need to see that they are getting tangible benefits from the planning session. When people help design particular program components, they tend to be more enthused and active in implementing the intervention. After a series of core group meetings, additional sponsors might be invited to contribute to the self-help intervention.

We have worked with these types of planning groups to develop community-owned and implemented, large-scale, self-help, media interventions (Jason, 1997). Self-help groups can be assembled to watch the programs together, or viewers of these programs can receive additional support to deal with their problems by actually being put in contact with self-help group members or other community agencies. Programs have been developed in the Chicago area to deal with diverse types of issues including smoking cessation and prevention, drug abuse prevention, weight reduction, stress management, and aids prevention (Jason, 1997). We believe that the future will see more of these types of adventuresome new ways of getting the self-help message out to the community.

**References**
Jason, L. A. (1998). Tobacco, drug, and HIV preventive media interventions. American Journal of Community Psychology, 26(2), 151-173.

Jason, L. A., & Hanaway, L. (1997). Remote control. A sensible approach to kids, TV, and the electronic media. Sarasota, FL: Professional Resource Press.

Jason, L. A., & Salina, D. (1993). Quality media connections. Another look at successful interventions. Prevention Forum, 13, 2-8.

# Internet Terms and Web Sites

## Jargon

### Chat Groups

Online meetings with numerous people signing on at the same time.

### Email

Electronic mail sent as private mail between two or more individuals.

### File Transfer Protocol

FTP allows you to place or retrieve digital computer files on an Internet site. You can use a browser to transfer files (download) from an FTP site, but you need an FTP tool to upload files.

### Home Page

A major document on a WWW page.

### Internet

A collection of networks and computers all over the world, all of which share information, or at least email, by agreed-upon Internet protocols.

### Internet Address

A place on the Internet where the computer user accesses the Internet. It is denoted by a Domain Name System consisting of three sections (for example, jsmith@library.uiuc.edu).

### Link or Hyperlink

A word (underlined in blue or other color different from the rest of the text) or image that when selected with the mouse takes a Web browser to a new page or other destination.

### Mailing Lists

With an email account, you can subscribe to a mailing list through the list's manager and communicate to everyone on the list at the same time; you will read everyone's message.

### Usenet Newsgroup

An interactive forum, similar to digital bulletin boards; you can post informal email messages and read what others have written; Newsgroups organized hierarchically by topics and broken down further by subject; See sci.med.nutrition, alt.support.cancer, misc.kids, misc.kids.pregnancy; misc.health.diabetes.

### World Wide Web

A section of the Internet with resources reached by HTTP protocol or other Internet protocols that Web browsers can understand; WWW: organizes and accesses text, graphics, audio, movies.

### Internet Search Engine

Helps organize information by searching for key words or concepts (examples of search engines: Yahoo, Alta Vista, Web Crawler). It is easiest to find information through a search engine, but try different ones if you don't get what you need since the selections vary on each search engine. Examples include:

www.yahoo.com/
Yahoo health indexes: At the search engine site, browse topics from alternative resources to women's health.

www.lycos.cs.cmu.edu/

www.infoSeek.com/Home

www.dogpile.com
Research on multiple search engines

## Self-Help Clearinghouses

www.cmhc.com/selfhelp/
National list of self-help groups and clearinghouses.

www.selfhelp-illinois.org
Illinois Self-Help Coalition's online directory of 2500 Illinois support groups.

www.prairienet.org/selfhelp
Family Services/Self-Help Center of Champaign County maintains support group lists for Central Illinois.

## "Just in Time" Health Information

www.nlm.nih.gov
The National Library of Medicine's MEDLINEplus offers quality information and links. MEDLINE, the database used by librarians and health professionals for nearly 30 years, is now available at no cost, 24 hours a day, seven days a week, throughout the world. Two web-base interfaces for searching MEDLINE are available: PubMed and Internet Grateful Med. The NLM is available to help people find information from MEDLINE at 1-888-FIND-NLM during business hours Monday through Friday, or by email at custserv@nlm.nih.gov. Questions can also be faxed to NLM staff at 301/402-1384. The NLM provides reliable medical information.

www.healthfinder.gov
Provides a secure gateway to thousands of sites listed by the Department of Health and Human Service.

www.aafp.org/family/patient.html
Offers consumer health information for 250 topics.

www.ama-assn.org
Contains resources for consumers as well as professionals, including doctor finder, hospitals finder, and American Medical News and journal information.

www.MedWeb.Emory.Edu/MedWeb/
Browse this extensive index of health sciences resources, societies, associations and agencies, including alternative medicine and directories of organizations.

www.betterhealth.com/healthwise
Healthwise Handbook Includes topics included are researched by a national medical review board for accuracy and understandability. Users explore health topics and problems, employ tactics for staying healthy, home self-care, determine when you need to seek medical attention, prepare for a physician visit.

www.goaskalice.columbia.edu
Go Ask Alice at Columbia University allows you to email questions and search its database of answers.

www.thriveonline
A one-stop healthy living resource that is a joint venture between AOL and Time Incorporated.

www.rxlist
Provides general drug information on over 4000 US drug products and is intended to supplement the advice of a physician.

www.reutershealth.com
Offers 20 full-text news items published online every day containing the latest news from the medical world.

## Disease Management Web sites

www.shn.net
A free health community providing information and support for people with serious and chronic illnesses. Requires completion of a registration.

www.seals.com
Offers rehabilitation and support services to meet the needs of people with disabilities.

www.cancercare.org
Offers one-hour conference calls where you can hear the latest information from experts in oncology, social work, public policy, and other fields. These teleconference programs feature coping strategies and updates on specific cancers. You can register for these programs online or by phone at 1-800-813-HOPE. Also provides information about clinical trials and referrals to related web sites and provides online support groups for patients, partners, and bereavement groups.

www.cmhc.com/
Mental health links.

www.coil.com/~grohol/
John Grohol's extensive mental health page

www.cancer.med.upenn.edu/
OncoLink offers cancer information screened by a medical advisory.

www.cybertowers.com/selfhelp
*Self-Help & Psychology Magazine* articles on a wide range of self-help topics.

www.Quackwatch.com
Steven Barret, MD provides cautions for self-help and self-care users. His reservation to some therapies, and to some extent those that work to heal emotions, is to caution against using those therapies if they consume time and energy that interfere with effective conventional treatment.

www.recoverynetwork.com
Recovery Network is committed to serving the 100 million Americans it identifies in its mission affected by alcoholism, drug abuse, eating disorders, child abuse, depression, or gambling problems. In delivering programming for these populations, this site encourages the partnership of public radio, cable television, and other media. On its Internet site, Recovery Network links hundreds of self-help organizations, 12 step groups, national hotlines, and resources.

## Web Site Lists

http:Dejanews.com
Lists of newsgroups and also archives past messages.

http://www.liszt.com
Lists of mailing lists.

## Prevention

www.youfirst.com
Allows you to fill out a short questionnaire and then it creates a health assessment report. The report is free, personalized, confidential and includes healthy lifestyle recommendations.

# Resources

Tom Ferguson, MD, *Health Online, How to Find Health Information, Support Groups, and Self-Help Communities in Cyberspace*, Addison-Wesley, Massachusetts, 1996.
Ferguson invites the reader on a personal tour to discover his fascination, with the online world.

Also helpful:

Butler, *How to Use the Internet, Ziff-Davis Press,* Berkeley, 1994

Hoben, *1996 Guide to Health Care Resources on the Internet*, Faulkner & Gray, New York, 1996

Linden, Tom, MD, *Dr. Tom Linden's Guide To Online Medicine*, McGraw-Hill, New York, 1995

# SECTION II:

# REGISTER OF
# SELF-HELP GROUPS
# IN ILLINOIS

# Addictions

## Alcohol

### Alcoholism-General

**Dual Diagnosis Anonymous** *Area Served: Cook and DuPage Counties* Fellowship of men and women who meet to share their experience,strength and hope with each other so they may solve their common problems and to help those still suffering from mental disorders and alcoholism and/or drug addictions. Uses the 12 Steps of AA. *Meetings*: Weekly for patients—open meetings for all interested also. *Write*: Alexian Brothers Medical Center, 800 Biesterfield Rd, Elk Grove Village, IL 60007-3397 *Call*: 708/437-5500 4646

**Dual Disorders Anonymous** *Area Served: Cook County* A fellowship of men and women who meet to sharetheir experience, strength and hope with each other so they may solve their common problems and to help those still suffering from mental disorders and alcoholism and/or drug addictions. Uses the 12 Steps of AA. *Meetings*: Weekly for patients—open meetings for all interested also. *Services*: Mutual aid, educational program or material, telephone support. *Write*: 13136 S Western, Blue Island, IL 60406 *Call*: 708/371-5170 *Fax*: 708/371-0466

**Rational Recovery Self-Help Network** *Area Served: National* Provides teaching for lifetime abstinence from alcohol/drugs in a mercifully brief period of time; non 12-step teaches addictive voice recognition technique. *Services*: Materials, meetings, book-$12.00. *Meetings*: Weekly; call for time, date, and location. Nationwide. In IL, call 1/847/328-0100 or 1/800/303-CURE (2873). *Write*: PO Box 800, Lotus, CA 95651 *Call*: 916/621-4374 *Fax*: 916/622-4296*Email*: rr@rational.org *Web site*: http://www.rational.org/recovery

**Women for Sobriety** *Area Served: Cook, Kane and DuPage Counties* Self-help group for women with drinking problems. Designed to help women make a decision to stop drinking and work on their self-esteem. Teaches a philosophy based on abstinence. *Meetings*: Weekly for women. *Services*: Mutual aid, educational program or material. *Write*: 405 Washington St, Elmhurst, IL 60126 *Call*: 800/333-1606

**Women for Sobriety, Inc** *Area Served: National* Offers a self-help program for women alcoholics to stop drinking and start a new life in recovery. Building a firm foundation through self-esteem, positive attitude, goal setting, meditation, daily positive affirmations, journaling.

*Services*: New life program statements; referral for WFS meetings nearest your location; Wisconsin pen pal support. *Meetings*: Depends on each meeting location, and accessibility will differ at each location. See IL. *Write*: PO Box 618, Quakertown, PA 18951-0618 *Call*: 215/536-8026 *Fax*: 215/536-8026 *Email*: WFSobriety@aol.com *Web site*: www.mediapulse.com/wfs/

**Moderation Management** *Area Served: National* Support for problem drinkers who want to reduce their drinking, quit, and make other changes. Not intended for alcoholics. Literature, support meetings, online group, handbook available. *Write*: PO Box 27558, Golden Valley, MN 55427 *Call*: 612/512-1484 *Email*: bkishlin@isd.net *Web site*: http://comnet.org/mm/

### Alcoholism-Alcoholics Anonymous

**Alexian Brothers Medical Center** *Area Served: Cook County* Alcoholics Anonymous is for people with an alcohol problem. *Meetings*: Weekly. *Services*: Mutual aid. *Write*: 800 W Biesterfield, Elk Grove Village, IL 60007 *Call*: 708/437-5500 4646

**Beginning Group** *Area Served: Cook County* *Write*: St Francis Hospital, 355 Ridge Ave, Evanston, IL 60202 *Call*: 847/492-6385

**Carbondale Intergroup** *Area Served: Jackson and Williamson Counties* *Write*: 301 W Elms St, Carbondale, IL 62901 *Call*: 618/549-4633

**Central DuPage County Hospital** *Area Served: DuPage County* *Write*: Behavioral Health Services, 27 W 350 High Lake Rd, Winfield, IL 60190 *Call*: 630/653-4000

**Chicago Area Central Office** *Area Served: Chicagoland* *Call*: 312/346-1475

**District 51 Northern IL** *Area Served: Will County* Makes referrals to 99 meetings weekly. *Services*: Mutual aid. *Write*: 256 Republic, Joliet, IL 60433 *Call*: 815/741-6637

**District 52 AA** *Area Served: Kankakee and Iroquois Counties* *Write*: PO Box 265, Bradley, IL 60915 *Call*: 815/935-6923

**District 91** *Area Served: Knox County* *Write*: Builders of Hope, 1290 W Main St, Galesburg, IL 61401 *Call*: 309/343-1530

**For Gays and Lesbians** *Area Served: Champaign County Call*: 217/384-8040

**LaGrange Memorial Hospital** *Area Served: Cook County Write*: Health Education Dept, 5101 Willow Springs Rd, LaGrange, IL 60525 *Call*: 408/354-7070

**North IL District 11** *Area Served: McHenry Write*: PO Box 37, Crystal Lake, IL 60014 *Call*: 815/455-3311

**Rock Island County Intergroup** *Area Served: NW IL Write*: 2320 16th St, Rock Island, IL

**Rockford Area Intergroup** *Area Served: NW-IL* Help for the person who wants to stop drinking. Refers to 330 AA meetings. *Meetings*: Daily for anyone who shares the concern. *Services*: Mutual aid, educational program or material, advocacy, telephone hotline, home or hospital visitation, social activities, newsletter, written information. *Write*: 319 W Jefferson St, Rm 212, Rockford, IL 61101 *Call*: 815/968-0333

**St Elizabeth's Hospital** *Area Served: IL Write*: 211 S 3rd St, Belleville, IL 62222 *Call*: 618/234-2121 1555

**St Mary's Hospital** *Area Served: LaSalle and Livingston Counties Write*: 111 E Spring St, Streator, IL 61364 *Call*: 815/672-9810

## Alcoholism-Family

**Adult Children of Alcoholics** *Area Served: McLean County* A fellowship of men and women who share their experience, strength and hope to recover from the effects of having been brought up in an alcoholic household or dysfunctional family. We practice a program of recovery based on the 12 steps and 12 traditions of AA. *Meetings*: Weekly. *Services*: Mutual aid, educational program or material, telephone support, written information. *Write*: Bloomington, IL *Call*: 309/827-4005

**Adult Children of Alcoholics St. Mary's Hospital** *Area Served: Kankakee County Write*: Kankakee, IL 60901 *Call*: 815/935-1660

**Al-Anon-Alateen** *Area Served: St Clair County* Refers to meetings in area. *Meetings*: Weekly. *Services*: Mutual aid. *Write*: 15 Johnson Pl, Belleville, IL 62223 *Call*: 618/398-9400

**Al-Anon-Alateen Palos Community Hospital** *Area Served: Cook County* Self-help for teenagers affected by another's alcoholism. Membership intended for persons age 11-18 who have been affected. *Services*: Mutual aid. *Write*:12251 80th Ave, Palos Heights, IL 60463 *Call*: 708/923-4000

**Al-Anon-Alateen** *Area Served: Stephenson County Call*: 815/233-8988 Answer Mach

**Al-Anon-Alateen District 5A** *Area Served: Grundy and Will Counties Write*: 265 Republic, Joliet, IL 60435 *Call*: 815/744-2992 Answer Mach

**Al-Anon-Alateen St Francis Hospital** *Area Served: Cook County Meetings*: Bi-weekly. *Write*: 355 Ridge Ave, Evanston, IL 60202 *Call*: 847/492-6385

**Al-Anon-Alateen** *Area Served: McHenry Write*: PO Box 1527, Crystal Lake, IL 60039 *Call*: 815/459-6190 Answer Mach

**Al-Anon-Alateen Alateen Family Groups Al-Anon Info Service Office** *Area Served: Macon County Write*: PO Box 3223, Decatur, IL 62526 *Call*: 217/423-8214

**Al-Anon-Alateen Northern IL AFG** *Area Served: Cook County, NW, SW Write*: PO Box 1332, Galesburg, IL 61402 *Call*: 708/848-2707

**Al-Anon-Alateen District 6B** *Area Served: Kane and Kendall Counties Write*: PO Box 422, Geneva, IL 60134-0422 *Call*: 630/896-5552

**Al-Anon-Alateen** *Area Served: Lake County Write*: PO Box 974, Libertyville, IL 60048-0974 *Call*: 847/680-4640

**Al-Anon-Alateen** *Write*: PO Box 35, Addison, IL 60101 *Call*: 630/627-4441

**Al-Anon-Alateen** *Area Served: IL-N* Hotline, service center, meetings, and disseminates information. Spanish- and Polish-speaking groups on referral. *Write*: 4259 S Archer Ave, Chicago, IL 60632 *Call*: 773/890-1141

**Al-Anon-Alateen Peoria Chapter** *Area Served: Peoria Write*: Peoria, IL 61637 *Call*: 309/655-0051

**Al-Anon-Alateen Central DuPage County Hospital** *Area Served: DuPage County Write*: Behavioral Health Services, 27 W 350 High Lake Rd, Winfield, IL 60190 *Call*: 630/653-4000

**Al-Anon-Alateen Canton Al-Anon Family Group** *Area Served: Fulton County* Cal I.A.2 Alcohol Alcoholism l: 309/649-9605

**Family Outreach Team Orland Park Christian Reformed Church** *Area Served: Cook County* Meet with individuals or family members to confidentially discuss any questions they may have about alcohol, drugs, the symptoms of problem drinking, etc. Two team members work with those interested in learning about the various treatment alternatives available and the facilities and self-help groups in the area. *Services*: Speakers bureau, written information, referral to other services, educational program or material, home or hospital visitation. *Write*: 7500 W Sycamore Dr, Orland Park, IL 60462 *Call*: 708/532-4900 *Fax*: 708/532-4971

**Support Group for Adult Children of Alcoholic Or Other Dysfunctional Families Ravenswood**
*Area Served: Cook County Write*: Community Mental Health Center, 2312 W Irving Park Rd, Chicago, IL 60618 *Call*: 773/463-7000 1455

# Co-Dependency

**Co-Dependents Anonymous** *Area Served: Lake and Cook Counties* Fosters healthy relationships with oneself and others. *Write*: St Michael's Church, 647 Dundee Ave, Barrington, IL 60010 *Call*: 847/304-0135

**The Brady St 12 Step Family Group St Paul Lutheran Church** *Area Served: Rock Island County* 12 Step-based program of recovery and support for adult survivors of trauma and/or dysfunctional relationships. Concerns include substance abuse; physical, emotional or sexual abuse; workaholism; perfectionism; eating disorders; and childhood shame, guilt, grief, rage or chronic illness. *Meetings*: Weekly. *Services*: Mutual aid, speakers bureau, written information, telephone support, referral to other services. *Write*: 2136 Brady St, Davenport, IA 52803 *Call*: 319/326-3547

**CODA** Fosters healthy relationships with ourselves and others. There are many groups in IL. *Write*: PO Box 33577, Phoenix, AZ 85067-3577 *Call*: 602-277-7991

**Co-Dependents Anonymous National Service Office** *Area Served: National* Fosters healthy relationships with ourselves and others. Close to 100 groups in IL. *Meetings*: Weekly. *Services*: MA/written information, newsletter. *Write*: PO Box 33577, Phoenix, AZ 85067 *Call*: 602/277-7991

**Co-Dependents Anonymous IL Office** *Area Served: IL Write*: PO Box 641973, Chicago, IL 60664 *Call*: 312/609-3100

**Co-Dependency Support Group Richland Memorial Hospital** *Area Served: Richland, Lawrence and Jackson Counties Write*: 154 Glenwood, Olney, IL 62450 *Call*: 618/392-2785

**Codependency Support Group Ravenswood CMHC** *Area Served: IL Write*: 2312 W Irving Park Rd, Chicago, IL 60618 *Call*: 773/463-7000 1455

**Love-N-Addiction** *Area Served: National* Support groups help love-addicted people heal by understanding the reasons they seek out or remain in a relationship that is unhealthy and painful. Provides assistance in starting meetings, including a $10 starter packet. One known IL group. *Services*: Mutual aid, speakers bureau, telephone support, referral to other services, educational program or material. *Write*: PO Box 759, Willimantic, CT 06226 *Call*: 203/423-2344

**Relationships Anonymous** *Area Served: Cook County* RA is a 12-step program dedicated to helping in the support/recovery of people addicted to another person and suffering from a disease process that affects every area of their lives in a disastrous way. *Meetings*: Weekly, but restricted to persons sharing the concern. *Services*: Mutual aid, written information, referral to other services, speakers bureau, telephone support *Write*: 5225 Fair Elms, Western Springs, IL 60558 *Call*:708/246-6992

**Women Who Love Too Much Iris Garden Bookstore** *Area Served: Winnebago County Write*: 124 N Main, Rockford, IL 61103 *Call*: 815/968-4321

**Women Who Love Too Much St Francis Hospital** *Area Served: Cook County* Deals with issues of abandonment, rejection, anger, conflict, depression, self-esteem, dysfunctional families, relationship addiction and healing the child within. *Meetings*: Weekly for those affected with the concern. *Services*: Home visitation, member education, professional services, referrals, hotline, mutual aid, self-help groups, printed information, social activities, phone support. Special accessibility; mobility impaired, hearing impaired. *Write*: 335 Ridge, Evanston, IL 60202 *Call*: 847/332-1552

# Drugs

## Drugs-General

**Alcohol, Drugs and Pregnancy Help-Line NAPARE** *Area Served: National Write*: 200 N Michigan Ave, Ste 300, Chicago, IL 60611 *Call*: 800/638-2229 *Fax*: 312/541-1271

**Bill's Family Recovering Communities** *Area Served: Cook and Kankakee Counties Write*: 1257 N Pulaski, Chicago, IL 60651 *Call*: 773/276-5883

**Center for Substance Abuse Treatment National Drug Information Treatment and Referral Hotline** *Area Served: National Write*: 11426 Rockville Pike, Ste 410, Rockville, MD 20852 *Call*: 800/662-4357

**Cocaine Anonymous Alexian Brothers Medical Center** *Area Served: Cook County Write*: 800 W Biesterfield, Elk Grove Village, IL 60007 *Call*: 708/437-5500 4646

**Cocaine Anonymous Central DuPage County Hospital** *Area Served: DuPage County Write*: Behavioral Health Services, 27 W 350 High Lake Rd, Winfield, IL 60190 *Call*: 630/653-4000

**Cocaine Anonymous IL Referral** *Area Served: IL Call*: 773/202-8898

**Cocaine Anonymous National Referral** *Area Served: IL*
*Call*: 800/347-8998 *Fax*: 310/559-2554
*Email*: caqso@ca.org *Web site*: http//www.ca.org

**Cocaine Phoenix House** *Area Served: National*
Substance abuse service that offers information by phone
or mail and makes referrals to local self-help groups and
treatment centers. *Services*: Written information, referral
to other services, hotline. *Write*: 164 W 74th St, NY, NY
10023-0100 *Call*: 800/262-2463

**Gateway Foundation** *Area Served: IL* Helps individuals
effectively deal with their chemical misuse and promotes
their recovery. *Services*: Mutual aid, referral to other
services, professional service. *Write*: 819 S Wabash Ave,
Ste 300, Chicago, IL 60605 *Call*: 312/663-1130

**NARCON Support Group Evanston Hospital**
*Area Served: Cook County Write*: Chapman Center,
2650 Ridge Ave, Evanston, IL 60201 *Call*: 847/570-2834
*Fax*: 847/570-2939

**Narcotics Anonymous Alexian Brothers Medical
Center** *Area Served: Cook County Write*: 800 W
Biesterfield, Elk Grove Village, IL 60007
*Call*: 708/437-5500 4646

**Narcotics Anonymous** *Area Served: Cook, Lake,
Winnebago and DeKalb Counties* Fellowship of
recovering addicts who meet regularly to help each other
stay clean. NA is composed of men and women of all
ages from all walks of life. Main goal is to carry the
message of recovery to those still suffering from
addiction. *Meetings info*: English hotline 1-708-848-4884;
Spanish hotline
1-708-848-5194; meetings are monthly. Call for specific
dates and times. (400 meetings weekly in the Chicago and
suburb areas.) *Write*: 212 S Marion St, Ste 27, Oak Park,
IL 60302 *Call*: 708/848-4884 *Fax*: 708/848-2263

**Narcotics Anonymous** *Area Served: DeKalb*
*Call*: 815/964-5959

**Narcotics Anonymous** *Area Served: IL Write*: Alton, IL
*Call*: 618/398-9409

**Narcotics Anonymous** *Area Served: IL*
*Write*: PO Box 1332, Champaign, IL 61824-1332
*Call*: 217/373-2063

**Narcotics Anonymous** *Area Served: Kankakee*
*Call*: 815/935-0396

**Narcotics Anonymous Central DuPage County
Hospital** *Area Served: DuPage County Write*:
Behavioral Health Services, 27 W 350 High Lake Rd,
Winfield, IL 60290 *Call*: 630/653-4000

**Narcotics Anonymous Chemical Dependency Program**
*Area Served: La Salle Meetings*: Weekly. *Services*:
Mutual aid, educational program or material, written

information, referral to other services, hotline, social
activities, home or hospital visitation. *Write*: 111 E Spring
St, Streator, IL 61364 *Call*: 815/672-2568

**Narcotics Anonymous Support Group Victory
Memorial Hospital** *Area Served: IL Write*: 1324
Sheridan, Waukegan, IL 60085 *Call*: 847/360-4090

**Narcotics Anonymous World Service Office**
*Area Served: National* 12-step program for persons
desiring to recover from drug addiction and live a
drug-free life. Refers to 6 regional help-lines listed below.
More information on Internet. *Write*: PO Box 9999,
Van Nuys, CA 91409 *Call*: 818/773-9999 148
*Email*: LManches@M1.InterServ.com
*Web site*: http://www.wsoinc.com

**Pills Anonymous Lutheran General Health System**
*Area Served: Cook County Write*: 1775 Dempster St,
Park Ridge, IL 60068-1174 *Call*: 847/696-6050

**Rational Recovery** *Area Served: Cook, DuPage and Will
Counties Write*: 204 Green Bay Rd, Evanston, IL 60201
*Call*: 847/328-0100

**Recovering Couples Anonymous** *Area Served: National*
*Write*: PO Box 11872, St Louis, MO 63105
*Call*: 314/830-2600

**New Town Alano Club** *Area Served: Cook County*
Recovery club for gay men and lesbians seeking 12-step
meetings in an alcohol and drug-free environment. 83
meetings per week of AA, Al-Anon, ACOA, OA, DA,
NA, SCA and other 12-step programs. Membership open
to those in 12-step programs. Mutual aid, educational
program or material, social activities. *Write*: 4407 N Clark
St, Chicago, IL 60640 *Call*: 773/271-6822
*Fax*: 312/728-8293

**Substance Abuse Program Holy Family Medical
Center** *Area Served: IL Write*: 100 N River Rd,
Des Plaines, IL 60016 *Call*: 847/297-1800 1742
*Fax*: 847/298-3732

**Healthcare Alternative Systems, Inc** *Area Served:
Chicago Write*: 4534 S Western, Chicago, IL 60609
*Call*: 773/252-5141 *Fax*: 312/254-5753

## Drugs-Children

**Kids Like Us** *Area Served: Cook County* Provides
support, help and understanding to children from the ages
of 3 to 14 who live in the homes of addicted adults.
Different age groups meet separately. Individual and
group meetings. *Services*: Mutual aid. *Write*: 180 N
Michigan Ave, Ste 1013, Chicago, IL 60601 *Fax*:
312/263-1463

**Children's Support Group MacNeal Memorial
Hospital** *Area Served: Cook County* Support group for

children of alcoholics or drug addicts. This is not a 12-step group. *Services*: Mutual aid. *Write*: 3249 S Oak Park Ave, Berwyn, IL 60402 *Call*: 708/795-3056

## Drugs-Family

**Families Anonymous Alexian Brothers Medical Center**
*Area Served: Cook County* Families Anonymous is for family members of addicts. *Meetings*: Weekly. *Services*: Mutual aid. *Write*: 800 W Biesterfield, Elk Grove Village, IL 60007 *Call*: 708/437-5500 4646 *Fax*: 708/981-2059

**Families Anonymous** *Area Served: Winnebago County* Independent, non-profit self-help program patterned after Al-Anon for those concerned about drug abuse and related behavior problems of a relative or friend. No advance arrangements necessary to attend weekly meetings. *Services*: Mutual aid, hotline, telephone support, educational program or material, written information, speakers bureau, referral to other services, telephone support, professional service. *Write*: Christ United Methodist Church, 4515 Highcrest, Rockford, IL 61107 *Call*: 815/964-4044

**Families Anonymous Bethel Reform Church**
*Area Served: IL Write*: 5433 S Austin, Basement, Chicago, IL 60638 *Call*: 773/777-4442

**Families Anonymous Central DuPage Hospital**
*Area Served: DuPage County Write*: Behavioral Health Services, 27 W 350 High Lake Rd, Winfield, IL 60190 *Call*: 630/777-4442

**Families Anonymous Christ Church Parish Hall**
*Area Served: Cook and Lake Counties Write*: Oak and Maple Sts, Winnetka, IL 60093 *Call*: 847/777-4442

**Families Anonymous Faith Lutheran Church**
*Area Served: Cook County Write*: 41 Park Blvd, Upstairs Rear, Glen Ellyn, IL 60137 *Call*: 773/777-4442

**Families Anonymous, Inc** *Area Served: National* Fellowship of 12 Step self-help recovery support groups for parents, spouses, family members and friends of someone else who has a current, suspected, or past abuse of drugs, alcohol, or has behavior problems. Our program helps us regain some serenity and sanity in our chaotic lives caused by this other person's behavior. Referral to support groups and sales of literature. *Meetings*: Generally weekly, call for dates and times. *Write*: PO Box 3475, Culver City, CA 90231-3475 *Call*: 800/736-9805 *Fax*: 310/313-6841 *Email*: famanon@aol.com

**Families Anonymous LaGrange Memorial Health System** *Area Served: Cook County Write*: 5105 Willow Springs Rd, Health Education, LaGrange, IL 60525 *Call*: 708/354-7070 *Fax*: 708/579-4930

**Families Anonymous Lifeway Chemical Dependency for Adolescents** *Area Served: IL Write*: Lifeway Chem Dependency Prog, 600 S 13th St, 4-N, Pekin, IL 61554 *Call*: 800/543-3929

**Families Anonymous St Mark's Lutheran Church**
*Area Served: Kane County Write*: Galena and Edgelawn, Aurora, IL 60506 *Call*: 630/777-4442

**Families Anonymous St Luke's Lutheran Church**
*Area Served: Cook County Write*: 205 N Prospect Cedar, Street Entrance, Park Ridge, IL 60068 *Call*: 847/777-4442

**Families Anonymous The Lighthouse** *Area Served: McLean Write*: R1 Box 276, Hudson, IL 61748 *Call*: 309/827-6026

**Families Anonymous Victory Memorial Hospital**
*Area Served: Lake County Write*: 1324 N Sheridan Rd, Ground Fl, Waukegan, IL 60085 *Call*: 847/623-7914

**Families Anonymous Village of Morton Grove Senior Citizen Center** *Area Served: Cook County Write*: 6101 Capulina, Rear Entrance, Morton Grove, IL 60053 *Call*: 847/777-4442

**Nar-Anon Family Group Nar-Anon Friday Night Step-In** *Area Served: Cook and Will Counties* Help the family and friends of addicts understand that addiction is a disease that they are powerless over. Emphasis on helping them learn a better way to live. *Meetings*: Weekly, but are restricted to persons sharing the concern. *Services*: Mutual aid, hotline, telephone support, written information. *Write*: 7631 S Prairie, Chicago, IL 60619 *Call*: 773/714-5516

## Drugs-Specific Populations

### ALUMNI ASSOCIATIONS

**CDP Alumni Assn St Elizabeth's Hospital**
*Area Served: Sangamon, Madison and Monroe Counties Write*: 211 S 3rd St, Belleville, IL 62222-0694 *Call*: 618/234-2120 1555

### CHRISTIAN

**Christian Chemical Dependency Support Group**
*Area Served: Peoria and Tazewell Counties Write*: 417 N Adams, Peoria, IL 61603 *Call*: 309/655-7272

**Overcomers Victory Through Christ** *Area Served: National* Offers Christ-centered recovery from addiction and dysfunction. *Meetings*: Weekly. One known IL group. *Services*: Mutual aid. *Write*: 4905 N 96th St, Omaha, NE 68134 *Call*: 402/397-3317

**Calix Society** *Area Served: National* Providing help for Catholics in AA with the 3rd and 11th Steps of AA recovery. *Services*: Literature and newsletter-$15.00/year. Concerned with total abstinence, spiritual development, and sanctification of the person. *Meetings*: Call 1-800-398-0524 for specific information on time and location. *Write*: 7601 Wayzata Blvd, Minneapolis, MN 55426 *Call*: 612/546-0544

## FARMERS

**Farm Resource Center** *Area Served: IL* Provides financial information and referral as well as referrals to counselors, mental health agencies, ministers, etc., for stress, alcoholism, drug abuse, marital difficulties, physical abuse, suicide, etc. *Services*: Written information, referral to other services. *Write*: PO Box 87, Mound City, IL 62963 *Call*: 800/851-4719

## HISPANIC

**Hispanic Alcohol Program Healthcare Alternative Systems, Inc** *Area Served: Cook County* Provides alcohol and other drug abuse treatment and prevention services to Hispanics in the Chicagoland area. *Services*: 16-bed residential program; intensive outpatient program; aftercare; toxicology/drug testing program County-312/814-4718; Suburban Chicago- 708/530-6985; Rockford- 815/987-7694; Springfield- 217/782-2850; and Mt Vernon- 618/242-4840. *Services*: Provides information. *Write*: 100 W Randolph St, Ste 5-600, Chicago, IL 60601 *Call*: 312/814-3840 *Fax*: 312/814-2419

**Support Group-El Grupo University of IL West Side Outreach** *Area Served: Chicago* *Write*: 1612 N Kedzie, Chicago, IL 60647 *Call*: 773/252-4422 *Fax*: 312/252-1153

## JEWISH

**Chai-Jacs Ezra** *Area Served: Cook County* CHAI JACS: Chicago Area Involved Jewish Addictive and Compulsive Persons and Significant Others is concerned with the disease of addiction and compulsive behavior among Jews. Provides spiritual and communal support for addicts and their families and serves as a resource center. Supplements and complements the 12-step recovery program. Support groups, public education and information, social activities. *Write*: 3701 W Devon, Chicago, IL 60659-1101 *Call*: 800/248-1818 *Web site*: http://www.jacsweb.org

## LAWYERS

**Lawyers' Assistance Program, Inc** *Area Served: IL* LAP consists of lawyers and judges helping members of their own profession who are impaired by alcoholism, drug abuse or physical and emotional problems, which interfere with his/her ability to practice law. LAP is voluntary and confidential. *Meetings*: Quarterly for attorneys, judges and law students. *Services*: Mutual aid, speakers bureau, written information, telephone support, referral to other services, hotline. *Write*: 321 S Wacker Dr,

Ste 800, Chicago, IL 60604 *Call*: 312/922-7332 *Fax*: 312/922-7339 *Email*: illap@aol.com

## LESBIANS/GAY

**Intergroup** *Area Served: McLean County* Our primary purpose is to carry the message to alcoholics in and out of the 12 Step program. *Services*: Mutual aid, educational program or material. *Write*: 501 N Main, #7, Bloomington, IL 61701 *Call*: 309/828-7092

**Liontamers Anonymous** *Area Served: Knox County* A Christian group practicing the 12 Steps of Alcoholics Anonymous. For recovering alcoholics, adult children of alcoholics, co-dependents, persons with eating disorders. Ties the 12 Steps to Biblical principles and the higher power to Jesus Christ. *Meetings*: Weekly. *Services*: Mutual aid, written information. *Write*: 116 NE Perry Ave, Peoria, IL 61603 *Call*: 309/673-3641 *Fax*: 309/673-3644

## NURSES

**International Nurses Anonymous** *Area Served: National* Provide networking and mutual support for nurses in recovery from addictive disease and/or co-dependence. Membership is limited to RNs, LPNs or nursing students who consider themselves a member of a 12-step group. *Services*: Mutual aid. *Write*: 1020 Sunset Dr, Lawrence, KS 66044 *Call*: 913/842-3893

**Peer Assistance Network for Nurses (PANN) IL Nurses Assn** *Area Served: IL* A peer assistance network and intervention program for nurses under stress or at risk for drug abuse or other problems which impair their performance and threaten their well-being. Support and referral. *Services*: Mutual aid. *Write*: 300 S Wacker, Ste 2200, Chicago, IL 60606 *Call*: 800/262-2500 *Fax*: 312/360-9380

## PHYSICIANS

**Physician Assistance Program IL State Medical Society** *Area Served: IL* For individual physicians, family, friends or colleagues concerned about a physician or medical student at risk for alcoholism, drug abuse or any other cause of physical or mental impairment. Provides referrals, advocacy, monitoring, interventions, general counseling, and advice. No treatment. *Services*: Educational program or material, advocacy, telephone support, written information, referral to other services. *Write*: 20 N Michigan Ave, Ste 700, Chicago, IL 60602 *Call*: 312/580-2499 *Fax*: 708/318-0966

**American Society for Handicapped Physicians** *Area Served: National* Provide support and advocacy for handicapped people who have chosen a career in medicine primarily, through referrals to others with similar handicaps. *Meetings*: Annually. *Services*: Mutual aid, educational program or material, telephone support, newsletter, written information, referral to other services.

*Write*: 105 Morris Dr, Bastrop, LA 71220
*Call*: 318/281-4436

# Gambling

**Gamblers Anonymous** *Area Served: Peoria Write*: 600 Fayette, Peoria, IL 61613 *Call*: 309/655-0217

**Gamblers Anonymous International Service Office** *Area Served: National Write*: PO Box 17173, Los Angeles, CA 90017

**Gamblers Anonymous** *Area Served: IL* Help people who gamble compulsively. Also has information on Gam-Anon (spouse group) and Young Gamblers Anonymous (for those in their 30's and under). Refers to 17 GA meetings and 10 Gam-Anon meetings in IL. *Meetings*: Weekly. *Services*: Mutual aid, educational program or material, telephone support, hotline. *Write*: PO Box 3233, Chicago, IL 60690 *Call*: 312/346-1588

**IL Council on Compulsive Gambling, Inc** *Area Served: Cook County Write*: PO Box 6489, Evanston, IL 60204 *Call*: 800/426-2546

# Overspending

**Debtors Anonymous Great Lake Counties Debtors Anonymous** *Area Served: Cook, DuPage and Kankakee Counties Write*: PO Box 4982, Chicago, IL 60680 *Call*: 773/274-3328

**Debit-Anon, DA** *Area Served: Lake & Cook Counties Call*: 708/945-9106

**Debtors Anonymous Lombard Community Center** *Area Served: DuPage County Write*: 205 W Maple, Lombard, IL 60148 *Call*: 630/274-3328

# Prevention

**Mothers Against Drunk Driving (MADD)** *Area Served: IL* Assist the victims of drunk driving and to end the tragedies of drunk driving. MADD works in 4 program areas: victim services, public awareness, youth education and laws and legislation. 21 chapters in IL. *Meetings*: For victims and families. *Services*: Mutual aid, educational program or material, written information, advocacy, referral to other services, speakers bureau, fundraising, social activities, newsletter. *Write*: 203 N Wabash, #2118, Chicago, IL 60601 *Call*: 800/253-6233 *Fax*: 312/782-5130 *Web site*: http://www.madil.com

*Area Served: Champaign County Write*: PO Box 6543, Champaign, IL 61826 *Call*: 217/356-6233 Answer Mach

*Area Served: Christian County Write*: PO Box 228, Taylorville, IL 62568 *Call*: 217/623-4279

*Area Served: Coles County Write*: PO Box 1691, Mattoon, IL 61938 *Call*: 217/235-283

*Area Served: Cook County Write*: 13492 Lydia, Robbins, IL 60472 *Call*: 708/489-6233

*Area Served: Cook County Write*: PO Box 438274, Chicago, IL 60643 *Call*: 773/881-8804 *Fax*: 312/881-8804

*Area Served: Douglas County Write*: PO Box 55, Villa Grove, IL 61956 *Call*: 217/832-8590

*Area Served: DuPage County Write*: 2900 Ogden Ave, Ste 106, Lisle, IL 60532 *Call*: 630/369-6233 *Fax*: 630/369-6233

*Area Served: Fox Valley Write*: 2934 N 4370 Rd, Sheridan, IL 60551 *Call*: 815/496-2754

*Area Served: Fulton County Write*: 128 Pecan, Canton, IL 61520 *Call*: 309/647-6892

*Area Served: Henry/Rock Island Counties Write*: PO Box 45 Silvis, IL 61282 *Call*: 309/792-8159 *Fax* 309/792-8159 *Web site*: http://www.madil.com

*Area Served: Jackson County Write*: 103 W Walnut St, Ste 116 R#1 Box 492, Carbondale, IL 62901 *Call*: 618/549-8249

*Area Served: Jersey County Write*: 110 S State St, PO Box 137, Jerseyville, IL 62052 *Call*: 618/498-6233

*Area Served: Kane County Write*: 366 Washburn, Elgin, IL 60123 *Call*: 847/741-7540

*Area Served: Livingston County Write*: PO Box 311, Dwight, IL 60420 *Call*: 815/584-1090

*Area Served: Macon County Write*: PO Box 233, Decatur, IL 62521 *Call*: 217/422-4860

*Area Served: Macoupin County Write*: PO Box 307, Bunker Hill, IL 62014 *Call*: 618/585-3385

*Area Served: Madison County Write*: PO Box 224, Wood River, IL 62095 *Call*: 618/251-6222

*Area Served: McLean County Write*: PO Box 794, Bloomington, IL 61702-0794 *Call*: 309/862-2008

*Area Served: Montgomery County Write*: PO Box 148, Raymond, IL 62095 *Call*: 217/324-6883

*Area Served: Morgan County* Stop drunk driving and help the victims of this violent crime. *Meetings*: Monthly for anyone interested. *Services*: Mutual aid, speakers bureau, written information, telephone support, professional service, educational program or material, hotline, home or hospital visitation, newsletter, referral to other services. *Write*: PO Box 265, Jacksonville, IL 62651 *Call*: 217/243-7570

*Area Served: Peoria Write*: PO Box 3226, Peoria, IL 61612 *Call*: 309/688-0047

*Area Served: Quincy Write*: 1258 S Park Terrace, Quincy, IL 62301 *Call*: 217/224-3617

*Area Served: Rock Island/Henry Counties Write*: PO Box 45, Silvis, IL 61282 *Call*: 309/792-8159 *Fax* 309/792-8159 *Web site*: http://www.madil.com

*Area Served: Sangamon County Write*: PO Box 5516, Springfield, IL 62705 *Call*: 217/498-7718

*Area Served: St Clair County Write*:140 Iowa, Ste 7, Belleville,IL 62221 *Call*: 618/277-6222

*Area Served: Tazewell County Write*: PO Box 2186, E Peoria, IL 61611 *Call*: 309/695-1449

*Area Served: Williamson County Write*: PO Box 307, Herrin, IL 62948 *Call*: 618/942-6233

**Remove Intoxicated Drivers, Inc RID-USA, Inc**
*Area Served: National Write*: PO Box 520, Schenectady, NY 12301 *Call*: 518/393-4357 Answer Mach

**Students Against Drunk Driving SADD** *Area Served: IL Write*: 100 N First St, Springfield, IL 62777 *Call*: 217/782-2826

**Alliance Against Intoxicated Motorists AAIM Fox Valley Chapter** Dedicated to combating drunk and drugged driving in IL and giving comfort and aid to victims of drunk driving. 5 chapters in IL. *Meetings*: Monthly for all interested. *Services*: Mutual aid, educational program or material, advocacy, telephone support, newsletter, written information, speakers bureau, hotline. *Write*: 870 E Higgins Rd, Ste 131, Schaumburg, IL 60173 *Call*: 847/240-0027 *Fax*: 847/240-0028

**Deerfield Citizens for Drug Awareness** *Area Served: Lake County* Promote substance-free living through education and prevention. *Meetings*: Monthly for anyone interested. *Services*: Mutual aid, educational program or material, advocacy, newsletter, written information, referral to other services. *Write*: PO Box 607, Deerfield, IL 60015 *Call*: 847/945-7010

**IL Alcoholism and Drug Dependence Assn** *Area Served: National Write*: 500 W Monroe, Springfield, IL 62704 *Call*: 800/252-6301

**Just Say No International** *Area Served: National* Help callers create Just Say No clubs. Foundation puts out a $10 book on starting anti-drug abuse groups. *Services*: Written information, educational program or material. *Write*:

2101 Webster St, Ste 1300, Oakland, CA 94612 *Call*: 800/258-2766

**Northbrook Citizens for Drug and Alcohol Awareness** *Area Served: Cook County–N* Primarily community awareness—to inform and assist those who are involved with youth drug and alcohol abuse. 12 committees run by volunteer parents assist in making the individual and the public aware of the problems and the needs. Courses in parenting provided. *Meetings*: Vary, call for information. *Services*: Educational program or material, written information, referral to other services, newsletter. *Write*: 1364 Shermer, Northbrook, IL 60062-2517 *Call*: 847/272-7870

**We're Into Health (WITH)** *Area Served: Champaign County* A citizen's org. focused on education to create a total community social climate in which we are encouraged to be free of drug and alcohol abuse. *Meetings*: Quarterly. *Services*: Educational program or material. *Write*: Mohomet Seymour Jr HS, Mahomet, IL 61853 *Call*: 217/586-4415

**Parents' Resource Institute for Drug Education Pride** *Area Served: National* Make referrals to drug abuse agencies. *Services*: Referral to other services. *Write*: 50 Hurt Plaza, Ste 210-The Hurt Building, Atlanta, GA 30303 *Call*: 404/577-4500

# Prostitution

**Prostitutes Anonymous** *Area Served: National Write*: 11225 Magnolia Blvd #181, North Hollywood, CA 91601 *Call*: 818/905-2188

**Children of The Night, Inc** *Area Served: National* Provide effective intervention in the lives of children ages 11-17 who are coerced into prostitution for pornography. 24-hour toll-free national hotline 1-800-551-1300. St program throughout western region of US. 24-hour bed shelter home receiving children around the clock. *Write*: 14530 Sylvan St, Van Nuys, CA 91411 *Call*: 818/908-4474 *Fax*: 818/908-1468 *Email*: COTNLL@AOL.COM

**The Pride Program Family and Children's Service** *Area Served: National Write*: 3125 E Lake St, Minneapolis, MN 55406 *Call*: 612/728-2062

**Prostitutes Anonymous Genesis House** *Area Served: Cook County Write*: 911 W Addison, Chicago, IL 60613 *Call*: 773/281-3917

**Genesis House** *Area Served: Chicago* Nurture women who are/have been involved in prostitution through offering friendship, shelter in time of need, counseling and referral to appropriate agencies for housing, legal employment, training, psychological and social needs. *Meetings*: As needed. *Services*: Mutual aid, educational program or material, social activities, referral to other services. *Write*: 911 W Addison, Chicago, IL 60613 *Call*: 773/281-3917

# Sexual

**Quad Cities Sexaholics Anonymous (QCSA) Courage to Change QCSA** *Area Served: Iowa* Provide support for men and women recovering from compulsive/addictive sexual behavior. *Services*: 12 Step meetings, sponsorship, and literature. *Meetings*: Sunday-7 pm, Wednesday-7 pm, Thursday-12 noon, and Saturday-8 am. New meetings established to meet needs/demands. *Write*: PO Box 4533, Davenport, IA 52808

**S-Anon International Family Groups** *Area Served: DuPage County* *Write*: PO Box 183, Glen Ellyn, IL 60138 *Call*: 630/545-7110

**S-Anon International Family Groups** S-Anon family groups consist of families and friends of sexaholics who come together to share their experience, strength and hope. S-Anon is a 12-step recovery program. Some groups across the country have their own hotline numbers. We have printed literature and a newsletter that is issued quarterly to subscribers. *Write*: PO Box 5117, Sherman Oaks, CA 91413 *Call*: 818/990-6910 *Email* saif@sanon.org *Web site*: http://www.sanon.org

**Sex Addicts Anonymous International Service Org. of SAA** *Area Served: National* SAA exists to help sex addicts achieve freedom from compulsive behavior and become sexually healthy and self confident people. Literature, videos, and audio tapes available at minimal cost. Self-help meetings conducted locally conference information available. Call us for help in the beginning or for joining a local group. *Write*: PO Box 70949, Houston, TX 77270-0949 *Call*: 713/869-4902 *Web site*: www.saa-recovery.org

**Sex Addicts Anonymous** *Area Served: Rock Island and Scott (IA) Counties* *Write*: PO Box 4165, Davenport, IA 52808

**Sex and Love Addicts Anonymous** *Area Served: IL-NE* SLAA is a 12-step oriented fellowship based on the principles of AA. The only qualification for membership is a desire to stop living out a pattern of sex and love addiction. 15 groups in Chicago area. *Meetings*: Weekly. *Services*: Mutual aid, educational program or material. *Write*: PO Box 14071, Chicago, IL 60614 *Call*: 312/409-0771

**Sex and Love Addicts Anonymous The Augustine Fellowship** *Area Served: National* A 12 Step group, modeled after Alcoholics Anonymous to deal with sex, love, fantasy and romantic addiction. 13 groups in IL. *Services*: Mutual aid, speakers bureau, written

information, telephone support, newsletter. *Write*: PO Box 119, New Town Branch, Boston, MA 02258 *Call*: 617/332-1845

**Sexaholics Anonymous Chicago SANON Office** *Area Served: DuPage County* SA is a fellowship for men and women who want to stop their sexually self-destructive thinking and behavior. *Services*: 12 Step groups, national conferences, sponsorships, literature (some book fees). *Meetings*: 6 Chicago area groups; 2 Indiana groups; call for times and dates. *Write*: PO Box 183, Glen Ellyn, IL 60138 *Call*: 630/545-7110

**Sexaholics Anonymous SANON Central Office** *Area Served: National* SA is a fellowship for men and women who want to stop their sexually self-destructive thinking and behavior. 12 Step groups, sponsorship, national conferences, literature (some book fees). *Meetings*: Call or write for information on local meetings in locations nearest you. *Write*: PO Box 111242, Nashville, TN 37222 *Call*: 615/833-3152

**Sexual Compulsives Anonymous** *Area Served: Cook County* *Call*: 312/935-3573

# Smoking

**Chicago Lung Assn Smoking Cessation Program** *Area Served: Cook County* Makes referrals to self-help groups. Also publishes literature on classes to stop smoking. *Services*: Educational program or material referral to other services. *Write*: 1440 W Washington Blvd, Chicago, IL 60607-1878 *Call*: 312/243-2000 263 *Fax*: 312/243-3954

**Ex-Smokers Support Group** *Area Served: Cook County* *Write*: Weiss Memorial Hospital, 4646 N Marine Dr, Chicago, IL 60640 *Call*: 773/549-2322

**Freedom From Smoking** *Area Served: Lake and McHenry Counties* *Write*: Saint Theresa Medical Center, 2615 Washington St, Waukegan, IL 60085 *Call*: 847/360-4988

**Groups Against Smokers' Pollution, INC-GASP** *Area Served: National* *Write*: PO Box 632, College Park, MD 20741-0632 *Call*: 301/459-4791

**Nicotine Anonymous White Oaks Center** *Area Served: IL* A 12-step self-help group for anyone who has a desire to stop using nicotine. *Meetings*: Weekly. *Services*: Mutual aid, written information. *Write*: New Leaf Ln, Peoria, IL 61615 *Call*: 309/699-8635

**Nicotine Anonymous Chicagoland Intergroup of Nicotine Anonymous** *Area Served: Cook County* *Write*: Cina PO Box 784, Northbrook, IL 60065 *Call*: 773/509-6373 *Email*: nica@onramp.net *Web site*: http://rampages.onramp.net/~nica

**Nicotine Anonymous** *Area Served: Boone County*
*Write*: 1625 S State, Belvedere, IL *Call*: 815/544-5804

**Smokers Anonymous** *Area Served: Tazewell County*
Peer support group for recovery from nicotine addiction.
*Meetings*: Weekly for anyone seeking recovery from
nicotine dependency. *Services*: Mutual aid, written
information, telephone support. *Write*: Lifeway Chem
Dependency Prog, 600 S 13th St, Pekin, IL 61554
*Call*: 800/543-3929

**Smokers Anonymous Lifeway Chemical Dependency
Program** *Area Served: Tazewell County Write*:
600 S 13th St, Pekin, IL 61554 *Call*: 800/543-3929

## Work

**Workaholics Anonymous (WA) World Service Office**
*Area Served: International* WA is a fellowship of persons
who share their experience, strength and hope with each
other, to help each other solve and recover from
workaholism. Requirement to join is a desire to stop
working compulsively. WA is not allied with any sect,

org., or institution; neither does it endorse or oppose any
causes. *Write*: PO Box 661501, Los Angeles, CA 90066
*Call*: 312/409-0596

**Workaholics Anonymous** *Area Served: Cook County*
*Write*: PO Box 289, Menlo Park, CA 94026-0289
*Call*: 773/281-6782

## Youth

**Peer Support Group Universal Family Connection, Inc**
*Area Served: Chicago-S* To strengthen families and
improve quality of life for disadvantaged Chicago
residents. Addresses issues including alcohol and
substance abuse, teenage pregnancy, infant mortality and
unemployment. 2 support groups for teenagers. *Services*:
Mutual aid, educational program or material, advocacy,
referral to other services, professional service, speakers
bureau, referral to other services, telephone support, social
activities, home or hospital visitation, newsletter.
*Write*: 7949 S Western Ave, Chicago, IL 60620
*Call*: 773/925-2222

# Education & Employment

## Literacy

**Waubonsee Adult Literacy Project** Volunteer tutors
assist adults in learning to read and/or speak English.
*Services*: Reading and writing English instruction.
Training of volunteer tutors. *Meetings*: Weekly, call for
specific information. *Write*: 5 E Galena Blvd, Aurora, IL
60506 *Call*: 630/801-7900 1107 *Fax*: 630/906-4127
*Email*: LVAWCC@AOL.CO M

## Salespersons

**First IL Sales Club At Large** Fiscal support and
education group for sales personnel. Speakers and
discussion of topics of interest. *Meetings*: Weekly for
salespersons. *Services*: Mutual aid, educational program or
material, social activities. *Write*: 115 N Marion St, Oak
Park, IL 60301-1004 *Call*: 708/383-5981

## Professionals, Childcare

**Provider Networking Night (PNN) YWCA of The Sauk
Valley** Reassures childcare providers that their services
are vital, equips them to provide quality programs, and
allows them to build mentoring relationships with other
providers. Provide satellite office for 4-C, comm.
Coordinated childcare services offered include: toy and
resource library, training and technical assistance for
childcare providers, workshops, seminars, food programs
and referral service. *Meetings*: 3rd Tuesday, monthly,
7-8:30 pm. *Write*: 412 First Ave, Sterling, IL 61081
*Call*: 815/625-0333

# Family

## Adoption

**Adoptees In Search** *Area Served: National Write*:
PO Box 41016, Bethesda, MD 20824 *Call*: 301/656-8555
*Fax*: 301/652-2106 *Email*: ais20824@aol.com

**Adoptees Liberty Movement Assn Chicago Chapter**
*Area Served: IL Write*: PO Box 59345, Chicago, IL
60659 *Call*: 773/631-5816

**Adoptees Liberty Movement Assn** *Area Served: IL*
*Write*: PO Box 81, Bloomington, IL 61702
*Call*: 309/828-2217

**Adoption Triangle (CHASI)** *Area Served: Champaign
County Write*: 1819 S Neil St, Ste D, Champaign, IL
*Call*: 219/365-0574

**Adoption Triangle** *Area Served: Cook County Write*:
PO Box 384, Park Forest, IL 60466 *Call*: 708/481-8916

**Adoptive Families of America Adoptive Families** *Area
Served: National Write*: 2309 Como Ave, St Paul, MN,
55113 *Call*: 800/372-3300 *Fax*: 612/645-0055
*Web site*: http://www.adoptivefam.org

**Birth-Wise NAPSAC** *Area Served: Cook County*
*Write*: 15522 S Dearborn St, South Holland, IL 60473
*Call*: 708/333-5579

**Chicago Area Families for Adoption (CAFFA)** *Area
Served: IL Write*: 534 Castle Ct, Bolingbrook, IL 60440
*Call*: 630/739-6576

**Healing Hearts Inc** *Area Served: IL Write*: PO Box 606,
Normal, IL 61761 *Call*: 309/692-3028

**IL Parents for Black Adoption** *Area Served: IL*
Recruits families for black and minority adoptions and to
give necessary ongoing services and support after
placement. *Meetings*: Monthly. *Services*: Mutual aid,
educational program or material, advocacy, telephone
support, written information. *Write*: 7930 S Colfax Ave,
Chicago, IL 60617 *Call*: 773/734-2305

**Liberty Godparent Home** *Area Served: National Write*:
1000 Villa Rd, Lynchburg, VA 24503 *Call*: 804/384-3043

**Truth Seekers In Adoption** *Area Served: IL*
*Write*: Lutheran General Health System, 1775 Dempster
St, Park Ridge, IL 60068 *Call*: 847/342-8742

## Child Custody

**Provider Networking Night (PNN) YWCA of The Sauk
Valley** Reassures childcare providers that their services
are vital, equips them to provide quality programs, and
allows them to build mentoring relationships with other
providers. Provide satellite office for 4-C, comm.
Coordinated childcare services offered include: toy and
resource library, training and technical assistance for
childcare providers, workshops, seminars, food programs
and referral service. *Meetings*: 3rd Tuesday, monthly,
7-8:30 pm. *Write*: 412 First Ave, Sterling, IL 61081
*Call*: 815/625-0333

## Childhood Loss

**Rainbows** *Area Served: IL* Support groups for children
who have experienced the loss of a parent through death
or divorce. 675 Rainbow groups in IL. Call one of eight IL
offices. *Services*: Mutual aid, educational program or
material, written information, speakers bureau. *Write*:
2100 Golf Rd, Ste 370, Rolling Meadows, IL 60008
*Call*: 847/952-1770

## Divorce

**Adults Whose Parents Have Divorced Jewish Family
and Community Service** *Area Served: Cook County*
*Write*: 205 W Randolph St, Ste 1100, Chicago, IL 60606
*Call*: 312/263-5523

**Christian Single Helpmate Groups, Inc Northern Ill
Dist Lutheran Church-Missouri Synod***Area Served:
DuPage, Cook and Peoria Counties* Assists singles in
making the transition from married life to a positive single
lifestyle. 16 chapters in IL. *Meetings*: Weekly, but
restricted to persons sharing the concern. *Services*: Mutual
aid, newsletter. *Write*: 6418 Bradley, Woodridge, IL
60517 *Call*: 630/969-0679

**Coping with Separation and Divorce Southwest
Women Working Together** *Area Served: Chicago-S*
Aids recently divorced women and those in the process of
divorce. Will provide opportunity to share experiences and
to gain support from others in making transition to single
life. *Meetings*: Weekly. *Services*: Mutual aid, educational
program or material. *Write*: 3201 W 63rd St, Chicago, IL
60629 *Call*: 773/582-0550

**Divorce Adjustment Group** *Area Served: DuPage County Write*: DuPage County YWCA, 739 Roosevelt Rd, Bldg 8, Ste 8, Glen Ellyn, IL 60137 *Call*: 630/790-6600

**Divorce Anonymous** *Area Served: Cook County* Telephone referral network for divorced women and men. *Services*: Telephone support, written information, referral to other services. *Write*: 4848 N Central, #309, Chicago, IL 60630 *Call*: 773/685-3447 Evening

**Divorce Group** *Area Served: Cook County-SW Write*: Worth United Methodist Church, 100 W 112 St, Worth, IL 60482 *Call*: 708/448-6682

**Divorce Support Group Ravenswood CMHC** *Area Served: IL* Group members gain support through sharing experiences, feelings and ways to cope. Leaders are peer trained to facilitate a format that provides safety and support for group members. *Meetings*: 6-week groups, but restricted to persons sharing the concern. *Services*: Mutual aid. *Write*: 2312 W Irving Park Rd, Chicago, IL 60618 *Call*: 773/463-7000 1455

**Divorce Support, Inc** *Area Served: IL* Support group for divorced, separated and those with marital relationship problems. To help explore the physical, emotional and spiritual aspects and develop coping skills. Allows members to make friends in a non-threatening situation. *Meetings*: Weekly. *Services*: Mutual aid, educational program or material, telephone support, social activities, newsletter. *Write*: 5020 W School St, Chicago, IL 60641 *Call*: 773/286-4541

**Divorce Support Inc Our Lady of The Resurrection Medical Center** *Area Served: Local* Support group for divorced, separated and those with marital relationship problems. To help explore the physical,emotional and spiritual aspects and develop coping skills. Allows members to make friends in a non-threatening situation. *Meetings*: Weekly. *Services*: Mutual aid, educational program or material, telephone support, social activities, newsletter. *Write*: 5645 W Addison, Chicago, IL 60634 *Call*: 773/286-4541 *Email*: Windycity@worldnet.att.net

**Helpmates** *Area Served: Lake County Write*: 4206 W Elm, McHenry, IL 60050 *Call*: 815/385-0859

**Partners In Transition** *Area Served: Cook-N and Lake County Write*: 3330 Old Glenview Rd, Ste 15, Wilmette, IL 60091 *Call*: 847/256-2300

**Phoenix Ministry for Separated and Divorced Catholics** *Area Served: Chicago, Cook and Lake Counties* Addresses the realities of separation and divorce in their pastoral, practical and emotional aspects. No one who was formerly married should feel cut off from the supportive and growth-enabling hand of the Church. An ecumenical ministry to provide service, support, challenge and education. *Services*: Mutual aid, telephone support, social activities, newsletter, home or hospital visitation. *Write*: Family Ministries/Archdiocese, 155 E Superior St, Chicago, IL 60611 *Call*: 312/751-8353

**Prism Rainbows** *Area Served: IL* Support groups for persons who have experienced the loss of a spouse either through death or divorce. 8 offices in IL. *Services*: Mutual aid, educational program or material, written information, speakers bureau. *Write*: 1111 Tower Ln, Schaumburg, IL 60173 *Call*: 847/310-1880

**Separated and Divorced Group St Patrick's Roman Catholic Church** *Area Served: Kane, DuPage and DeKalb Counties* Provides support and social activity for those people experiencing the trauma of separation or loss of a spouse. It is a non-denominational group. *Meetings*: Monthly. *Services*: Mutual aid, social activities, written information, telephone support, referral to other services. *Write*: 408 Cedar St, St Charles, IL 60174 *Call*: 630/584-0092

**Separated and Divorced Support Group Our Lady of The Wayside Church** *Area Served: Cook County NW* Our purpose is to read, study, and integrate into our lives the 12-step program, thereby gaining inner strength to accept ourselves and to continue to grow through our painful experiences. *Meetings*: Weekly. *Services*: Mutual aid, speakers bureau. *Write*: 432 W Park, Arlington Heights, IL 60005 *Call*: 847/253-5353

**Separation and Divorce Support Groups Center for Family Ministry** *Area Served: Will, DuPage and Kendall Counties* Provides referrals to support groups for separated and divorced persons in a 7-county area. Also offers peer support group facilitator training twice a year. *Services*: Referral to other services, newsletter, educational program or material. *Write*: Joliet Diocese, 402 S Independence Blvd, Romeoville, IL 60441-2299 *Call*: 815/838-5334

**Share and Care, Separated, Divorced, Widowed** *Area Served: St Clair and Madison Counties Write*: Our Lady of the Snows, 9500 W IL Hwy 15, Belleville, IL 62223 *Call*: 618/397-6700

**Surviving Separation and Divorce Jewish Family and Community Service** *Area Served: Lake and Cook Counties* 6-week series at several locations throughout the year. Practical matters as well as many feelings experienced will be addressed to help people through the separation and divorce process and to deal with the life after divorce-especially relationships within the family and outside the family. *Services*: Mutual aid, educational program or material, written information. *Write*: 210 Skokie Valley Rd, Highland Park, IL 60035 *Call*: 847/831-4225

**Surviving Separation and Divorce Jewish Family and Community Service** *Area Served: Cook and Lake Counties* 6-week series at several locations throughout the year. Practical matters as well as many feelings experienced will be addressed to help people through the separation and divorce process and to deal with life after divorce-especially relationships within the family and outside the family. *Services*: Mutual aid, educational program or material, written information. *Write*: 1250 Radcliffe Rd, #206, Buffalo Grove, IL 60089 *Call*: 847/392-8820

**Surviving Separation and Divorce Jewish Family and Community Service** *Area Served: Chicago*
*Write*: 205 W Randolph, Ste 1100, Chicago, IL 60606
*Call*: 312/263-5523

# Foster Parent

**Foster Parent Training La Ribida Children's Hospital**
*Area Served: Cook County Write*: E 65th St At Lake Michigan, Chicago, IL 60649 *Call*: 773/363-6700 415

**IL Foster Parent Assn** *Area Served: IL* Work toward making happy foster homes; inform foster parents about legal problems, current legislation and their rights. Newsletter goes to all foster parents in the state. *Meetings*: Monthly for family and friends in various locations. *Services*: Mutual aid, educational program or material, advocacy, telephone support, newsletter, written information, speakers bureau, social activities, referral to other services, fundraising, home or hospital visitation, professional service. *Write*: 1444 E County Rd, 2710 N, Niota, IL 62358 *Call*: 217/448-4191

# Grandparents as Parents

**Grandchildren's Rights to Grandparents** *Area Served: Cook County Write*: 5234 W Oak, Oak Lawn, IL 60304 *Call*: 708/422-3336

**Grandparents Anonymous, Inc** *Area Served: National* Encourage grandparents to secure visitation privileges for their grandchildren. Advocate for grandparents' visitation rights and encourage schools to sponsor grandparents programs. Successfully lobbied for a Grandparents and Grandchildren's Day (March 18th) in Michigan. No known IL groups. *Services*: Advocacy, telephone support, home or hospital visitation, social activities. *Write*: 461 Huron, Pontiac, MI 48341 *Call*: 800/422-4453

**Grandparents As Parents** *Area Served: Chicago, Cook County* A self-help group of grandparents facing the issues of being a parent to their grandchildren. *Meetings*: Weekly for grandparents. *Services*: Mutual aid, telephone support. *Write*:9107 Keating, Skokie, IL 60076 *Call*: 847/676-1320

**Grandparents Raising Grandchildren** *Area Served: IL-Central* To make the world a safer place for our grandchildren. Moral support and help for each other. Guidance and advice with assistance. Legislation as needed. *Meetings*: Monthly. *Services*: Mutual aid, telephone support, referral to other services, advocacy, newsletter. *Write*: 535 W Grove St, Bloomington, IL 61701 *Call*: 309/888-4265

# Homeless

**Gospel League for Homeless Women and Children** *Area Served: Chicago* Offers food, clothing, shelter and medical care for women and children. Christian counseling for battered and homeless women. Intermediate facility to assist in restoration. *Services*: Mutual aid, written information, referral to other services, telephone support. *Write*: 955 W Grand Ave, Chicago, IL 60622
*Call*: 312/243-2480

**Home of the Sparrow** *Area Served: McHenry County Write*: PO Box 343, McHenry, IL 60050
*Call*: 815/344-5171

**Homeless Hotline** *Area Served: Chicago* Gives referrals to shelters in the city of Chicago; if these are full, then caller will be referred to a warming center. *Services*: Referral to other services. *Write*: 510 N Peshtigo Ct, Chicago, IL 60611 *Call*: 800/654-8595

**Institute for Women Today Maria Shelter-Casa Notre Dame** *Area Served: Chicago Write*: 7315 S Yale, Chicago, IL 60621 *Call*: 773/994-5350

**Maria Shelter Institute for Women Today** *Area Served: Chicago* Transitional shelter for 60 mothers and children. Offers alcohol support group, counseling, assistance in apartment and job placement, parenting classes, educational workshops. *Services*: Mutual aid, professional service, referral to other services. *Write*: 7300 S Yale, Chicago, IL 60621 *Call*: 773/651-8372

**St Martin De Porres Shelter House of Hope** *Area Served: Cook County* Shelter for homeless women and children for whatever reason. Can stay up to 120 days. Has programs which are designed to help the person avoid becoming homeless again, such as individual and group counseling, GED, etc. *Services*: Mutual aid, educational program or material, advocacy, professional service. *Write*: 6423 S Woodlawn, Chicago, IL 60637 *Call*: 773/643-5843

**The Olive Branch** *Area Served: Chicago* Provide morning and evening shelter for homeless persons (no overnight). Meals, showers, clothing and haircuts are also available. *Write*: 1047 W Madison County St, Chicago, IL 60607 *Call*: 312/243-3373

# Interracial

**Biracial Family Network** *Area Served: National* Conducts educational forums on interracialism; to eliminate prejudice and discrimination; to advocate racial integration; and to provide support for one another. *Meetings*: Monthly. *Services*: Mutual aid, written information, referral to other services, speakers bureau, referral to other services, social activities, newsletter. *Write*: PO Box 3214, Chicago, IL 60654 *Call*: 773/288-3644

**Interracial Family Alliance** Strengthens the interracial family unit and promote its acceptance by the public. *Services*: Mutual aid, educational program or material, advocacy, telephone support, social activities, speakers bureau, newsletter, referral to other services, written information. *Write*: PO Box 20290, Atlanta, GA 30325 *Call*: 404/696-8113

**Interracial Family Network** *Area Served: Cook, DuPage and Lake Counties* Affirms the dignity and equality of every racial and cultural group; supports and serves the interracial/intercultural family and multiracial individuals; nourishes a positive sense of identity and self-esteem in multiracial children; serves as a centralized resource. Childcare and children's activities provided at each meeting. *Meetings*: Monthly. *Services*: Mutual aid, educational program or material, social activities. *Write*: PO Box 5380, Evanston, IL 60204-5380 *Call*: 847/491-9748

# Latch Key Children

**Grandma, Please Hull House** *Area Served: Chicago and Cook County* Telephone hotline M-F 3 pm-6 pm for latch key children. Trained older adults provide comfort and reassurance to children after school. Grandma, Please encourages communication between children and parents and promotes home safety for children at home alone. *Services*: Telephone support. *Write*: 4520 N Beacon St, Chicago, IL 60640 *Call*: 773/271-0000

# Marriage

**Courage to Love** *Area Served: Chicago Write*: 1660 Lorraine, Wheaton, IL 60187

**For Better** *Area Served: Chicago and Suburbs* Mutual growth group for co-dependent individuals who are in a marital relationship that is in transition. Emphasizing self-awareness, personal growth, and the belief that quality of a marriage is dependent upon the health and welfare of the individuals in the marriage. 12-step program. *Meetings*: Monthly, but restricted to persons in a marital

relationship. *Services*: Mutual aid. *Write*: 413 N Winston Dr, Palatine, IL 60067 *Call*: 847/359-3141

**We Saved Our Marriage, Inc (WESOM, Inc)** A 12 Step support group for married people who have been emotionally harmed by infidelity. 3 meeting locations of WESOM: 2 in the Chicago and 1 in San Francisco, CA. *Services*: phone support, nationally and internationally, and support group. *Meetings*: Every Wednesday in Park Ridge, IL; every other Monday in Palatine, IL; every Tuesday in San Francisco, CA; call for specific times. *Write*: PO Box 46312, Chicago, IL 60646-0312 *Call*: 773/792-7034

# Missing Children

**Child Find of America, Inc** To register and locate missing children; to use mediation as a forum to return parentally abducted children; to prevent parental abduction, and promote child safety and public information about the issue of missing children. *Services*: Mutual aid, educational program or material, written information, referral to other services, speakers bureau, hotline, newsletter. *Write*: PO Box 277, New Paltz, NY 12561 *Call*: 800/426-5678

# Mothers

**A Time for Mom** *Area Served: Peoria, Tazewell and Woodford Counties* A support group for the mothers of pre-schoolers who have chosen to stay at home during their children's early years. Professionals speak on a variety of topics providing insights on womanhood, marriage and children based on Judeo-Christian family values. Sponsored by Catholic Social Service, but all denominations welcome. Babysitting available at no charge. *Services*: Mutual aid, educational program or material. *Write*: 5819 N Rosemead, Peoria, IL 61614 *Call*: 309/691-2035

**Formerly Employed Mothers At Loose Ends FEMALE** Through its monthly newsletter and network of local chapters, FEMALE offers support to women making the transition from paid employment to at-home motherhood and advocacy of more family-friendly public policies and private business practices. 11 chapters in IL. *Meetings*: Bi-monthly. *Services*: Mutual aid, written information, advocacy, referral to other services, speakers bureau, social activities, newsletter. *Write*: PO Box 31, Elmhurst, IL 60126 *Call*: 630/279-8862

# Parenting

**Discipline Without Hitting, Screaming Or Bribing Jewish Family and Community Service** *Area Served:*

*Cook County Write*: 205 W Randolph St, Ste 1100, Chicago, IL 60606 *Call*: 312/263-5523

**Family Education Centers Adler School of Professional Psychology** *Area Served: Lake, Cook and DuPage Counties* Community education division sponsors free and low-cost family education lectures, panel discussions, live and taped family counseling demonstrations through the various family education centers. Trains and provides parent education/study groups and parent support groups. *Meetings*: Weekly for parents. *Services*: Mutual aid, educational program or material, newsletter, written information. *Write*: 65 E Wacker Pl, Ste 2100, Chicago, IL 60601 *Call*: 312/201-5900 226

**Family Resources Coalition** *Area Served: National* Primarily serves social service professionals working with families. FRC's mission is to build support and resources within communities that strengthen and empower families, enhance the capacities of parents, and foster the optimal development of children and youth. Offers information on family resource programs, training, and publishes resources. *Services*: Written information, advocacy. *Write*: 200 S Michigan Ave, Ste 1520, Chicago, IL 60604 *Call*: 312/341-0900

**Latina Parenting Travelers and Immigrants Aid Women's Program** *Area Served: Cook County Write*: 1950 W Pershing Rd, Chicago, IL 60609 *Call*: 773/847-4417

**Northside Parents Network** *Area Served: Chicago-N* Network dedicated to helping raise happy, active, and involved children in the city. NPN was created and managed by parents. NPN is a source of information, support and fun for families. Monthly newsletter, new moms groups, babysitting coops, drop-in center, holiday parties, information booklets and brochures, and many other programs. *Write*: 1218 W Addison, Chicago, IL 60613 *Call*: 312/409-2233

**Parent Support Group** *Area Served: Cook County* 15-week support groups provide parenting skills for Latino parents of adolescents and grammar school children. Ongoing groups for parents completing the 15-week program. Groups are given only in Spanish. *Meetings*: Weekly for Spanish-speaking parents. *Services*: Mutual aid, educational program or material. *Write*: 1823 W 17th St, Chicago, IL 60608 *Call*: 312/226-1544

**Parent Support Group Family Services and Mental Health Center of Cicero** *Area Served: Cook County Write*: 5341 Cermak, Cicero, IL 60650 *Call*: 708/656-6430

**Parental Stress Group Erie Family Health Center** *Area Served: Chicago-N and NW* Helps parents (or childcare providers) to deal with stress related to children's discipline, behavior problems and school problems. English and Spanish. Hotline. *Meetings*:

Weekly for parents, children, and anyone taking care of children. *Services*: Mutual aid, educational program or material, telephone support, written information, hotline. *Write*: 1656 W Chicago Ave, Chicago, IL 60622 *Call*: 312/666-3488

**Parental Stress Services Child Abuse Prevention Service** *Area Served: Chicago* 24-hour crisis hotline for parents under stress or at the point of losing control with their children. Understanding volunteers give support and referrals. Parenting classes to develop parenting skills. Parents Anonymous support groups for parents under stress and who haveor feel they may abuse their children. *Meetings*: Weekly. *Services*: Mutual aid, written information, referral to other services, speakers bureau, hotline, newsletter. *Write*: 600 S Federal, Ste #205, Chicago, IL 60605 *Call*: 312/427-1102

**Parenthesis Parent-Child Center** *Area Served: Cook-W* Support groups for families at risk: premature infants; single families; and teen parents. *Services*: Mutual aid, educational program or material, fundraising, referral to other services, telephone support, home or hospital visitation, social activities, newsletter, information. *Write*: 405 S Euclid Ave, Oak Park, IL 60302 *Call*: 708/848-2227

**Parenting Skills for Hispanic Women Travelers and Immigrants Aid-Women's Program** *Area Served: Chicago Write*: 1950 W Pershing Rd, Chicago, IL 60609 *Call*: 773/847-5602 hotline

**Parents Group-Single, Married, Remarried Jewish Family and Community Service** *Area Served: Lake and Cook Counties Write*: 210 Skokie Valley Rd, Highland Park, IL 60035 *Call*: 847/831-4225

**The Get Together Virginia Frank Child Development Center** *Area Served: Cook County* Drop-in center group for mothers of 0-3 year olds; an opportunity to meet with other mothers and professional staff whose skills are in family and child development. *Meetings*: Weekly. *Write*: 3033 W. Touhy, Chicago, IL 60645 *Call*: 773/761-4550

**The Parent Group** *Area Served: Lake County Write*: 641 Lorraine Ave, Waukegan, IL 60085 *Call*: 847/263-7272

# Single Parents

**Parenting Apart Parents Not Living Together** Provide psycho social and emotional support. Resource info available for education. Encouragement from facilitator and group members. Referrals for other help. Focus on the parenting role for parents not living together. *Meetings*: monthly, 2nd Thursday at 7 pm; English; no transportation; accessible. *Write*: St Margaret's Hospital, 600 E 1st St,

Spring Valley, IL 61362 *Call*: 815/664-1132
*Fax*: 815/664-1188

**Parents Support Group Community Crisis Center**
*Area Served: Kane County Write*: PO Box 1390, Elgin, IL 60121 *Call*: 847/697-2380

**Parents Without Partners** *Area Served: Cook County Write*: 8050 S Kilpatrick, Chicago, IL 60652
*Call*: 773/371-3610

**Parents Without Partners Ogden Trails** *Area Served: DuPage County Write*: PO Box 37, Downers Grove, IL 60515 *Call*: 630/932-1615 Answer Mach.

**Parents Without Partners Western Springs**
*Area Served: Cook and DuPage Counties Services*:
Mutual aid, social activities, telephone support, referral to other services, educational program or material,
newsletter. *Write*: PO Box 3, Western Springs, IL 60558
*Call*: 708/246-7840 Answer Mach.

**Single Fathers Jewish Family and Community Service**
*Area Served: Cook County Write*: 205 W Randolph, Ste 1100, Chicago, IL 60606 *Call*: 312/263-5523

**Single Mothers By Choice Midwest Chapter** *Area Served: IL* Provide support and information to women who have chosen to be single parents--whether through natural means, artificial insemination or adoption; and whether or not they are already parenting, actively trying or merely considering motherhood. Provides a peer group for the children through monthly meetings, outings, socials and childcare co-op. *Services*: Mutual aid, speakers bureau, written information, social activities, referral to other services, newsletter. *Write*: 1020 W Altgeld St, Chicago, IL 60614-2209 *Call*: 773/920-5113

**Single Mothers Support Group DePaul Community Health Center** *Area Served: Cook County* A 10-week group to offer emotional support and information to single mothers over the age of 21. The goal is to enhance ability of single moms to cope with stress and demands of parenting. Individual interview required before joining the group. *Meetings*: Weekly. *Services*: Mutual aid, referral to other services, speakers bureau. *Write*: 2219 N Kenmore, Chicago, IL 60614 *Call*: 312/362-8292

**Single Parents and Their Children Virginia Frank Child Development Center** *Area Served: Chicago-N*
Evening supper discussion group for single parents and their children, 0-5 years old. 8-week series held 3 to 4 times a year. *Services*: Mutual aid, educational program or material, social activities, newsletter. *Write*: 3033 W Touhy, Chicago, IL 60645 *Call*: 773/761-4550

**Single Parents and Their Children Jewish Family and Community Service** *Area Served: Lake and Cook Counties Write*: 1250 Radcliffe Rd, #206, Buffalo Grove, IL 60089 *Call*: 847/392-8820

**Single Parents Group Jewish Family and Community Service** *Area Served: Chicago Write*:3033 W Touhy, Chicago, IL 60645 *Call*: 773/761-4550

**Society for the Preservation of Human Dignity** *Area Served: Cook, Lake and DuPage Counties* Offers single mothers groups. *Services*: Mutual aid, educational program or material, written information, referral to other services. *Write*: 37 N Plum Grove Rd, Palatine, IL 60067
*Call*: 847/359-4919

**Span-Single Parent Support Group Village of Mount Prospect** *Area Served: Cook County Write*: Human Resources Dept, 50 S Emerson, Mt Prospect, IL 60056
*Call*: 847/870-5680

**Unwed Parents Anonymous, Inc** A spiritual self-help support group which has adapted the 12-steps and 12-traditions from AA to the problems attending out-of-wedlock pregnancy. To bring serenity to members by practicing sexual abstinence and chastity. Brochures and video tapes available. *Meetings*: For anyone affected by an out-of-wedlock pregnancy; childcare provided.
*Services*: Mutual aid, educational program or material.
*Write*: PO Box 15466, Phoenix, AZ 85064
*Call*: 602/952-1463

**Young Single Parents of America, Inc Chapter 115**
*Area Served: Kane, DuPage and Kendall Counties* Org. of young single parents (21-45), educational, dedicated to overcoming the complex hardships for single parents and their children. *Meetings*: Weekly for parents. *Services*:
Mutual aid, educational program or material, telephone support, social activities, newsletter, referral to other services. *Write*: Box 1682, Aurora, IL 60507
*Call*: 630/859-8890

## Stepfamilies

**Stepfamily Assn of IL, Inc** *Area Served: IL-N*
SAI, INC. Aims to educate, counsel, and support
Stepfamilies; to reduce the confusions, frustrations, and
isolation felt in Stepfamilies. Provide lay and professional
materials, support self-help chapters, publishes Stepfamily
bulletin, guest speakers, classes, consultation, and
professional training. Warm line phone: 708/848-0909.
*Meetings*: Call for information. *Internet news group*:
alt.support.Stepparents (use all small letter for news
group). *Write*: PO Box 3124, Oak Park, IL 60303
*Call*: 708/848-0909 *Email*: Pilgrim27@aol.com
*Web site*: http://members.aol.com/pilgram27/

## Teen Parents

**Greater DuPage County Mym, Inc** *Area Served:
DuPage, Cook and Kane Counties* Provide peer support
groups for adolescent parents, both moms and dads.
Deliver parenting education through groups. Home visits
to teen parents; peer presented prevention program,
support/education groups for teen mothers and
fathers-facilitated by former teen parents. Weekly
meetings; transportation costs can be covered, childcare
and meals provided at group meetings. *Write*: 739
Roosevelt Rd, Bldg 8, Ste 202, Glen Ellyn, IL 60137
*Call*: 630/790-8433 *Fax*: 630/790-8024

**Parenteen Parenthesis Parent-Child Center**
*Area Served: Cook-W* Special program for teen parents.
*Meetings*: Weekly. *Services*: Mutual aid, educational
program or material, fundraising, referralto other services,
telephone support, home or hospital visitation, social
activities, newsletter, written information. *Write*: 405 S
Euclid Ave, Oak Park, IL 60302 *Call*: 708/848-2227

**Teen Parents-Lawndale Family Focus, Inc**
*Area Served: Chicago-W* Support, information and
resources to meet the special needs of teen parents and
teens who are expecting to become parents. *Services*:
Mutual aid, educational program or material, telephone
support, social activities, Home or hospital visitation,
professional service. *Write*: 3600 W Ogden Ave, Chicago,
IL 60623 *Call*: 773/521-3306

**Teen Parents-Our Place Family Focus, Inc**
*Area Served: Cook-N* Support, information and resources
to meet the special needs of pregnant and parenting teens.
*Meetings*: Weekly. *Services*: Mutual aid, educational
program or material, telephone support. *Write*: 2010
Dewey, Evanston, IL 60201 *Call*: 847/475-7570

**Young Parents Center Chicago Urban League**
*Area Served: Cook County Write*: 226 W Jackson, 4th Fl,
Chicago, IL 60606 *Call*: 312/357-0470 *Fax*:
312/357-0492

## Troubled Children

**Aunt Martha's Youth Service Center** *Area Served:
Cook, Will and Kankakee Counties* Community based
comprehensive youth service helping youth and families.
24-hour crisis intervention. *Services*: Professional service.
*Write*: 4343 Lincoln Hwy, #340, Matteson, IL 60443
*Call*: 708/747-2701

**National Runaway Switchboard** *Area Served: National*
Provide information, referral and crisis intervention to
runaways and other homeless youth and their families on a
24-hour, 7 day a week telephone hotline serving the entire
US. *Services*: Written information, referral to other
services, telephone support, hotline. *Write*: 3080 N
Lincoln Ave, Chicago, IL 60657 *Call*: 800/621-4000

**Parenting Adolescents Without Losing Your Cool
Jewish Family and Community Service** *Area Served:
Cook and Lake Counties Write*: 5050 Church St, Skokie,
IL 60077 *Call*: 847/675-0390

**Tough Love** *Area Served: IL* Open to all parents, family
members and professionals who encounter unacceptable
behavior from children (ages 9-40), such as drug or
alcohol abuse, running away, school failure, gangs and
violence. 22 chapters in IL. *Meetings*: Weekly. *Services*:
Mutual aid, written information, telephone support,
educational program or material, advocacy, newsletter,
speakers bureau, social activities, referral to other
services, referral to other services, hotline. *Write*: 6111
Springside, Downers Grove, IL 60516 *Call*: 800/926-5437
or
800/333-1069

**National Runaway Switchboard** *Area Served: National*
Provide information, referral and crisis intervention to
runaways and other homeless youth and their families on a
24-hour, 7 day a week telephone hotline serving the entire
US. *Services*: Written information, referral to other
services, telephone support, hotline. *Write*: 3080 N
Lincoln Ave, Chicago, IL 60657 *Call*: 800/621-4000

## Twins

**Double Headers** *Area Served: Cook County Write*:
Swedish Covenant Hospital, 5145 N California Ave,
Chicago, IL 60625 *Call*: 773/769-6564

**IL Org of Mothers of Twins Clubs, Inc** *Area Served: IL*
Members clubs exist throughout IL for the purpose of
exchanging information pertaining to the rearing,
development and recognition of the individuality of twins
as may be forthcoming from parents, doctors, educators
and other appropriate sources. 25 chapters in IL.
*Meetings*: Monthly for mothers. *Services*: Mutual aid,
educational program or material, fundraising, written

information, advocacy, referral to other services, referral to other services, telephone support, social activities, newsletter. *Write*: 415 Spaulding Rd, Bartlett, IL 60103 *Call*: 630/876-1205

**Parents of Twins Club Northwestern Memorial Hospital** *Area Served: Chicago* Provide ongoing educational and support programs for parents of multiples. Meet other parents of multiples and address the special needs of group members. *Meetings*: Monthly. *Services*: Mutual aid, educational program or material. *Write*: 333 E Superior St, Ste 161, Chicago, IL 60611 *Call*: 312/908-8400

## Young Children

**Early Years Program Orchard Mental Health Center** *Area Served: IL* Family support program serving families with newborns and children through age 4. Provide families with support and information designed to enhance the experience of the early years, thus helping to lay a solid foundation for future development. *Meetings*: Weekly, but restricted to persons sharing the concern. *Services*: Mutual aid, educational program or material, written information, advocacy, referral to other services, speakers bureau, home or hospital visitation, newsletter. *Write*: 8324 Skokie Blvd, Skokie, IL 60077 *Call*: 847/933-0051

**Family Focus, Inc Central Administrative Office** *Area Served: Chicago* 5 Chicago-area offices. Programs address parenting, including teen pregnancy and parenting. *Write*: 310 S Peoria St, Ste 401, Chicago, IL 60607-3534 *Call*: 312/421-5200

**Family Focus, Inc Chicago-Lawndale** *Area Served: Chicago* Family support org. and drop-in center for parents of young children (infancy through 3 years). Purpose is to strengthen and support families in effort to prevent the occurrence of mental, emotional, and social

problems. Various programs and services. Support group and workshops for parents and children. *Meetings*: Weekly.*Services*: Mutual aid, educational program or material, telephone support *Write*: 3600 W Ogden Ave, Chicago, IL 60623 *Call*: 773/521-3306

**Family Focus, Inc District 65** *Area Served: Cook-N* Family support org. and drop-in center for parents of young children (infancy through 5 years) in School District 65. Purpose is to strengthen and support families in effort to prevent the occurrence of mental, emotional, and social problems. Various programs and services. Group and workshops for parents and children. *Services*: Mutual aid, educational program or material, telephone support. *Write*: 1942 Dempster, Evanston, IL 60202 *Call*: 847/869-1800

**Family Focus, Inc Evanston-Our Place** *Area Served: Cook-N Write*: 2010 Dewey, Evanston, IL 60201 *Call*: 847/475-7570

**Parents Concern** *Area Served: Cook County* Support for parents of young children. Programs of an educational nature for parents; a babysitting co-op; rap groups; newsletter. *Meetings*: Bi-weekly for parents. *Services*: Mutual aid, educational program or material, advocacy, telephone support, social activities, newsletter, written information. *Write*: 824 Milburn St, IL 60201 *Call*: 847/256-7048

Parents, Infants and Preschoolers Drop-In Center Family Service Center *Area Served: Cook County* Drop-in center for parents, infants and preschoolers once a week. Play activities for youngsters; discussion support group for mothers. *Meetings*: Weekly. *Services*: Mutual aid. *Write*: 1167 Wilmette Ave, Wilmette, IL 60091 *Call*: 847/251-7350

# Health

## Acoustic Neuroma
## -See *Hearing Impairment*

## Adrenal Disease-Kidney

**Addison's Disease Support Group for Northern IL** *Area Served: Chicago* Mutual self-help group for people with adrenal diseases Addison's disease, Cushing's

syndrome, pheochromocytoma. Interested family members and friends are welcome. *Services*: Newsletters,support, information resources, guest speakers and group discussions. This group does not offer medical advice. *Meetings*: 4 meetings a year, usually at local hospitals in the metro-Chicago area, in English, 2:30-5 pm, we try to arrange transportation. *Write*: 115 Pebble Creek Dr, Lake Zurich, IL 60047 *Call*: 847/394-5308 *Email*: IL Adrenal@aol.com *Web site*: http://home.aol.com/iladrenal

**National Adrenal Diseases Foundation** *Area Served: IL* We are a national org. dedicated to serving the needs of those with adrenal diseases and their families, through education, support groups and buddy arrangements. Research is a planned goal. One support group in IL. *Services*: Mutual aid, telephone support, newsletter. *Write*: 505 Northern Blvd, Great Neck, NY 11021 *Call*: 516/487-4992

**National Adrenal Diseases Foundation Addison's Disease Support Group/Northern IL** *Area Served: IL-N* To increase public awareness of Addison's disease; to learn more about the disease; and to offer encouragement to all Addisonians. Does not offer medical advice. *Meetings*: Quarterly for anyone with Addison's disease or any adrenal dysfunction and for anyone close to such a person. *Services*: Mutual aid, educational program or material, written information, advocacy, speakers bureau, telephone support, social activities, newsletter. *Write*: 942 Michigan Ave, c/o Courtney P Paddock, Evanston, IL 60202 *Call*: 847/864-6604

# Aging

## Aging-General

**American Assn of Retired Persons AARP- Regional Headquarters** *Area Served: IL* Non-profit membership assn, which helps persons age 50 and older to help themselves and their communities through programs such as Health Education, Crime Prevention, Tax-Aide, 55 Alive/Mature Driving, Consumer Affairs, Widowed Persons Service, Institute of Lifetime Learning, Inter-generational Programs and Legislative advocacy. *Services*: Educational program or material, advocacy, fundraising, social activities, newsletter, written information. *Write*: 8750 W Bryn Mawr Ave, Chicago, IL 60631 *Call*: 773/714-9800 *Fax*: 312/714-9927

**Central IL Area Agency on Aging Area 4** *Area Served: Peoria, Tazewell and Fulton Counties Write*: 700 Hamilton Blvd, Rm 300, Peoria, IL 62603

**Chicago Department of Aging Area 12** *Area Served: Cook County Write*: 510 N Peshtigo, Chicago, IL 60611 *Call*:312/744-4016 *Fax*: 312/744-1022

**Christmas in April, USA** *Area Served: National Write*: 1225 Eye St NW, Ste 601, Washington, DC 20005 *Call*: 800/473-4229

**East Central IL Agency on Aging Area 5** *Area Served: McLean, Vermillion and Cumberland Counties Write*: 1003 Maple Hill Rd, Bloomington, IL 61704-9008

**Health Committee of Gray Panthers** *Area Served: Chicago Write*: 5757 N Sheridan Rd, Apt 8D, Chicago, IL 60660 *Call*: 773/561-3195

## Aging-Healthy

**Access Wisdom, Inc** *Area Served: Cook, DuPage and Will Counties Write*: 288 N Addison, Elmhurst, IL 60126

**Acting Up! Acting Up Too!** *Area Served: Cook-N* Acting Up! and Acting Up Too! are 2 separate and distinct special performing companies of people over age. *Call*: 800/562-5555 *Email*: greta@netexpress.net *Web site*: http://www.wiaaa.org

**Healthy Transitions Membership Program Northwestern Memorial Hospital** *Area Served: Cook County Write*: Dept of Geriatric Services, Superior and Fairbanks Ct, Chicago, IL 60611 *Call*: 312/908-4335 *Fax*: 312/908-8066

**IL Department on Aging** *Area Served: IL Write*: 421 E Capital, #100, Springfield, IL 62701-1789 *Call*: 800/252-8966

**Lake County Council for Seniors** *Area Served: Lake County* To serve the needs and concerns of senior citizens; to protect the rights and promote the general welfare of the senior community. *Meetings*. Monthly. *Services*: Advocacy, telephone support, newsletter, written information. *Write*: 414 S Lewis, Waukegan, IL 60085 *Call*: 847/244-1720

**Midland Area Agency on Aging Area 9** *Area Served: Marian, Clay and Effingham Counties Write*: PO Box 1420, Centralia, IL 62801 *Call*: 618/532-1853

**New City YMCA Programs for Seniors** *Area Served: Chicago Write*: 1515 N Halsted, Chicago, IL 60622 *Call*: 312/266-1249

**Niles Senior Center** *Area Served: Cook County Write*: 8060 Oakton, Niles, IL 60648 *Call*: 847/967-6100 *Fax*: 847/692-3297

**Northeastern IL Area Agency on Aging Area 2** *Area Served: IL Write*: PO Box 809, Kankakee, IL 60901 *Call*: 800/528-2000 *Fax*: 815/939-0022

**Northwestern IL Area Agency on Aging Area 1** *Area Served: Winnebago, Lee and Ogle Counties Write*: 638 Holister, Rockford, IL 61108 *Call*: 815/226-4901

**Older Women's League OWL IL** *Area Served: IL* OWL was founded in 1980 to focus on key issues for olderwomen including access to health care insurance, social security reform, and pension rights. Today, OWL carries the message of midlife and older women for caregiving, job discrimination, financial planning, staying in control during periods of fixed income. Provides support, education, advocacy, and newsletters. 12 chapters in IL. *Write*: 332 S Michigan, #1050, Chicago, IL 60604-0011

*Call*: 312/347-0011  *Fax*: 312/347-1003
*Web site*: http://members.aol.com/owlil/owlil.htm

**Older Women's League Chicago/Hyde Park**
*Area Served: Chicago-S* OWL is an educational,
advocacy and Mutual support org focusing on the issues of
midlife and older women including: caregiving, the image
of the older woman, job discrimination, financial
planning, social Security, pension reform, staying in
control of one's life during periods of fixed income.
*Services*: Mutual aid, educational program or material,
written information, referral to other services, advocacy,
social activities, newsletter, speakers bureau. *Call*:
312/347-0011
*Web site*: http://members.aol.com/owlil/owlil.htm

**Older Women's League Chicago Southeast Chapter**
*Area Served: Chicago-SE  Call*: 312/347-0011

**Older Women's League Chicago North Chapter**
*Area Served: Chicago-N  Call*: 312/347-0011

**Older Women's League Danville Chapter**
*Area Served: Central IL  Call*: 312/347-0011
*Web site*: http://members.aol.com/owlil/owlil.htm

**Older Women's League DuPage County Area Chapter**
*Area Served: DuPage County  Call*: 312/347-0011

**Older Women's League Fox Valley Chapter**
*Area Served: Kane County* Support, education and
advocacy for midlife and older women. *Meetings*:
Monthly for all interested. Support group, education,
and advocacy. *Call*: 312/347-0011
*Web site*: http://members.aol.com/owlil/owlil.htm

**Older Women's League Hyde Park Owl** *Area Served:
Chicago-S* Write: 5235 S University Ave, Chicago, IL
60615 *Call*: 773/324-5116

**Older Women's League Near West Chapter**
*Area Served: Chicago-W  Call*: 312/347-0011

**Older Women's League North Suburban Chapter**
*Area Served: Chicago-N  Call*: 312/347-0011

**Older Women's League Quad Cities Chapter**
*Area Served: Quad Cities  Call*: 312/347-0011
*Web site*: http://members.aol.com/owlil/owlil.htm

**Older Women's League River Valley**
*Area Served: River Valley  Call*: 312/347-0011
*Web site*: http://members.aol.com/owlil/owlil.htm

**Older Women's League South Suburban Chapter**
*Area Served: South Suburban  Call*: 312/347-0011

**Our World Senior Support Center**  *Write*: 624 E State
St, O'Fallon, IL 62269 *Call*: 618/632-3674

**Programs and Services for Older Persons Belleville
Area College Prog and Svcs**  *Area Served: St Clair*

*County  Write*: 201 N Church, Belleville, IL 62220
*Call*: 618/234-4410 31  *Fax*: 618/234-8634

**Project Life Area Agency on Aging Area 9**
*Area Served: Sangamon, Morgan and Mason Counties*
*Write*: 2141 W White Oak Ave, Ste C, Springfield, IL
62704 *Call*: 217/787-9234

**Reminiscing Southwest Suburban Center on Aging**
*Area Served: DuPage County  Write*: 111 W Harris Ave,
LaGrange, IL 60525 *Call*: 708/354-1323
*Fax*: 708/354-0282

**River Forest Township Community Center**
*Area Served: Cook County  Write*: 8020 Madison, River
Forest, IL 60305 *Call*: 708/771-5820 *Fax*: 708/771-8958

**Royalty Club Carlinville Area Hospital Community
Relations**  *Area Served: Macon and Monroe Counties*
*Write*: 1001 E Morgan, Carlinville, IL 62626
*Call*: 800/828-9923 354

**Senior Citizens' Center** *Area Served: Henry County* To
enrich the lives of our senior citizens with meals, van
service, education and recreation. Our goal is to be able to
continue these services and find others we can be of
service to support.*Services*: Mutual aid, educational
program or material, written information, advocacy,
telephone support, social activities, newsletter, Home or
hospital visitation. *Write*: 541 E North St, Geneseo, IL
61254 *Call*: 309/944-3793

**Sharing and Caring Ravenswood CMHC** *Area Served:
Cook County  Write*: 2312 W Irving Park Rd, Chicago, IL
60618 *Call*: 773/463-7000 1455

**Southeastern IL Area Agency on Aging Area 10** *Area
Served: Edwards, Crawford and Lawrence Counties*
*Write*: 35 W Main St, Albion, IL 62806
*Call*: 800/635-8544

**Southwestern IL Area Agency on Aging Area 8**
*Area Served: Scott Bond and Madison Counties*
*Write*: 331 Salem Pl, Ste 170, Fairview Heights, IL 62208
*Call*: 800/326-3221

**Suburban Area Agency on Aging Area 13** *Area Served:
Cook County  Write*: 1146 W Gate, Oak Park, IL 60301
*Call*: 708/383-0258

**Telecare Elmhurst Memorial Hospital** *Area Served:
DuPage County  Write*: 200 Berteau, Elmhurst, IL 60126
*Call*: 630/833-1400 4095

**Telecare Holy Family Hospital** *Area Served: Cook
County Services*: Telephone support. *Write*: 100 N River
Rd, Des Plaines, IL 60016 *Call*: 847/297-1800 1160

**Telecare Northwest Community Hospital** *Area Served:
Cook County* Telecare is a special service for senior
citizens or disabled who live alone. It is a friendly, reliable

means of verifying your well-being thru daily phone conversations with caring hospital volunteers. *Services*: Telephone support. *Write*: 800 W Central Rd, Arlington Heights, IL 60005 *Call*: 847/577-4045

**Telecare St Anthony's Memorial Hospital** *Area Served: Effingham* *Write*: Effingham, IL 62401
*Call*: 217/342-2121

**Telecare St Francis Hospital** *Area Served: Cook County* *Services*: Telephone support. *Write*: Volunteer Dept, 355 Ridge, Evanston, IL 60202 *Call*: 847/492-2255

**Telecare St Joseph Hospital** *Area Served: Chicago* Special service for senior citizens or disabled who live alone. A friendly, reliable means of verifying the senior's well-being through daily phone conversations with caring hospital volunteers. *Services*: Telephone support. *Write*: 2900 N Lake Shore Dr, Chicago, IL 60657 *Call*: 773/975-3167

**Telecare Swedish American Hospital** *Area Served: Winnebago County* Telecare is a special service for senior citizens or disabled who live alone. It is a friendly, reliable means of verifying your well-being thru daily phone conversations with caring hospital volunteers. *Services*: Telephone support. *Write*: 1400 Charles St, Rockford, IL 61104 *Call*: 815/968-4400

**West Central IL Area Agency on Aging Area 6** *Area Served: Adams, Schuyler and Brown Counties* *Write*: PO Box 428, Quincy, IL 62306-0428

**Western IL Area Agency on Aging Area 3** *Area Served: Rock Island, Putnam and Warren Counties* *Write*: 729 34th Ave, Rock Island, IL 61201 *Call*: 309/793-6800 *Fax*: 309/793-6807

# AIDS

**AIDS Action Project Howard Brown Memorial Clinic** *Area Served: Chicago* Psycho-social services for AIDS patient and loved ones—not exclusively gay. Buddy program provides one-on-one support. Also provides home visitation, legal services, bereavement group, and nutritional counseling. *Meetings*: Call for information. *Services*: Mutual aid, educational program or material, advocacy, telephone support, written information, home or hospital visitation, professional service. *Write*: 945 W George St, Chicago, IL 60657-9974 *Call*: 773/871-5777

**AIDS Care Network** *Area Served: Winnebago County* Community based org. dedicated to working with people with AIDS/HIV, their families, partners and friends. The main purpose of ACN is to provide people affected by AIDS with support—especially emotional and educational. *Meetings*: Weekly but restricted to persons sharing the concern. *Services*: Mutual aid, educational program or material, written information, advocacy,

referral to other services, speakers bureau, referral to other services, telephone support, social activities, home or hospital visitation, newsletter. *Write*: 221 N Longwood, Ste 105, Rockford, IL 61107-1573 *Call*: 815/968-5181

**AIDS Legal Council of Chicago** *Area Served: Cook County* *Write*: 220 S State, Ste 1330, Chicago, IL 60604 *Call*: 312/427-8990

**AIDS Support Group** *Area Served: DuPage County* *Write*: Edward Hospital, 801 S Washington, Naperville, IL 60566 *Call*: 630/527-3572

**AIDS Support Group McLean County AIDS Task Force** *Area Served: McLean* Discussion, support, contacts. *Services*: Mutual aid, educational program or material. *Write*: PO Box 304, Bloomington, IL 61702 *Call*: 309/827-2437

**AIDS Support Group Wellness Center SIU-Carbondale** *Write*: SIU Regional Effort for AIDS, Jackson County Health Dept, Murphysboro, IL 62966 *Call*: 618/684-3143

**AIDS Support Group Wellness Center SIU-Carbondale** Provides support, for those living with HIV infection (within a safe, confidential environment) by allowing for expression of feelings and one's changing life situations that are a result of infection with HIV. *Meetings*: Weekly but restricted to persons sharing the concern. *Services*: Mutual aid, educational program or material, written information, advocacy, referral to other services, professional service, speakers bureau, referral to other services, telephone support, social activities. *Write*: Counseling Center, Carbondale, IL 62901 *Call*: 708/453-5371

**AIDS Support Network** *Area Served: DuPage County* *Write*: PO Box 254, Naperville, IL 60566 *Call*: 630/585-3810

**Bonaventure House** *Area Served: Chicago* *Write*: PO Box 148187, Chicago, IL 60614

**Buddy System Support Group Springfield Area AIDS Task Force** Support group for anyone who is HIV positive. *Meetings*: Weekly. *Services*: Mutual aid, educational program or material. *Write*: PO Box 6219, Springfield, IL 62708 *Call*: 217/789-2437

**Calor** *Area Served: Cook County* *Write*: 2013 W Division, 2nd Fl, Chicago, IL 60622 *Call*: 773/235-3161 *Fax*: 312/772-0484

**Caregivers Groups Gay Community AIDS Project** *Area Served: Champaign County* *Write*: PO Box 713, Champaign, IL 61824 *Call*: 217/356-4138

**Central IL HIV Care Consortium SIU-School of Medicine** *Area Served: Cent IL* Please call 217/782-7683 for further information. *Write*: PO Box 19230, Springfield, IL 62794-1311 *Call*: 217/782-7683 *Fax*: 217/788-5504

**Chicago House and Social Service Agency, Inc** *Area Served: Chicago Write*: PO Box 14728, Chicago, IL 60614-0728 *Call*: 773/248-5200

**El Groupo Women Support Group U of I, NW Site** *Area Served: Cook County Write*: 1612 N Kedzie, Chicago, IL 60647 *Call*: 773/252-4422

**Family Support Group Bethany Place** *Area Served: IL* Support group for family members who are living with a person who has AIDS. *Meetings*: Bi-monthly for those with the concern. *Services*: Mutual aid, educational program or material, written information, advocacy, referral to other services, speakers bureau, telephone support, newsletter, home or hospital visitation, professional service. *Write*: 224 W Washington St, Belleville, IL 62220 *Call*: 618/234-0291

**Family Support Group Kupona Network** *Area Served: Cook County* Support group for the family and friends of persons who are HIV positive or who have AIDS. *Meetings*: Twice a month. *Services*: Mutual aid, educational program or material, written information. *Write*: 4611 S Ellis, Chicago, IL 60653 *Call*: 773/536-3000 *Fax*: 312/536-8355

**Gay Community AIDS Project** *Area Served: Champaign County* To provide education to the people of East Central IL and support services to the men and women who are, or are close to, HIV positive individuals. *Meetings*: Weekly for anyone interested. *Services*: Mutual aid, educational program or material, information referral to other services, speakers bureau, telephone support, social activities, home or hospital visitation, newsletter. *Write*: PO Box 713, Champaign, IL 61824 *Call*: 217/351-AIDS

**HIV-AIDS Support Group The Carle Pavilion** *Area Served: Champaign County Write*: 602 W University, Champaign, IL 61801-3399 *Call*: 217/383-3180

**HIV-AIDS Women's Support Group Calor** *Area Served: Cook County Write*: 2013 W Division, Chicago, IL 60622 *Call*: 773/235-3161 *Fax*: 312/772-0484

**HIV Positive and AIDS Support for Patients-Others** *Area Served: IL Write*: Columbus Hospital, 2520 N Lakeview, Chicago, IL 60614 *Call*: 773/883-6400 260

**HIV Positive Support Group Humana Hospital-Michael Reese HIV Clinic** *Area Served: Cook County* To offer support to gay and bisexual men who have HIV positive. *Meetings*: Bimonthly. Mutual aid, written information. *Write*: 2929 S Ellis, Chicago, IL 60616 *Call*: 312/791-3104

**HIV PWA Support Group Bethany Place** *Area Served: IL Write*: 224 W Washington St, Belleville, IL 62220 *Call*: 618/234-0291

**HIV Support Group St Thomas Community Center** *Area Served: Central IL* Our group was founded by HIV positive individuals who saw a need to share concerns and resource information with others who are HIV positive. Our coordinator and contact person compiles resources and facilitates discussion. *Meetings*: Twice a month but restricted to persons sharing the concern. *Services*: Mutual aid, educational program or material, written information, referral to other services, speakers bureau. *Call*: 217/429-2148

**Horizons Community** *Services Area Served: Cook County* Offers 2 peer-led self-help groups with 2 trained co-facilitators for each: Living Positive, for persons who have tested positive for HIV; and HIV and Couples, for couples where one or both persons have tested positive. Offered in 10-12 week sessions throughout the year, based on demand. *Services*: Mutual aid. *Write*: 961 W Montana, Chicago, IL 60614 *Call*: 773/472-6469 250

**IL AIDS Hotline Department of Public Health** *Area Served: IL* Makes referrals to self-help groups and services throughout IL and answers medical questions concerning AIDS-HIV. *Services*: Hotline, written information, referral to other services. *Write*: Chicago, IL *Call*: 800/AID-AIDS

**Joshua Northwest Community Hospital** *Area Served: Cook County* A support group for family, friends and caregivers of persons HIV positive or persons with AIDS. *Services*: Mutual aid, written information, referral to other services, educational program or material. *Write*: 800 W Central Rd, Arlington Heights, IL 60005 *Call*: 847/259-7080

**Kupona Network** *Area Served: Cook County Write*: 4611 S Ellis Ave, Chicago, IL 60653 *Call*: 773/536-3000 *Fax*: 312/536-8355

**Madison County AIDS Program (MADCAP)** Prevents the spread of HIV/AIDS and to respond to the needs of those affected by HIV-AIDS. Case management/referrals, financial assistance, counseling, support groups, volunteer opportunities, advocacy, AIDS-HIV information, speakers bureau. Serves anyone in Madison County and surrounding areas outside St Louis. *Meetings*: Call for information. *Write*: 2016 Madison Ave, Granite City, IL 62040 *Call*: 618/877-5110 42 *Fax*: 618/876-4952

**National AIDS Clearinghouse** *Area Served: National Write*: PO Box 6003, Rockville, MA 20849-6006 *Call*: 800/458-5231

**National AIDS Hotline Center for Disease Control** *Area Served: National* Information, education, and referral hotline. Spanish-language hotline

1-800-344-7432. Open 7 days a week, 9 am-3 pm. Not a crisis line. *Services*: Hotline, written information, referral to other services. *Write*: PO Box 13827, Research Triangle Pk, NC 27709 *Call*: 800/342-2437

**One-To-One Gay Community AIDS Project** *Area Served: Champaign County Write*: PO Box 713, Champaign, IL 61814-0713 *Call*: 217/351-2437

**Positive Attitudes to HIV Northwest Community Hospital** *Area Served: Cook-NW* A self-help group for men and women who are HIV-positive or have AIDS. The group provides a warm environment of acceptance with a positive approach to the disease. It is facilitated by a RN and a psychologist. *Meetings*: Twice a month. *Services*: Mutual aid, written information, referral to other services. *Write*: 800 W Central Rd, Arlington Heights, IL 60005 *Call*: 847/259-1000 5060

**Professional AIDS Caregivers Champaign County Urbana Public Health** *Area Served: IL Write*: 710 N Neil St, PO Box 1488, Champaign, IL 61824 *Call*: 217/352-7961 124 *Fax*: 217/352-0126

**PWA Friends and Family** *Area Served: Peoria County Write*: 415 St Marks Ct, Ste 504, Peoria, IL 61603 *Call*: 309/671-2144

**PWA Heterosexual Group** *Area Served: Peoria County Write*: 415 St Marks Ct, Ste 504, Peoria, IL 61603 *Call*: 309/671-2144 *Fax*: 309/671-8363

**Saint Louis Effort for AIDS** *Area Served: St Clair County* Provides social, psychological and financial support to qualifying persons with AIDS. Offers publiceducation on AIDS prevention. Raises funds for those activities. Advocacy for the AIDS issue. *Meetings*: Weekly restricted to persons sharing the concern. *Services*: Mutual aid, educational program or material, written information, advocacy, referral to other services, speakers bureau, referral to other services, social activities, home or hospital visitation, newsletter. *Write*: 5622 Delmar, Ste 104E, St Louis, MO 63112 *Call*: 314/367-2382 *Fax*: 314/367-5985

**Stop AIDS** *Area Served: Chicago Write*: 909 W Belmont, Chicago, IL 60657

**Support Group for Persons Living with AIDS Madison County AIDS Programs** *Area Served: Madison County* To educate the public, advocate and provide emergency assistance to people with AIDS, and network with other entities which provide services beneficial to people with HIV infection. *Meetings*: Monthly. The support group offers a place for people with AIDS to share their concerns. *Services*: Mutual aid, educational program or material, written information, advocacy, professional service, speakers bureau, telephone support, social activities, newsletter. *Write*: 1254 Niedringhaus Ave, Granite City, IL 62040 *Call*: 618/877-5110

**Support Groups for Significant Others Madison County AIDS Programs** *Area Served: Madison County Write*: 2016 Madison Ave, Granite City, IL 62040 *Call*: 618/877-5110 *Fax*: 618/877-0772

**Test Positive Aware Network** *Area Served: Cook, DuPage and Will Counties* Our group is a non-therapeutic support, fellowship and information network for people impacted by HIV. *Services*: Mutual aid, written information, advocacy, referral to other services, speakers bureau, referral to other services, hotline, social activities, newsletter. *Write*: 1258 W Belmont, Chicago, IL 60657 *Call*: 773/404-8726 *Fax*: 312/472-7505

**The HIV Coalition and Network** *Area Served: Cook, Lake and Kendall Counties Write*: 1471 Business Center Dr, #500, Mt Prospect, IL 60056 *Call*: 847/294-6186 *Fax*: 847/294-6467

**Turning Point St. Margaret's Hospital** Provide psychosocial and emotional support. Resource information available. Encouragement from facilitator and group members. Referrals for other help. *Meetings*: Twice monthly, 1st and 3rd Monday at 6 pm; English; no transportation; accessible. *Write*: 600 E 1st St, Spring Valley, IL 61362 *Call*: 815/664-1132 *Fax*: 815/664/1188

**United Counties AIDS Network Whiteside County Health Department** *Area Served: Whiteside County* Provides education to youth and community on AIDS and provides community services to PWAs and their families. *Meetings*: Quarterly for anyone interested. *Services*: Mutual aid, educational program or material, referral to other services, professional service, speakers bureau, home or hospital visitation. *Write*: 18929 E Lincoln, Morrison, IL 61270 *Call*: 815/772-7411 26

**Women's Support Group Chicago Women's AIDS Project** *Area Served: Chicago* Open meeting for any woman who is HIV Positive or who has AIDS. *Meetings*: Twice a month, open to both English and Spanish-speaking women. *Services*: Mutual aid, educational program or material, written information, referral to other services, newsletter. *Write*: 5249 N Kenmore, Chicago, IL 60640 *Call*: 773/271-2070

**Women's Support Group Chicago Women's AIDS Project** *Area Served: Cook County Write*: UI Northwest Outreach Project, 1612 N Kedzie, Chicago, IL 60647 *Call*: 773/252-4422

**Women's Support Groups Kupona Network** *Area Served: Cook County Write*: 4611 S Ellis, Chicago, IL 60653 *Call*: 773/536-3000

# Alzheimer's Disease

**Alzheimer's and Related Disease Family Support Group Family Service Agency** *Area Served: DeKalb*

*County* To support caregivers of families with Alzheimer's. *Services*: Mutual aid. *Write*: Senior Citizens Center, 330 Grove, DeKalb, IL 60115 *Call*: 815/758-8616 *Fax*: 815/758-7569

**Alzheimer's Assn Alzheimer's Family Support Group**
*Area Served: Champaign County* Offers up-to-date information and a forum for mutual help and support. Founded by families of patients with the disease. *Meetings*: Monthly. *Services*: Mutual aid, educational program or material, telephone support, referral to other services. *Write*: 1701 E Main St, Urbana, IL 61801 *Call*: 217/384-3784 44

**Alzheimer's Assn** *Area Served: Kankakee, Will and Grundy Counties* *Write*: PO Box 377, Kankakee, IL 60901 *Call*: 800/332-4495

**Alzheimer's Assn** *Area Served: Peoria, Bureau and LaSalle Counties* *Write*: 2524 W Farley, Peoria, IL 61615 *Call*: 309/681-1100

**Alzheimer's Assn Corn Belt Chapter** *Area Served: McLean, Woodford and Livingston Counties* Provides services for patients and families in the McLean, DeWitt, Livingston and Woodford counties. To educate and support patients and families who face the limitations of Alzheimer's Disease. *Services*: Support groups for patients/caregivers; 24 hr. helpline; individual counseling; lending library; bi-monthly newsletter and educational materials. *Meetings*: Bi-monthly board and monthly support group meetings. Call for specific dates and times.*Write*: 807 N Main St, Bloomington, IL 61702-2850 *Call*: 800/627-0747 *Fax*: 309/827-0734

**Alzheimer's Assn East Central IL Chapter** *Area Served: Champaign, Vermilion, Piatt and DeWitt Counties* *Write*: PO Box 962, Champaign, IL 61824-0962 *Call*: 217/351-1726

**Alzheimer's Assn Support Group Gibson Community Hospital** *Write*: 1120 N Melvin St, Gibson City, IL 60936 *Call*: 217/784-4251

**Alzheimer's Caregivers Support Group** *Area Served: Henry County* *Write*: Kewanee Hospital, 719 Elliott St, Kewanee, IL 51433 *Call*: 309/853-6051 6029

**Alzheimer's Caregivers Support Group Little Company of Mary Hospital** *Area Served: Cook County* To assist spouses, adult children and other family members in caring for the Alzheimer patient. Persons caring for those with other types of dementia are also welcomed. *Meetings*: Monthly. *Services*: Mutual aid. *Write*: 2800 W 95th St, Evergreen Park, IL 60642 *Call*: 708/422-6200 5700

**Alzheimer's Disease and Related Disorders Assn Rockford Chapter** *Area Served: Winnebago, Boone and DeKalb Counties* Provides support and information for

family members of Alzheimer's Disease patients. 8 chapters in IL. Meetings for all interested. *Services*: Mutual aid, educational program or material, advocacy, referral to other services, telephone support, newsletter, written information. *Write*: Swedish American Hospital, Dorm 3, 1400 Charles St, Rockford, IL 61104 *Call*: 815/963-3510

**Alzheimer's Disease and Related Disorders Assoc** *Area Served: National* Founded in 1980 as a national voluntary health org. dedicated to research for the case, cure and prevention of Alzheimer's disease and related disorders and to providing support services to America's 4 million Alzheimer's patients, their families and caregivers. 8 chapters in IL. *Services*: Mutual aid, educational program or material, referral to other services, referral to other services, speakers bureau, newsletter, advocacy. *Write*: 919 N Michigan Ave, Ste 1000, Chicago, IL 60611 *Call*: 800/272-3900

**Alzheimer's Disease Assn Alzheimer's Disease Support** *Area Served: Cook, Lake-S County* Provide mutual support and information to family caregivers of persons with memory loss from Alzheimer's Disease or related disorders. Referrals to other services can be made by group leader. *Meetings*: Twice monthly. *Services*: Mutual aid, referral to other services. *Write*: North Shore Senior Center, 7 Happ Rd, Northfield, IL 60093 *Call*: 847/441-7775 *Fax*: 847/446-8762

**Alzheimer's Disease Assn Chicago Chapter**
*Area Served: Cook, Lake and DuPage Counties* Provides support and information for family members of Alzheimer's disease patients. Meetings for all interested. *Services*: Mutual aid, educational program or material, advocacy, referral to other services, telephone support, newsletter, written information. *Write*: 4709 Golf Rd, Ste 1015, Skokie, IL 60076 *Call*: 847/933-1000 *Fax*: 847/933-2417

**Alzheimer's Disease Assn Quad Cities Chapter** *Area Served: Iowa* Provides family support information and referral, education and training, advocacy and guidance to families and caregivers of Alzheimer's or similar disorders patients. *Meetings*: Twice a month. *Services*: Mutual aid, educational program or material, written information, advocacy, referral to other services, speakers bureau, referral to other services, hotline, telephone support, social activities, newsletter. *Write*: 111 E 3rd St, Davenport, IA 52801 *Call*: 319/324-1022

**Alzheimer's Disease Assn Springfield Area Chapter** *Area Served: Central IL* Educate and inform lay and professional people and interested agencies and groups; and to provide guidance and support for families primarily through support group. Encourage and support research. *Services*: Mutual aid, educational program or material, written information, advocacy, referral to other services, professional service, speakers bureau, referral to other services, newsletter. *Write*: 530 S Grand Ave, West, Springfield, IL 62704 *Call*: 217/522-8518

**Alzheimer's Disease Assn Central IL Chapter Support Group** *Area Served: Central IL* Provides an opportunity for caregivers and others whose lives are affected by Alzheimer's disease and other related illnesses to share feelings, coping techniques and solutions to practical problems, while learning more about the disease and available resources. *Meetings*: Monthly. *Services*: Mutual aid, written information. *Write*: Pekin Hospital, 600 S 13th St, Pekin, IL 61554 *Call*: 309/353-0206

**Alzheimer's Disease Support Group Riverside Medical Center** *Area Served: Kankakee and Iroquois Counties* Allow caregivers to share stresses, experiences, information; contact with supportive professionals and service providers; disseminate reliable, timely information about research, treatment and interventions. *Services*: Mutual aid, educational program or material. *Write*: 350 N Wall St, Kankakee, IL 60901 *Call*: 815/935-1671

**Alzheimer's Disease Support Group St Elizabeth's Hospital** *Area Served: St. Clair, Madison and Monroe Counties* *Write*: 220 W Lincoln, Belleville, IL 62222 *Call*: 618/234-4410 33

**Alzheimer's Disease Support Group Passavant Area Hospital** *Area Served: Morgan County Write*: 1600 W Walnut, Jacksonville, IL 62650 *Call*: 217/245-9541 3594

**Alzheimer's Disease Support Group WestLake County Pavilion** *Area Served: Cook County Write*: 10500 Grand Ave, Franklin Park, IL 60131 *Call*: 708/451-1520 35 *Fax*: 708/451-1503

**Alzheimer's Disease Support Group St Joseph's Hospital** *Area Served: Madison, Bond and Clinton Counties* Education, group support and discussion. *Meetings*: Monthly. *Services*: Mutual aid, educational program or material, written information, advocacy. *Write*: 1515 Main St, Highland, IL 62249 *Call*: 618/654-7421 2231 *Fax*: 618/654-5065

**Alzheimer's Disease Support Group South Suburban Hospital** *Area Served: Cook County Write*: Social Services Dept, 17800 S Kedzie Ave, Hazel Crest, IL 60429 *Call*: 708/799-8000 3022 *Fax*: 708/799-0178

**Alzheimer's Educational Forum McDonough Dist Hosp Alzheimer's Resource** *Area Served: McDonough County Write*: 525 E Grant St, Macomb, IL 61455 *Call*: 309/833-4101 3056

**Alzheimer's Family Support Group Family Alliance** *Area Served: McHenry County* Meeting structure: First-half educational information and the second-half support group. *Services*: Mutual aid, educational program or material. *Write*: 670 S Eastwood Dr, Woodstock, IL 60098 *Call*: 815/338-3590 *Fax*: 815/337-4406

**Alzheimer's Family Support Night St Anthony's Health Center** *Area Served: Madison County Write*: St Anthony's Way, PO Box 340, Alton, IL 62002 *Call*: 618/463-5333

**Alzheimer's Support Group Act II Club** *Area Served: Cook County Write*: LaGrange Memorial Health Sys, 5107 Willow Springs Rd, LaGrange, IL 60525 *Call*: 708/579-4989 *Fax*: 708/579-4991

**Alzheimer's Support Group Alzheimer's Assn** *Area Served: Cook County Write*: 1038 Harbour Ct, Wheeling, IL 60090 *Call*: 847/870-0794

**Alzheimer's Support Group Alzheimer's Assn** *Area Served: Cook County Write*: Meadowbrook Manor, 431 W Remington, Bolingbrook, IL 60440 *Call*: 630/759-1112 *Fax*: 708/759-5473

**Alzheimer's Support Group Alzheimer's Assn** *Area Served: Cook County Write*: Slame United Methodist Church, 115 W Lincoln, Barrington, IL *Call*: 847/933-1000

**Alzheimer's Support Group American Health Center** *Area Served: Peoria County Write*: 5600 N Glen Elm Dr, Peoria, IL 61614 *Call*: 309/693-8777

**Alzheimer's Support Group** *Area Served: Richland, Clay, Crawford and Effingham Counties Write*: Southeastern IL Counsel Ctrs, Drawer M, Olney, IL 62450 *Call*: 618/395-4306

**Alzheimer's Support Group** *Area Served: Champaign County Write*: 302 Burwash Ave, Savoy, IL 61874-3399 *Call*: 217/383-3090

**Alzheimer's Support Group** *Area Served: McLean County Write*: 509 S Buck Rd, PO Box 149, Leroy, IL 61752 *Call*: 800/446-9047 *Fax*: 309/962-6227

**Alzheimer's Support Group Blessing Hospital and Area Agency on Aging** *Area Served: Adams County Meetings*: Monthly. *Services*: Mutual aid, social activities, newsletter. *Write*: PO Box 428, Quincy, IL 62306 *Call*: 800/252-9027

**Alzheimer's Support Group Grundy County Health Department** *Area Served: Grundy County Write*: 1320 Union St, Morris, IL 60450 *Call*: 815/941-3138

**Alzheimer's Support Group LaGrange Memorial Hospital** *Area Served: IL Write*: 5101 S Willow Springs Rd, LaGrange, IL 60525 *Call*: 708/579-2627

**Alzheimer's Support Group Snyder Village** *Area Served: Woodford County Write*: 1200 E Partridge, Metamora, IL 61548 *Call*: 309/367-4300 *Fax*: 309/367-2325

**Alzheimer's Support Group St Elizabeth Medical Center** *Area Served: Madison County Write*: 2100 Madison Ave, Granite City, IL 62040 *Call*: 618/798-3477

**Alzheimer's Support Group Union County Hospital** *Area Served: Union County Write*: Rt 1, Box 91, Jonesboro, IL 62952 *Call*: 618/833-7016

**Alzheimer's Support Group Wellness Promotion** *Area Served: Will County Write*: Silver Cross Hospital, 1200 Maple Rd, Joliet, IL 60432 *Call*: 815/740-1100 7629

**Caregivers of Memory-Impaired Loved Ones Southwest Suburban Center on Aging** *Area Served: Cook County Write*: 111 W Harris Ave, LaGrange, IL 60525 *Call*: 708/354-0826

**Caregivers' Alzheimer's Support Group Community Hospital of Ottawa** *Area Served: LaSalle County Write*: 219 W Lafayette St, Ottawa, IL 61350 *Call*: 815/434-4234

**Early Alzheimer's Disease Support Group CNS Adult Day Care** *Area Served: DuPage County Write*: 1260 Iroquois Dr, Ste 300, Naperville, IL 60563 *Call*: 630/357-8300

**Families of Alzheimer's Coping Together** *Area Served: LaSalle, Bureau and Putnam Counties Write*: 600 E 1st St, Spring Valley, IL 61362 *Call*: 815/664-1546

**Hoopeston Area Alzheimer's Support Group Hoopeston Hospital and Nursing Home** *Area Served: Vermilion County Write*: 701 E Orange, Hoopeston, IL 60942 *Call*: 217/283-5531 243 *Fax*: 217/283-8249

**Macon County Alzheimer's Support Group** *Area Served: Macon County Call*: 217/428-3075

**Memory Disorder Support Group McDonough District Hospital Alzheimer's Resource** *Area Served: McDonough County Write*: 525 E Grant St, Macomb, IL 61455 *Call*: 309/833-4101 3056

**Peoria Area Alzheimer's Support Group** *Area Served: Central IL* Provide understanding, education, sharing and support. *Meetings*: Monthly for relatives and caregivers of persons with Alzheimer's disease. *Services*: Mutual aid, written information. *Write*: 7202 N Miramar, Peoria, IL 61614 *Call*: 309/692-2465

**West Central IL Alzheimer's Support Group West Central IL Area on Aging** *Area Served: Adams County* Provides support and information for family members of Alzheimer's Disease victims. Meetings for all interested. *Services*: Mutual aid, educational program or material, advocacy, referral to other services, telephone support, newsletter, written information. *Write*: Senior Center, 1125 Hampshire, Quincy, IL 62301 *Call*: 217/223-5811 1560

# Amputation

**A-SCIP Plus Maine Township Town Hall** *Area Served: Cook County* For family members and friends of persons who have lost a limb or use of a limb. Meets concurrently with A-SCIP. *Meetings*: Monthly. *Services*: Mutual aid, educational program or material. *Write*: 1700 Ballard Rd, Park Ridge, IL 60068 *Call*: 847/297-2510 229

**American Amputee Foundation, Inc** *Area Served: National* A national information clearinghouse and referral center serving primarily amputees and their families. Local chapters provide various forms of peer support. No known IL groups. *Write*: PO Box 250218, Little Rock, AR 72225 *Call*: 501/666-2523 *Fax*: 501/666-8367

**Amputee Coalition of America** *Area Served: National Write*: 6300 River Rd, Ste 727, Rosemont, IL 60018 *Call*: 847/698-1633

**Amputee Support Group** *Area Served: DuPage County Write*: Marianjoy Hospital, 26 W 171 Roosevelt Rd, Wheaton, IL 60187 *Call*: 630/462-4134 *Fax*: 708/462-4441

**Amputee Support Group** *Area Served: Cook County Write*: Hines Veteran Hospital, 112 H-1, Hines, IL 60141 *Call*: 708/216-2407

**Amputee Support Group Copley Memorial Hospital** *Area Served: Kankakee, Kendall, DeKalb and DuPage Counties Write*: 502 S Lincoln Ave, Aurora, IL 60505-4690 *Call*: 630/844-1030 4479

**Amputee Support Group Johnston R Bowman Center for The Elderly** *Area Served: Cook County Write*: 710 S Paulina St, Chicago, IL 60612 *Call*: 312/942-7010

**Amputee Support Group Paulson Rehab Network** *Area Served: IL Write*: Hinsdale Hospital Rehab Svcs, 120 N Oak St, Hinsdale, IL 60521 *Call*: 630/856-3144 *Fax*: 708/856-7938

**Amputee Support Group St Elizabeth's Hospital** *Area Served: St. Clair and Madison County Write*: 211 S 3rd St, Belleville, IL 62222-0694 *Call*: 618/234-2120 1575

**Families and Amputees In Motion, Inc** *Area Served: IL Write*: 1639 N Paulina St, Chicago, IL 60622 *Call*: 708/349-6378

**Families of Amputee Children Together Facts** *Area Served: Cook County* Supplies information and support for the family of a child with an amputation. To provide an opportunity for group interaction for the children and siblings and to provide information on facilities and financial help available. *Meetings*: As needed for parents and siblings. *Services*: Mutual aid, advocacy, telephone

support. *Write*:12403 71$^{st}$ Ave, Palos Heights, IL 60463
*Call*: 708/354-8398

# Amyloidosis

**Amyloidosis Network International** *Area Served: National Write*: 7118 Cole Creek Dr, Houston, TX 77092 *Call*: 713/466-4351

# Amyotrophic Lateral Sclerosis (ALS)

**ALS Assn University of Chicago Hospital Support Group** *Area Served: Cook County* Support and education for families, friends, patients. *Meetings*: Monthly with speakers. *Services*: Mutual aid, educational program or material, referral to other services, social activities,newsletter, written information. *Write*: PO Box 425, Chicago, IL 60637 *Call*: 773/702-1747

**Les Turner ALS Foundation (Lou Gehrig's Disease)** *Area Served: IL* Foundation provides support research and services for people with amyotrophic lateral sclerosis, better known as Lou Gehrig's disease. *Services*: Research labs and outpatient clinics at Northwestern Medical School; support groups; communication and durable medical equipment; home liaison; inservices and educational materials. *Meetings*: 4-5 monthly support group meetings. Call for times and dates. *Write*: 3325 W Main St, Skokie, IL 60076 *Call*: 847/679-3311 *Fax*: 847/679-9109 *Email*: cowen@lturnerals.org

# Ankylosing Spondylitis

**Ankylosing Spondylitis Assn** *Area Served: National* Enhances the well-being of persons affected by AS and related diseases; to promote early diagnosis and effective treatment; to support the advancement of research. No known IL chapters. *Services*: Mutual aid, written information, newsletter, telephone support, referral to other services, educational program or material, advocacy. *Write*:PO Box 5872, Sherman Oaks, CA 91413 *Call*: 800/777-8189

# Aplastic Anemia

**Aplastic Anemia Foundation of America** *Area Served: National* Provides emotional support for aplastic anemia patients and families; provide education and awareness of aplastic anemia; and to support research to find a cure. One group in IL. *Services*: Mutual aid, educational program or material. *Write*: PO Box 22689, Baltimore, MD 21203 *Call*: 800/747-2820

**Earl J. Goldberg Plastic Anemia Foundation** *Area Served: IL* Supports families and patients at their time of need and to raise funds for research. 2 chapters in IL. *Services*: Mutual aid, educational program or material, written information, telephone support, newsletter. *Write*: PO Box 2231, Glenview, IL 60025 *Call*: 847/559-0688 Answer Mach.

# Arthorogryposis

**Aves** *Area Served: National* Connects families with arthorogryposis for mutual support and sharing of information. Educates medical and social service professionals regarding the disease. *Services*: Mutual aid, educational program or material. *Write*: PO Box 5192, Sonora, CA 95370 *Call*: 209/928-3688

# Arthritis

**Arthritis Education** *Area Served: Cook County* Mission: Provides mutual support and education to arthritis sufferers. Meets the last Wednesday of each month from 1:15-2:30. Group is open to arthritis victims over the age of 60. *Write*: 1415 W Foster, Chicago, IL 60640 *Call*: 773/769-5500 127 *Fax*: 312/769-5500

**Arthritis Foundation** *Area Served: IL* Provides education and support for people with arthritis. *Write*: 807 N Main, Bloomington, IL 61701 *Call*: 309/829-0752

**Arthritis Foundation** *Area Served: Winnebago County and NW IL* Class provides general information, education and support to anyone who has or is concerned about arthritis. On-going support group available after completion. *Meetings*: Monthly. *Services*: Mutual aid, educational program or material, advocacy, referral to other services, telephone support, social activities, newsletter, written information. *Write*: 2500 N Rockton Ave, Ste 215, Rockford, IL 61103-3667 *Call*: 815/961-6380

**Arthritis Foundation** *Area Served: Cook County* Offers education and support of people with arthritis. *Write*: 303 E Wacker Dr, Ste 300, Chicago, IL 60601 *Call*: 312/616-3470 *Fax*: 312/616-9281

**Arthritis Foundation Blessing Hospital** *Area Served: Adams County Write*: 1415 Vermont, Quincy, IL 62301 *Call*: 217/228-3208

**Arthritis Foundation Central IL Chapter** *Area Served: IL* Women's support group. *Write*: 2621 N Knoxville, Peoria, IL 61604 *Call*: 309/682-6600 *Fax*: 309/682-6732

**Arthritis Foundation Champaign County Branch** *Area Served: Champaign County and E IL Services*:

educational program or material, mutual aid, speakers bureau, written information, telephone support, referral to other services, fundraising. *Write*: Carle Medical Supply, 810 W University, Urbana, IL 61801 *Call*: 217/367-0988

**Arthritis Foundation Quad City Arthritis Support Groups** *Area Served: Iowa* 6 support groups for adults and youth. Additionally, 6-week self-help classes and 4 water exercise programs. *Services*: Mutual aid, speakers bureau, written information, telephone support, educational program or material. *Write*: 2116 W 34th St, Davenport, IA 52806 *Call*: 319/391-3193

**Arthritis Foundation Share** *Area Served: Central IL* Provides support, information and education for arthritis patients and their families. *Meetings*: Monthly. *Services*: Mutual aid, speakers bureau, written information, social activities, telephone support, professional service, referral to other services, educational program or material, referral to other services, advocacy, hotline, newsletter. *Write*: 1800 Lake Shore Dr, Rm 462, Decatur, IL 62521 *Call*: 217/422-1740

**Arthritis Support Group** *Area Served: Kankakee County* Copes with arthritis, provides support group, public education, awareness, printed brochures/information, advocacy, and telephone support. *Services*: Mutual aid, educational program or material, information, advocacy, telephone support *Write*: 475 W Merchant St, Kankakee, IL 60901 *Call*: 815/937-2461

**Arthritis Support Group IL Valley Community Hospital** *Area Served: LaSalle and Bureau Counties* *Write*: 925 West St, Peru, IL 61354 *Call*: 815/223-3300 216

**Arthritis Support Group Iroquois Memorial Hosp Ed Dept** *Area Served: Iroquois and Newton Ind Counties* *Write*: 200 Fairman, Watseka, IL 60970 *Call*: 815/432-5841 4429

**Arthritis Support Group Rush North Shore Medical Center** *Area Served: Cook County-N* Provides peer support, speakers, information and education about arthritis and its treatment. *Services*: Mutual aid, telephone support, professional service, referral to other services. *Write*: 9600 Gross Point Rd, Skokie, IL 60076 *Call*: 847/933-6663 *Fax*: 847/933-6887

**Juvenile Rheumatoid Arthritis Support Group Arthritis Foundation** *Area Served: Rock Island County* One of 6 support groups for adults and youth. Also, 6-week self-help classes and 4 water exercise programs. *Services*: Mutual aid, speakers bureau, written information, telephone support, educational program or material. *Write*: 2116 W 34th St, Davenport, IA 52806 *Call*: 319/324-4767

**Young Adult Support Group St Mary's Hospital** *Area Served: Macon, DeWitt and Moultrie Counties*

*Write*: 1800 E Lake Shore Dr, Rm T-312, Decatur, IL 62521 *Call*: 217/422-1740

# Asbestos

**Asbestos Victims of America AVA National Headquarters** *Area Served: National* AVA provides services to asbestos disease victims, their families, and survivors, including: medical/legal referrals, counseling, educational materials, and support groups. In addition to assisting those already affected, AVA is dedicated to prevent future disease especially through public education on the hazards of asbestos. *Services*: Mutual aid, educational program or material, advocacy, telephone support, written information. *Write*: 4622 W Walnut, Soquel, CA 95073 *Call*: 408/476-3646

# Asthma and Allergy

**Allergy and Asthma Network Mothers of Asthmatics, Inc** *Area Served: National* Educates those who suffer from allergies and asthma, and their families, about their illnesses. *Services*: Written information, referral to other services, speakers bureau, newsletter. *Write*: 3554 Chair Bridge Rd, #200, Fairfax, VA 22030 *Call*: 703/385-4403

**Asthma and Allergy Foundation of America Parents of Asthmatic/Allergic Children of DuPage County** *Area Served: DuPage County* Gives parents of children with asthma and/or allergies information and the support of other parents. Physicians and others speak every other month. Group open to parents of asthmatic and/or allergic children and interested others. *Meetings*: Monthly. *Services*: Mutual aid, written information, telephone support. *Call*: 708/393-1379

**Asthma and Allergy Foundation of America** *Area Served: National* Educate about asthma and allergies; offer emotional support. *Services*: Groups for parents, pre-teens, teens and adults with asthma allergies. *Meetings*: vary, call for more information. *Write*: 1125 15th NW, Ste 502, Washington, DC 20005 *Call*: 970/221-9165 *Fax*: 970/407-9885 *Email*: aafasupgr@aol.com

**Asthma Parents Support Group** *Area Served: Cook County* Assists parents with an asthmatic child and helps the child participate irregular activities. *Services*: Mutual aid, written information, hotline, telephone support. *Write*: PO Box 195, Streamwood, IL 60107 *Call*: 630/289-7150

**Asthmatic Children's Aid** *Area Served: IL-N* Raises funds to help children with asthma. ACA raises funds for research, scholarships and individual aid. Helps afflicted and family. *Meetings*: Monthly. *Services*: Mutual aid, educational program or material, fundraising, referral to other services, telephone support, social activities, written information, referral to other services. *Write*: 5875 N Lincoln Ave, Chicago, IL 60659 *Call*: 773/271-3110

**Family Asthma Support Group** *Area Served: Peoria and Tazewell Counties Write*: 5409 N Knoxville Proctor Prof Bldg, Peoria, IL 61614 *Call*: 309/691-1041 *Fax*: 309/689-6009

**Lungline National Jewish Center Immunology-Respiratory Medicine** *Area Served: National Write*: 1400 Jackson St, Denver, CO 80206 *Call*: 800/222-5864

**Parents of Asthmatic Children Support Group** *Area Served: Cook, Lake and McHenry Counties Write*: Good Shepherd Hospital, 450 W Hwy 22, Barrington, IL 60010 *Call*: 847/381-9600 5024

**Parents of Asthmatic Children Chicago Lung Assn** *Area Served: Cook-SW* Offers support, education, and information to parents of children with asthma or any interested persons. *Services*: Mutual aid, educational program or material, written information, speakers bureau, referral to other services, telephone support, social activities, newsletter. *Write*: 1440 W Washington Blvd, Chicago, IL 60607 *Call*: 773/239-7209

**Parents of Asthmatic Kids American Lung Assn of Middlesex County** *Area Served: Middlesex* Education, support group meetings, and telephone networking to help parents cope with asthmatic kids. Model org. serving Middlesex County, MA; will provide chapter development help and telephone assistance nationwide. *Services*: Mutual aid, educational program or material, telephone support, newsletter, written information. *Write*: PO Box 265, Burlington, MA 01803 *Call*: 847/272-2866 *Fax*: 617/273-2846

**Parents of Children with Asthma and Allergies** *Area Served: Stephenson, Ogle and Winnebago Counties* Separate support groups for parents, youth (10-18 years) and children (age 9 and younger). Educates parents, children and the community about what asthma is, how to treat it, how to recognize the early warning signs of an attack and how to prevent an attack. *Meetings*: Monthly. *Services*: Mutual aid, speakers bureau, written information, telephone support, educational program or material. *Write*: 1322 S Blackhawk Rd, Freeport, IL 61031 *Call*: 915/232-7410

# Ataxia

**National Ataxia Foundation** *Area Served: National* National group to combat all types of hereditary ataxia (HA). Also is concerned with closely-related conditions, such as peroneal muscular atrophy, hereditary spastic paraplegia, ataxia telangiectasia, and hereditary tremor. Provides support to patients and families and referrals to

clinics in some locations. *Services*: Educational program or material, MA/written information, referral to other services, referral to other services, newsletter. *Write*: 15500 Wayzata Blvd, 750 Twelve Oaks Center, Wayzata, MN 55391 *Call*: 612/473-7666 *Fax*: 612/473-9289 *Email*: NAF@Mr.NET *Web site*: http://WWW.ATAXIA.ORG

# Balance Disorders

**Vestibular Disorders Assn** *Area Served: National* National org. Veda provides information and support to people with inner ear balance disorders. Veda link list connects people to other members, offers quarterly newsletter, and material on positional vertigo, meuniere's disease, labyrinthitis, perilymph fistular, diagnostic tests, managing dizziness attacks. Books and tapes: balancing act: for people with dizziness and balance disorders, staying even: how to cope, and bibliography. *Write*: PO Box 4467, Portland, OR 97208-4467 *Call*: 503/229-7705 *Fax*: 503/229/8064 *Email*: VEDA@TELEPORT.COM *Web site*: HTTP://WWW.TELEPORT.COM/~VEDA

# Baldness

**Bald Headed Men of America** *Area Served: National* No known IL Chapters. A national group to eliminate the vanity associated with the loss of one's hair and to instill pride and dignity in being bald-headed. It is more important what's inside the head than what's on top of it! To provide support to men, women, children, and cancer patients who have loss of hair. *Meetings*: Annually. *Services*: Mutual aid, telephone support, social activities, newsletter, written information. *Write*: 102 Bald Dr, Morehead City, NC 28557 *Call*: 919/726-1855

**National Alopecia Areata Foundation** *Area Served: Cook, Lake and DuPage Counties* Promotes research, works to serve those with alopecia areata, educate government officials about the need for fair insurance laws and greater government-sponsored research and an ongoing public awareness program. 2 IL support groups. *Services*: Mutual aid, educational program or material, written information, advocacy, referral to other services, social activities, newsletter. *Write*: 3211 Glenbrook Dr, Northbrook, IL 60062 *Call*: 847/456-4644 *Fax*: 847/480-1873

**National Alopecia Areata Foundation** *Area Served: National* Promotes research, works to serve those with alopecia areata, educated government about the need for fair insurance laws, sponsor research, and create ongoing public awareness.*Services*: Mutual aid, self-help groups, public education, printed material, advocacy, social, newsletter. National org. IL has 2 chapters. *Write*: 710 C

St, #11, San Rafael, CA 94901 *Call*: 415/456-4644
*Fax*: 415/456-4274

# Batten's Disease

**Children's Brain Disease Foundation** *Area Served: National* Funds research worldwide for Batten's disease. *Services*: Advocacy, fundraising. *Write*: 350 Parnassus Ave, Ste 900, San Francisco, CA 94117 *Call*: 415/565-6259

# Beckwith Wiedemann Syndrome

**Beckwith-Wiedemann Support Network** *Area Served: National* It is a national org. of parents who have children with Beckwith-Wiedemann Syndrome. The network is setup to provide moral support and to facilitate the flow of information between parents and interested medical professionals. *Services*: Written information, telephone support, newsletter. *Write*: 3206 Braeburn Circle, Ann Arbor, MI 48108 *Call*: 800/837-2976 *Fax*: 313/973-9721

# Birth Defects

**Assn of Birth Defect Children, Inc** *Area Served: National* A national org. committed to overcoming birth defects by educating the public, professional community and government as to the many toxins in the environment that are leading to birth defects. *Services*: Educational program or material written information, newsletter. *Write*: 827 Irma Ave, Orlando, FL 32803 *Call*: 407/245-7035 *Fax*: 407/629-1466

**March of Dimes Birth Defects Foundation** *Area Served: IL* The March of Dimes Birth Defects Foundation is a unique partnership of volunteers and professionals that provide leadership and the treatment and prevention of birth defects and prematurity. *Services*: Mutual aid, educational program or material, written information, referral to other services, speakers bureau, newsletter. *Write*: 111 W Jackson, 22 Fl, Chicago, IL 60604 *Call*: 312/435-4007

# Blood Disorders

**Lean on Me Rush-Presbyterian-St Luke's Medical Center** *Area Served: Chicago, IN Write*: Rush Cancer Center-Hematology, 1725 W Harrison, #862, Chicago, IL 60612 *Call*: 312/942-5982

**Parent Networking Group Children's Memorial Hospital** *Area Served: Cook County Write*: 2300 Children's Plaza, Chicago, IL 60614 *Call*: 773/880-4489

# Brain Tumor

**American Brain Tumor Assn** *Area Served: National* ABTA not-for-profit org. *Services*: 20 publications which address brain tumors, their treatment, and coping with the disease; nationwide resource listings of support groups and physicians offering investigative treatments; pen-pal program; national symposium for patients and their families and a tri-annual newsletter. *Meetings*: Mon-Fri, 9-5 pm, central standard time. *Write*: 2720 River Rd, Ste 146, Des Plaines, IL 60018-4106 *Call*: 800/886-2282 *Fax*:847/827-9918 *Email*:ABTA@aol.com *Web site*: http://pubweb.acns.nwu.edu/~lberko/abta_html/abta1.htm

**American Brain Tumor Assn** *Area Served: National* 800/886-2282 *Write*: 2720 River Rd, Des Plaines, IL 60018 *Call*: 847/827-9910

**Brain Tumor Network Columbus Hospital** *Area Served: Cook County Write*: 2520 N Lakeview, Chicago, IL 60614 *Call*: 773/883-6400 490

**Brain Tumor Support Central DuPage County Hospital, Dept of Neurosurgery** Provide resources, education and support to people with tumors and their significant others and family. *Services*: Education-specific to brain tumor patients. newsletter and resource information also available. *Meetings*: Every other Tuesday at 7:30 pm, handicapped accessible. *Write*: 25 N Winfield Rd, Winfield, IL 60190 *Call*: 630/682-1600 6955 *Fax*: 630/260-2671

**Brain Tumor Support Group Lutheran General Hospital** *Area Served: Cook County* Offer support and education to persons with brain tumors and their families and friends. Facilitated by a social worker. *Meetings*: Monthly for patient, family and friends. *Services*: Mutual aid, educational program or material. *Write*: 1775 Dempster St, Park Ridge, IL 60068 *Call*: 847/696-5475

**Brain Tumor Support Group Northwestern Memorial Hospital** *Area Served: Cook County Write*: 303 E Superior, Chicago, IL 60611 *Call*: 773/907-2348

**Parents of Children with Brain Tumor Support Group The Children's Hospital** *Area Served: IL Write*: 2300 Children's Plaza, Chicago, IL 60614 *Call*: 708/232-6518

# Breast Feeding

**Breast Feeding Support Group** *Area Served: Cook County Write*: Northwest Community Hospital, 800 W

Central Rd, Arlington Heights, IL 60005
*Call*: 708/259-1000 4544

**La Leche League** *Area Served: Champaign County*
*Write*: 208 Arcadia Dr, Champaign, IL 61820
*Call*: 217/359-3923

**La Leche League** *Area Served: McLean County Write*:
9616 Minneapolis Ave, PO Box 1209, Franklin Park, IL
60131 *Call*: 309/454-3285

**La Leche League Passavant Area Hospital**
*Area Served: Morgan County Write*: 1600 W Walnut,
Jacksonville, IL 62650 *Call*: 217/245-9541 3594

# Breast Implants

**Breast Implant Information Exchange** *Area Served: IL*
*Write*: 9746 W Reeves Ct, Franklin Park, IL 60131
*Call*: 708/678-5934

# Burns

**Alisa Ann Ruch California Burn Foundation** *Area
Served: National* Support group for burn survivors and
their families, facilitated by psychologists. Starting
hospital-based self-help group for adult burn survivors and
California telephone network. Available for consultation
on starting burn survivors self-help group. Has wide
variety of burn prevention/fire safety materials available
nationwide. *Services*: Mutual aid, educational program or
material, telephone support, home or hospital visitation,
social activities, newsletter, written information. *Write*:
20944 Sherman Way, Ste 115, Canoga Park, CA 91303
*Call*: 818/883-7700

**Burn United Support Groups, Inc** Provide common
support for burn survivors (children and adults), their
families and friends. No matter how major or minor the
burn. *Services*: videos, library, speakers, support groups,
printed information, etc. *Meetings*: 1st Monday of each
month. Call for specific times. *Write*: PO Box 36416,
Grosse Pointe Farms, MI 48236-2819 *Call*: 313/881-5577
*Fax*: 313/417-8700 *Email*: 1561@concentric.net

**National Burn Victim Foundation** *Area Served:
National* Assists burn victims and their families dealing
with the trauma of disability and disfigurement. Conducts
back to school and back to work programs. *Services*:
Mutual aid, educational program or material, advocacy,
telephone support, home or hospital visitation, newsletter,
written information. *Write*: 32-34 Scotland Rd, Orange,
NJ 07050 *Call*: 201/676-7700

# Cancer

## Cancer-General

**American Cancer Society Area 4 Western** *Area
Served: Sangamon County Write*: 1305 Wabash Ste J,
Springfield, IL 62704 *Call*: 800/252-5302

**American Cancer Society Area 5 Southwest** *Area
Served: Coles County Write*: 201 N Logan, PO Box 813,
Mattoon, IL 61938 *Call*: 800/252-8809

**American Cancer Society Area 6 Southern** *Area
Served: Williamson County Write*: 121 N 13th St, Herrin
County *Area Served: Lake County Write*: 2835 Belvidere
Rd, Waukegan, IL 60085 *Call*: 800/942-6641

**American Cancer Society Area 3 West Central** *Area
Served: Peoria County Write*: 3118 N University, Peoria,
IL 61604 *Call*: 800/322-4577

**American Cancer Society Area 1 Northern** *Area
Served: Winnebago County Write*: 850 N Church St,
Rockford, IL 61103 *Call*: 800/892-9296

**American Cancer Society** *Area Served: National*
*Write*: 118 S Seminary, Collinsville, IL 62234
*Call*: 618/345-7911

**American Cancer Society Area 2 Northwest** *Area
Served: IL Write*: 3727 Blackhawk Rd, Ste 101, Rock
Island, IL 61201 *Call*: 800/322-4337

**American Cancer Society Cancer Information and
Counseling Line** *Area Served: National Write*: 1600
Pierce St, Denver, CO 80214 *Call*: 800/525-3777

**American Cancer Society IL Division** *Area Served: IL*
*Write*: 77 E Monroe, Chicago, IL 60603
*Call*: 800/227-2345

**Can Cope American Cancer Society** *Area Served: Rock
Island, Henderson and Henry Counties Write*: 3727
Blackhawk Rd, Rock Island, IL 61201 *Call*: 309/784-0601

**Can Cope Foster McGaw Hospital** *Area Served: Cook
and DuPage Counties* 6-week educational program,
professionally-led for cancer patients and their families.
Runs twice yearly. *Services*: Mutual aid, educational
program or material. *Write*: Social Work Dept, 2160 S 1st
Ave, Maywood, IL 60153 *Call*: 708/216-4044

**Cancer Care Foundation** *Area Served: Cook and Lake
Counties* Help make living with cancer and its treatment
as least impactful as possible for those who have cancer,
for those who care for, and for those whose lives are
intertwined with people who have cancer. Services include
cancer information help line, support groups, crisis
counseling and nutritional support services. *Services*:
Mutual aid, educational program or material, written

information, speakers bureau, telephone support.
*Write*: 615-19 Milwaukee, Ste 21, Glenview, IL 60025
*Call*: 847/256-2428

**Cancer Care Institute Support Group Decatur Memorial Hospital Cancer Care Institute** Help cancer patients adjust to the changes that occur after a diagnosis of cancer, to offer an opportunity for patients to share experiences and concerns, to meet theemotional and spiritual needs of cancer patients and their families. Provide peer and professional support, lending library, and educational resources. *Meetings*: 2$^{nd}$ Wednesday of each month; handicapped accessible; language-English.
*Write*: 2300 N Edward St, Decatur, IL 62526-4193
*Call*: 217/876-2380  *Fax*: 217/876-2387

**Cancer Care Support Groups Trinity Medical Center** *Area Served: Rock Island County* Cancer care support groups, including a children's group, for patients and their families. *Meetings*: Twice monthly. *Services*: Mutual aid, written information, social activities, telephone support, referral to other services, educational program or material. *Write*: Pastoral Care, 501 10$^{th}$ Ave, Moline, IL 61265
*Call*: 309/757-2696

**Cancer Education and Support Northwest Community Hospital** *Area Served: Local* Series of 12 educational programs help patients, their families and friends become knowledgeable about the disease and treatment. Helps manage day-to-day problems and maintain the highest possible quality of life. *Write*: 800 W Central Rd, Arlington Heights, IL 60005 *Call*: 847/618-6665

**Cancer In The Family Methodist Medical Center** *Area Served: Peoria County* *Write*: 221 NE Glen Oak, Peoria, IL 60636 *Call*: 309/672-4110

**Cancer Information Service IL Cancer Council** *Area Served: IL* *Write*: 200 S Michigan Ave, Ste 1700, Chicago, IL 60604 *Call*: 800/422-6237

**Cancer Information Service National Cancer Institute** *Area Served: National* Offers information on diagnosis treatment, prevention, research studies and referrals to cancer centers and resources. *Services*: Educational program or material written information, telephone support, hotline, speakers bureau, referral to other services. *Write*: U of Kansas Cancer Center, 3901 Rainbow Blvd, Kansas City, KS 66160 *Call*: 800/422-6237

**Cancer Patient and Family Support Group Columbus Hospital** *Area Served: IL* Provides information and emotional support to cancer patients and their families and friends. *Meetings*: Twice monthly for all interested. *Services*: Mutual aid, educational program or material. *Write*: 2520 N Lakeview, Chicago, IL 60614
*Call*: 773/883-6400 260

**Cancer Resource Center Northwest Community Hospital** Provides over 300 publications and reference materials. Each has been reviewed and evaluated for its readability and benefit to cancer patients, families and friends. On-line educational program, cancer help contains up-to-date and comprehensive information from the national cancer inst. An easy touch screen prompter retrieves information immediately. Hours open: M-F (no holidays); 8-4:30 pm; handicap accessible bldg and parking; in English. *Write*: 800 W Central Rd, Arlington Heights, IL 60005 *Call*: 847/618-6665

**Cancer Support Center Chicago-Southland Area** *Area Served: Cook and Will Counties, and Indiana  Write*: 2028 Elm St, Glenwood, IL 60430 *Call*: 708/798-9171

**Cancer Support Group Carle Cancer Center** *Area Served: IL  Write*: 602 W University Ave, Urbana, IL 61801 *Call*: 217/383-3119

**Cancer Support Group Community Hospital** *Area Served: LaSalle County  Write*: 1100 E Norris Dr, Ottawa, IL 61350 *Call*: 815/433-3100 442

**Cancer Support Group Elmhurst Memorial Hospital** *Area Served: DuPage County  Write*: 200 Berteau Ave, Elmhurst, IL 60126 *Call*: 630/833-1400 4691

**Cancer Support Group Grundy *County* Community Hospice** *Area Served: Grundy County  Write*: 1802 N Division, Ste 307, Morris, IL 60450 *Call*: 815/942-1499

**Cancer Support Group Iroquois Memorial Hospital and Resident Home** *Area Served: IL  Write*: 200 Fairman, Watseka, IL 60970 *Call*: 815/432-5841 4309

**Cancer Support Group Kewanee Hospital** *Area Served: Henry County  Write*: 719 Elliott St, Kewanee, IL 61443 *Call*: 309/853-3361

**Cancer Support Group Kishwaukee Community Hospital** *Area Served: DeKalb County* *Write*: 626 Bethany Rd, PO Box 707, DeKalb, IL 60115 *Call*: 815/756-1521

**Cancer Support Group Lake County Forest Hospital** Provides support to cancer patients and their families and friends. *Meetings*: Monthly. *Services*: Mutual aid. *Write*: 660 N Westmoreland, Lake Forest, IL 60045 *Call*: 847/234-5600 6445

**Cancer Support Group Resurrection Medical Center** *Area Served: Chicago* Support group for patients with cancer and their families. *Services*: Mutual aid, educational program or material, telephone support, social activities, written information. *Write*: Cancer Treatment Center, 7435 W Talcott, Chicago, IL 60631 *Call*: 773/792-5116

**Cancer Support Group Richland Memorial Hospital** *Area Served: Richland, Edwards, Clay and Wayne*

*Counties Write*: 800 E Locust St, Olney, IL 62350
*Call*: 618/395-2131 4279

**Cancer Support Group St Anthony's Memorial Hospital** *Area Served: Effingham, Jasper, Clay and Fayette Counties Write*: 1901 S 4ᵗʰ, Ste 17, Effingham, IL 62401 *Call*: 217/347-0343

**Cancer Support Group St Francis Hospital and Health Center** *Area Served: Cook and Will Counties*
*Write*: 12935 S Gregory St, Blue Island, IL 60406
*Call*: 708/597-2000 5521

**Cancer Support Network** *Area Served: McLean County*
Offer support and encouragement to cancer patients, their families, and friends through a cancer hotline, lending library, wig bank, music, and art therapy programs and support groups. *Meetings*: Weekly. *Services*: Mutual aid, educational program or material, written information, advocacy, referral to other services, speakers bureau, referral to other services, hotline, telephone support, social activities. *Call*: 309/829-2273

**Cancer Support Palos Community Hospital** *Area Served: IL* For people who have been diagnosed with cancer and their family members who are having a difficult time dealing with the situation. Provide cancer support group;mutual aid; self-help groups; and phone support. *Meetings*: 2ⁿᵈ Monday of every month at 7:30 pm., Conference Rm B. *Write*: 12251 S 80ᵗʰ Ave, Palos Heights, IL 60463 *Call*: 708/923-4028

**Cancer Survivors' Club St James Hospital** *Area Served: Cook County Write*: 1423 Chicago Rd, Chicago Heights, IL 60411 *Call*: 708/756-1000

**Cancer Wellness Center** *Area Served: IL* We offer cancer patients and their families an environment where comprehensive psychological, social and emotional support is available on a continual basis. Peer hotline, cancer library, education, self-help and professionally led support groups, groups for metastatic illness, new diagnosis, and t'ai chi. *Write*: 215 Revere Ct, Northbrook, IL 60022 *Call*: 847/509-9595

**Cansurmount Division of American Cancer Society** *Area Served: National* A visitation/referral program for newly diagnosed cancer patients linking them with former cancer patients with a similar diagnosis. *Services*: Mutual aid, educational program or material, home or hospital visitation. *Write*: 2255 S Oneida, Denver, CO 80224 *Call*: 303/758-2030

**Cansurmount St Elizabeth Medical Center** *Area Served: Madison and St Clair Counties Write*: 2100 Madison Ave, Granite City, IL 62040 *Call*: 618/798-3510

**Care and Share Methodist Medical Center** *Area Served: Peoria County Write*: 221 NE Glen Oak, Peoria, IL 60636 *Call*: 309/672-4110

**Care and Share Saint James Hospital** *Area Served: Cook and Will Counties* Provides an opportunity for cancer patients and their families and concerned persons to discuss their worries, concerns, and problems living with cancer with a social worker as facilitator. *Services*: Mutual aid, written information. *Write*: 1423 Chicago Rd, Chicago Heights, IL 60411 *Call*: 708/756-1000 6177

**Community Cancer Support and Breast Cancer Support Good Shepherd Hospital** *Area Served: Lake County Write*: 450 Hwy 22, Barrington, IL 60010 *Call*: 847/381-9600 5592

**Coping with Cancer Stress Foster McGaw Hospital** *Area Served: Cook County* Education sessions and support group meetings for patients, their family members and friends. Speakers will address cancer and its treatments, physical, sexual and emotional and social changes. Informal self-help sessions determined by the needs of those attending. *Meetings*: Weekly. *Services*: Mutual aid. *Write*: Social Work Dept, 2160 S 1ˢᵗ Ave, Maywood, IL 60153 *Call*: 708/216-4044

**Coping with Cancer Support Group Rockford Memorial Hospital** *Area Served: IL* Provides an opportunity for cancer patients and their families and concerned persons to discuss their worries, concerns, and problems living with cancer with a social worker as facilitator. *Services*: Mutual aid, written information. *Write*: 2400 N Rockton Ave, Rockford, IL 61103 *Call*: 815/969-6189

**Exceptional Patient Group** *Area Served: Regional* Provide psycho social and emotional support. Resource information available for education. Encouragement from facilitator andgroup members. referrals for other help. Serves persons facing any life threatening disease with a focus on survivorship skills. *Support group meetings*: twice monthly conducted by professional staff and long-term cancer survivors. 2ⁿᵈ Monday at 2 pm and 4ᵗʰ Monday at 7 pm; accessible. *Write*: St Margaret's Hospital, 600 E 1ˢᵗ St, Spring Valley, IL 61362 *Call*: 815/664-1132 *Fax*: 815/644-1188

**Help St Joseph's Hospital** *Area Served: Clinton, Madison and Bond Counties Write*: 9515 Holy Cross Ln, PO Box 99, Breese, IL 62230 *Call*: 618/526-4511 327

**Hinsdale Hospital Support Group** Provide emotional support, enhance coping skills and provide resource information to patients and their families living with cancer. Peer support is encouraged. Meetings are run in a self-help format. Monday evenings 1-9 pm; speakers are scheduled for the last Monday night of each month. Topics include stress management, nutrition, etc. *Write*:

120 N Oak St, Hinsdale, IL 60521 *Call*: 630/856-7094 *Fax*: 630/856-7099

**I Can Cope Little Company of Mary Hospital** *Area Served: Cook County Write*: 2800 W 95th St, Evergreen Park, IL 60642 *Call*: 708/422-6200 5480

**I Can Cope Methodist Medical Center** *Area Served: Peoria County Write*: 221 NE Glen Oak, Peoria, IL 60636 *Call*: 309/672-4110

**I Can LaGrange Memorial Health Center** *Area Served: Cook County Write*: Health Education Dept, 5101 Willow Springs Rd, LaGrange, IL 60525 *Call*: 708/354-7070

**International Assn of Cancer Victims and Friends, Inc** *Area Served: International* Restores the right to life for cancer victims, encourages and supports independent research, studies all of the aspects of cancer, cancer therapies, and clinical tests of great promise which have been suppressed. *Services*: Information, education and support. *Meetings*: 2nd Tuesday of each month from 7-9 pm at 7222 W Cermak Rd-lower level. *Write*: 5508 W 19th St, PO Box 347, Cicero, IL 60804-2202 *Call*: 708/780-6188

**Lesbian Community Cancer Project** *Area Served: IL* Provides support, information, education, advocacy, and direct services to lesbian and non-lesbians living with cancer or cancer histories and to their self-identified families. The project doesn't discriminate and is open to all women who support our goals. Services include a freegyn. clinic, professionally facilitated survivors and caregivers support groups; volunteer practical support prog.; smoking cessation clinic; spiritual support program. *Write*: 4753 N Broadway, Ste 602, Chicago, IL 60640 *Call*: 773/561-4662 *Fax*: 773/561-1830

**Living with Cancer Central DuPage County Hospital** *Area Served: DuPage County Write*: Behavioral Health Sciences, 25 N Winfield Rd, Winfield, IL 60190 *Call*: 630/682-1600 2136

**Living with Cancer Hinsdale Hospital** *Area Served: DuPage County* Provides emotional support and information and to teach coping skills to patients and families who are living with cancer. Nutrition, stress management, communication, are available. Community resources are also discussed. *Meetings*: Weekly for patient, family, and friends. *Services*: Mutual aid. *Write*: 120 N Oak, Hinsdale, IL 60521 *Call*: 630/856-7094

**Living with Cancer Passavant Area Hospital** *Area Served: Morgan, Scott and Cass Counties Write*: 1600 W Walnut, Jacksonville, IL 62650 *Call*: 217/245-9541 3594

**Living with Cancer Support Group McDonough District Hospital Center for Wellness** *Area Served: McDonough, Hancock and Schuyler Counties* Assists persons and families afflicted with cancer to learn to live more effectively within the parameters of the disease. Meets twice a month. *Services*: Mutual aid, educational program or material, advocacy, telephone support, home or hospital visitation, written information. *Write*: 525 E Grant St, Macomb, IL 61455 *Call*: 309/833-4101 3483

**Living with Cancer Support Group Swedish American Hospital** *Area Served: Winnebago, Boone, Ogle and Stephenson Counties* This group is for people with cancer and their family members or support person. The group discusses living with the disease and coping with problems and treatments. The emphasis is on living. *Meetings*: Weekly. *Services*: Mutual aid, advocacy, referral to other services, speakers bureau, social activities. *Write*: 1400 Charles St, Rockford, IL 61104 *Call*: 815/968-4400

**Look Good...Feel Better Northwest Community Continuing Care Center** 12 Step beauty program by a certified professional cosmetologist, especially for women undergoing radiation and chemotherapy. Discussion of wigs, turbans and other beauty tips (nails, etc.). *Meetings*: 3rd Tuesday of each month at 7:00 pm, in English, handicap accessible building and parking. To register, please call 847/618-3460. *Write*: 901 W Kirchoff, Arlington Heights, IL 60005 *Call*: 847/618-6665

**Macon County Support Group Network** *Area Served: Macon County* Help patients in their fight against cancer and help family and friends to cope and understand. Wheelchair accessible. Also available: books, pamphlets, health care newsletters. *Meetings*: Weekly. *Services*: Mutual aid, written information, social activities, telephone support, educational program or material, home or hospital visitation. *Write*: 1221 E Condit, Decatur, IL 62522 *Call*: 217/429-4357

**Make Today Count Alexian Brothers Medical Center** *Area Served: Cook-NW and DuPage Counties* Mutual support org. that brings together those persons affected by a life threatening illness so they may helpeach other learn to live in a positive, meaningful manner. Meetings have educational and mutual aid components. *Meetings*: Twice monthly. *Services*: Mutual aid. *Write*: 800 Biesterfield Rd, Elk Grove Village, IL 60007-3397 *Call*: 708/981-3675

**Make Today Count** *Area Served: St. Clair County Write*: St Elizabeth's Hospital, 211 S 3rd St, Belleville, IL 62222 *Call*: 618/234-2120 1240

**Make Today Count** *Area Served: Macon County Write*: Decatur Memorial Hospital, 23400 N Edward, Decatur, IL 62526 *Call*: 217/764-5006

**Make Today Count CGH Medical Center** *Area Served: Whiteside County Write*: 100 E Lefevre Rd, Cancer Dept, Sterling, IL 61081 *Call*: 815/625-0400 4415

**Make Today Count Condell Memorial Hospital** *Area Served: Lake County Write*: 900 Garfield, Libertyville, IL 60048 *Call*: 847/362-2900 5285

**Make Today Count Edward Hospital** *Area Served: DuPage County* Support group for persons facing a life-threatening illness and for their families and friends. *Services*: Mutual aid. *Write*: Pastoral Care Dept, 801 S Washington, Naperville, IL 60540-7499 *Call*: 630/527-3564

**Make Today Count Fox Valley Chapter** *Area Served: Kane County Write*: Delnor Community Hospital, 300 Randall Rd, Geneva, IL 60134 *Call*: 630/208-3084

**Make Today Count Northwest Community Hospital. Continuing Care Center** Support for all cancer patients, family and friends. Support group and newsletters/flyers. *Meetings*: Every other Thursday evening at 7:30 pm, in English, handicap accessible building and parking. 24 hour voice mail service. *Write*: 901 W Kirchoff Rd, Arlington Heights, IL 60005 *Call*: 847/618-6665

**Make Today Count St Catherine's Hospital** *Area Served: Cook-SE and Will-E Counties Write*: 4321 1ˢᵗ St, East Chicago, IN 46312 *Call*: 219/392-7197

**Make Today Count St. Joseph Hospital** *Area Served: Kane County* By using the supportive atmosphere of the group, individuals learn how to better cope with their illness, related difficulties, and share insights, ventilate feelings engage in problem solving and give support. *Meetings*: Twice a month for family and friends. *Services*: Mutual aid. *Write*: 77 N Airlite, Elgin, IL 60123-4912 *Call*: 847/695-3200 5245

**Make Today Count St Margaret's Hospital** *Area Served: LaSalle County* A national self-help/mutual aid group that provides psycho social and emotional support for persons and their families facing serious illness. Members receive encouragement from facilitators and group members. *Meetings*: Monthly. 1ˢᵗ and 3ʳᵈ Thursday; 7:00 pm; English; accessible; no transportation. *Write*: 600 E 1ˢᵗ St, Spring Valley, IL 61362 *Call*: 815/664-1132 *Fax*: 815/664-1188

**Make Today Count Support Group Saint Joseph Hospital** *Area Served: Kane County Write*: 77 N Airlite, Elgin, IL 60123 *Call*: 847/695-3200 5245

**Northwest Community Continuing Care Center Cancer Support** A series of 12 educational programs help patients, their families and friends become knowledgeable about the disease and treatment. Helps manage day-to-day problems and maintain the highest possible quality of life through working hand-in-hand with their health professionals. *Meetings*: 12 educational programs on Tuesday and Thursday, English, handicap accessible building and parking. Call for flyer. *Write*: 901

W Kirchoff, Arlington Heights, IL 60005 *Call*: 847/618-6665

**Oncology Support Group Swedish Covenant Hospital** *Area Served: Cook County Write*: 5145 N California Ave, Chicago, IL 60625 *Call*: 773/878-8200

**Oncology Support Group Thorek Hospital** *Area Served: Cook County Write*: 850 W Irving Park Rd, Chicago, IL 60613 *Call*: 773/975-6776

**Outpatient Cancer Support Group Palos Community Hospital-Social Services** *Area Served: Cook County Write*: 80ᵗʰ Ave and McCarthy Rd, Palos Heights, IL 60463 *Call*: 708/923-4840

**Patient/Family Cancer Support Group Rush-Pres-St. Luke's Hospital** Primarily for Rush-Pres in-patients and their families, although out-patients are also welcome. The group provides emotional peer support, and informal patient education given by a nurse, social worker, and a chaplain. *Meetings*: Weekly for patient, family. *Services*: Mutual aid, educational program or material. *Write*: 1653 W Harrison, Chicago, IL 60612 *Call*: 312/942-5358

**People Against Cancer** *Area Served: National* Encourages innovation in prevention and therapy of cancer. Offers educational lectures, counseling services and an alternative therapy program. O'Neill chapter. *Services*: Speakers bureau, written information, telephone support, professional service, educational program or material, advocacy, hotline, newsletter. *Write*: PO Box 10, Otho, IA 50569 *Call*: 515/972-4444

**People Against Cancer IL Chapter** *Area Served: IL Write*: 420 Wilshire Dr E, Wilmette, IL 60091 *Call*: 847/251-1121

**Person to Person Cancer Patient-Family Support Group** *Area Served: Cook County Write*: The MacNeal Cancer Center, 3340 S Oak Park, Berwyn, IL 60402 *Call*: 708/795-0300

**Positive People Support Group Silver Cross Hospital** *Area Served: Will County Write*: 1200 Maple Rd, Joliet, IL 60432 *Call*: 815/740-1100 7629

**Room to Talk Support Group Northwestern Memorial Hospital** *Area Served: Cook County Write*: Cancer Dept, Superior and Fairbanks Ct, Chicago, IL 60611 *Call*: 312/908-9400

**Stress Management Methodist Medical Center** *Area Served: Peoria County Write*: 221 NE Glen Oak, Peoria, IL 60636 *Call*: 309/672-4110

**Strive to Survive First United Methodist Church** *Area Served: Ogle County Write*: Mason and Congress Sts, Polo, IL 61064 *Call*: 815/946-2678 Evening

**Support Group for Children with Ill Parent Lutheran General Hospital** *Area Served: Cook County* Support for children and teens whose parent(s) have cancer. *Meetings*: Monthly. *Services*: Mutual aid, educational program or material, written information, referral to other services, telephone support. *Write*: Dept of Pastoral Care, 1775 Dempster St, Park Ridge, IL 60068 *Call*: 847/696-6395

**The Cancer Support Group Carle Clinic Assn** *Area Served: Champaign County Write*: 2300 N Vermilion, Danville, IL 61832 *Call*: 217/431-7825

**Time Out Christ Hospital** *Area Served: Cook County* This group setting has been designed to assist family members and friends of patients with cancer in talking about their concerns in dealing with the disease. *Meetings*: Weekly for patient, family and friends. *Services*: Mutual aid. *Write*: 4440 W 95th St, Oak Lawn, IL 60453 *Call*: 708/857/51

**Time Out Edward Hospital** *Area Served: IL  Write*: 801 S Washington St, Naperville, IL 60566 *Call*: 630/527-3140

**Together We Share Lutheran General Hospital** *Area Served: Cook County* Provide support and friendship, share experiences, help those involved to feel less alone and to do fun, diversionary activities. *Meetings*: Monthly but semi-restricted to persons sharing the concerns. *Services*: Mutual aid, social activities. *Write*: 1775 Dempster #402, Park Ridge, IL 60068 *Call*: 847/696-7747

**Triumph Over Cancer University of Chicago Hospitals** *Area Served: IL  Write*: 5841 S Maryland, MC 1098, Chicago, IL 60637 *Call*: 773/569-0913

**We Can Weekend Getaway Methodist Medical Center** *Area Served: Peoria County  Write*: 221 NE Glen Oak, Peoria, IL 60636 *Call*: 309/672-4110

**We're Movin' on West Suburban Hospital Medical Center** *Area Served: Cook County* Promote mutual support, share information and resources in helping individuals cope with cancer. *Services*: Mutual aid, written information. *Write*: Erie at Austin, Oak Park, IL 60302 *Call*: 708/383-6200 2221

**Wellness House** *Area Served: IL  Write*: 131 N County Line Rd, Hinsdale, IL 60521 *Call*: 630/323-5150

**Wellness House** *Area Served: Local* Offers emotional support and educates cancer patient and families, time-limited psycho social support groups, workshops, presentations including medical lectures, exercise courses, relaxation techniques, discussion groups and social events and referral services. *Write*: 131 N County Line Rd, Hinsdale, IL 60521 *Call*: 630/323-5150 *Fax*: 630/654-5346

**Wellness Resources Center Rush Cancer Institute** *Area Served: Cook County  Write*: 1725 W Harrison St, #863, Chicago, IL 60612 *Call*: 312/563-2350

**Women Aware of Breast Cancer Methodist Medical Center** *Area Served: Peoria County  Write*: 221 NE Glen Oak, Peoria, IL 60636 *Call*: 309/672-4100

## Cancer-Breast

**ABC Support Group (After Breast Cancer) Pekin Hospital** *Area Served: Tazewell, Peoria, Mason and Fulton Counties  Write*: 600 S 13th St, Pekin, IL 61554 *Call*: 309/353-0807 807

**Breast Cancer Support Erie Family Health Center** *Area Served: Chicago* For Spanish speaking only. Educational presentations about breast cancer, detection and treatment. Learn about breast self-examination. Also emotional aspects of it. *Services*: Mutual aid, educational program or material, telephone support, written information. *Write*: 1656 W Chicago Ave, Chicago, IL 60622 *Call*: 312/666-3488

**Breast Cancer Support Group Delnor-Community Hospital** *Area Served: Kane County* Support group for women with breast cancer. Also provides education about breast cancer and available resources. *Meetings*: Monthly. *Services*: Mutual aid, educational program or material. *Write*: The Women's Center, 300 Randall Rd, Geneva, IL 60134 *Call*: 630/208-3999 3995

**Breast Cancer Support Group EHS Christ Hospital** *Area Served: Will, Cook and DuPage Counties  Write*: Health Advisor, 4440 W 95th St, Oak Lawn, IL 60453 *Call*: 708/346-5091 5890

**Breast Cancer Support Group for Women Under 50 Rockford Memorial Hospital** *Area Served: Winnebago, Stephenson and Boone Counties  Write*: Women's Health Advantage, 2350 N Rockton Ave, Rockford, IL 61103 *Call*: 815/961-6215

**Breast Cancer Support Group Mason District Hospital** *Area Served: Mason, Fulton and Tazewell Counties  Write*: 520 E Franklin St, Box 530, Havana, IL 62644 *Call*: 309/543-4431 312

**Breast Cancer Support Group McDonough District Hospital Women's Resource Center** *Area Served: McDonough County  Write*: 525 E Grant St, Macomb, IL 61455 *Call*: 309/833-4101 3198

**Breast Cancer Support Group Bromenn Healthcare** *Area Served: McLean County  Write*: Virginia and Franklin, Normal, IL 61761 *Call*: 309/888-0917

**Breast Cancer Support Group Good Samaritan Hospital** Information and support for women diagnosed with breast cancer. *Meetings*: 3rd Tuesday of every month from 7:00-8:30 pm. Handicapped accessible, easy parking. All information shared in this group is confidential. *Write*: Blue Oak Room, 3815 Highland Ave., Downers Grove, IL 60515-1500 *Call*: 630/275-1270 *Fax*: 630/963-6078

**Breast Cancer Support LaGrange Memorial Hospital** *Area Served: IL Write*: 5101 S Willow Springs Rd, LaGrange, IL 60525 *Call*: 708/354-7070

**Community Cancer Support and Breast Cancer Support Good Shepherd Hospital** *Area Served: Lake County Write*: 450 Hwy 22, Barrington, IL 60010 *Call*: 847/381-9600 5592

**Encore YWCA** *Area Served: Winnebago, Ogle and Boone Counties Write*: 220 S Madison St, Rockford, IL 61104 *Call*: 815/968-9681

**Encore YWCA** *Area Served: Whiteside and Lee Counties Write*: 412 1st Ave, Sterling, IL 61081 *Call*: 815/625-0333

**Mastectomy and Breast Cancer Support Group Highland Park Hospital** *Area Served: Lake County* Help cancer patients and their families to cope with the changes in their lives. *Services*: Mutual aid, educational program or material. *Write*: 718 Glenview Ave, Highland Park, IL 60035 *Call*: 847/432-8000 5032

**Mastectomy Club St Elizabeth's Hospital** *Area Served: St Clair County Write*: 211 S 3rd, Belleville, IL 62222 *Call*: 618/234-2120

**Mastectomy Support Group St Elizabeth Medical Center** *Area Served: Madison and St Clair Counties Write*: 2100 Madison Ave, Granite City, IL 62040 *Call*: 618/798-3510

**Reach for Recovery American Cancer Society** *Area Served: McLean County* Volunteers who have had a mastectomy call on patients in hospitals or in their homesafter they have had a breast(s) removed to give out brochures, a temporary prosthesis, and talk and give support. *Services*: Written information, Home or hospital visitation. *Write*: 1312 E Vernon, Normal, IL 61761 *Call*: 800/252-1646

**Reach for Recovery American Cancer Society** *Area Served: LaSalle County Write*: St Mary's Hospital, 111 E Spring St, Streator, IL 61364 *Call*: 800/325-7699

**Reach for Recovery American Cancer Society** *Area Served: IL Write*: 77 E Monroe, Chicago, IL 60603 *Call*: 800/227-2345

**Reach for Recovery Blessing Hospital** *Area Served: Adams County Write*: Broadway and 11th, Quincy, IL 62301 *Call*: 217/223-2726

**Reach for Support Northwest Community Commoving Care Center** *Area Served: Cook County* Provides

support for breast cancer patients, their families and friends. *Services*: Support group and prosthesis display. *Meetings*: 1st Wednesday of each month, 6-7:30 pm is the prosthesis display and the support group meeting starts at 7:30 pm; handicap accessible building and parking; language spoken-English. *Write*: 901 W Kirchoff, Arlington Heights, IL 60005 *Call*: 847/618-6665

**Reach to Recovery American Cancer Society** *Area Served: Peoria, Fulton and Mason Counties Write*: 3118 N University, Peoria, IL 61604 *Call*: 309/688-3488

**Reach to Recovery** *Area Served: Winnebago County Write*: 850 N Church St, Rockford, IL 61103 *Call*: 815/962-0604

**Reach to Recovery Northwestern Memorial Hospital** *Area Served: Cook County Write*: Cancer Dept, Superior and Fairbanks Ct, Chicago, IL 60611

**Rebound St Margaret's Hospital** Provide psycho social and emotional support. Resource information available for education. Encouragement from facilitator and group members. Referrals for other help. Serves persons affected by breast cancer. Support group meetings monthly; 3rd Monday at 7 pm; English; no transportation; accessible. *Write*: 600 E 1st St, Spring Valley, IL 61362 *Call*: 815/664-1132 *Fax*: 815/664-1188

**The Komen Group At DMH: Breast Cancer Support Group Decatur Memorial Hospital Cancer Care Institute** *Area Served: Macon County* Provides peer support, professional support and education. Each session is facilitated by a professional from the DMH cancer care institute and includes an educational presentation, an opportunity to meet others with the same personal experiences. Lending library available. *Meetings*: 2nd Thursday of each month at 7 pm. Location is handicapped accessible; English. *Write*: 2300 N Edward St, Decatur, IL 62526-4193 *Call*: 217/876-2380 *Fax*: 217/876-2387

**Together Edward Hospital** *Area Served: IL Write*: 801 S Washington St, Naperville, IL 60566 *Call*: 630/527-3140

**Y-Me? National Org for Breast Cancer Information and Support, Inc** *Area Served: IL* Provides information, referral and emotional support to individuals concerned about or diagnosed with breast cancer. National toll-free hotline staffed by trained staff and volunteers who have experienced breast cancer. Promotes breast cancer awareness. Wig and prosthesis bank available. 13 groups in IL. *Services*: Mutual aid, educational program or material, written information, referral to other services, speakers bureau, hotline, telephone support, newsletter. *Write*: 212 W Van Buren, Chicago, IL 60607 *Call*: 800/221-2141 *Fax*: 312/986-0020

# Cancer-Children

**Cancer Care Support Group Iroquois Memorial Hospital and Resident Home** *Area Served: IL Write*: 200 Fairman, Watseka, IL 60970 *Call*: 815/432-5841 4309

**Candlelighters** *Area Served: IL Write*: 14424 Knoxville Rd, Milan, IL 61264 *Call*: 309/787-3791

**Candlelighters CCCF** *Area Served: Cook, DuPage, Kane and Lake Counties* Candlelighters is a self-help/mutual aid support group for parents who have children with cancer or blood disorders, infancy thru teenage. It is part of a nationwide org. Meetings, library, phone link-ups, social activities, newsletter, speakers. *Meetings*: For all interested. *Services*: Mutual aid, educational program or material, telephone support, social activities, newsletter, written information. *Write*: PO Box 957253, Hoffman Estates, IL 60195 *Call*: 708/495-2777

**Candlelighters CCCF** *Area Served: Cook, DuPage, Kane and Will Counties* A self-help/mutual aid support group for parents who have children with cancer or blood disorders, infancy through teenage; part of a nationwide org. Offers library, phone link-ups, social activities, newsletter, speakers. *Meetings*: For all interested. *Services*: Mutual aid, educational program or material, telephone support, social activities, newsletter, written information. *Write*: PO Box 98, Downers Grove, IL 60515 *Call*: 630/985-7430

**Candlelighters CGH Medical Center** *Area Served: Whiteside and Lee Counties Write*: 100 E Lefevre Rd, Sterling, IL 61081 *Call*: 815/625-0400

**Lean on Me Rush-Presbyterian-St Luke's Medical Center** *Area Served: Chicago, Indiana Write*: Rush Cancer Center-Hematology, 1725 W Harrison, #862, Chicago, IL 60612 *Call*: 312/942-5982

**Many Involved Towards Cancer Help** *Area Served: Cook County* Fund raising for peer-counseling program at Children's Memorial Hospital. *Meetings*: Monthly for public. *Services*: Referral to other services, fundraising. *Write*: Mitch 2550 Queens Way, Northbrook, IL 60062 *Call*: 847/564-1239

**Pediatric Cancer Support Group Foster McGaw Hospital** *Area Served: Cook County Write*: Social Work Dept, 2160 S 1st Ave, Maywood, IL 60153 *Call*: 708/216-3639

**Together We Share Lutheran General Hospital** Provide support and activity group for teens and young adults who have, or have had, cancer or a tumor. The group is affiliated with Lutheran General Hospital; however, members do not have to be associated with the hospital or one of their doctors. *Services*: Quarterly activity get-togethers; support group meetings as needed;

connect teens who are or have been in similar situations. *Meetings*: Call for dates and times; English; location varies. *Write*: 1775 Dempster, Rm E261, Park Ridge, IL 60068 *Call*: 847/723-8336

# Cancer-Colon-Polyposis

**Inherited Colorectal Cancer Registries Department of Colorectal Surgery Desk A-111** *Area Served: National Write*: Cleveland Clinic Foundation 9500 Euclid Ave, Cleveland, OH 44195 *Call*: 216/444-9052

# Cancer-Leukemia

**Leukemia Society of America Family Support Group Program** *Area Served: National* Addresses the special psycho social needs of the patient/family member affected by the leukemias, Hodgkins disease, lymphomas and multiple myeloma. Support groups led by professional health specialists encourage better communication between the patient and his/her family, medical team and friends. *Meetings*: Monthly. *Services*: Mutual aid. *Write*: 733 3rd Ave, Ste 1400, NY, NY 10017 *Call*: 800/284-4271 126

**Leukemia Support Group Northwest Community Hospital** *Area Served: IL* Provides support for leukemia patients, their families and friends to help them deal with concerns about leukemia. *Services*: Support group and flyers. *Meetings*: 2nd Wednesday of each month at 7:30 pm, English speaking, handicapped accessible building and parking. 24 hour voice mail service. *Write*: 800 W Central Rd, Arlington Heights, IL 60005 *Call*: 847/618-6665

# Cancer-Prostate

**Central Illinois Us Too Prostate Cancer Support Group DMH Cancer Care Institute** Provide forum in which participants can discuss problems and anxieties. org. serves as a source of up-to-date medical information. The group is registered with the American Foundation for Urologic Disease, Inc (AFUD). Open to prostate cancer survivors, their spouses, family and friends. Interactive facilitators, educational programs and special guests. *Meetings*: 4th Tuesday, monthly; handicapped accessible; language- English. *Write*: 2300 N Edward St, Decatur, IL 62526-4193 *Call*: 217/876-2380 *Fax*: 217/876-2387

**Patient Advocates for Advanced Cancer Treatment** *Area Served: National Write*: PO Box 141695, Grand Rapids, MI 49514 *Call*: 616/453-1477

**Prostate Cancer Support Group Northwest Community Hospital Continuing Care Center** *Area Served: Cook and Lake Counties* Provides education and support for prostate cancer patients, their families and friends. *Services*: Support group, education, and flyer materials. *Meetings*: 1st Tuesday of each month at 7:30 pm., English speaking, handicap accessible building and parking. 24 hour voice mail service. *Write*: 901 W Kirchoff, Arlington Heights, IL 60005 *Call*: 847/618-6665 4172

**Us Too American Urological Assn** *Area Served: National Write*: Amer Fund-Urological Disease, 300 W Pratt St, Baltimore, MD 21201 *Call*: 800/822-5277

**Us Too Elmhurst Memorial Hospital** *Area Served: DuPage County Write*: 200 Berteau, Elmhurst, IL 60126 *Call*: 630/831-1400 4691

**Us Too Evanston Hospital** *Area Served: Cook County Write*: 2650 Ridge Ave, Evanston, IL 60201 *Call*: 847/570-2110 *Fax*: 847/570-2918

**Us Too Prostate Cancer Ingalls Memorial Hospital** *Area Served: Cook County Write*: One Ingalls Dr, Harvey, IL 60426 *Call*: 708/333-2300 6380

**Us Too Prostate Cancer Support Group Good Samaritan Hospital** *Area Served: DuPage and Cook Counties* Provide information, education, and support for men diagnosed with prostate cancer, and support for their families and friends. Meetings alternate between a speaker on a prostate cancer related topic or networking and sharing information on an informal basis. *Meetings*: 1st Thursday of every month from 7:00-9:00 pm. Handicapped accessible, easy parking. *Write*: Blue Oak Room, 3815 Highland, Downers Grove, IL 60515-1500 *Call*: 630/275-1270 *Fax*: 630/963-6078

**Us Too St James Hospital** *Area Served: Cook County Write*: 1423 Chicago Rd, Chicago Heights, IL 60411 *Call*: 708/756-1000

**Us Too Weiss Memorial Hospital** *Area Served: Cook County Write*: 4646 N Marine Dr, Chicago, IL 60640 *Call*: 773/878-8700 1023 *Fax*: 312/561-9426

# Caregivers

**Care of the Caregivers Good Samaritan Mental Health Center** *Area Served: DuPage and Cook Counties Write*: 3815 Highland Ave, Downers Grove, IL 60515 *Call*: 630/257-6384

**Caregiver Connection Riverside Medical Center** *Area Served: Kankakee and Will Counties* Inform caregiversabout available resources and support; educate in care giving skills; provide environment and format for information, mutual support among caregivers; a designed interactive forum in which professional service providers and caregivers may share informally, non-threateningly. *Services*: Mutual aid, educational program or material,

written information. *Write*: 350 N Wall St, Kankakee, IL 60901 *Call*: 815/933-1671

**Caregiver Support Group St Mary's Hospital** *Area Served: IL Write*: 111 E Spring St, Streator, IL 61364 *Call*: 800/325-7699

**Caregivers Group** *Area Served: Stark County* Our purpose is to provide support and maintenance to persons of observed need for caregivers. Both short-term relief and long-term support is practiced. We have a referral system to assist us in helping in other ways. *Meetings*: Monthly. *Services*: Mutual aid, referral to other services, educational programs and materials, home visits, social activities. *Write*: 102 N 7th St, Wyoming, IL 61491 *Call*: 309/695-5660

**Caregivers of the Elderly** *Area Served: Coles, Moultrie and Douglas Counties Write*: 1000 Health Center Dr, PO Box 372, Mattoon, IL 61938 *Call*: 217/348-2525 2392

**Caregivers Support and Peer Support Group Palatine Senior Center** *Area Served: Cook County Write*: 721 S Quentin Rd, Palatine, IL 60067

**Caregivers Support Group** *Area Served: Macon, Piatt and DeWitt Counties Write*: Prime Time Resource Center, 3140 N Water St, Decatur, IL 62526

**Caregivers Support Group Community Hospital of Ottawa** *Area Served: LaSalle County Write*: 219 W Lafayette St, Ottawa, IL 61350 *Call*: 815/433-6090

**Caregivers Support Group Family Alliance** *Area Served: McHenry County* Provides basic information on resources needed by caregivers and a supportive atmosphere where caregivers can gather and share their problems while learning more about various approaches/ solutions to their situations. *Meetings*: Monthly for anyone caring for a physically or emotionally frail elderly relative. Mutual aid, educational program or material. *Write*: 670 S Eastwood Dr, Woodstock, IL 60098 *Call*: 815/338-3590

**Caregivers Support Group Richland Memorial Hospital** *Area Served: Richland, Jasper and Crawford Counties Write*: 800 E Locust St, Olney, IL 62450 *Call*: 618/395-2131 4302

**Caregivers Support Group Village of Mount Prospect** *Area Served: IL Write*: 50 S Emerson St, Mt Prospect, IL 60056 *Call*: 847/870-5680

**Caregivers Support McDonough District Hospital** *Area Served: McDonough and Hancock Counties* Provide opportunity to learn about caregiving, and to provide opportunity for sharing and mutual support among caregivers. 2 groups: one for spouse or sibling caregivers, and another group for adult children with elderly parents. *Meetings*: Monthly for all interested. *Services*: Mutual aid, educational program or material, referral to other services, professional service. *Write*: 525 E Grant, Macomb, IL 61455 *Call*: 309/833-4101 3415

**Caregiving for Aging Relatives Ravenswood CMHC**
*Area Served: Cook County Write*: 2312 W Irving Park Rd, Chicago, IL 60618 *Call*: 773/463-7000

**Caregiving Friends** *Area Served: Cook County Write*: 105 S Oak Park Ave, Oak Park, IL 60302 *Call*: 708/383-1324 *Fax*: 708/386-1399

**Caring for the Caregiver LaGrange Hospital**
*Area Served: Cook County Write*: 5101 Willow Springs Rd, LaGrange, IL 60525 *Call*: 708/354-7070

**Caring for the Elderly Park Place Senior Center**
*Area Served: Cook and Lake Counties* Help the caregiver betterunderstand the feelings and needs of the person they are caring for. Develop a greater awareness of their own needs and responses to their situation. *Meetings*: Twice monthly. *Services*: Mutual aid, referral to other services. *Write*: Lutheran Community Services, 306 W Park St, Arlington Heights, IL 60005 *Call*: 847/253-3710 3387

**Children of Aging Parents CAPS Woodbourne Office Campus** *Area Served:* Caps provides information and supportive data to caregivers of elderly parents. *Services*: Information and referral, network of support groups, and public education. Bi-monthly newsletter and fact sheets. *Meetings*: Call for specific dates and times of locations near you. *Write*: 1600 Woodbourne Rd, Ste 302A, Levittown, PA 19057-1511 *Call*: 800/227-7294 *Fax*: 215/945-8720

**Children of Aging Parents Support Group Methodist Medical Center** *Area Served: Peoria and Tazewell Counties Write*: 221 NE Glen Oak Ave, Peoria, IL 61636 *Call*: 309/672-5571

**Children of Dependent Parents** *Area Served: Cook and Lake Counties Write*: Arlington Countryside Church, 916E, Arlington Heights, IL 60004 *Call*: 847/255-2140

**Client Assistance Line Ill Dept of Mental Health and Developmental Disabilities** *Area Served: IL* Client Assistance Line to help parents, guardian, families to find residential placement, funding possibilities, respite care, and to handle complaints about services. Will take questions and pass it along to appropriate agency. *Services*: Written information, referral to other services, advocacy. *Write*: Stratton Bldg, Rm 405, Springfield, IL 62765
*Call*: 800/843-6154

**CO-OP Network (Caregivers of Older Persons) St Elizabeth's Hospital-Belleville Area College**
*Area Served: St Clair and Madison Counties Write*: 201 N Church St, Belleville, IL 62220 *Call*: 618/234-4410 33 *Fax*: 618/234-8634

**Concerned Relatives of Nursing Home Patients Nursing Home Advisory and Research Council, Inc**
*Area Served: National Write*: PO Box 18820, Cleveland, OH 44118-0820 *Call*: 216/321-0403

**In Touch Lutheran Social Services** *Area Served: Rock Island, Knox and Warren Counties* Groups for family members and interested public at a day center for the elderly. Alzheimer Unit meets twice a month and over 60 Unit meets every month. *Services*: Mutual aid, educational program or material, advocacy, written information. *Write*: 3520 53$^{rd}$ St, Moline, IL 61265 *Call*: 309/344-2520

**My Aging Parents and I St Joseph Medical Center**
*Area Served: Cook, Will and DuPage Counties* Provides emotional support and information to those concerned about older persons and their families/support systems. *Meetings*: Monthly for all interested. *Services*: Mutual aid, educational program or material, written information. *Write*: 333 N. Madison, Joliet, IL 60435
*Call*: 815/725-7133 3175

**Respite Care** *Area Served: Chicago Write*: 2032 N Clybourn, Chicago, IL 60614 *Call*: 773/929-8200 292

**Shares** *Area Served: Cook County Write*: Swedish Covenant Hospital, 5145 N California, Chicago, IL 60625 *Call*: 773/878-8200 5365

**Skokie Office of Human Services** *Area Served: Cook County* Provide emotional support as well as referrals to community resources. *Services*: Mutual aid, referral to other services, professional service, social activities, newsletter. *Write*: 5120 Galitz, Skokie, IL 60077 *Call*: 847/673-0500

**Sterling Rock Falls Provider Support Group** *Area Served: Whiteside and Lee Counties Write*: YWCA, 412 1$^{st}$ Ave, Sterling, IL 61081 *Call*: 815/625-0333

**Village of Mount Prospect Human Services Department** *Area Served: IL* Help caregivers deal with the many emotions of giving care, such as anger, anxiety, frustration, feeling trapped, sorrow, etc. In addition to offering monthly outlet, the nurse and social worker (facilitators of group) are available for more hands on help. Outreach nursing and social work, advocacy, assist with paperwork, etc. *Meetings*: 2$^{nd}$ Friday every month from 10:00-11:30 am. *Write*: 50 S Emerson St, Mt Prospect, IL 60056 *Call*: 847/870-5680 *Fax*: 847/818-5321

**Well Spouse Foundation** *Area Served: National* Supports the well spouse while dealing with the chronic illness of a husband or wife. Offers self-help groups, educates about the hidden role, advocates for insurance coverage and new programs for families with a chronic illness. Publications: newsletters and information. 2 Illinois chapters. *Write*: PO Box 801, NY, NY 10023 *Call*: 212/724-7209

# Celiac Sprue

**American Celiac Society Dietary Support Coalition** *Area Served: National Write*: 58 Musano Ct, West Orange, NY 07052 *Call*: 201/325-8837

**Celiac-Sprue Assn of Greater Chicago** *Area Served: Cook, DuPage and Lake Counties Write*: PO Box 7021, Villa Park, IL 60181 *Call*: 630/972-1476

**Gluten Intolerance Group of North America** *Area Served: National* Provides information and support to those with celiac sprue and/or dermatitis herpetiformis, their families and healthcare professionals. Offers a variety of printed materials. Annual meeting, regional seminars and local support groups provide opportunities for increasing one's knowledge base and networking with other members. *Services*: Mutual aid, educational program or material, written information, telephone support. *Write*: PO Box 23053, Seattle, WA 98102-0353 *Call*: 206/325-6980

**Midwestern Celiac-Sprue Assn IL Chapter** *Area Served: IL Write*: 710 5th St and Greenrock, Green Rock, IL 61241 *Call*: 309/796-2010

# Cerebral Palsy

**Able Disabled United Cerebral Palsy of Central IL** *Area Served: McLean, Livingston and Woodford Counties Write*: 808 Eldorado Rd, Ste C-3, Bloomington, IL 61704 *Call*: 309/663-8275

**Assn for Special Families** *Area Served: Chicago, Cook County* Provide support and information to those interested in cerebral palsy and for families of children with multiple handicaps. *Services*: Mutual aid, educational program or material, written information, social activities, referral to other services, TEL hotline. *Write*: 10054 S Princeton, Chicago, IL 60628 *Call*: 773/995-9368

**United Cerebral Palsy Blackhawk Region** *Area Served: Winnebago County* Provides general services for children and adults handicapped by cerebral palsy and their families. Provides education, transportation, training, therapy, counseling to help the individual reach his/her maximum potential. *Services*: Educational program or material, advocacy, provide professional service. *Write*:7399 Forest Hills Rd, Love Park, IL 61111 *Call*: 815/282-8824

**United Cerebral Palsy Marion County UCP of Southern IL** *Area Served: IL-S Write*: PO Box 1066, 115 S Lincoln, Centralia, IL 62801 *Call*: 800/332-9745

**United Cerebral Palsy Parent Support Group** *Area Served: Will, Grundy and Kankakee Counties* Provides general services for children and adults handicapped by cerebral palsy and their families. Provides education, transportation, training, therapy, counseling to help the individual reach his/her maximum potential. *Services*: Educationalprogram or material, advocacy, provide professional service. *Write*: 311 S Reed St, Joliet, IL 60436 *Call*: 815/744-3500

**United Cerebral Palsy Sangamon County UCP Land of Lincoln** *Area Served: Sangamon County and IL-CE Write*: 130 N 16th St, PO Box 19494, Springfield, IL 62794 *Call*: 217/525-6522

**United Cerebral Palsy St Clair County Cerebral Palsy of SW IL** *Services*: Mutual aid, advocacy. *Write*: 211 Lebanon Ave, Belleville, IL 62220 *Call*: 618/233-6576 TDD

**United Cerebral Palsy UCP of Central IL** *Area Served: Peoria County—C Write*: 320 E Armstrong, Peoria, IL 61603 *Call*: 309/672-6325

**United Cerebral Palsy UCP of Mississippi Valley** *Area Served: Rock Island County and IL NW Write*: 4709 44th St, Ste 8, Rock Island, IL 61201 *Call*: 309/788-0851

# Charcot Marie Tooth Disorder

**Charcot-Marie-Tooth International** *Area Served: International Write*: 1 Springbank Dr, St Catharine's, Ontario, Canada, L2S 2K1 *Call*: 905/687-3630

**Charcot-Marie-Tooth Assn** *Area Served: National* Provide information and support to patients/families with Charcot-Marie-Tooth disorder (aka Peroneal Muscular Atrophy and Hereditary Motor Sensory neuropathy). Provide referrals, sponsor patient and professional conferences, support groups and a VCR tape program. Meeting in late 1992 to form an IL chapter. *Services*: Mutual aid, educational program or material, written information, advocacy, referral to other services, speakers bureau, referral to other services, telephone support, newsletter. *Write*: 601 Upland Ave, Upland, PA 19015 *Call*: 800/606-8682 *Fax*: 610/499-7487

# Chemical Sensitivity

**Chicago Area Environmental Illness-Multiple Chemical Sensitivities (EI/MCS) Support Group** *Area Served: IL* Provide education, information and support to persons with MCS and those sensitive to chemicals. Our org. advocates for public policies and collaborates with local, state, and national orgs on issues of the chemically injured. *Services*: Newsletters; resource guide/info-line (773) 227-5059; physician and lawyer referrals; and a lending library. *Meetings*: Monthly, call for dates and times. Near public transportation. *Write*: 1404 Judson Ave, Evanston, IL 60201-4722 *Call*: 630/529-1342

# Chronic Fatigue Syndrome

**Chronic Fatigue Syndrome Society of IL, Inc**
*Area Served: IL* Support group that tries to help
individuals through meetings with guest speakers, through
a quarterly newsletter, and through physician referrals.
Meetings are open to the public. *Services*: Mutual aid,
social activities, telephone support, referral to other
services, educational program or material, advocacy,
newsletter, written information. *Write*: PO Box 10139,
Chicago, IL 60610 *Call*: 312/280-6987 *Fax*:
312/644-4316

**Chicago Chronic Fatigue Syndrome Assn** *Area Served:
Cook and DuPage Counties* Provide emotional support
and to share information about all methods of treatment.
Open to people with the syndrome and their supporters.
*Meetings*: Monthly. *Services*: Written information, mutual
aid, newsletter. *Write*: 818 S Wenonah Ave, Oak Park, IL
60304 *Call*: 773/334-3504

**Chronic Fatigue and Fibromyalgia Support Group
Bromenn Lifecare Center** *Area Served: McLean County*
*Write*: 807 N Main, Bloomington, IL 61701
*Call*: 309/829-5020

**The CFIDS Assn of America** *Area Served: National*
National voluntary org. dedicated to conquering chronic
fatigue and immune dysfunction syndrome. Services
include brochures that are free and fee based, funding for
research projects to identify causes and effective
treatments, and education of government officials about
importance of disease. Membership includes a
subscription to the CFIDS chronicle, directory of local
support groups, guide for physician referral. *Write*: PO
Box 220398, Charlotte, NC 28222-0398 *Call*:
800/442-3437
*Fax*: 704/365-9755 *Email*: cfids@vnet.net
*Web site*: http://cfids.org.cfids

**The CFIDS Assn** *Area Served: National Write*: PO Box
220398, Charlotte, NC 28222 *Call*: 800/442-3437

**CFIDS Support** *Area Served: DuPage County* Place for
CFIDS patients to share and learn with others. Both
speaker and support meetings are available as is an
extensive reprint library and newsletter. *Meetings*:
Monthly for anyone who suffers from CFIDS, CFS, ME,
EBV, CEBV, PVFS, FM. *Services*: Mutual aid, speakers
bureau, written information, telephone support, referral to
other services, educational program or material, advocacy,
hotline, home or hospital visitation, newsletter. *Write*:
PO Box 10, Naperville, IL 60566-0010

# Chronic Pain

**American Chronic Pain Assn** *Area Served: National*
Offers help and hope to those suffering from chronic pain
(pain that lasts 6 months or longer). Support groups offer
positive and constructive methods of dealing with pain. 15
IL groups. *Services*: Mutual aid, written information,
telephone support, educational program or material,
newsletter. *Write*: PO Box 850, Rocklin, CA 95677
*Call*: 916/632-0922

**Chronic Pain Outreach** *Area Served: IL* To support
people living with chronic pain and their families.
Emphasis on establishing positive attitudes and to help
people regain control of their lives. *Services*: Mutual aid.
*Write*: 28 Bay Shore, Lacon, IL 61540 *Call*: 309/246-8963

**Chronic Pain Outreach** *Area Served: DuPage County*
*Write*: 5525 King Arthur Ct, #1, Westmont, IL 60559
*Call*: 630/963-6292

**Chronic Pain Outreach** *Area Served: Peoria, Tazewell
and Woodford Counties Write*: 28 Bay Shore Dr, Lacon,
IL 61540 *Call*: 309/246-8963

**Chronic Pain Outreach** *Area Served: LaSalle County*
Self-help group offering emotional support system,
practical help to individuals and families trying to cope
with chronic pain. *Services*: Mutual aid, educational
program or material. *Write*: RR 4, 2558 N IL 23, Ottawa,
IL 61350 *Call*: 815/434-1804

**Marianjoy Pain Support Group Marianjoy Rehab
Hospital and Clinics** *Area Served: IL* Offers peer
support and information to pain individuals, their families,
friends, and the community at large. Professionals
specializing in chronic pain treatment speak frequently.
*Meetings*: Twice monthly for anyone interested. *Services*:
Mutual aid, written information. *Write*: PO Box 795,
Wheaton, IL 60189 *Call*: 630/629-8538

# Circumcision

**Recap** *Area Served: National Write*: 3205 Northwood
Dr, Ste 209, Concord, CA 94520 *Call*: 510/827-4077

# Cleft Palate

**About Face Support Group Carle Clinic** *Area Served:
Champaign County Write*: 602 W University, W-4,
Champaign/Urbana, IL 61802 *Call*: 217/383-3130

**Cleft Lip and Palate Support Group** *Area Served:
Adams County* Provide educational programs and services
for people with diabetes, healthcare professionals and the
general public. Raise funds to support research. *Services*:

Mutual aid, educational program or material, advocacy. *Write*: 2580 Federal Dr, Ste 403, Decatur, IL 62526 *Call*: 800/445-1667

**Cleft Lip and Palate Support Group Lutheran General Health System** *Area Served: Cook County Write*: 1775 Dempster St, Park Ridge, IL 60068 *Call*: 847/696-7705

**Cleft Palate Foundation** *Area Served: National* Provides 24-hour phone service, group or professional referrals, publications, information and brochures. *Meetings*: Referral to group or professionals in caller's state. *Write*: 1829 E Franklin St, #1022, Chapel Hill, NC 27514 *Call*: 800/24CLEFT *Fax* 919/933-9604 *Web site*: http://www.cleft.com

**Cleft Palate Institute Parent Support Northwestern University** *Area Served: Chicago Write*: 240 E Huron St, Chicago, IL 60611 *Call*: 312/908-5955

# Colitis Ileitis and Crohn's Disease

**Crohn's and Colitis Foundation of America, Inc IL Carol Fisher Chapter** *Area Served: IL Write*: 2200 E Devon, Ste 364, Des Plaines, IL 60018 *Call*: 847/827-0404 *Fax*: 847/827-6563

# Cooley's Anemia

**Thalassemia Action Group National Cooley's Anemia Foundation** *Area Served: National* A network of Thalassemia patients 13 years old and over who have joined together to develop support groups around the country. We reach out to all Thalassemia patients to offer love, support, and a learning experience. to work for therapy compliance and a better life. *Meetings*: Monthly for anyone interested. One IL chapter. *Services*: Mutual aid, educational program or material, written information, referral to other services, speakers bureau, referral to other services, telephone support, newsletter. *Write*: 105 E 22nd St, Ste 911, NY, NY 10010 *Call*: 800/221-3571

# Cornelia De Lange Syndrome

**Cornelia De Lange Syndrome Foundation, Inc** *Area Served: National Write*: 60 Dyer Ave, Collinsville, CT 06022 *Call*: 800/223-8355

# Cri Du Chat Syndrome

**5-P Society** *Area Served: DuPage County Write*: 416 Menominee, Naperville, IL 60563 *Call*: 630/357-8408

# Cystic Fibrosis

**Cystic Fibrosis Center Children's Hospital of IL** *Area Served: IL* Provide information about support groups to parents of children with cystic fibrosis. Also telephone network in some groups. *Meetings*: For patients, parents, and siblings. *Services*: Mutual aid, educational program or material, advocacy, telephone support, written information. *Write*: 530 NE Glen Oak, Peoria, IL 61637 *Call*: 309/655-4063

**Cystic Fibrosis Clinic St Francis Medical Center** *Area Served: IL Write*: 530 NE Glen Oak, Peoria, IL 61637 *Call*: 309/655-6753

**Cystic Fibrosis Foundation Greater IL Chapter** *Area Served: IL Write*: 150 N Michigan Ave, Ste 410, Chicago, IL 60601 *Call*: 312/236-4491

# Cystinosis

**Cystinosis Foundation, Inc** *Area Served: National Write*: 1212 Broadway, Oakland, CA 94612 *Call*: 800/392-8458

# Death, Suicide

**Hemlock Society Hemlock of IL** *Area Served: IL* Group believes adults have the right to some control over their own dying and should plan ahead for the inevitable event of their own death. Educates the general public on physician-aided dying. *Services*: Mutual aid, educational program or material, written information, newsletter, speakers bureau, advocacy, referral to other services, telephone support, home or hospital visitation. *Write*: PO Box A3883, Chicago, IL 60690-3883 *Call*: 773/477-7228 Answer Mach.

# DES (Diethylstilbestrol)

**DES Action National** No known IL chapters. A national group to inform DES exposed individuals, health professionals, and others concerned about the health care needs of people exposed to the drug diethylstilbestrol (DES), prescribed to women during pregnancy from 1938 into the early 1970s. *Services*: Educational program or material advocacy, telephone support, newsletter, referral to other services, written information. *Write*:

1615 Broadway, Ste 510, Oakland, CA 94612
*Call*: 510/465-4011  *Fax*: 510/465-4815

# Diabetes

**American Diabetes Assn Adams County Chapter**
*Area Served: Adams County  Call*: 800/445-1667

**American Diabetes Assn** *Area Served: National*
General information and referrals to 24 groups in the
Chicago area and 28 groups elsewhere. *Services*: Written
information, referral to other services. *Write*: 1660 Duke
St, Alexandria, VA 22314 *Call*: 312/346-1805

**American Diabetes Assn Downstate IL Affiliate**
*Area Served: Downstate  Write*: 2580 Federal Dr, Ste 403,
Decatur, IL 62526 *Call*: 217/875-9011

**American Diabetes Assn Lee and Whiteside Counties
Chapter** *Area Served: Whiteside and Lee Counties*
Improve the health and well being of all people with
diabetes and their families. *Meetings*: Twice monthly for
family and friends. *Services*: Mutual aid, educational
program or material, advocacy, fundraising. *Write*: 100 E
Lefevre Rd, Sterling, IL 61081 *Call*: 815/625-0400 4415

**American Diabetes Assn North IL Affiliate, Inc** *Area
Served: IL-N* Mutual aid and support for individuals with
diabetes. Also, groups for family members and spouses,
and parents of children with diabetes. Emotional support
to deal with feelings related to the disease and promote
coping. No formal education about diabetes. *Meetings*:
Monthly for those with diabetes or family members at
various community locations. *Services*: Mutual aid,
educational program or material, written information.
*Write*: 6 N Michigan Ave, Ste 1202, Chicago, IL 60602
*Call*: 800/433-4966

**Community Diabetic Series** *Area Served: Kankakee,
Iroquois and Will Counties  Write*: Riverside Medical
Center, 350 N Wall St., Kankakee, IL 60901
*Call*: 815/935-3276

**Community Diabetic Series Riverside Medical Center**
*Area Served: Kankakee, Iroquois and Will Counties*
Support group for patient education, advocacy, and
awareness. *Services*: Mutual aid, advocacy. *Write*: 350 N
Wall St, Kankakee, IL 60901 *Call*: 815/936-6515

**Diabetes Adult Support Group** *Area Served: Cook-S
and Will Counties  Write*: South Suburban Hospital,
17800 S Kedzie Ave, Hazel Crest, IL 60429
*Call*: 708/799-8000 3481

**Diabetes Parents of Youths Support Group** *Area
Served: Cook-S and Will Counties  Write*: South Suburban
Hospital, 17800 S Kedzie Ave, Hazel Crest, IL 60429
*Call*: 708/799-8000 3481

**Diabetes Support and Education Group** *Area Served:
Cook and Will Counties  Write*: St James Hospital, 1423
Chicago Rd, Chicago Heights, IL 60411
*Call*: 708/709-2010  *Fax*: 708/709-2053

**Diabetes Support Group** *Area Served: Cook and
DuPage County  Write*: Gottlieb Memorial Hospital,
701 W North Ave, Melrose Park, IL 60160
*Call*: 708/681-3200 2410  *Fax*: 708/681-5412

**Diabetes Support Group** *Area Served: Madison and
Jersey Counties  Write*: Alton Memorial Hospital,
1 Memorial Dr, Alton, IL 62002 *Call*: 618/463-7526

**Diabetes Support Group** *Area Served: Henry County
Write*: Henry County Kewanee Hospital, Kewanee, IL
61443 *Call*: 309/853-3361 283

**Diabetes Support Group** *Area Served: DeWitt  Write*:
Dr John Warner Hospital, 422 W White, Clinton, IL
61727 *Call*: 217/935-9571 9570

**Diabetes Support Group** *Area Served: Henry County
Write*: Henry County Kewanee Hospital, Kewanee, IL
61443 *Call*: 309/853-3361 283

**Diabetes Support Group** *Area Served: Jackson County
Write*: PO Box 10000, Carbondale, IL 62902
*Call*: 618/549-0721 5167

**Diabetes Support Group Highland Park Hospital** *Area
Served: Cook, Lake and McHenry Counties* Developed to
continue the patient's education on diabetes management.
Educational offerings include a physician lecture monthly
on such topics as diabetes and heart disease, insulin pump
therapy, diabetes and neuropathy. Following lectures, the
group interacts with facilitators. *Meetings*: Monthly for all
interested. *Services*: Mutual aid, educational program or
material, telephone support, written information.
*Write*: 718 Glenview, Highland Park, IL 60035
*Call*: 847/432-8000 4327

**Diabetes Support Group Iroquois Memorial Hospital
and Resident Home** *Area Served: Iroquois County*
*Write*: 200 Fairman, Watseka, IL 60970
*Call*: 815/432-5841 4320

**Diabetes Support Group Lake Grange Memorial
Hospital** *Area Served: Cook County  Write*: 5105 Willow
Springs Rd, LaGrange, IL 60525 *Call*: 708/354-1200 4784

**Diabetes Support Group McDonough District Hospital
Center for Wellness** *Area Served: McDonough County*
*Write*: 525 E Grant St., Macomb, IL 61455
*Call*: 309/833-4101 3483

**Diabetes Support Group Palos Community Hospital
Social Services Dept** *Area Served: Cook County*
*Write*: 12251 S 80th Ave, Palos Heights, IL 60463
*Call*: 708/361-4500 5054  *Fax*: 708/923-4849

**Diabetes Support Group St. Francis Hospital of Evanston** *Area Served: Cook and Lake Counties* Self-help group with open discussion format allowing members to share concerns, knowledge, and learning experiences regarding their adjustment to diabetes and diabetes maintenance. *Meetings*: Monthly. *Services*: Mutual aid. *Write*: 355 Ridge Ave, Evanston, IL 60202 *Call*: 847/492-7337

**Diabetes Support Group St Joseph's Hospital of Highland** *Area Served: Madison County Write*: 1515 Main St, Highland, IL 62249 *Call*: 618/654-7421 2396

**Diabetes Support Groups Silver Cross Hospital** *Area Served: Will County Write*: New Lenox Medical Center, 250 E Maple St, New Lenox, IL 60451 *Call*: 815/740-1100 7629

**Diabetes Support Groups/Supper Club** *Area Served: McLean, Livingston and Logan Counties Write*: Bromenn Healthcare, Bloomington-Normal, IL 61702 *Call*: 309/888-0952

**Diabetic Club MacNeal Memorial Hospital** *Area Served: Cook-W* Provide information and support to those in the surrounding areas who have diabetes or an interest in diabetes; subject matter is different each month. *Meetings*: Monthly. *Services*: Mutual aid, educational program or material. *Write*: 3249 S Oak Park Ave, Berwyn, IL 60402 *Call*: 708/795-9100 3511

**Diabetic Education Support Group Covenant Medical Center** *Area Served: Champaign County* Designed to educate diabetics and the general public about diabetes. Provide current knowledge about diabetes and furnish support to the members. *Services*: Mutual aid, educational program or material. *Write*: Urbana Campus, 1400 W Park St, Urbana, IL 61801 *Call*: 217/337-2381

**Diabetic Support and Education Group Condell Medical Center** *Area Served: Lake County Write*: Allen Conference Center, 900 Garfield Ave, Libertyville, IL 60048 *Call*: 847/362-2905 5122 *Fax*: 708/362-5529

**Diabetic Support Group Christ Hospital Ophthalmology Dept** *Area Served: Cook County* This group was established to help diabetics manage their diabetes while feeling better about themselves. We discuss topics that range from glucose monitoring to holiday dinner planning. Our meetings are open to anyone interested. *Meetings*: Monthly. *Services*: Mutual aid, educational program or material, written information, speakers bureau, referral to other services. *Write*: 4440 W 95th St, Oak Lawn, IL 60453 *Call*: 708/346-5903

**Diabetic Support Group Christ Hospital and Medical Center** *Area Served: Chicago-SW Write*: 4440 W 95th St, Oak Lawn, IL 60453 *Call*: 708/346-5432

**Diabetic Support Group-Gibson City** *Area Served: Ford and McLean Counties Write*: 1120 N Melvin, Gibson City, IL 60936 *Call*: 217/784-4251

**Diabetic Support Group Johnston R Bowman Center for The Elderly** *Area Served: Cook County Write*: 710 S Paulina St, Chicago, IL 60612 *Call*: 312/942-7010 *Fax*: 312/942-2323

**Highland Park Hospital Diabetes Support Group Highland Park Hospital** Provide physician lectures on diabetes self management and facilitators, RN and RD, available for questions and support at coffee hour following lecture. *Services*: Support, lectures, and handouts. *Meetings*: 3rd Tuesday evening from 7:30-9:30 pm of each month, meeting rooms II HPH. (No meetings in August or January.) *Write*: 718 Glenview Ave, Highland Park, IL 60035 *Call*: 847/432-8000 5032 *Fax*: 847/480-3944

**Joslin Center for Diabetes MacNeal Medical Center** *Area Served: Cook County Write*: 7020 W 79th St, Bridgeview, IL 60455 *Call*: 708/430-0730 *Fax*: 708/430-7379

**Juvenile Diabetes Foundation Greater Chicago Chapter** *Area Served: Cook County Write*: 70 W Hubbard St, Chicago, IL 60610 *Call*: 312/670-0313

**Parents of Diabetic Children** *Area Served: Cook-S Write*: Palos Community Hospital, 80th Ave and McCarthy Rd, Palos Heights, IL 60463 *Call*: 708/361-4500

**Quad Cities Diabetes Assn** *Area Served: Rock Island County* Support persons with diabetes, to share with medical professionals, and to provide education and information. *Meetings*: Twice a month for all interested. *Services*: Mutual aid, educational program or material, written information, newsletter. *Write*: 1001 16th St, Rm 204, Moline, IL 61265 *Call*: 309/762-0357

**Viviendo Con Diabetes Saint Therese Medical Center** *Area Served: Lake and McHenry Counties Write*: Home Health Dept, 2615 Washington St, Waukegan, IL 60085 *Call*: 847/249-5897

# Digestive Disease

**Kids Connection Pediatric Outpatient Subspecialty Clinic** *Area Served: Cook County Write*: 1255 N Milwaukee Ave, Glenview, IL 60027 *Call*: 847/318-2903

# Disability

## Disability-General

**A-SCIP Persons with Disabilities Support Group** *Area Served: Cook-W* Offer group support and education to persons with a disability. Sponsored by Maine Township government. *Meetings*: Monthly. *Services*: Mutual aid, educational program or material. *Write*: Maine Township Town Hall, 1700 Ballard Rd, Park Ridge, IL 60068 *Call*: 847/297-2510  *Fax*: 847/297-1335

**Able Data Information System Springfield Center for Independent Living** *Area Served: IL Write*: 426 W Jefferson, Springfield, IL 62702 *Call*: 800/447-4221

**Council for Disability Rights** *Area Served: IL* The mission of CDR is to provide individuals with disabilities, their families, and the general public with information (and other forms of support) on the rights of people with disabilities and how to implement those rights. *Services*: Educational program or material written information, advocacy, newsletter. *Write*: 176 W Adams, Ste 1830, Chicago, IL 60603 *Call*: 312/444-9484

**Equip for Equality, Inc** *Area Served: Rock Island County Write*: PO Box 3753, Rock Island, IL 61204 *Call*: 800/758-6869

**Equip for Equality Inc  Jackson County** *Area Served: Jackson County Write*: 103 S Washington, Ste 202, Carbondale, IL 62901 *Call*: 618/457-3304

**Health Resource Center for Women with Disabilities Rehab Institute of Chicago** *Area Served: National Write*: 345 E Superior, Chicago, IL 60611 *Call*: 312/908-7997

**Les-Bi-Gay People with Disabilities Social Support Group/Fox River Valley** *Area Served: Kankakee and Kendall Counties Write*: Center for Independent Living, 730 W Chicago Ave, Elgin, IL 60123 *Call*: 847/695-5818

**Protection and Advocacy Inc Sangamon County** *Area Served: Sangamon County Write*: 427 E Monroe, Ste 302, PO Box 276, Springfield, IL 62705 *Call*: 217/544-0464

**Protection and Advocacy, Inc** *Area Served: IL* Advocates legal and human rights of persons with disabilities. Specific services include: information and referral, legal advice and representation in negotiations, administrative hearings in court if necessary. *Meetings*: As needed for all interested. *Services*: Mutual aid, educational program or material, advocacy, referral to other services, written information. *Write*: 11 E Adams, Ste 1200, Chicago, IL 60603 *Call*: 800/537-2632

**Schaumburg Township Disabled Services Office Schaumburg Township, Disabled Services** *Area Served: Cook-NW* Provide support groups for: mobility limited, visually impaired, diabetics, and counseling. Provide information and referral, newsletter, ITAC TTY distribution and repair, and transportation. *Meetings*: Call for scheduling and to get on mailing list. Deaf services coordinator: TTY 847/884-1560. *Write*: 1 IL Blvd, Hoffman Estates, IL 60194 *Call*: 847/884-0030 *Fax*: 847/884-0194

**Sertoma Centre, Inc** *Area Served: Cook and Will Counties* Provides programs and services to help persons with disabilities, maximize their independence, productivity and integration in the community. We offer job training and job placement services. Provide vocational evaluation, work adjustment and job training, supported employment, school transition, developmental training, and community and residential services and programs. *Meetings*: Mon-Fri, 8:30 am to 3:30 pm, provide transportation. *Write*: 4343 W 123$^{rd}$, Alsip, IL 60658 *Call*: 708/387-2542  *Fax*: 708/371-9747

**Speaking for Ourselves** *Area Served: National* Act as an advocacy group for people with developmental disabilities. Members help each other resolve problems, gain self-confidence, learn leadership skills. No known IL groups. *Services*: Mutual aid, educational program or material, advocacy, written information. *Write*: 1 Plymouth Meeting, Ste 430, Plymouth Meeting, PA 19462 *Call*: 610/825-4592

**Special Directions** *Area Served: Cook-W* Encourages fraternization and exchange of ideas regarding the growth, development and education of special needs children. The org. offers support through member rap sessions, guest speakers, telephone inquiries, social activities and quarterly newsletters. *Meetings*: Monthly for all interested. *Services*: Mutual aid, educational program or material, advocacy, telephone support, social activities, newsletter. *Write*: 6413 W 102$^{nd}$ Pl, Chicago Ridge, IL 60415 *Call*: 708/848-5326

**Special People, Inc Human Resources-City Hall** Helps people with disabilities in solving related problems and provide information and referral, community education on disability issues, co-sponsor disabled job fair, quarterly newsletter, sign language classes and social events. *Meetings*: 3$^{rd}$ Thursday of every month, interpreter present, accessible, call for specific times. *Write*: 1420 Miner St, Des Plaines, IL 60016 *Call*: 847/827-1893

**Springfield Center for Independent Living** *Area Served: Sangamon County* Disability research network program. An information and referral service for disability topics. Use computer listings and our own library files to provide the most accurate information. Obtain info about: agencies, education, employment, adaptive equipment, funding and financial resources, law, personal care, recreation/travel, standards, statistics, surveys, disabilities, conditions, diseases, syndromes. *Meetings*: None, we are a resource. *Write*: 426 W Jefferson St, Springfield, IL 62702 *Call*: 847/447-4221 *Fax*: 217/523-0427 *Email*: CHAASIS@PRAIRIENET.ORG

**Suburban Service League for The Disabled**
*Area Served: Cook, DuPage and Lake Counties*
*Write*: PO Box 8760, Rolling Meadows, IL 60008
*Call*: 847/991-7945

**Vent Developmental Services Center** *Area Served: Champaign County Write*: 1304 W Bradley, Champaign, IL 61821 *Call*: 217/356-9176

**Workers Support Group Kreider Services, Inc**
*Area Served: Lee County Write*: 500 Anchor Rd, PO Box 366, Dixon, IL 61021 *Call*: 815/288-6691

# Disability-Autism

**Autism Society of IL Northeastern IL Chapter**
*Area Served: Lake County and McHenry Counties*
*Write*: Box 6779 RFD, Long Grove, IL 60047
*Call*: 847/949-8721

**Autism and Related Disorders Support Group Passavant Area Hospital** *Area Served: Morgan County*
*Write*: 1600 W Walnut, Jacksonville, IL 62650
*Call*: 217/245-9541 3594

**Autism Society of IL Chicago/South Suburban Chapter** *Area Served: Cook-S, Will Counties* Support and further education and understanding of autism. *Meetings*: Monthly. *Services*: Mutual aid, educational program or material. *Write*: 414 Watseka St, Park Forest, IL 60466 *Call*: 708/747-0694

**Autism Society of IL Autism Society of The Quad Cities** *Area Served: Iowa* Provides parent support, information and referral, public awareness and advocacy about autism. *Meetings*: Monthly. *Services*: Mutual aid, educational program or material, written information, advocacy, referral to other services, speakers bureau, referral to other services, hotline, telephone support, social activities, newsletter. *Write*: PO Box 472, Bettendorf, IA 52722 *Call*: 309/762-3995

**Autism Society of IL Peoria Chapter** *Area Served: Peoria, Woodford and Tazewell Counties* Dedicated to the education, welfare, rights, and cure of people developmentally disabled by severe disorders of communication and behavior. Provides legal advocacy, support groups, helps those affected by autism meet their own and family needs. *Meetings*: Bimonthly for all interested. *Services*: Mutual aid, educational program or material, advocacy, telephone support, newsletter, written

information. *Write*: 502 Sunset, Eureka, IL 61530 *Call*: 309/467-4050

**Autism Society of IL Northwest Suburban IL Chapter**
*Area Served: Cook and DuPage Counties Meetings*:
Monthly. *Services*: Mutual aid. *Write*: 254 Brookhaven Dr, Elk Grove Village, IL 60007 *Call*: 708/364-4743

**IL Center for Autism** *Area Served: IL Write*: 548 S Ruby Ln, Fairview Heights, IL 62208 *Call*: 618/398-7500

**Parents of Children with Persuasive Developmental Disorders (PDD)/Autism/Jayne Shover Easter Seal** *Area Served: Kane County Write*: Rehab Center, 799 S McLean Blvd. PO Box 883, Elgin, IL 60121 *Call*: 847/742-3264 123

# Disability-Children

**Birth-To-Three Livingston County Salem Children's Home** *Area Served: Livingston County Services*: Mutual aid. *Write*: RR1 Box 64, Flanagan, IL 61740 *Call*: 815/796-4561

**Core Champaign County Developmental Services Center** *Area Served: Champaign County Write*: 1304 W Bradley, Champaign, IL 61821 *Call*: 217/356-9176

**County Parent Infant Education Program Chicago Board of Education Program** *Area Served: Chicago* *Write*: Skinner School, 111 S Throop St, Chicago, IL 60607 *Call*: 773/534-7863

**Early Childhood Research and Intervention Programs** *Area Served: Chicago Write*: 1640 W Roosevelt Rd, Chicago, IL 60608 *Call*: 312/413-1567

**Fathers Group Winnebago County Children's Developmental Center** *Area Served: Winnebago, Boone and Ogle Counties* Our group focuses on the unique perspective that fathers have in responding to the need and care of the special needs child. *Meetings*: Twice monthly and open to all interested fathers. *Services*: Mutual aid, educational program or material, referral to other services, telephone support, social activities. *Write*: 650 N Main St., Rockford, IL 61103 *Call*: 815/965-6745

**Keshet Jewish Parents of Children with Special Needs** *Area Served: Cook-N Write*: 3210 Dundee Rd, Northbrook, IL 60062 *Call*: 847/205-0274

**Lekotek Center National Center** *Area Served: National* Provides play libraries and resources for families with children with developmental disabilities. Offers play counseling, education, toys, information and social activities. *Write*: 2100 Ridge Ave, Evanston, IL 61201 *Call*: 847/328-0001

**Lekotek Center Peoria County Easter Seal Rehab Center** *Area Served: Peoria County Write*: 320 E Armstrong Ave, Peoria, IL 61603 *Call*: 309/672-6330

**Lekotek Center Sangamon County UCP Land of Lincoln** *Area Served: Sangamon, Montgomery and Christian Counties Write*: 130 N 16th St, Springfield, IL 62701 *Call*: 217/525-6522

**Lekotek Center West Suburban Special Recreation Assn** *Area Served: Regional* Search for LEKOTEK *Write*: 2915 Maple St, Franklin Park, IL 60131 *Call*: 708/455-2100 *Fax*: 708/455-2157

**Lekotek Center Winnebago County Early Education Center** *Area Served: Winnebago County Write*: 512 S Fairview, Rockford, IL 61108 *Call*: 815/229-4230

**National Lekotek Center** *Area Served: National* Provides direct services, support and information to children with special needs and their families in resource and play centers that can be found worldwide. NLC is a non-profit org. with a network of 46 centers housing family play facilities and toy lending libraries, 18 compuplay sites (computer resource centers), help lines, workshops, and family literacy programs. *Meetings*: Contact your local sites for dates and times. *Write*: 2100 Ridge Ave, Evanston, IL 60201-2796 *Call*: 800/366-7529 *Fax*: 847/328-5514 *Email*: lekok@interaccess.com

**Parents Helping Parents-Special Winnebago County Rockford Memorial Hospital** *Area Served: Northern. IL Write*: 2400 N Rockton Ave, Rockford, IL 61103 *Call*: 815/969-5186

**Pilot Parents Program GOARC** *Write*: 3610 Dodge St, Omaha, NE 61831 *Call*: 402/346-5220

**William M Bedell Achievement and Resource Center Madison County** *Area Served: Madison County* Offers support groups for parents of developmentally disabled children, as well as complete services for children ages birth to 21 and case management for developmentally disabled adults. *Meetings*: Monthly. *Services*: Mutual aid, educational program or material, written information, referral to other services, advocacy. *Write*: 400 S Main St, Wood River, IL 62095 *Call*: 618/251-2175

## Disability-Children Recreation

**West Suburban Special Recreation Assn** Provide fun for children and respite for parents through after-school and Saturday therapeutic recreation programs. *Services*: Away and day camps every summer; swim lessons, athletics, drama, nature, art, music and scout activities. *Meetings*: Usually once a week with close supervision by trained staff. Call for specific dates and times. *Write*: 2915 Maple St, Franklin Park, IL 60131 *Call*: 847/455-2100 *Fax*: 847/455-2157

## Disability-Family

**Disabilities Access Network DeKalb County Family Service Agency** *Area Served: DeKalb County Write*: 14 Health Services Dr, DeKalb, IL 60015 *Call*: 815/758-8616

**Early Intervention Parent Support Groups Winnebago County Children's Development Center** *Area Served: Winnebago, Boone and Ogle Counties Write*: 650 N Main St, Rockford, IL 61103 *Call*: 815/965-6745 146

**Family Resource Center on Disabilities** *Area Served: National, Cook, DuPage and Lake Counties* Coalition of parents and professionals working to improve services for disabled children. Among free services offered are assistance in organizing parent groups; information/referral/linkage services; training on special education rights, advocacy, assertiveness, organizing; awareness activities. *Services*: Mutual aid, educational program or material, advocacy, telephone support, newsletter, written information, professional service. *Write*: 20 E Jackson, 9th Fl, Chicago, IL 60604 *Call*: 312/939-3513 *Fax*: 312/939-7297

**Mothers United for Moral Support Inc (MUMS)** *Area Served: National Write*: 150 Custer Ct, Green Bay, WI 54301 *Call*: 414/336-5333

**Parent Support Group 5010 St Charles Rd** *Area Served: Cook-W Write*: Bellwood, IL 60104 *Call*: 708/547-3557

**Parent Support Group Jayne Shover Easter Seal Rehab Center** *Area Served: Kane County Write*: 799 S McLean Blvd, PO Box 883, Elgin, IL 60121 *Call*: 847/742-3264 123

**Parent to Parent Champaign County Developmental Services Center** *Area Served: Champaign and Ford Counties Write*: 1304 W Bradley, Champaign, IL 61821 *Call*: 217/359-0287

**Parents Helping Parents** *Area Served: National* Resource center for families who have children with special needs. It covers any and all handicapping conditions; supports and provides information and training to help families cope with having a special child. Also provides education and training for professionals on breaking the news, resources, and communicating with special needs families. Offers program for siblings and single parents. *Services*: Mutual aid, educational program or material, telephone support, home or hospital visitation, social activities, newsletter, written information. *Write*: 535 Race St, Ste 140, San Jose, CA 95126 *Call*: 408/288-5010

**Patient-Family Education Classes** *Area Served: Cook County Write*: Alexian Brothers Medical Center, 800 W Biesterfield Rd, Elk Grove Village, IL 60007 *Call*: 708/437-5500 4684

**Pediatric Family Forum Rock Island County Mercy Hospital** *Area Served: Rock Island County Write*: 1401 W Central Park, Davenport, IA 52804 *Call*: 319/383-1255

**Sibling Information Network The A.J. Pappanikou Center** *Area Served: National* Provides information relative to siblings who have a brother/sister with a developmental disability. Provides a quarterly newsletter, bibliographies and a listing of sibling groups. *Services*: Mutual aid, newsletter, referral to other agencies. *Write*: 62 Washington St, Middletown, CT 06457 *Call*: 203/344-7500 *Fax*: 203/344-7595

**Single Parents of Children with Special Needs Jayne Shover Easter Seal Rehab Center** *Area Served: Kane County Write*: 799 S McLean Blvd, PO Box 883, Elgin, IL 60121 *Call*: 847/742-3264 123

**Support Kenneth Young Center** *Area Served: Cook and DuPage Counties* Provides support to parents who have handicapped children. *Meetings*: Weekly. Mutual aid. *Write*: 1001 Rohlwing Rd, Elk Grove Village, IL 60007 *Call*: 708/364-4743

## Disability-Learning

**Attention Deficit Parent Support Group St Mary's Hospital** *Write*: 1800 E Lake Shore Dr, Decatur, IL 62521 *Call*: 217/422-1903

**Attention Disorders Assn of Parents-Professionals** *Area Served: Cook, Will and DuPage Counties* Provide a support group for parents who have children with attention disorders, provide information on attention disorders to families, professionals and the public, and protect the best interest of persons with ADD through public awareness and lobbying efforts. *Meetings*: Monthly. *Services*: Mutual aid, educational program or material, written information, referral to other services, speakers bureau, social activities, newsletter. *Write*: ADAPPT, PO Box 293, Oak Forest, IL 60452 *Call*: 708/361-3387

**Children and Adult with Attention Deficit Disorder North Suburban CHADD** *Area Served: Chicago, Cook and LaSalle Counties* Search concern 'attention deficit' and IL. *Write*: PO Box 99, Winnetka, IL 60093 *Call*: 847/501-5662

**Children and Adults with Attention Deficit Disorders National Org** *Area Served: National* Provides family support and advocacy, public and professional education and encouragement of research. CHADD provides monthly meetings, newsletter, information. *Write*: 499 NW 70th Ave, Plantation, FL 33317 *Call*: 305/587-3700

**Children and Adults with Attention Deficit Disorder Parents of Attention Deficit Disorder Children** *Area Served: Winnebago County* Support and education for parents; educate school system and make them aware of availability of groups; change legislation so that these children are covered by the school system. *Services*: Mutual aid, educational program or material, advocacy, written information, referral to other services, telephone support, social activities, newsletter. *Write*: 972 N Main St, Rockford, IL 61103-7061 *Call*: 815/963-5095

**Children and Adults with Attention Deficit Disorder Kendall County** *Area Served: Kendall County Write*: 220 N Sleight St, Naperville, IL 60540 *Call*: 630/357-4791

**Children and Adults with Attention Deficit Disorder Lake County Chapter** *Area Served: Lake County* Search concern 'attention deficit' and IL *Write*: 516 Beck Rd, Lindenhurst, IL 60046 *Call*: 708/356-6286

**Children and Adults with Attention Deficit Disorder** Search for concern 'attention deficit' and IL *Write*:114 Delta Dr, Poplar Grove, IL *Call*: 815/765-3593

**Children and Adults with Attention Deficit Disorder CHADD** *Area Served: IL* Through family support and advocacy, public and professional education and encouragement of research. CHADD works to ensure that those with attention deficit disorder reach their interest potential. *Meetings*: Once or twice a month for family,teachers and interested others. *Services*: Mutual aid, educational program or material, written information, advocacy, newsletter, telephone support.

**Children and Adults with Attention Deficit Disorder Kendall Co Special Ed Co-Op** *Area Served: Kendall County Write*: 507 Hatcher Dr, Yorkville, IL 60560 *Call*: 630/553-5833

**Children with Attention Deficit Disorder** *Area Served: Central IL* Through family support and advocacy, public and professional education and encouragement of research, CHADD works to ensure that those with attention deficit disorder reach their inherent potential. *Meetings*: Monthly, open to family, teachers and others interested in the concern. *Services*: Mutual aid, educational program or material. *Write*: 208 S 6th St, Box 375, Riverton, IL 62561 *Call*: 217/498-7833

**Feingold Assn of The US (FAUS)** *Area Served: National* Non-profit volunteer org. of parents organized for the treatment of hyperactivity, ADD, and food sensitivity through the use of diet management (without drugs). *Meetings*: For child and family. *Services*: Mutual aid, educational program or material, referral to other services, telephone support, social activities, newsletter, written information. *Write*: PO Box 6550, Alexandria, VA 22306 *Call*: 800/312-3287

**Learning Disabilities Assn of IL** *Area Served: Champaign County Write*: 1009 W Daniel, Champaign, IL 61820 *Call*: 217/356-1921

**Learning Disabilities Assn of IL Chicago Assn for Children with Learning Disabilities** *Area Served: Chicago-N* Promote awareness and understanding of learning disabilities. Inform teachers and professionals of this parent group and to provide information and educational materials. *Meetings*: For all interested. *Services*: Mutual aid, educational program or material, written information. *Write*: ACLD North, PO Box 59433, Chicago, IL 60659 *Call*: 773/338-5441 *Fax*: 312/744-5544

**Learning Disabilities Assn of IL South Suburban Help** *Area Served: Cook-S and Will Counties Write*: PO Box 663, Park Forest, IL 60466 *Call*: 708/747-2632 Answer Mach. *Fax*: 708/672-7516

**Learning Disabilities Assn of IL** *Area Served: IL* Non-profit org. dedicated to the advancement of the education and general welfare of children and youth of normal or potentially normal intelligence who have learning disabilities of a perceptual, conceptual or coordinative nature or related problems. *Meetings*: Monthly for those interested. *Services*: Mutual aid, educational program or material, written information, telephone support, advocacy, newsletter. *Write*: 10101 S Roberts Rd, Ste 205, Palos Hills, IL 60465 *Call*: 708/430-7592 *Fax*: 708/430-7592

**Learning Disabilities Assn of IL United Chapter** *Area Served: McHenry, Cook & Lake Counties Write*: PO Box 9414, Crystal Lake, IL 60014 *Call*: 815/455-2817 am.

**Learning Disabilities Assn of IL Lake County** *Area Served: Lake County Write*: PO Box 595, Waukegan, IL 60079 *Call*: 847/249-0886

**Learning Disabilities Assn of IL Council on Understanding Learning Disabilities** *Area Served: Cook-NW* COULD is dedicated to the advancement of the educational and general welfare of children and adults with learning disabilities. Speaker as well as parent support meetings. *Meetings*: Monthly for anyone interested. *Services*: Mutual aid, written information, telephone support, referral to other services, newsletter. *Write*: PO Box 704, Arlington Heights, IL 60006 *Call*: 847/255-5428

**Parent Support Group St Elizabeth Medical Center** *Area Served: St Clair and Madison Counties Write*: 2100 Madison Ave, Granite City, IL 62040 *Call*: 618/288-5500

**Time Out to Enjoy, Inc** *Area Served: Cook-N Write*: Council For Disability Rights, 176 W Adams, Ste 1830, Chicago, IL 60603 *Call*: 312/444-9484 *Fax*: 312/444-1977

# Disability-Physical

**Accent on Information Cheever Publishing Inc** *Area Served: McLean County* Provides information about assistive devices and coping with a physical disability. *Write*: Gillum Rd and High Dr, PO Box 700, Bloomington, IL 61702 *Call*: 309/378-2961

**Access Living Independent Living Center** *Area Served: Chicago* Provides creative alternatives to the housing crisis of people with disabilities. Provides a peer support program. Public education and systemic advocacy on the rights of the disabled, peer counseling on independent living skills training for disabled, etc. *Meetings*: To be announced, call for dates and times. Sign language interpreter, TTY: 312-226-1687. *Write*: 310 S Peoria, Ste 201, Chicago, IL 60607 *Call*: 312/226-5900 *Fax*: 312/226-2030

**Center for Independent Living Fox River Valley Center** *Area Served: Kane, McHenry and Kendall Counties* Consumer-controlled, community-based, private, non-for-profit organization. committed to the independent living, movement and empowerment of persons with disabilities and equal access in society. *Services*: Mutual aid, speakers bureau, written information, social activities, professional service, referral to other services, educational program or material, referral to other services, advocacy, newsletter. *Write*: 730B W Chicago St, Elgin, IL 60123 *Call*: 847/695-5818 *Fax*: 847/695-5892

**Center for Independent Living Access Living of Metropolitan Chicago** *Area Served: Chicago* Helps disabled people reach their maximum potential for living independently in the community. Services include personal care assistant training, disability rights counsel, peer counseling program, domestic violence counseling and referral, and deaf services program. Battered women's support group meets as needed. *Services*: Mutual aid, educational program or material, advocacy, telephone support, newsletter, written information, referral to other services, professional service. *Write*: 310 S Peoria, Ste 201, Chicago, IL 60607 *Call*: 312/226-5900 TTY 312/226-1687 656 *Fax*: 312/226-2030

**Coalition for Disabled Musicians, Inc** Using individual adaptive techniques, CDM Inc gives physically challenged musicians the opportunity to develop skills, join performing groups and entertain and inspire all audiences. No IL groups. *Services*: Mutual aid. *Write*: PO Box 1002M, Bay Shore, NY 11706 *Call*: 516/586-0366

**Easter Seal Handicapables Club-Rehab Center** Support group for physically disabled adults. Members participate in social, educational and recreational activities. Family members are also invited to participate. Club members help each other out through their sharing of similar experiences. *Meetings*: Monthly for patient and family. *Services*: Mutual aid, educational program or material, telephone support, social activities, newsletter, written information. *Write*: 1230 N Highland Ave, Aurora, IL 60506 *Call*: 630/896-1961

**Easter Seal Society** Provides a wide range of services and therapies for disabled people including amputees, developmentally disabled, laryngectomy, and post-polio. Offers parent education, referral and self-help groups. Special accessibility for mobility impaired.

**Friendship Handicapped Club Christ Hospital**
*Area Served: Cook-SW* Education and support for the physically handicapped in their daily lives with a variety of activities. *Meetings*: Monthly for anyone over 18 with handicaps and their families. *Services*: Mutual aid, educational program or material, advocacy, social activities, written information. *Write*: 4440 W 95th St, Oak Lawn, IL 60453 *Call*: 708/346-5264

**Gazette International Networking Institute**
*Area Served: National* Encourages community-based orgs dedicated to education on disability issues and works to improve health care delivery and brings together concerned persons to address issues confronting the disabled. Promotes self-help groups, provides education, information, and referral. Publications, including a newsletter. *Write*: 4207 Lindell Blvd, #110, St Louis, MO 63108-2915 *Call*: 314/534-0475 *Email*: GINI_INTL@MSN.COM

**Helping Hands of Bloom Township** *Area Served: Cook-S* Assists residents with disabilities in advocacy, housing, recreational activities, and educational issues. *Meetings*: Monthly for anyone who shares the concern. *Services*: Mutual aid, educational program or material, written information, advocacy, referral to other services, speakers bureau, referral to other services, telephone support, social activities, newsletter. *Write*: 425 S Halsted, Chicago Heights, IL 60411 *Call*: 708/754-9400 TDD

**Independent Friends Alumni Club Michael Reese Hospital** *Area Served: Cook County* For those who have experienced a physical disability. Our mission is mutual support for common challenges, thru educational and social activities. *Meetings*: Bi-monthly. *Services*: Mutual aid, educational program or material, social activities. *Write*: 31st St at Lake Shore Dr, Chicago, IL 60616 *Call*: 312/791-2321

**Leaning Tower Y Conquerors** *Area Served: IL-N* The Conquerors' program provides recreational, therapeutic physical activities and swimming for handicapped persons of all ages. social events for conquerors and their families also provided. *Services*: Mutual aid, social activities. *Write*: 6300 W Touhy Ave, Niles, IL 60714 *Call*: 847/647-8222

**Life Center for Independent Living McLean County**
*Area Served: McLean, Ford, DeWitt and Logan Counties*

*Write*: 1328 E Empire, Bloomington, IL 61701 *Call*: 309/663-5433

**Life Goes On St Elizabeth's Hospital** *Area Served: St Clair and Madison Counties M* *Write*: 211 S 3rd St, Belleville, IL 62222-0694 *Call*: 618/234-2120 1519

**LINC Center for Independent Living** *Area Served: St Clair County* *Write*: 10 E Washington, Ste 101, Belleville, IL 62220 *Call*: 618/235-9988

**Macoupin County Assn for Retardation Macoupin County** *Area Served: Macoupin County* *Write*: 700 E Elm, PO Box 596, Carlinville, IL 62626 *Call*: 217/854-4060

**Maine-Niles Assn of Special Recreation** *Area Served: Cook-N County* Provides a wide variety of social/ therapeutic recreation for all types of handicapped, children, teens and adults. We teach skills for constructive use of leisure time including appropriate social behaviors, community awareness. We also teach swimming and many other sports for the disabled individual. *Meetings*: An 8-week schedule for all interested. Educational program or material advocacy, telephone support, home or hospital visitation, social activities, newsletter, social activities. *Write*: 8950 Grosse Point Rd, Skokie, IL 60077 *Call*: 847/966-5522

**Malcolm Eaton Enterprise Stephenson County** *Area Served: Stephenson County* *Write*: 570 W Lamm Rd, Freeport, IL 61032 *Call*: 815/235-7181

**National Shut-In Society Wings** *Area Served: Chicago* To see that physically handicapped and elderly have an opportunity to socialize. Volunteer drivers pick up members for meetings and bring them home. *Meetings*: Bi-monthly. Mutual aid, telephone support, social activities, newsletter *Write*: 2235 W Fletcher, Chicago, IL 60618 *Call*: 773/248-8283

**National Shut-In Society Wings** *Area Served: Chicago* To see that the physically handicapped and elderly have an opportunity to socialize. Volunteer drivers pick up members for meetings and bring them home. *Meetings*: Bi-monthly. *Services*: Mutual aid, telephone support, social activities, newsletter. *Write*: 300 S Damen, #1802, Chicago, IL 60612 *Call*: 773/248-8283

**New Year Coeds Evanston-North Shore YWCA** *Area Served: Cook County* Bring mentally handicapped adults together in a social club meeting, usually on Saturdays, for dances, theater, bowling, sporting events, trips to museums, fairs, etc. for women and men, ages 21 and up. Our chaperones are all non-professional volunteers. Our goal is to foster independence by giving our members necessary but light supervision. *Meetings*: Weekly. *Services*: Social activities. *Write*: 2143 Pioneer Rd, Evanston, IL 60201 *Call*: 847/475-8529

**Northwestern IL Center for Independent Living** *Area Served: Whiteside, Ogle and Carroll Counties* Peer support groups for epilepsy, head injury and general disability. *Meetings*: Monthly. *Services*: Mutual aid, professional service. *Write*: 229 1ˢᵗ Ave, Ste 2, Rock Falls, IL 61071 *Call*: 815/625-7860 *Fax*: 815/625-7876

**Options Center for Independent Living** *Area Served: Kankakee and Iroquois Counties* Assists persons with disabilities to become as independent as they desire through training of independent living skills. Advocacy of disability issues. Community awareness of disability issues. Offers two support groups: one for persons with any disability, one for hearing impaired. *Meetings*: Weekly/monthly. *Services*: Mutual aid, educational program or material, written information, advocacy, referral to other services, referral to other services, social activities, home or hospital visitation, newsletter. *Write*: 51 Meadowview Center, Kankakee, IL 60901 *Call*: 815/936-0100 4362

**PACE, Inc** *Area Served: Champaign and Vermilion Counties Write*: Sunnycrest Mall, 1717 Philo Rd, Urbana, IL 61801 *Call*: 217/344-5433

**PACT, Inc** *Area Served: Cook, DuPage and Lake Counties* Provides comprehensive guardianship, advisory and case advocacy as well as life care planning. As a not-for profit private agency, PACT can serve as guardian of person and/or estate or assist families being appointed guardian. Populations served are the developmentally disabled, mentally ill and elderly disabled. *Services*: Educational program or material advocacy, professional service. *Write*: 555 E Butterfield Rd, Ste 201, Lombard, IL 60148 *Call*: 630/960-9700

**Regional Access and Mobilization Project, Inc (RAMP)** *Area Served: Winnebago, Boone and DeKalb Counties* Community-based, non-profit, non-residential program controlled by and serving people with disabilities. Advocate for civil rights, benefits, community accessibility, housing and employment. Information and referral, peer counseling, skills training, support and mutual aid groups for people with disabilities. *Services*: Mutual aid, educational program or material, advocacy, written information, speakers bureau, social activities, telephone support, referral to other services, home or hospital visitation, newsletter. *Write*: 1040 N 2ⁿᵈ St, Rockford, IL 61107 *Call*: 815/968-7467 TDD

**Rehab Institute of Chicago Alexian Brothers Physical Rehab** *Area Served: Cook County Write*: Recreation Therapy, Elk Grove, IL 60007 *Call*: 847/437-5500 4844

**Second Chance Society-Marcy Barish, Centers Alexian Brothers Medical Center** Provides a social support group for all persons with physical disabilities and their families. Opportunities for social, recreational and educational activities for persons who have sustained a stroke, amputation or other physical impairments. Provides support and encouragement through group interaction and sharing, speakers, community involvement, and outings. *Meetings*: Monthly-at various times (call to get on mailing), handicapped accessible. *Write*: 955 Beisner Rd, Elk Grove Village, IL 60007 *Call*: 847/437-5500 4844 *Fax*: 847/981/6554

**Support Group SBLHC** *Area Served: Coles County Write*: 1000 Health Care Dr, Mattoon, IL 61938 *Call*: 217/258-2392

**Take Time for Fun! West Suburban Special Recreation Assn** *Area Served: Cook-W Write*: 2915 Maple St, Franklin Park, IL 60131 *Call*: 708/455-2100

**The Assn for People with Severe Handicaps Madison County Southern IL University** *Area Served: Madison County Write*: Box 1147, Edwardsville, IL 62026 *Call*: 618/692-3896

**The Innovators Holy Cross Hospital** *Area Served: Chicago* Provides information and opportunities to socialize and support one another. Presentations are primarily suggested and/or approved by the membership. Much interest is shown in options to improve function and information regarding better, more convenient ways to achieve needs. *Meetings*: Monthly for patients. *Services*: Mutual aid, educational program or material, advocacy, social activities, newsletter, written information. *Write*: 2701 W 68ᵗʰ St, Chicago, IL 60629 *Call*: 773/471-5652

**West Lake Community Hospital** *Area Served: Cook County Write*: 1111 Superior Prof Bldg, Melrose Park, IL 60160 *Call*: 708/681-3000 2421

**Western DuPage County Special Recreation Assn** *Area Served: DuPage-W* Provides recreational opportunities for children, teens and adults with special needs and abilities. *Meetings*: Weekly but restricted to persons sharing the concern. *Services*: Educational program or material written information, advocacy, referral to other services, professional service, speakers bureau, social activities. *Write*: 671 Crescent Blvd, Glen Ellyn, IL 60137 *Call*: 630/790-9370

## Disability-Services

**Easter Seal Adult and Child Rehab Center** *Area Served: McHenry and Boone Counties Write*: 708 Washington St, Woodstock, IL 60098 *Call*: 815/338-1707

**Easter Seal Jayne Shover Rehab Center, Inc** *Area Served: Cook-NW and Kane County Write*: 799 S McLean Blvd, Elgin, IL 60123 *Call*: 847/742-3264

**Easter Seal Rosalie Dold Center for Children** *Area Served: DuPage County* Outpatient therapy program. Physical, occupational and speech therapy. Audiology, day care, social work, technology resource. A variety of support groups offered through the social department. *Services*: Mutual aid, professional service. *Write*: 830 S Addison Rd, Villa Park, IL 60181 *Call*: 630/620-4433

**Easter Seal Society of Mid-Eastern IL, Inc**
*Area Served: Iroquois, Ford and Kankakee Counties*
*Write*: 895 S Washington Ave, Kankakee, IL 60901-5052
*Call*: 815/932-0623 *Fax*: 815/932-0623

**Easter Seal Society of Metro Chicago, Inc** *Area Served: Cook and Lake Counties* *Write*: 220 S State St, Ste 312, Chicago, IL 60604 *Call*: 312/939-5115

**Easter Seal Society Rehab Center** *Area Served: Will and Grundy Counties* Has a wide range of services and therapies for disabled people, including laryngectomy, stroke, amputees, post-polio, developmentally disabled children and physical disabilities of all kinds. Information and referral, parent education classes. *Services*: Mutual aid, educational program or material, written information, referral to other services. *Write*: 212 Barney Dr, Joliet, IL 60435 *Call*: 815/725-2194

**Evanston Special Recreation Civic Center** *Area Served: Cook-N County* Year-round program for youth and adults. Philosophy that through good leadership and supervision all handicapped people can develop life-long recreation skills. Also sponsors social clubs. Program services Evanston residents only. *Services*: Social activities.
*Write*: 2100 Ridge Ave, Evanston, IL 60204
*Call*: 847/866-2910 2499

**Handicapped Program New City YMCA** *Area Served: Chicago-N* We offer programs for disabled and senior citizens in aquatics. *Meetings* Weekly for all interested. *Services*: Social activities. *Write*: 1515 N Halsted, Chicago, IL 60622 *Call*: 312/266-1242

**Northeast DuPage County Special Recreation Assn NEDSRA** *Area Served: DuPage County* *Write*: 644 S Ardmore Ave, Addison, IL 60101 *Call*: 630/620-4500

**Northern Suburban Special Recreation Assn NSSRA** *Area Served: Cook-N, Lake County* NSSRA is a community-based therapeutic recreation program serving the leisure needs of disabled individuals of all ages and all disabilities. *Services*: Educational program or material home or hospital visitation, social activities. *Write*: 636 Ridge Rd, Highland Park, IL 60035 *Call*: 847/831-2450

**Resources for Retarded and Autistic Families** *Services*: Provides developmental training and in-home support services for adults with developmental disabilities. *Meetings*: Support services. *Write*: 590 S York, Unit B, Elmhurst, IL 60126-4466 *Call*: 630/279-2441 *Fax*: 630/279-2441

# Down Syndrome

**Central IL Down Syndrome Org. McLean County**
*Area Served: McLean County* Provide parent support and public awareness regarding all aspects of Down Syndrome. *Services*: Mutual aid, educational program or material. *Write*: PO Box 595, Normal, IL 61761 *Call*: 309/452-3264

**Down Development Council** *Area Served: IL* Non-profit org. open to parents of children with Down Syndrome, friends and professionals. Group activities include new parent counseling, information exchanges, advocacy and fund raising for research and self-help, as well as social activities for families. *Services*: Mutual aid, advocacy, referral to other services, social activities, written information, newsletter, telephone support, home or hospital visitation. *Write*: PO Box 118, Grays Lake, IL 60030 *Call*: 847/537-9297

**Down Syndrome Assn of Champaign County** *Area Served: Champaign, Piatt and Vermilion Counties* *Write*: PO Box 797, Mahomet, IL 61853 *Call*: 217/586-3166

**Down Syndrome Parent Support Group Rock Island County** *Area Served: Rock Island, Henry and Scott Counties* *Write*: 116 E 5th St, Coal Valley, IL 61240 *Call*: 309/799-8126

**Elgin Area Down Syndrome Parent Support Group Jayne Shover Easter Seal Rehab Center** *Area Served: Kane County* This group is educational, social and support oriented. The group is active in the Rehab Center's activities as well as NADS. They also participate in community education and have developed a packet about Down Syndrome which they send to doctors and hospitals in the area. *Meetings*: Monthly. *Services*: Mutual aid, telephone support, home or hospital visitation, social activities, written information. *Write*: 799 S McLean Blvd, Elgin, IL 60123 *Call*: 847/742-3264

**HOI Down Syndrome Support Group Peoria County** *Area Served: Central IL* *Write*: 320 E Armstrong, Peoria, IL 61603 *Call*: 309/672-6308

**Keeping Involved with Down Syndrome - KIDS Immanuel Lutheran Church** Provides a support group for parents of children with down syndrome. Families, friends and interested persons are also welcome. *Services*: Support, education and informational needs. Folders with information, personal experiences, and other parents phone numbers are available upon request. *Meetings*: 2nd Saturday of each month at 10:00 am in English. *Write*: Kennedy Dr and 16th Ave, East Moline, IL 61244 *Call*: 796-1609

**Mothers of Children with Down Syndrome Support Winnebago County Children's Development Center** *Area Served: Winnebago, Boone and Ogle Counties*

Self-help group for parents, family, or friends of a person with Down Syndrome. *Meetings*: Bi-monthly. *Services*: Mutual aid, educational program or material, referral to other services, telephone support, social activities, home or hospital visitation, newsletter, speakers bureau. *Write*: 650 N Main St, Rockford, IL 61103 *Call*: 815/965-6745

**National Assn for Down Syndrome** *Area Served: National* Create better understanding and acceptance of children and adults who have Down Syndrome. Provide support and information to parents. Provide up-to-date information to professionals. Referral to local support groups. *Meetings*: Annually. *Services*: Mutual aid, educational program or material, advocacy, referral to other services, speakers bureau, referral to other services, telephone support, home or hospital visitation, newsletter. *Write*: PO Box 4542, Oak Brook, IL 60522-4542 *Call*: 630/325-9112

**National Down Syndrome Congress** *Area Served: IL/Nation Write*: 605 Chantilly Dr, Ste 250, Atlanta, GA 30324 *Call*: 800/232-6372 *Email*: ndsc@charitiesusa.com; *Web site*: http://www.coral.net/~ndsc/

**National Down Syndrome Society** Provide people with Down Syndrome with the opportunity to achieve their full potential in community life. Provides information, referral, research, advocacy, conferences, materials available free of charge. Fees for some materials and videos. *Meetings*: Call for information. *Write*: 666 Broadway, Ste 800, NY, NY 10012-2317 *Call*: 800/221-4602 *Fax*: 212-979-2873 *Web site*: http://www.ndss.org

**Parents Assn for Down Syndrome Jackson County Archway** *Area Served: Jackson and Perry Counties Write*: PO Box 1180, Carbondale, IL 62903 *Call*: 618/549-4442

**Riverbend Down Syndrome Parent Support Group** *Area Served: SW IL* Provides support for parents of Down Syndrome children. Contact: Victor J. Bishop. *Call*: 618/462-0521 *Email*: bishop@ezl.com *Web site*: www.altpmweb.com/cs/downsyndrome

# Dysautonomia

**Dysautonomia Foundation, Inc IL Chapter** *Area Served: IL* Familial Dysautonomia is an often fatal Jewish genetic disorder. Our purpose is to raise funds for medical research and clinical care for the victims of this disease. In addition, it is our purpose to make the community aware of the disorder and advise them on the support and care presently available. *Meetings*: Bi-monthly for all interested. *Services*: Mutual aid, educational program or material, referral to other services, telephone support, social activities, newsletter, written information. *Write*: 7033 N Kedzie Ave, Ste #401, Chicago, IL 60645 *Call*: 773/764-8224

# Dyslexia

**Orton-Dyslexia Society IL Branch** *Area Served: IL* Org. of professionals, parents of dyslexics and adults with dyslexia. Main goal is to foster research into the causes and treatment of dyslexia. In the process of developing a tutor referral service. *Meetings*: For all interested twice a year plus conferences. *Services*: Educational program or material referral to other services, telephone support, newsletter, written information, MA. *Write*: 529 W Roosevelt Rd, Wheaton, IL 60187 *Call*: 630/668-4800 *Fax*: 708/662-5782

# Dystonia

**Dystonia Medical Research Foundation National Chapter** Works to advance medical research, creating public and physician awareness of this genetic disorder, and sponsoring patient and family support groups. *Services*: Quarterly newsletter, news group and Web page, physician referral list, educational symposia, awareness campaigns, legislative initiatives, research and treatment updates, 100 support groups nationwide. *Meetings*: Please contact local individual group for further information. *Write*: One E Wacker Dr, Ste 2430, Chicago, IL 60601-1905 *Call*: 312/755-0198 *Fax*: 312/803-0138 *Email*:dystfndt@aol.com *Web site*: www.ziplink.net/users/dystonia/

**Dystonia Medical Research Foundation South Suburban Chapter** Works to advance medical research, creating public and physician awareness of this genetic disorder, and sponsoring patient and family support groups. *Services*: Quarterly newsletter, news group and web page, physician referral list, educational symposia, awareness campaigns, legislative initiatives, research and treatment updates, 100 support groups nationwide. *Meetings*: Please contact local individual group for further information. *Call*: 708/758-0481 *Email*: dystfndt@aol.com *Web site*:http://www.ziplink.net/users/dystonia/

**Dystonia Medical Research Foundation Southern IL Chapter** *Area Served: IL* Works to advance medical research, creating public and physician awareness of this genetic disorder, and sponsoring patient and family support groups.*Services*: Quarterly newsletter, news group and WWW page, physician referral list, educational symposia, awareness campaigns, legislative initiatives, research and treatment updates, 100 support groups nationwide. *Meetings*: Please contact local individual group for further information. *Call*: 618/755-0198 *Email*: dystfndt@aol.com *Web site*: http://www.ziplink.net/users/dystonia/

**Dystonia Medical Research Foundation Chicago Chapter** *Area Served: Chicago* Works to advance

medical research, creating public and physician awareness of this genetic disorder, and sponsoring patient and family support groups. *Services*: Quarterly newsletter, news group and web page, physician referral list, educational symposia, awareness campaigns, legislative initiatives, research and treatment updates, 100 support groups nationwide. *Meetings*: Please contact local individual group for further information. *Write*: 170 Lakeside Pl, Highland Park, IL 60035 *Call*: 847/433-2405
*Email*: dystfndt@aol.com
*Web site*: http://www.ziplink.net/users/dystonia/

**Dystonia Medical Research Foundation Springfield Chapter** *Area Served: Springfield, IL* Works to advance medical research, creating public and physician awareness of this genetic disorder, and sponsoring patient and family support groups. *Services*: Quarterly newsletter, news group and WWW page, physician referral list, educational symposia, awareness campaigns, legislative initiatives, research and treatment updates, 100 support groups nationwide. *Meetings*: Please contact local individual group for further information. *Call*: 217/529-3357
*Email*: dystfndt@aol.com
*Web site*: http://www.ziplink.net/users/dystonia/

# Eating Disorders

## Eating Disorders-Anorexia

**American Anorexia/Bulemia Assn** Give support to those affected by bulemia, anorexia and compulsive eating through support groups. Provide referrals and public education and promote research. No known IL groups. *Services*: Mutual aid, educational program or material, written information, referral to other services, advocacy, newsletter. *Write*: 418 E 76th St, NY, NY 10021
*Call*: 212/734-1114

**Anorexia Nervosa and Associated Disorders (ANAD) Green Bay Pavilion** *Area Served: Lake County* Founded in 1976, ANAD is the first national non-profit educational and self-help org. in America dedicated to alleviating the problems of eating disorders. *Services*: Counseling; information and referrals; self-help groups for victims and families; educational programs; and a listing of therapists, hospitals and clinics treating eating disorders. The group also encourages research. *Meetings*: Tuesdays at Highland Park Hospital-call 847/480-2617. *Write*: 1936 Green Bay Rd, Highland Park, IL 60035 *Call*: 847/831-3438
*Fax*: 847/433-4632 *Web site*: http://www.hphospitalorg

**Anorexia Nervosa and Associated Disorders Evanston Support Group** *Area Served: Cook-N County* Our group's primary objective is to provide support and education for people who suffer from eating disorders and their families. *Meetings*: Weekly for all interested. *Services*: Mutual aid, educational program or material,

telephone support, written information. *Write*: 636 Church St, Evanston, IL 60201 *Call*: 847/869-0539

**Anorexia Nervosa and Bulemia Support Group Good Samaritan Hospital** *Area Served: IL Write*: Center for Mental Health, 3815 Highland Ave, Downers Grove, IL 60515 *Call*: 630/653-1923 *Fax*: 630/653-8592

**Anorexia Nervosa and Bulemia Support Group** *Area Served: IL Write*: 2238 Appleby Dr, Wheaton, IL 60187 *Call*: 630/653-1923 *Fax*: 630/653-8592

**Compulsive Eaters Therapy Group Turning Point Behavioral Health Care Center** *Area Served: Cook County Write*: 8324 Skokie Blvd, Skokie, IL 60077-2545 *Call*: 847/933-0051

**Eating Disorders Family Awareness Group** *Area Served: Peoria, Woodford and Tazewell Counties Write*: St Francis Medical Center, 530 NE Glen Oak Ave, Peoria, IL 61637 *Call*: 309/655-2738

**Eating Disorders Support Group McDonough District Hospital Recovery Center** *Area Served: McDonough County Write*: 525 E Grant St, Macomb, IL 61455 *Call*: 309/833-4101 3270

**Eating Disorders Support Group** *Area Served: Champaign County Write*: 1802 S Mattis Ave, Champaign, IL 61821 *Call*: 217/373-1402

**Eating Disorders Support Group Sallas Center** *Area Served: Cook County* For individuals with eating disorders, their families and friends. to disseminate information about eating disorders and their treatment; assist all in their understanding of these problems and their feelings about them; discuss alternativeconstructive solutions. *Meetings*: Monthly for all interested. *Services*: Mutual aid, educational program or material. *Write*: 401 N Michigan Ave, #818, Chicago, IL 60611
*Call*: 312/222-9060

**National Assn of Anorexia Nervosa** *Area Served: National* National, non-profit, educational and self-help org. dedicated to alleviating problems of eating disorders such as anorexia nervosa and bulemia. Meetings are for sufferer and family. Call to receive a referral to one of 35 chapters in IL. *Services*: Mutual aid, educational program or material, fundraising, referral to other services, telephone support, newsletter, written information. *Write*: PO Box 7, Highland Park, IL 60035 *Call*: 847/831-3438

**O-Anon General Service Office** *Area Served: National* Self-help 12 Step-oriented support group for friends and family members of persons with eating disorders. 2 IL groups. *Meetings*: Weekly for anyone interested. *Services*: Mutual aid, written information, telephone support, educational program or material. *Write*: PO Box 748, San Pedro, CA 90733 *Call*: 310/547-1570

**Patient Support Group St Francis Medical Center**
*Area Served: Peoria County Write*: 530 NE Glen Oak, Peoria, IL 61637 *Call*: 309/655-2809

## Eating Disorders-Family

**Family Awareness Support Group St Francis Medical Center** *Area Served: Peoria County Write*: 530 NE Glen Oak, Peoria, IL 61637 *Call*: 309/655-2738

## Eating Disorders-Weight Control

**Fight The Fat Clinic Francis Nelson Health Center**
*Area Served: Champaign County Write*: 1306 Carver Drive, Champaign, IL 61820 *Call*: 217/356-1558

**Food Addicts Anonymous** *Area Served: National*
International org. founded in 1987; a fellowship of men and women willing to recover from the disease of food addiction. Our purpose is to stay abstinent feeding our bodies with a plan of sound food nutrition and to help other food addicts achieve abstinence. A 12 Step program. Provides self help group meetings, information, and support. 2 meetings in IL. *Write*: 4623 Forest Hill Bl, Ste 109-4, West Palm Beach, FL 33415-9120
*Call*: 561/967-3871 Answer Mach. *Fax*: 561/967-3871

**Food Addicts Anonymous** See Food Addicts Anonymous national listing. *Call*: 847/726-0334

**Food Addicts Anonymous** See Food Addicts Anonymous national listing. *Write*: 1460 Fairlane Dr, Buzz #193, Schaumburg, IL 60193 *Call*: 708/351-2327

**Herscher Weight Loss Support Group Herscher United Methodist Church** *Area Served: Kankakee County* Helps individuals with their weight loss programs. *Services*: Mutual aid. *Write*: 274 N Elm St, Herscher, IL 60941 *Call*: 815/426-6278

**Letting Go of Compulsive Eating Support Group Ravenswood CMHC** On-going group if sufficient leadership is available. Otherwise intermittent 6-week group meets quarterly. *Meetings*: Weekly. *Services*: Mutual aid. *Write*: 2312 W Irving Park Rd, Chicago, IL 60618 *Call*: 773/463-7000 1455

**Overeaters Anonymous** *Area Served: Champaign County Write*: 2022 Cureton Dr, Urbana, IL 61801 *Call*: 217/384-6383

**Overeaters Anonymous** *Area Served: Cook County Write*: St Francis Hospital, 355 Ridge Ave, Evanston, IL 60202 *Call*: 847/492-6385

**Overeaters Anonymous** *Area Served: DeKalb County Write*: Kishwaukee Hospital, 626 Bethany Rd, DeKalb, IL 60115 *Call*: 815/756-7658

**Overeaters Anonymous** *Area Served: LaSalle County Write*: St Mary's Hospital, 111 E Spring St, Streator, IL 61364 *Call*: 815/672-8797

**Overeaters Anonymous** *Area Served: National Write*: PO Box 92870, Los Angeles, CA 90009 *Call*: 310/618-8835

**Overeaters Anonymous** *Area Served: Winnebago County Write*: Rockford, IL *Call*: 815/962-4664

**Overeaters Anonymous Decatur Outreachers Intergroup** *Area Served: Macon County Write*: PO Box 414, Decatur, IL 62526 *Call*: 217/429-1263

**Overeaters Anonymous First Presbyterian Church** *Area Served: Morgan County* 3 meetings weekly. *Write*: 870 W College, Jacksonville, IL 62650 *Call*: 217/243-4970

**Overeaters Anonymous, Inc Region 4 Office**
*Area Served: Regional* OA is a fellowship of individuals who, through shared experience, strength and hope, are recovering from overeating. OA is based on the 12 Steps and 12 traditions originating in Alcoholics Anonymous. OA provides and offers information and group meetings to assist people toward their own recovery and dealing with physical and emotional symptoms. *Meetings*: Call OA world service office, 1-508-891-2644, for meetings nearest you. *Write*: 9907 Gravois Rd, Ste E, St. Louis, MO 63123 *Call*: 314/638-6070

**Overeaters Anonymous, Inc World Service Office**
*Area Served: National* OA is a fellowship of individuals who through shared experience, strength and hope, are recovering from compulsive overeating. OA is based on the 12 Steps and 12 traditions originating in Alcoholics Anonymous. Provide information and group meetings to assist people toward recovery. Meetings are confidential. Literature provided. *Meetings*: Call the OA world service office for the meetings nearest you. *Write*: 6075 Zenith Court NE, Rio Rancho, MN 87124 *Call*: 505/891-2664

**Overeaters Anonymous Little Company of Mary Hospital** *Area Served: Cook County Write*: 4544 W 103 St, Oak Lawn, IL 60453 *Call*: 708/346-6000

**Overeaters Anonymous Path Crisis Center**
*Area Served: McLean County Write*: PO Box 1961, Bloomington, IL 61702 *Call*: 309/827-4005

**Overeaters Anonymous Quad Cities** *Area Served: Rock Island Write*: 1852 16th St, Ste 7, Moline, IL 61265 *Call*: 309/762-1747

**Take Off Pounds Sensibly Central Office** *Area Served: IL* International non-profit self-help org. to help people take off pounds sensibly. Members must be in contact with a doctor. 7 regional coordinators in IL. Refer to local groups. *Meetings*: Weekly. *Services*: Mutual aid, educational program or material, telephone support. *Write*: 5519 W 87th St, Oak Lawn, IL 60453 *Call*: 708/499-5255

**Take Off Pounds Sensibly** *Area Served: Tazewell County* *Write*: 208 Wagner Rd, Washington, IL 61571 *Call*: 217/743-6336

**Take Off Pounds Sensibly** *Area Served: Vermilion County* *Write*: 104 Delmar Dr, Box 219, Catlin, IL 61817 *Call*: 217/427-5919

**Weight Loss Support Group St Elizabeth's Hospital** *Area Served: St Clair and Madison Counties* *Write*: 211 S 3rd St, Belleville, IL 62222-0694 *Call*: 618/234-2120 1156

**Weight Support Group Pavilion Senior Center** *Area Served: Cook-NW* Promotes good nutrition and a healthy life style. Weight support—not a diet program. *Services*: Mutual aid, educational program or material. *Write*: 199 N 1st St, Wheeling, IL 60090 *Call*: 847/459-2670

# Ectodermal Dysplasia

**National Foundation for Ectodermal Dysplasia** *Area Served: IL* NFED is a nonprofit org. serving individuals affected by Ectodermal Dysplasia, 1,660 families in 33 countries. Mission: to assist people with ED and their families to live not only normal life spans but nearly normal life-styles. *Services*: Scholarship and dental implant programs; family conferences; publications on treatment and care; treatment and research fund and newsletter. *Meetings*: Family conferences-annual. *Write*: 219 E Main St, Box 114, Mascoutah, IL 62258-0114 *Call*: 618/566-2020 *Fax*: 618/566-4718 *Email*: nfed2@aol.com *Web site*: http://www.nfed.org

# Ehlers Danlos Syndrome

**Ehlers-Danlos National Foundation** *Area Served: National* Provides updated information and emotional support to those suffering from Ehlers-Danlos Syndrome. Publishes quarterly newsletter, offers physician referral assistance, provides a forum whereby interested members may communicate with one another. Sponsors an annual learning conference. *Services*: Educational program or material written information, advocacy, referral to other services, speakers bureau, referral to other services, telephone support, newsletter. *Write*: PO Box 1212, Southgate, MI 48195 *Call*: 313/282-0180

# Endometriosis

**Choices In Family Building** *Area Served: Champaign County* *Write*: 704 S Charter St, Monticello, IL 61856 *Call*: 217/762-8326

**Endometriosis Assn Headquarters** *Area Served: National* Provide information and support to women with endometriosis; educate the public and the medical community about the disease; conduct research. Provide newsletter, support groups, crisis call, hotline, networks, prescription drug savings plan. *Meetings*: Contact headquarters, chapter coordinator. *Write*: 8585 N 76th Pl, Milwaukee, WI 53223 *Call*: 414/355-2200 *Fax*: 414/355-6065

**Endometriosis Group Christ Hospital Women's Health Center** *Area Served: Cook County* *Write*: 16325 S Harlem Ave, Tinley Park, IL 60477 *Call*: 708/532-6194

**Endometriosis Group Northwestern Memorial Hospital** *Area Served: Cook County* *Write*: Prentice Women's Hospital, 333 E Superior St, Chicago, IL *Call*: 312/908-7503

**Endometriosis Group Wellspring Women's Health Center** *Area Served: Lake County* *Write*: 825 N Quentin Rd, Palatine, IL 60067 *Call*: 847/364-5139

**Endometriosis Group Women's Health Care and Wellness Center** *Area Served: Cook County* *Write*: 965 Lake St, Oak Park, IL 60301 *Call*: 708/484-6801

**Endometriosis Group** *Write*: Condell Medical Center, 900 S Garfield Ave, Libertyville, IL 60048 *Call*: 847/940-0718

# Epilepsy

**Blackhawk Epilepsy Self Help** *Area Served: IL N* Encouraging clients to cope with their seizure activity, three education and treatment plans using individual and family counseling. Supply a facilitator and speakers from the community for a social exchange of ideas. We hope to remove the stigma associated with epilepsy. *Meetings*: Monthly. *Services*: Mutual aid, educational program or material, written information, advocacy, referral to other services, speakers bureau, home or hospital visitation. *Write*: 1518 5th Ave, Ste 410, Moline, IL 61265 *Call*: 309/762-3668

**Decatur Epilepsy Support Group Epilepsy Assn** *Area Served: Macon County* *Write*:206 S 6th St, Springfield, IL 62907 *Call*: 217/789-8911

**Epilepsy Assn of America** *Area Served: IL-SW* *Write*: 1200 Caseyville Ave, Swansea, IL 62220 *Call*: 618/236-2181

**Epilepsy Assn of Southwestern IL Epilepsy Assn Office** Support group to share experiences, strength and hope about living with epilepsy. Peer support through discussion. *Meetings*: Monthly, some transportation provided, fully accessible, group engages in many social and recreational activities. *Write*: 1200 Caseyville Ave, Swansea, IL 62226 *Call*: 618/236-2181

**Epilepsy Foundation of America Epilepsy Assoc of Rock Valley** *Area Served: Winnebago County and IL-NW* Inform and share experiences in coping with the various aspects of epilepsy. Topics of discussion include family and psychological problems, the treatment of epilepsy, vocational problems, insurance, and social security problems. *Meetings*: For individuals with seizure disorders and their family. *Services*: Mutual aid, referral to other services, educational program or material, social activities, written information, newsletter, speakers bureau.
*Write*: 321 W State St, Ste 208, Rockford, IL 61101 *Call*: 815/964-2689

**Epilepsy Foundation of Greater Chicago National Epilepsy Self Help** *Area Served: Chicago and Cook County* *Write*: 20 E Jackson Blvd, Ste 1300, Chicago, IL 60604 *Call*: 312/939-8622 131 *Fax*: 312/939-1117

**Epilepsy Foundation of Greater Chicago Heights Epilepsy Self-Help Group** *Area Served: Will County* Group self-support and information concerning epilepsy. Educating general public about epilepsy. *Services*: Mutual aid, educational program or material, written information, telephone support, social activities, speakers bureau. *Write*: PO Box 541, Beecher, IL 60401 *Call*: 708/946-6286

**Epilepsy Resources of North Central IL Kishwaukee Hospital** *Area Served: DeKalb, Kane and Kendall Counties* *Write*: Bethany Rd, DeKalb, IL 60115 *Call*: 815/756-8554

**Epilepsy Support Group Rush-Presbyterian-St Luke's Medical Center** *Area Served: IL* *Write*: 1725 W Harrison, Ste 755, Chicago, IL 60612 *Call*: 312/942-2363 *Fax*: 312/942-2238

**Epilepsy Support Group South Suburban Hospital** *Area Served: Cook County* *Write*: Marketing Dept, 17800 S Kedzie Ave, Hazel Crest, IL 60429 *Call*: 708/799-8000 3006

**Epilepsy Support Group The Carle Pavilion** *Area Served: Champaign County* *Write*: 809 W Church St, Champaign, IL 61820 *Call*: 217/383-3440

**Parents of Children with Seizure Disorders Epilepsy Foundation of Greater Chicago** *Area Served: DuPage and Cook County* Supports parents with children who have seizures. Helps parents provide an environment that allows children to achieve independence and autonomy.

*Services*: Mutual aid, written information, telephone support, advocacy. *Write*: 159 Pebblecreek Ter, Carol Stream, IL 60188 *Call*: 630/653-3239

**Parents Support Group Epilepsy Services for Northeastern IL** *Area Served: Cook-N and Lake County* Parent and family support network. *Write*: 1698 1st St, Highland Park, IL 60035 *Call*: 847/433-8960

# Esophageal Atresia

**Esophageal Atresia/Tef Family Support Org.** *Area Served: IL* *Write*: 921 Acorn Dr, Sleepy Hollow, IL 60118 *Call*: 847/426-9486

# Fibromyalgia

**Fibromyalgia Assn of DuPage County** *Area Served: Cook and DuPage Counties* *Write*: 870 Lively Blvd, Elk Grove Village, IL 60007 *Call*: 708/665-9365 Evenings

**Fibromyalgia Support Group Iroquois Memorial Hospital** *Write*: 200 Fairman Ave, Watseka, IL 60970 *Call*: 815/432-5841 *Fax*: 815/432-6052

**Fibromyalgia Support Group Lutheran General Health System** *Area Served: Cook County* *Write*: 1775 Dempster St, Park Ridge, IL 60068 *Call*: 847/616-3470

**Fibromyalgia Support Highland Park Hospital** Provide support, resources, education for Fibromyalgia sufferers. Family members participate on intermittent schedule by invitation. *Services*: Education and support. Facilitator at meetings is a registered physical therapist. *Meetings*: 2nd Wednesday of each month from 7:30-8:30 pm, handicap accessible, language-English. *Write*: 718 Glenview Ave, Highland Park, IL 60035 *Call*: 847/432-8000 5027 *Fax*: 847/480-3962

**Fibromyalgia Support Group Arthritis Foundation** *Area Served: IL* *Write*: 111 E Wacker Dr, Ste 1928, Chicago, IL 60601 *Call*: 800/735-0096

# Fragile X Syndrome

**National Fragile X Foundation** *Area Served: National* Provides information to promote education and research for Fragile X Syndrome, a hereditary condition which can cause learning problems. *Write*: 1441 York St, #303, Denver, CO 80206 *Call*: 800/688-8765 *Fax*: 303/333-4369 *Email*: natfx@aol.com

# Gaucher Disease

**National Gaucher Foundation** *Area Served*: *National* Information and assistance for those affected by Gaucher Disease. Provides education and outreach to increase public awareness, and support networks. Bimonthly newsletter, telephone support, medial board. *Write*: 11140 Rockville Pike, Ste 350, Rockville, MD 20852 *Call*: 800/925-8885 *Fax*: 301/816-1516 *Web site*: www.gaucherdisease.org *Email*: sadamsng@aol.com

# Graves Disease

**National Graves' Disease Foundation** *Area Served*: *National* *Write*: 2 Tsitsi Ct, Brevard, NC 28712-3221 *Call*: 904/724-0770

# Guillain-Barre Syndrome

**Guillain-Barre Syndrome Foundation, International** *Area Served: National* An international org. that provides emotional support to victims and families of Guillain-Barre Syndrome; supplies literature about the condition; educates the public; and fosters research. 4 IL chapters. *Services*: Mutual aid, educational program or material, telephone support, home or hospital visitation, newsletter, written information. *Write*: PO Box 262, Wynnewood, PA 19096 *Call*: 610/667-0131 *Fax*: 610/667-7036

**Guillain-Barre Syndrome Foundation, International Guillain-Barre Syndrome Support Group** *Area Served: DuPage County and N IL* Provides moral support and information to persons afflicted with this disease. *Meetings*: Twice yearly. *Services*: Mutual aid, educational program or material, written information, telephone support, home or hospital visitation, newsletter. *Write*: 2 S 762 Ave, Barbizon, Oak Brook, IL 60521 *Call*: 630/279-5417

# Head Injury

**Coma Recovery Association** *Area Served: National* Support and advocacy for families of coma and traumatic brain injury survivors. Provides information and referrals, support meetings for recovering coma patients, case management, quarterly newsletter. *Write*: 100 E Old Country Rd, #9. *Call*: 561/746-7714

**Coma Support Group Oak Forest Hospital** *Area Served: Cook County and IL-NE* Provides emotional support and educational information to families of individuals in coma, through group sharing and guest speakers. *Meetings*: Monthly. *Services*: Mutual aid,

referral to other services, speakers bureau. *Write*: 15900 S Cicero Ave, Oak Forest, IL 60452 *Call*: 708/687-7200 4460

**Heart of IL Head Injury Support Group** *Area Served: IL Write*: 1101 Main St, Ste 202, Peoria, IL 61606 *Call*: 309/672-4400

**High Hopes Support Group Marianjoy Rehab Hospital** *Area Served: DuPage County Write*: 26 W 171 Roosevelt Rd, PO Box 795, Wheaton, IL 60189 *Call*: 630/462-5552 *Fax*: 708/462-4442

**IL Brain Injury Assn, Inc Head Winds** *Area Served: McHenry County* Focuses on providing mutual support, educationand information about head injuries, sharing of resources, and legislation information to survivors of head injuries, their families, and health care professionals and service providers. *Meetings*: Monthly for survivors and family members. *Services*: Mutual aid, written information, social activities, telephone support, referral to other services, educational program or material, advocacy, newsletter. *Write*: Pioneer Center, 3980 Albany St, McHenry, IL 60050 *Call*: 815/344-6228

**IL Brain Injury Assn, Inc Heads Up-Rehab Institute of Chicago** *Area Served: Chicago Write*: 300 W Hill St, Apt 923, Chicago, IL 60610 *Call*: 312/944-4762 *Fax*: 312/642-9263

**IL Brain Injury Assn, Inc IL State Headquarters** *Area Served: IL* Provides education, advocacy and referrals to support groups for the head injured and their families; and information regarding Rehab facilities for physical care. *Meetings*: Monthly for all interested. *Services*: Mutual aid, educational program or material, advocacy, referral to other services, telephone support, social activities, newsletter, referral to other services, written information, speakers bureau. *Write*: 8903 Burlington Ave, Brookfield, IL 60513 *Call*: 800/284-4442 800/444-NHIF (family helpline) *Web site*: www.biausa.org

**IL Head Injury Assn, Inc Kankakee Head Injury Support Group** *Area Served: Kankakee County* Mutual support group for head injury survivors and their families. The group is facilitated by professionals and addresses issues pertinent to families and survivors. *Meetings*: Monthly. *Services*: Mutual aid. *Write*: Riverside Head Injury Program, 350 N Wall St, Kankakee, IL 60901 *Call*: 815/265-7344

**IL Head Injury Assn, Inc Making Headway** *Area Served: Chicago* Provide support and education to the head injured individual and the family. *Meetings*: Monthly. *Services*: Mutual aid, educational program or material, advocacy. *Write*: Schwab Rehab Center, 1401 S California Blvd, Chicago, IL 60608 *Call*: 773/522-2010 5176

**IL Head Injury Assn, Inc Southwest Support Group**
*Area Served: Cook-S* Peer support group for family
members of head injury people. *Meetings*: Monthly for
family members. *Services*: Mutual aid. *Write*: 9959 S
Clifton Ave, Evergreen Park, IL 60642 *Call*:
708/422-1376

**IL Head Injury Assn, Inc Willowbrook-Southwest
Family Support Group** *Area Served: DuPage County*
*Write*: Paulson Center/Rehab Center, 619 Plainfield Rd,
Willowbrook, IL 60521 *Call*: 630/323-5656 400

**National Head Injury Foundation, Inc IL Chapter**
*Area Served: IL Write*: 1127 S Mannheim Rd, Ste 213,
Westchester, IL 60154 *Call*: 708/344-4646

**Wheeling Head Injury Support Group Rehab
Achievement Center** *Area Served: Cook and Lake
Counties* Peer and professional support for adjustment
after brain injury. *Meetings*: Monthly for those with brain
injury and their family members. *Services*: Mutual aid.
*Write*: 5150 Capitol Dr, Wheeling, IL 60090
*Call*: 847/215-9977

# Health Information

**Light for Health** *Area Served: National*
*Write*: 942 Twisted Oak Ln, Buffalo Grove, IL 60089
*Call*: 708/459-4455

**Mrs. Dash Sodium Information Hotline Alberto
Culver Company** *Area Served: National* Provides
nutrition information and recipes containing sodium
content for restricted diets. *Services*: Info/educational
program or material. *Write*: 2525 Armitage Ave, Melrose
Park, IL 60160 *Call*: 800/622-DASH

**National Pesticide Telecommunication Network
Oregon State University** *Area Served: National* Has a
library on pesticides and responds to questions about the
health effects of pesticides. A service of the
Environmental Protection Agency. *Services*: Written
information, hotline. *Write*: Ag and Life Sciences, #1007,
Corvallis, OR 97331 *Call*: 800/858-7378

**Public Health Hotline IL Department of Public Health**
*Area Served: IL Write*: 535 W Jefferson, Springfield, IL
62761 Health information on public health issues.
*Call*: 800/545-2200

**Uncommon Survivors** *Area Served: Cook and Lake
Counties* A self-help group for individuals dealing with
the difficulties of illness, recovery and/or maintaining
their health. *Meetings*: Twice monthly. *Services*: Mutual
aid. *Write*: 1800 Sherman, Ste 515, Evanston, IL 60201
*Call*: 847/492-3040 *Fax*: 708/492-3045

# Hearing Impairment

## Hearing Impairment-Loss of Hearing

**Assn for Late Deafened Adults ALDA** *Area Served:
Chicago-N* Offers help and encouragement to people who
have become deaf as adults. *Meetings*: Weekly. *Services*:
Mutual aid. *Write*: Ravenswood CMHC, 2312 W Irving
Park Rd, Chicago, IL 60618 *Call*: 773/463-7000 1455

**Catholic Office of the Deaf Archdiocese of Chicago**
*Area Served: Cook and Lake Counties* Provide for both
spiritual and social service needs of the deaf. Deaf persons
and/or families can contact office for services, including
counseling, advocacy, information and referral, spiritual
and personal guidance. Services offered to allpeople
regardless of religious affiliation; staff skilled in American
Sign Language. *Meetings*: Weekly for all interested, after
Sunday services. *Services*: Mutual aid, educational
program or material, advocacy, telephone support,
professional service. *Write*: 155 E Superior St, Chicago,
IL 60611 *Call*: 312/751-8370

**Children of Deaf Adults Chicagoland Chapter**
*Area Served: IL* Provide a clearinghouse of information,
support and advocacy for hearing children of deaf adults.
*Services*: Mutual aid, educational program or material,
advocacy, telephone support, newsletter, written
information, social activities. *Write*: PO Box 25140,
Chicago, IL 60625

**Deaf Parents Group Jewish Family and Community
Service** Promote interests of the deaf. *Services*: Call for
details. *Meetings*: Weekly, call for specific dates and
times. (847) 568-5240 TTY *Write*: Goldie Bachmann
Luftig Bldg, 5150 Golf Rd, 2nd Fl, Skokie, IL 60077
*Call*: 847/568-5200

**Deaf Senior Citizens** *Area Served: Chicago* Primarily a
social org. *Meetings*: Monthly. *Services*: Mutual aid,
educational program or material, social activities. *Write*:
Cathedral of St James, 65 E Huron St, Chicago, IL 60611
*Call*: 312/787-6410

**Hearing Health Awareness Group Louis A Weiss
Memorial Hospital** *Area Served: Cook County*
*Write*: 4646 N Marine Drive, Chicago, IL 60640
*Call*: 773/989-2621 *Fax*: 312/275-2275

**Hearing Impaired Support Group North Shore Senior
Center** *Area Served: Cook County* Offers information on
hearing and speech problems and ways to cope with those
problems. *Meetings*: Weekly. *Services*: Mutual aid. *Write*:
7 Happ Rd, Northfield, IL 60093 *Call*: 847/446-8751

**Hearing Loss Link** *Area Served: National Write*: 2600
W Peterson, Ste 202, Chicago, IL 60659
*Call*: 773/743-1032

**Hearing Program North Shore Senior Center** Provide a full range of opportunities for people with hearing loss. *Services*: Speech reading classes, Sound Offs support group, educational programs, chapter of SHHH, professional and peer counseling. *Meetings*: Sound Offs meets 1st, 3rd, and 4th Mondays, monthly, from 11-12 pm; Northshore chapter of SHHH (Self Help for Hard of Hearing) meets 2nd Monday, monthly, at 10 am. (No meetings in August.) *Write*: 7 Happ Rd, Northfield, IL 60093-3411 *Call*: 847/446-8751 *Fax*: 847/446-8762 *Web site*: http://www.ns sc.org

**Hearing Support Group** *Area Served: Chicago* Provides Mutual support to later life hearing impaired to provide education, speakers, presentations and instruction on use of assistive devices and fellowship. Group meets last Wednesday of the month at 10:00 am. Members must be over 60 years of age. *Write*: 1415 W Foster, Chicago, IL 60640 *Call*: 773/769-5500 127

**IL Acoustic Neuroma Assn** *Area Served: IL* Provides information and support for benign cranial nerve damage. Educates physicians and the public about acoustic neromas. Offers self-help groups, information, and social activities. Meetings 4 times a year. *Write*: 1336 NW Circle, Kankakee, IL 60901 *Call*: 815/937-4269

**IL Alliance of the Deaf and Hard of Hearing** Promote legislation in the interest of the deaf and hard of hearing. *Services*: Exchange information, expand and enhance services for the deaf and hard of hearing. *Meetings*: Call for information. Fees: ind-$10.00, govt. agencies-$20.00, org. membership-$30.00. *Write*: PO Box 643373, Chicago, IL 60664-3373

**IL Cochlear Implant Club** *Area Served: IL* Gives support and encouragement to people with cochlear implants and those thinking of having implants. Share information on coping strategies an hear professionals discuss the latest research and new assistive devices. *Meetings*: Every other month for all interested. *Services*: Mutual aid, newsletter. *Write*: 1255 Hailshaw Ct, Wheaton, IL 60187 *Call*: 630/653-9226 *Fax*: 708/653-9226

**Lipreading Support Group Smith Center** *Area Served: Cook-N* Help individuals remain in mainstream. *Meetings*: Weekly. *Services*: Mutual aid, social activities. *Write*: 5120 Galitz, Skokie, IL 60077 *Call*: 847/933-8208 4438 *Fax*: 708/673-0525

**Self Help for Hard of Hearing People, Inc SHHH West Suburban Chapter** *Area Served: IL* SHHH is a volunteer international org. of hard of hearing people, their relatives and friends. It is a non-profit, nonsectarian educational org. devoted to the welfare and interests of hearing impaired people. 11 Chapters in IL. *Meetings*: Monthly. *Services*: Mutual aid, educational program or material, advocacy, referral to other services, telephone

support, newsletter/written information. *Write*: 344 Ruby St, Clarendon Hills, IL 60514-1317

**Self Help for Hard of Hearing People, Inc** *Area Served: Cook County* Create awareness about hearing loss and to provide self help for the hearing impaired. to promote programs to prevent hearing loss, to publish sources for assistive hearing systems, coping strategies, etc., to advocate for hard of hearing people. Also to improve communicates access via the telephone and public space and to refer people to medical/professional services. *Meetings*: For anyone interested. *Services*: Mutual aid, educational program or material, written information, referral to other services, advocacy. *Write*: 9237 W 173rd St, Tinley Park, IL 60477 *Call*: 708/532-1956

**Self Help for Hard of Hearing People, Inc SHHH Chicago Northside Chapter** *Area Served: Chicago-N* Self-help group for those with hearing impairment. *Services*: Mutual aid, educational program or material, newsletter, social activities. *Write*: 5054 N St Louis, Chicago, IL 60625 *Call*: 773/539-2813

**Self Help for Hard of Hearing People, Inc SHHH Chicago North Shore Chapter** *Area Served: Cook-N* SHHH is a volunteer international org. of hard of hearing people, their relatives and friends. It is a non-profit, non-sectarian, educational org. devoted to the welfare and interests of hearing impaired people. *Meetings*: Monthly for all interested. *Services*: Mutual aid, educational program or material, advocacy, referral to other services, telephone support, newsletter, written information. *Write*: North Shore Senior Center, 7 Happ Rd, Northfield, IL 60093-3411 *Call*: 847/446-8750

**Self Help for Hard of Hearing People, Inc SHHH West Suburban Chapter** *Area Served: Cook, Will and DuPage Counties* Provides self help for people of all ages, communication styles and those who don't hear well. Primary purpose is to educate the hard of hearing, their families, friends, co-workers, teachers, etc. About hearing loss, advocacy, self-help groups, education, national programs, state and regional conferences, and discounted materials. *Meetings*: Call (for hearing impaired only TTY 301/657-2249). *Write*: 520 Heather Ln, Carol Stream, IL 60188-1722 *Call*: 301/657-2248

**Self Help for Hard of Hearing People, Inc SHHH Greater Chicago #1 Chapter** *Area Served: Cook County* *Write*: 600 W Rand Rd, Apt A305, Arlington Heights, IL 60004 *Call*: 708/259-0203

## Hearing Impairment-Tinnitus

**American Tinnitus Assn Melrose Tinnitus** *Area Served: Cook County* Support consists of supplying literature, inquiry and support over the phone and referrals to other groups holding meetings in the area. *Services*: Educational program or material, fundraising, referral to other services, telephone support. *Write*: 1303 N 17th Ave, Melrose Park, IL 60160 *Call*: 708/345-7642

**American Tinnitus Assn IL Contact** *Area Served: IL* Support tinnitus research, provide information about the condition to health professionals and to the public, and offer referral services and self-help groups to tinnitus sufferers. 4 contacts in IL. *Services*: Mutual aid, educational program or material, referral to other services, telephone support, newsletter, fundraising, written information, professional service. *Write*: 1931 Bradley Pl, Chicago, IL 60613 *Call*: 773/281-3750 *Fax*: 312/281-9187

**American Tinnitus Assn** *Area Served: National* Support tinnitus research, provide information about the condition to health professionals and to the public, and offer referral services and self-help groups to tinnitus suffers. 4 contacts in IL. *Services*: Mutual aid, educational program or material, referral to other services, telephone support, newsletter, written information, professional service. *Write*: PO Box 5, Portland, OR 97207 *Call*: 800/634-8978 16 *Fax*: 503/248-9985

# Heart Disease and Heart Surgery

**American Heart Assn Metropolitan Chicago Affiliate** *Area Served: Cook, Lake and DuPage Counties* Reduction of disability and death due to heart disease and stroke. *Services*: Advocacy. *Write*: 208 S LaSalle St, Ste 900, Chicago, IL 60604 *Call*: 312/346-4675 *Fax*: 312/346-7375

**Heart Talk-Alton (212) American Heart Assn** *Write*: 300 Charlene Ct, Alton, IL 62002 *Call*: 618/465-1952

**Heart Talk American Heart Assn** *Area Served: Cook-N* Provides opportunity to share one's experience with heart disease. Groups are intentionally small so that sharingcan take place. Encourages participants to reframe their lives and heal emotionally and physically. *Services*: Mutual aid, written information, telephone support, educational program or material. *Write*: Wm Rainey Harper College, 1200 W Algonquin Rd., Palatine, IL 60067 *Call*: 847/925-6281 6468

**Heart Talk American Heart Assn** Provides opportunity to share one's experience with heart disease. Groups are intentionally small so that sharing can take place. Encourages participants to reframe their lives and heal emotionally and physically. *Services*: Mutual aid, written information, telephone support, educational program or material. *Write*: Alexian Brothers Medical Center, 800 W Biesterfield Rd, Elk Grove Village, IL 60007 *Call*: 708/981-3653

**Heart Talk American Heart Assn** *Area Served: Cook-N* Let people share their experience with heart disease. Groups are intentionally small so that sharing can take place. The goal of the group is to help participants reframe their lives and heal emotionally and physically. *Services*: Mutual aid, written information, telephone support, educational program or material. *Write*: No Cook County Co Div, 9933 Lawler, Skokie, IL 60077 *Call*: 847/675-1535

**Heart Talk** *Area Served: Cook County* *Write*: Swedish Covenant Hospital, 5145 N California Ave, Chicago, IL 60628 *Call*: 773/878-8200 5097

**Heart Talk Aurora (57) American Heart Assn** *Write*: 40 N Bereman Rd, Montgomery, IL 60538 *Call*: 630/896-9707

**Heart Talk Belleville (226) American Heart Assn** *Write*: PO Box 780, Belleville, IL 62222 *Call*: 618/235-3064

**Heart Talk Central IL (250) American Heart Assn** *Area Served: Central IL* *Write*: 1717D King Dr, Normal, IL 61761 *Call*: 309/452-4191

**Heart Talk Chapter 213 American Heart Assn** *Area Served: Cook County* Provides opportunity to share one's experience with heart disease. Groups are intentionally small so that sharing can take place. Encourages participants to reframe their lives and heal emotionally and physically. *Services*: Mutual aid. *Write*: 6355 Nokomis Ave, Chicago, IL 60646 *Call*: 773/775-5593

**Heart Talk Chicago (106) American Heart Assn** *Area Served: Cook County* *Write*: 680 W Lake Shore Dr, #1524, Chicago, IL 60611 *Call*: 312/337-3251

**Heart Talk Chicago (169) American Heart Assn** *Area Served: Cook County* *Write*: 4447 W Cortland St, Chicago, IL 60639 *Call*: 773/772-0400

**Heart Talk Cook County(248) American Heart Assn** *Area Served: Cook County* *Write*: 1838 Schaumburg Rd, Schaumburg, IL 60193 *Call*: 847/882-5279

**Heart Talk Downers Grove (205) American Heart Assn** *Area Served: Cook County* *Write*: 4042 Elm, Downers Grove, IL 60515 *Call*: 630/964-1169

**The Mended Hearts Chapter #53 Elgin** *Area Served: Cook, DuPage and Kane Counties* *Write*: Sherman Hospital Cardio-Pulmanary Rehabilitation, 934 Center St, Elgin, IL 60120 *Call*: 847/888-8796

**Heart Talk Elgin (53) American Heart Assn** Meets at Sherman Hospital. *Write*: 5750-B Bavarian Ct, Hanover Park, IL 60103 *Call*: 630/289-1162

**Heart Talk Elk Grove (102) American Heart Assn**
*Area Served: Cook County Write*: 1823 Maryland Dr, Elk Grove, IL 60007 *Call*: 847/351-5879

**Heart Talk Elmhurst (218) American Heart Assn**
*Write*: 334 S Harvard Ave, Villa Park, IL 60181 *Call*: 630/834-6949

**Heart Talk Evanston/Glenbrook (217) American Heart Assn** *Area Served: Cook County Write*: 4604 Birchwood Ave, Skokie, IL 60076 *Call*: 847/674-3930

**Heart Talk Geneva (74) American Heart Assn**
*Write*: 4N463 Babson Ln, St Charles, IL 60175 *Call*: 630/584-4416

**Heart Talk Greater Chicago (36) American Heart Assn**
*Area Served: Cook County Write*: 3247 N Olcott, Chicago, IL 60634 *Call*: 773/889-3483

**Heart Talk Joliet (129) American Heart Assn** *Write*: 315 McKinley St, Morris, IL 60450 *Call*: 815/942-3413

**Heart Talk Naperville (232) American Heart Assn**
*Area Served: DuPage County Write*: 1609 Foxhorn Ct, Naperville, IL 60563 *Call*: 630/357-7751

**Heart Talk Park Ridge (80) American Heart Assn**
*Area Served: Cook County Write*: 401 Brookside Dr, Wilmette, IL 60091 *Call*: 847/256-2428

**Heart Talk West Suburban (196) American Heart Assn** *Write*: 560 Cherokee Ct, Carol Stream, IL 60188 *Call*: 630/668-7006

**Cardiac Support Group LaGrange Memorial Hospital**
*Area Served: Cook County Write*: 5101 Willow Springs Rd, LaGrange, IL 60525 *Call*: 708/354-7070

**CHAMP Rush-Presbyterian-St Luke's Medical Center**
*Area Served: Cook County Write*: 1725 W Harrison St, #120, Chicago, IL 60612 *Call*: 312/942-3487

**Coronary Club Mattoon Sarah Lincoln Health Center**
*Area Served: Coles County Write*: 1000 Health Care Dr, Mattoon, IL 61938 *Call*: 217/258-2293

**Heart and Sole Cardiac Rehab Support Group Olympia Fields Osteopathic Hospital and Medical Center** *Area Served: IL Write*: 20201 S Crawford Ave, Olympia Fields, IL 60461 *Call*: 708/747-4000 1225

**Heart At Work Support Group South Suburban Hospital** *Area Served: Cook County Write*: Cardiac Rehab Dept, 17800 S Kedzie Ave, Hazel Crest, IL 60429 *Call*: 708/799-8000 3104

**Heart Club** *Area Served: Lake and Cook Counties Write*: Good Shepherd Hospital, 450 W Hwy 22, 4E, Barrington, IL 60010 *Call*: 847/381-9600 5345

**The Mended Hearts** *Area Served: National* Support groups for persons who have heart disease, their families, and other interested persons. Quarterly magazine, chapter development kit. *Write*: Mended Hearts, 7272 Greenville Ave, Dallas, TX 752531 *Call*: 214/706-1442 *Fax*: 214/987-4334 *Web site*: http://www.mendedhearts.org

**The Mended Hearts Chapter #129** *Area Served: Will, Kendall and Kane Counties Write*: 315 McKinley, Morris, IL 60450 *Call*: 815/942-3413

**The Mended Hearts Chapter #169** *Area Served: Cook County* Members visit, with physician approval, patients and families in the Hospital prior to surgery or procedure and post op procedures. Visitors must undergo a training program and be reaccredited every year. Encompasses all cardiac conditions and procedures. *Meetings*: Open to all. 15 chapters in IL. *Services*: Mutual aid, written information, social activities, telephone support, referral to other services, educational program or material, home or hospital visitation, newsletter, speakers bureau. *Write*: 4447 W Cortland, Chicago, IL 60639 *Call*: 773/772-0400

**The Mended Hearts Chapter #102** *Area Served: Cook and DuPage Counties Services*: Mutual aid, educational program or material, fundraising. *Write*: 1823 Maryland Dr, Elk Grove Village, IL 60007 *Call*: 708/351-5879

**The Mended Hearts Chapter #196** *Area Served: DuPage County Write*: ON 463 Farwell St, Wheaton, IL 60187 *Call*: 630/668-7874

**The Mended Hearts Chapter #205** *Area Served: DuPage County Write*: Good Samaritan Hospital, 3815 Highland Ave, Downers Grove, IL 60515 *Call*: 630/964-1169

**The Mended Hearts Chapter #217** *Area Served: Cook-N and Lake County Write*: Evanston Hospital, 2650 Ridge, Rm 6302, Evanston, IL 60201 *Call*: 847/570-2155

**The Mended Hearts Chapter #218** *Area Served: DuPage County-E and Cook County-W Write*: 912 Chatham, Elmhurst, IL 60126

**The Mended Hearts Chapter #74** *Area Served: Kane and DuPage Counties Write*: 4N 463 Babson Lane, St Charles, IL 60174 *Call*: 630/584-4416

**The Mended Hearts Chapter #80** *Area Served: Cook, Lake and DuPage Counties* Allows those who have had heart surgery or any heart condition to come together in a self-help group and to provide post-heart surgery patients with up-to-date information. Members speak with patients and families before and at time of treatment when they want to talk to someone who has been through it. *Meetings*: Monthly for anyone interested. *Services*: Educational program or material advocacy, referral to other services, social activities, MA. *Write*: 401 Brookside Dr, Wilmette, IL 60091 *Call*: 847/256-2428

**The Mended Hearts Good Samaritan Hospital** *Area Served: Will and Cook Counties* *Write*: 3815 Highland Ave, Cardiac Rehab, 4ᵗʰ Fl NE, Downers Grove, IL 60515 *Call*: 630/275-4378

**The Mended Hearts Rush-Presbyterian-St Luke's Medical Center** *Area Served: Cook County* *Write*: Cardiology Dept, 1753 W Congress Pkwy, Chicago, IL 60612 *Call*: 312/563-2179

# Hemophilia

**Hemophilia Foundation of IL** *Area Served: IL* Hemophilia Foundation of IL was organized by families afflicted with hemophilia, a bleeding disorder which causes crippling arthritis because of hemorrhages into joints. Its purpose is to combine their resources for help with the medical, social, emotional, and financial stresses of the disorder. Its history includes responses to such stresses over a 40-year period. *Meetings*: For patient and family. *Services*: Mutual aid, educational program or material, referral to other services, telephone support, home or hospital visitation, newsletter, written information, advocacy, referral to other services. *Write*: 332 S Michigan Ave, #1720, Chicago, IL 60604 *Call*: 312/427-1495

**Hemophilia Patients The Children's Hospital** *Area Served: Cook, DuPage and Will Counties* *Write*: 2300 Children's Hospital, Chicago, IL 60614 *Call*: 773/880-4489

# Huntington's Disease

**Huntington's Disease Society of America** *Area Served: IL* Assists HD patients and their families in coping with the disease. Raise money for HD research. Educate HD families, medical professionals and the public on the nature of HD and the need to combat it. *Services*: Mutual aid, educational program or material, advocacy, referral to other services, telephone support, social activities, newsletter, written information. *Write*: PO Box 267987, Chicago, IL 60626 *Call*: 708/420-0418 *Email*: schoenberga@hdsa.ttisms.com *Web site*: hdsa.mgh.harvard.edu

# Hydrocephalus

**National Hydrocephalus Foundation** *Area Served: IL, National* Not-for-profit org. for parents of children or adults with hydrocephalus. Mainly an educational and referral org. People with similar concerns are linked; symposia are held and new groups formed. Parents and adults with hydrocephalus have formed their own sub-group and support systems. *Meetings*: Twice yearly.

*Services*: Mutual aid, educational program or material, telephone support, social activities, newsletter, written information. *Write*: 1670 Gree Oak Circle, Lawrenceville, GA 30243 *Call*: 800/431-9093, 562/402-3523 *Fax* 770/995-8982 *Email*: ann_liakos@atlmug.org

# Hyperthermia

**Malignant Hyperthermia Assn of The US MHAUS** *Area Served: National* Provide educational and supportive services to MH susceptible patients, their families, and physicians. No known IL groups. *Services*: Educational program or material, telephone support, newsletter, referral to other services, professional service. *Write*: PO Box 191, Westport, CT 06881-0191 *Call*: 203/847-0407

# Hypoglycemia

**Help, The Institute for Body Chemistry** *Write*: PO Box 1338, Bryn Mawr, PA 19010 *Call*: 215/525-1225

**National Hypoglycemia Assn** *Area Served: National* Provides education and information to hypoglycemics or related conditions, their families, friends, and the public. *Services*: Mutual aid, educational program or material, referral to other services, telephone support, home or hospital visitation, newsletter, written information, professional service. *Write*: PO Box 120, Ridgewood, NJ 07451 *Call*: 201/670-1189

# Hysterectomy

**Hysterectomy Educational Resources and Services HERS** *Area Served: National* HERS provides information and counseling about the alternatives to and consequences of hysterectomy. Publishes a quarterly newsletter and hosts semiannual conferences throughout the US. All counseling is by telephone and is free. Medical journal articles are available. Helps women start support groups. *Services*: Mutual aid, educational program or material, written information, referral to other services, speakers bureau, hotline, telephone support, newsletter. *Write*: 422 Bryn Mawr Ave, Bala Cynwyd, PA 19004 *Call*: 215/667-7757

**Hysterectomy Support Group Ravenswood CMHC** *Area Served: IL* *Write*: 2312 W Irving Park Rd, Chicago, IL 60618 *Call*: 773/463-7000 1455 *Fax*: 312/463-8938

# Ileitis, Colitis and Crohn's

**Crohn's and Colitis Support Group** *Area Served: Peoria County* *Write*: St Francis Medical Center, 530 NE Glen Oak, Peoria, IL 61637 *Call*: 309/692-8743

**Ileitis and Colitis Educational Foundation** *Area Served: Cook-W and DuPage Counties* Promotes better understanding of chronic digestive problems such as ileitis, colitis and Crohn's Disease through presentations and discussions on topics such as tests and therapies for digestive disorders, nutrition and stress management. *Meetings*: Quarterly for all interested. *Services*: Mutual aid, educational program or material, advocacy, telephone support, newsletter, written information. *Write*: 34 Princess Ct, Westchester, IL 60154 *Call*: 708/562-0424

**Reach Out for Youth with Ileitis and Colitis, Inc** *Area Served: National* *Write*: 15 Chemung Pl, Jericho, NY 11753 *Call*: 516/822-8010

# Immune Deficiency

**Immune Deficiency Foundation IL Affiliate** *Area Served: IL* Promotes goals of national foundation. Provides support groups and professionally-led educational programs quarterly for families with persons with immune deficiency diseases. *Meetings*: Bi-monthly. *Services*: Mutual aid, educational program or material, written information, newsletter, social activities, speakers bureau, advocacy, referral to other services, hotline, referral to other services, telephone support. *Write*: PO Box 801, Wheaton, IL 60189 *Call*: 630/260-9589

# Impotence

**Impotents Anonymous** *Area Served: DuPage County* Provide information and support. *Meetings*: Monthly. *Services*: Mutual aid, educational program or material. *Write*: 200 Berteau Ave, Deicke Medical Education Ctr, Elmhurst, IL 60126 *Call*: 630/941-2646

**Impotents Anonymous Concerned Partner IANON** Addresses the concerns of women with impotent spouses through meetings and literature. 2 chapters in IL. *Services*: Mutual aid, referral to other services, speakers bureau. *Write*: 119 S Ruth St, Maryville, TN 37801 *Call*: 615/983-6064

**Impotents Anonymous IANON Headquarters** Offer confidential help to impotent men through meetings and literature. Impotence is not unusual but a problem many men share. 2 groups in IL. *Services*: Mutual aid, educational program or material, telephone support, newsletter, written information. *Write*: 119 S Ruth St, Maryville, TN 37801 *Call*: 615/983-6064

**Impotence Information Center** *Area Served: National* Provide the public and professionals with information on the causes and treatments of impotence. *Services*: Written information, referral to other services, educational program or material. *Write*: Dept A, PO Box 9, Minneapolis, MN 55440 *Call*: 800/843-4315

# Inclusion Body Myositis

**Inclusion Body Myositis Support Group** *Area Served: IL Write*: 609 Forest Edge Land, Des Plaines, IL 60016 *Call*: 847/297-7685

# Incontinence

**Help for Incontinent People, Inc** *Area Served: National* An international org. designed to assist people who have bladder control problems and to promote public understanding and professional education about incontinence. *Services*: Educational program or material newsletter, written information, advocacy, referral to other services, speakers bureau, fundraising. *Write*: PO Box 544, Union, SC 29379 *Call*: 800/252-3337

**I Will Manage Simon Foundation for Continence** *Area Served: IL* Gives information on I Will Manage, a 5-session program designed to help people who have incontinence themselves and their significant others (spouses, friends and family). Available also for use by hospitals, clinics and long-term facilities. Quarterly newsletter available for free with a self-addressed stamped envelope. *Services*: Mutual aid, educational program or material, newsletter, written information. *Write*: PO Box 815, Wilmette, IL 60091 *Call*: 800/237-4666 *Fax*: 847/864-9758

# Infertility

**Infertility and Endometriosis Support Group** *Area Served: Champaign County* *Write*: 510 W Charles, Champaign, IL 61820 *Call*: 217/355-2004

**Infertility Information and Support Group** *Area Served: DeKalb County* *Write*: 1108 S 2$^{nd}$ St, DeKalb, IL 60115 *Call*: 815/758-2355 Evening.

**Infertility Support Group** *Area Served: Peoria County* *Write*: Methodist Medical Center, 221 NE Glen Oak, Peoria, IL 61637 *Call*: 309/672-4100

**Living with Infertility and Experimentation** *Area Served: Cook, DuPage and Lake Counties* Helps individuals/couples claim their experiences to these high-tech procedures; to avoid the often-felt isolation. Encourages a personal owning, sharing and caring for one's self and others with their desires for a family. *Meetings*: Twice monthly for those interested. *Services*: Mutual aid. *Write*: 2434 Ridgeway, Evanston, IL 60201 *Call*: 847/491-1870

**Resolve of IL, Inc** *Area Served: IL-NE,and Winnebago County Write*: 318 Half Day Rd, #300, Buffalo Grove, IL 60089 *Call*: 800/395-5522

# Joint Replacement

**Joint Replacement Support Group Elmhurst Memorial Hospital** *Area Served: DuPage County Write*: 200 Berteau Ave, Elmhurst, IL 60126 *Call*: 630/833-1400 4691
*Fax*: 630/941-4596

# Kidney Disease

**American Assn of Kidney Patients Mississippi Valley Support Group** *Area Served: Rock Island County Services*: Mutual aid. *Write*: 1706 41st St, Moline, IL 61265 *Call*: 309/797-5582

**American Kidney Fund** *Area Served: National* Provides direct financial assistance to kidney disease patients who cannot afford costs related to their treatment. Other program services include: education, research, community services, and kidney donor development. One chapter in IL. *Services*: Educational program or material written information, referral to other services, newsletter. *Write*: 6110 Executive Blvd, #1010, Rockville, MD 20852 *Call*: 800/638-8299

**Dialysis Patient and Family Support Group** *Area Served: IL-N Write*: Rockford Memorial Hospital, 2400 N Rockton, Rockford, IL 61103 *Call*: 815/969-5751

**Dialysis Support Group** *Area Served: Lake County Write*: Highland Park Hospital, 718 Glenview Ave, Highland Park, IL 60035 *Call*: 847/480-3700 *Fax*: 847/480-2726

**End Stage Renal Failure Education-Support MacNeal Hospital** *Area Served: Cook County* Discusses various topics pertaining to dialysis and in the process promote emotional support for patients and families in coping with End Stage Renal Disease. *Services*: Mutual aid, educational program or material. *Write*: 3722 S Harlem Ave, Riverside, IL 60546 *Call*: 708/442-0690

**Friends for Kidney** *Area Served: Adams County Write*: Blessing Hospital, Broadway at 11th St, Quincy, IL 62301 *Call*: 217/223-5811 1018

**National Kidney Foundation of IL** *Area Served: IL* Funds medical research, public information and education

and patient service programs. Provides telephone support to persons who call and want to speak with someone who shares their concern. *Services*: Mutual aid, educational program or material, referral to other services, telephone support, home or hospital visitation, social activities, newsletter, written information. *Write*: 600 S Federal, Chicago, IL 60605 *Call*: 312/663-3103

**Positive Renal Outreach Program** *Area Served: New York* Changes the negative image associated with people on dialysis. Offers support group, is becoming involved with transplant patients, and is putting together a spouse support group. *Meetings*: Monthly. *Services*: Mutual aid, speakers bureau, social activities, telephone support, referral to other services, educational program or material, hotline, Home or Hospital visitation, newsletter. *Write*: PO Box 32, Maryknoll, NY 10545-0032 *Call*: 914/739-6436 Evening

**Renal Dialysis Support Group** *Area Served: DuPage County Write*: Elmhurst Memorial Hospital, Elmhurst, IL 60126 *Call*: 630/833-1400 4691

# Kidney Transplant

**Friends for Kidney** *Area Served: Adams County Write*: Blessing Hospital Broadway at 11th St, Quincy, IL 62301 *Call*: 217/223-5811 1018

**Transplant Support Group** *Area Served: IL-N Write*: Rockford Memorial Hospital 2400 N Rockton Ave, Rockford, IL 61103 *Call*: 815/969-5751

# Klippel, Trenaunay Syndrome

**Klippel-Trenaunay Support Group (K-T Support Group)** *Area Served: National* National org. which serves as a clearinghouse for information. K-T syndrome is a rare congenital malformation. *Services*: Phone link to members; support group; list of medical literature including portwine stain, soft tissue or bony hypertrophy, venous and lymphatic abnormalities. *Meetings*: Every 2 years in Rochester, MN. Call for specific dates and times. *Write*: 4610 Wooddale Ave, Edina, MN 55424 *Call*: 612/925-2596 *Fax*: 612/925-4708 *Web site*: www.tc.umn.edu/nlhome/m474/vesse00l/k-t.html

# Laryngectomy, Voice Loss

**Greater Joliet Area Voice Club St Joseph Medical Center** *Area Served: Will County* Support people who have experienced laryngectomies, oral surgery where voice box is affected and support family members in meeting needs of that individual and help family members cope. Meeting: Every other month. *Services*: Mutual aid.

*Write*: 333 N Madison Ave, Joliet, IL 60435
*Call*: 815/725-7133 3180

**International Assn of Laryngectomees Chicago Assn of Laryngec-tomees** *Area Served: Cook-S* Provide support, encouragement and information to persons who have lost their natural voice due to cancer or other causes. *Meetings*: Monthly for all interested. *Services*: Mutual aid, educational program or material. *Write*: 11318 S Neenah Ave, Worth, IL 60482 *Call*: 708/448-7412

**International Assn of Laryngectomees New Voice Club of Central IL** *Area Served: IL-Central Write*: PO Box 27, Mt Zion, IL 62549 *Call*: 217/864-3992

**International Assn of Laryngectomees North Shore Lost Chords Club** *Area Served: Cook County* Provides education and support for persons who have lost their voice box. *Meetings*: Monthly (except Jan and Feb) for anyone interested. *Services*: Mutual aid, written information, social activities, telephone support, home or hospital visitation. *Write*: 1806 Welwyn Ave, Des Plaines, IL 60018 *Call*: 847/824-0885

**International Assn of Laryngectomees Nu-Voice Club Memorial Hospital-Speech** *Area Served: St Clair and Madison Counties Write*: 4500 Memorial Dr, Belleville, IL 62223 *Call*: 618/233-7750 5255

**International Assn of Laryngectomees Second Chance Club** *Area Served: DuPage County Services*: Mutual aid. *Write*: 1502 Sequoia Lane, Darien, IL 60561 *Call*: 630/968-1899

**International Assn of Laryngectomees Second Voice Assn** *Area Served: Cook-S and Will County* Support group to provide information, emotional and social support for Laryngectomees and their families. *Meetings*: Monthly. *Services*: Mutual aid, educational program or material, written information. *Write*: Oak Forest Hospital, 15900 S Cicero Ave, Oak Forest, IL 60452 *Call*: 708/687-7200 3360

**Laryngectomee Support Group Little Company of Mary Hospital** *Area Served: Cook, DuPage and Will Counties Write*: 2800 W 95<sup>th</sup> St, Evergreen Park, IL 60642 *Call*: 708/422-6200 5285

**Laryngectomy Club-Loyola New Voice Club Loyola University Medical Center** *Area Served: Cook, DuPage and Will Counties* Educate and support for laryngectomy patients, families and friends. *Meetings*: Monthly. *Services*: Mutual aid, speakers bureau, written information, social activities, professional service, home or hospital visitation. *Write*: Speech Pathology Dept, 2160 S 1<sup>st</sup> Ave, Maywood, IL 60153 *Call*: 708/216-3775

**Laryngectomy Support Group** *Area Served: IL-Central Write*: St Mary's Hospital, 111 E Spring St, Streator, IL 61364 *Call*: 800/325-7699

**New Voice Club** *Area Served: Cook County Write*: Swedish Covenant Hospital, 5145 N California Ave, Chicago, IL 60625 *Call*: 773/878-8200 5305

**New Voice Club** *Area Served: IL-Central Write*: Box 27, 320 May Ct, Mt Zion, IL 62549 *Call*: 217/864-2992

**New Voice Club** *Area Served: Peoria County Write*: Methodist Medical Center, 221 NE Glen Oak, Peoria, IL 60636-0002 *Call*: 309/672-4110

**New Voice Club** *Area Served: Woodford and Peoria Counties Write*: 1200 E Partridge, Apt 7B, Metamora, IL 61548 *Call*: 309/672-4971

**Second Chance Club-Laryngectomy Support Group** *Area Served: Cook County Write*: 1502 Sequoia, Darien, IL 60561 *Call*: 630/968-1899

---

# Leukodystrophy

**United Leukodystrophy Foundation, Inc** *Area Served: IL* Provides information about Leukodystrophy; to assist families in identifying sources of medical care, social services and genetic counseling; to establish a communication network; to increase public awareness; to act as a source of information for health care providers; and to promote research. *Meetings*: For all interested except young children. *Services*: Mutual aid, educational program or material, telephone support, newsletter, written information. *Write*: 2304 Highland Dr, Sycamore, IL 60178 *Call*: 800/728-5483

---

# Life Support Technology

**Care for Life** *Area Served: National* National resource and international networking org. which endeavors to improve the quality of life and reduce the cost for those persons with prolonged dependency on technical and nursing care. Works to develop alternatives to institutionalization. Encourages formation of self-help support groups. *Services*: educational program or material advocacy, referral to other services, speakers bureau, telephone support, HV. *Write*: 1018 W Diversey, Chicago, IL 60614 *Call*: 708/327-9114

**SKIP of IL, Inc Sick Kids New Educational Program or Material—Involved People, Inc** *Area Served: IL* Serves children who are dependent on medical technology and require ongoing medical and nursing management to live at home. Provides education for parents and professionals. Hosts an annual Skip Family Day for families. *Services*: Mutual aid, educational program or material, advocacy, newsletter. *Write*: 240 Clinton, Oak Park, IL 60302 *Call*: 708/848-0723

# Life-Threatening Illness

## Life-Threatening Illness—Children

**Alexian Brothers Medical Center Hospice** *Area Served: Cook County Write*: 800 W Biesterfield Rd, Elk Grove Village, IL 60007 *Call*: 708/981-5574

**A Wish with Wings, Inc** *Area Served: National Write*: PO Box 3479, Arlington, TX 76007-3479 *Call*: 847/469-9474

**Children's Hopes and Dreams Foundation, Inc** *Area Served: National Write*: 280 Rt 46, Dover, NJ 07801 *Call*: 201/361-7366

**Make-A-Wish Foundation Northern IL** *Area Served: IL-N* Grants wishes to children between the ages of 22 and 18 who suffer from life-threatening illnesses. *Services*: Social activities. *Write*: 640 N LaSalle, Ste 289, Chicago, IL 60610 *Call*: 312/943-8956

**Ronald McDonald Houses Golin Harris Communications** *Area Served: IL Write*: 500 N Michigan Ave, Chicago, IL 60611 *Call*: 312/836-7100 7384

**The KID Program Edward Hospital** *Area Served: IL Write*: 801 S Washington St, Naperville, IL 60566 *Call*: 630/527-3569

## Life-Threatening Illness—End Of Life

**Choice In Dying** *Area Served: National* Fosters educated choices in medical treatment wishes at the end of life by providing information and counseling services. Provides low cost, state-specific advance directives, a living will and a medical power of attorney; information on health care professionals and families updated. Videos available; counseling service: 1-800-989-WILL (9455). *Write*: 200 Varick St, 10th Fl, NY, NY 10014 *Call*: 212/366-5540 *Fax*: 212/366-5337 *Email*: cid@choices.org
*Web site*: www.choices.org

**Home Hospice Visiting Nurse Assn North** *Area Served: Cook-N Write*: 5215 Old Orchard, #700, Skokie, IL 60077 *Call*: 847/328-1900

**Homecare and Hospice Palliative Care Center of The North Shore** *Area Served: Cook and Lake Counties* Not-for-profit Medicare certified hospice which provides health care services including a variety of support groups for the terminally ill and their family. *Services*: Mutual aid. *Write*: 2821 Central St, Evanston, IL 60201 *Call*: 847/467-7423 *Fax*: 847/866-6023

**Hospice of DuPage County Community Nursing Service of DuPage County** *Area Served: Cook and DuPage Counties* Support groups for the terminally ill and their family. *Services*: Mutual aid. *Write*: 690 E North Ave, Carol Stream, IL 60188 *Call*: 630/690-9000

**IL State Hospice Org. University of IL at Chicago** *Area Served: IL* Makes referrals to hospice groups throughout IL. Promote the growth and development of quality hospice programs. Advocates for hospices and the concept of hospice care. *Services*: Referral to other services, written information, advocacy. *Write*: School of Public Health, 1525 E 53rd St, #720, Chicago, IL 60615 *Call*: 773/324-8844

**Palliative Care Unit Silver Cross Hospital** *Area Served: Will County* Support groups for the terminally ill and their family. Bereavement groups are open to the public. *Services*: Mutual aid. *Write*: 1200 Maple Rd, Joliet, IL 60432 *Call*: 815/740-7031

**St Thomas Hospice** *Area Served: DuPage County* Support groups for the terminally ill and their family. Bereavement groups are open to the public. *Meetings*: Twice weekly for those bereaved. *Services*: Mutual aid, written information, referral to other services, telephone support, home or hospital visitation. *Write*: 7 Salt Creek Lane, Hinsdale, IL 60521 *Call*: 630/850-3990

**VNHA of Rock Island County Pathway Hospice** *Area Served: Rock Island Write*: 500 42nd St, Ste 8, Rock Island, IL 61201 *Call*: 309/788-0600

# Liver Disease

**American Liver Foundation Chicago Metropolitan Chapter** *Area Served: Cook County* ALF is a national org. that focuses attention on the problems of liver disease, treatments and cures and to educate the public and professionals. Individuals in their chapters provide contact and support to each other. *Meetings*: Monthly. *Services*: Mutual aid, educational program or material, advocacy, telephone support, newsletter, written information, referral to other services, speakers bureau, hotline, social activities. *Write*: 67 Brandon, Northfield, IL 60093 *Call*: 847/446-7616

**Lowe's Syndrome Assn 222 Lincoln St** *Area Served: National Write*: West Lafayette, IN 47906 *Call*: 317/743-3634

# Lung

**Alpha-1 National Assn** *Area Served: IL, N Write*: 1829 Portland Ave, Minneapolis, MN 55404 *Call*: 612/871-7332

**Alpha-1 Support Group Quantum Health Resources** *Area Served: DuPage and Cook Counties* Support group for anyone with Alph-1 Anti-Trypsin Deficiency, their spouses, children and significant others. *Meetings*: Quarterly. *Services*: Mutual aid, speakers bureau, written information. *Write*: 1406 62$^{nd}$ St, Downers Grove, IL 60516 *Call*: 630/852-2368 Answer Mach.

**American Lung Assn of IL** *Area Served: Lake County* Provides education about the prevention and control of lunch disease. Areas of interest include smoking and health (smoking cessation programs for adults and teens), pediatric lung disease (camp for asthmatic children, asthma management program for children/parents), adult lung disease (information/referral), environmental and occupational health, research and professional education. *Services*: Speakers bureau, written information, referral to other services, educational program or material, advocacy. *Write*: 10 Phillip Rd, Ste 106, Vernon Hills, IL 60061 *Call*: 847/367-5864

**American Lung Assn of IL Chicago Lung Assn** *Area Served: Chicago and Cook County* Mission: alleviation and eradication of lung disease in Cook County. *Services*: Public education/public awareness; patient and public advocacy regarding smoking, environment, patient care and other items; professional education on lung disease; patient support groups; printed materials of various lung diseases; camp for severely asthmatic children; smoking cessation self-help programs; other. *Write*: 1440 W Washington Blvd, Chicago, IL 60607-1878 *Call*: 312/243-2000 244

**American Lung Assn of IL DuPage County and McHenry** *Area Served: DuPage and McHenry Counties* Dedicated to the prevention, cure and control of all lung diseases and their related causes, including smoking, air pollution and occupational lung hazards. Our public health education, research, and scholarship programs are supported by donations to Christmas Seals, grants, and by other voluntary contributions. *Services*: Educational program or material written information, advocacy. *Write*: PO Box 590, Glen Ellyn, IL 60138 *Call*: 630/469-2400

**American Lung Assn of IL Eastern Region** *Area Served: Bound County and IL-S Write*: 218 C N 2nd St, Rt 1 Box 84, Greenville, IL 62246-1535 *Call*: 618/664-1894

**Easy Breathers Support Group South Suburban Hospital** *Area Served: Cook County Write*: Respiratory Care Dept, 17800 S Kedzie Ave, Hazel Crest, IL 60429 *Call*: 708/799-8000 3255

# Lupus Erythematosus

**Lupus Support Group South Suburban Hospital** *Area Served: Cook County Write*: Marketing Dept, 17800 S Kedzie Ave, Hazel Crest, IL 60429 *Call*: 708/799-8000 3006

**Lupus Support Group** *Area Served: Cook County Write*: EHS Christ Hospital, 4440 W 95$^{th}$ St, Oak Lawn, IL 60453 *Call*: 773/445-7071

**Lupus Foundation of America, Inc IL Chapter** *Area Served: IL* Offers 16 peer-led support groups throughout IL. Works to increase awareness and understanding of lupus. Provides educational programs, informational services and emotional support. Supports research. Educational meetings open to the public. *Services*: Mutual aid, speakers bureau, written information, social activities, telephone support, educational program or material, hotline, newsletter. *Write*: 11102 S Artesian, Chicago, IL 60655 *Call*: 773/445-7071 *Fax*: 312/445-8254

# Marfan Syndrome

**National Marfan Foundation Chicago Chapter** *Area Served: IL Write*: 5015 River Rd, Schiller Park, IL 60176

**National Marfan Foundation** *Area Served: National* National org. with 75 chapters. A genetic connective tissue disorder. Provides, information, supports and fosters research, support groups, quarterly newsletter, awareness, education and fund-raising activities. Sponsors an annual conference. Publications: The Marfan Syndrome Booklet: $4, fact sheet: free, resource information and published research: prices vary. *Write*: 382 Main St, Pt Washington, NY 11050 *Call*: 516/883-8712 *Fax*: 516/883-8712 *Email*: STAFF@MARFAN.ORG *Web site*: HTTP://WWW.MARFAN.ORG

# Menopause

**Menopause Support Group Ravenswood CMHC** *Area Served: IL Write*: 2312 W Irving Park Rd, Chicago, IL 60640 *Call*: 773/463-7000 1455

**Menopause Support Women's Health Advantage** *Area Served: Winnebago County Write*:2350 Rockton, Rockford, IL 61103 *Call*: 815/961-6215

**The Menopause Support Group** *Area Served: Lake and Cook Counties Write*: 2955 Whispering Oaks Dr, Buffalo Grove, IL 60089 *Call*: 847/634-1852

**Women In Transition: Menopause Support Group Northwestern Memorial Hospital** *Area Served: Cook County Write*: Women's Health Dept, 333 E Superior, Chicago, IL 60611 *Call*: 312/908-9971

**Women of Change Menopause Support Group** *Area Served: Lake and Cook County Write*: 2955 Whispering Oaks Dr, Buffalo Grove, IL 60089 *Call*: 847/634-1852

# Mucopolysaccharidosis

**National MPS Society** *Area Served: IL* Provides information and support to people with MPS. *Services*: Mutual aid. *Write*: 14390 Streamwood Dr, Orland Park, IL 60462 *Call*: 708/403-2578

# Multiple Sclerosis

**Multiple Sclerosis Society Support Group Swedish Covenant Hospital** *Area Served: Cook County Write*: Anderson Pavilion, 2751 W Winona, Chicago, IL 60625 *Call*: 773/274-6913

**Multiple Sclerosis Society Support Group Evanston Hospital** *Area Served: Cook-N* Most importantly, group provides a supportive atmosphere and camaraderie among the members. Professional speakers also provide pertinent, updated information. *Meetings*: Monthly for individuals with MS, concerned family members and friends. *Services*: Mutual aid, speakers bureau. *Write*: 2650 Ridge, Evanston, IL 60201 *Call*: 847/570-2030

**Multiple Sclerosis Society Support Group** *Area Served: IL* Support group for persons with multiple sclerosis and their significant others. Provides educational information as well. *Meetings*: Monthly. *Services*: Mutual aid, educational program or material. *Write*: Holy Cross Hospital, 2701 W. 68th St, Chicago, IL 60629 *Call*: 773/471-7300

**Multiple Sclerosis Society Support Group** *Area Served: Cook County Write*: Holy Family Hospital, 100 N River Rd, Des Plaines, IL 60016 *Call*: 847/541-0659

**National Multiple Sclerosis Society Chicago Greater IL Chapter** *Area Served: IL* Referrals to diagnostic and medical exams, social service and therapy. Offers counseling, equipment loans, peer programs and therapeutic recreation. Monthly newsletter. Numerous support groups and educational meetings. *Meetings*: Monthly for all interested. *Services*: Mutual aid, educational program or material, advocacy, referral to other services, telephone support, home or hospital visitation, social activities, newsletter, written information. *Write*: 600 S Federal St, Ste 204, Chicago, IL 60605 *Call*: 800/922-0484

# Muscular Dystrophy

**Adult Muscular Dystrophy Club, Inc** *Area Served: Cook County* Social, recreational and educational outings (mostly once a month) for people handicapped by Muscular Dystrophy or related muscular disorders. Membership limited to 35 to provide space as needed for wheelchairs and volunteer attendants. New members are

accepted when an opening comes up. *Services*: Mutual aid, educational program or material, social activities. *Write*: 1986 W Algonquin, Apt 9C, Mount Prospect, IL 60056 *Call*: 847/364-1946

**Muscular Dystrophy Assn** *Area Served: Kane, Winnebago and DuPage Counties Write*: 800 W Roosevelt Rd, Ste C 12, Glen Ellyn, IL 60137 *Call*: 630/469-1310

**Muscular Dystrophy Assn Northern Cook County** *Area Served: Cook and Lake Counties* Support group established to provide an opportunity for individuals served by MDA to share concerns and experiences common to their disability. *Meetings*: Monthly for those with concern and family members. *Services*: Mutual aid, educational program or material. *Write*: 2101 S Arlington Hts Rd, Ste 112, Arlington Heights, IL 60005 *Call*: 847/290-0060

# Myasthenia Gravis

**Myasthenia Gravis Foundation Greater Chicago Chapter** *Area Served: IL* Non-profit org. involved in the support of patients and family members, professional and lay education, and medical research into the cause, treatment and cure of Myasthenia Gravis. *Meetings*: Several times yearly for patients and families. *Services*: Mutual aid, educational program or material, advocacy, referral to other services, telephone support, home or hospital visitation. *Write*: 2338 New St, Ste 200, Blue Island, IL 60406 *Call*: 800/888-6208 *Fax*: 708/385-0447

# Neurofibromatosis

**IL Neurofibromatosis, Inc** *Area Served: IL* Provides information and emotional support to patients and family living with the effects of neurofibromatosis. Also provides support for research into the cause, treatment and cure for neurofibromatosis. *Meetings*: Quarterly. *Services*: Mutual aid, educational program or material, written information, advocacy, speakers bureau, referral to other services, telephone support, social activities, newsletter. *Write*: 407 Indianapolis, Downers Grove, IL 60515 *Call*: 630/963-6040

# Neurological Disorders

**International Tremor Foundation** *Area Served: National* Provide quality, updated information about essential tremor (also called benign or familial tremor) to patients and their caregivers and also support research. *Services*: Quarterly newsletter; booklets on dealing with medications, therapies, coping strategies, etc.; and international referral services. Support groups being

formed. *Meetings*: Call for specific dates and times.
*Write*: 833 W Washington Blvd, Chicago, IL 60607
*Call*: 312/733-1893 *Email*: UPF_ITF@msn.com

# Organ Transplant

**United Network for Organ Sharing** *Area Served: National* Strives for continual improvement in transplantation through collective self-governance to benefit patients with organ failure. Provides public and patient education; transplant-related statistics and information. *Write*: 1100 Boulder Pkwy, Ste 500, PO Box 13370, Richmond, VA 23225 *Call*: 804/330-8500 *Fax*: 804/330-8507 *Email*: NEWMANJD@UNOS.ORG *Web site*: WWW.EW3.ATT.NET/UNOS

**The Living Bank** *Area Served: National* Operates a registry and referral service for people wanting to donate their tissues and vital organs for transplant or research. *Services*: Referral to other services. *Write*: PO Box 6725, Houston, TX 77265 *Call*: 800/528-2971

**Share Our Universal New Donors Blessing Hospital** *Area Served: IL* Provides education for public and health care professionals about transplantation from the donation family view point. Also provides support for donors. *Meetings*: Quarterly but restricted to persons sharing the concern. *Services*: Mutual aid, educational program or material, written information, advocacy, referral to other services, speakers bureau, hotline, telephone support. *Write*: PO Box C3, Quincy, IL 62305 *Call*: 217/223-5811 1405

**United Network for Organ Sharing** Strive for continual improvement in transplantation through collective self-governance to benefit patients with organ failure. Provide public and patient education; transplant related statistics and information. *Meetings*: None; to call for information: (800) 24-donor. *Write*: 1100 Boulder Parkway, Ste 500, PO Box 13770, Richmond, VA 23225-8770 *Call*: 804/330-8500 *Fax*: 804/330-8507 *Email*: newmanjd@unes. org *Web site*: http://www.ew3.att.net/unos

**Organ Transplant Support, Inc** *Area Served: DuPage County* Write: Good Samaritan Medical Center, 1020 E Ogden, Downers Grove, IL 60515 *Call*: 630/527-8640

**Transplant Recipients International Org. TRIO** *Area Served: National* Influences international issues in the field of transplantation. Provide support counseling, education and informational medical programs and materialson transplantation. Members include transplant recipients, candidates, their families and health care professionals. No known IL chapters. *Meetings*: Monthly. *Services*: Mutual aid, educational program or material, written information, advocacy. *Write*: 244 N Bellefield, Pittsburgh, PA 15213 *Call*: 412/687-2210

**Transplant Information and Resource Program Rush-Pres-St. Luke's Medical Center** *Area Served: Cook County* Promote public education of the need for organ donors and to serve as are source for transplant patients providing needed information about transplant centers, financing, legislation, transplant specialists, etc. Also has telephone and mail support and a support group. *Meetings*: Weekly for patient and family. *Services*: Mutual aid, educational program or material, telephone support. *Write*: 1753 W Congress, Chicago, IL 60612 *Call*: 312/942-6242

# Organic Acidemia

**Organic Acidemia Assn** *Area Served: National* *Write*: 2287 Cypress Ave, San Pablo, CA 94806 *Call*: 510/724-0297

# Osteogenesis Imperfecta

**Osteogenesis Imperfecta Foundation, Inc** *Area Served: National* *Write*: 5005 W Laurel St, Tampa, FL 33607 *Call*: 314/937-2699

# Osteoporosis

**National Osteoporosis Foundation** *Area Served: National* Reduces widespread incidence of osteoporosis through increasing public awareness and knowledge of osteoporosis; provides information to victims of osteoporosis; educates physicians and allied health care professionals; advocates for increased governmental support for research of osteoporosis; supports basic research. *Services*: Educational program or material referral to other services, telephone support, newsletter, written information. *Write*: 1150 17th St, NW, Ste 500, Washington, DC 20036 *Call*: 202/223-2226

**Osteoporosis Support Group Southwest Suburban Senior Center** Provides support and treatment information to women with osteoporosis. We sponsor monthly educational programs, peer support meetings and group facilitators. *Meetings*: Please call for dates and times. *Write*: 111 W Harris, LaGrange, IL 60525 *Call*: 708/354-9325 *Fax*: 708/354-9352

# Ostomy

## Ostomy-General

**United Ostomy Assn, National Office** *Area Served: National* Provide education and rehab and support to people who have had or will have intestinal or urinary diversions. *Services*: Monthly support/education meetings, monthly newsletter, magazine-6 times a year, advocacy, and literature. *Meetings*: Monthly; call for specific times, dates and locations near you. *Write*: 36 Executive Park, Ste 120, Irvine, CA 92614-6744 *Call*: 800/826-0826 *Fax*: 714/660-9262 *Email*: UOA@deltanet.com *Web site*: http://www.gulf.net/civic/org/uoa

**United Ostomy Assn** *Area Served: IL* Voluntary health org. dedicated to assisting people who have or will have intestinal or urinary tract diversions by providing psychological support and educational services, support to the family unit and advocacy. Also promotes the services of the org. to the public and professional communities. 33 groups in IL. *Services*: Mutual aid, educational program or material, written information. *Write*: 841 N Ottawa Ave, Park Ridge, IL 60068 *Call*: 847/823-6312 *Fax*: 708/692-9468

**United Ostomy Assn Alton IL Chpt #0601** *Write*: 2555 Benton, Granite City, IL 62040 *Call*: 618/876-0717

**United Ostomy Assn Aurora IL Chpt #0325** *Meetings*: Monthly. *Services*: Mutual aid. *Write*: 750 Blaine St, Batavia, IL 60510 *Call*: 630/879-7833

**United Ostomy Assn Bloomington/Normal IL Chpt #0519** *Write*: 205 W Chestnut, Bloomington, IL 61701 *Call*: 309/828-3836

**United Ostomy Assn Capitol IL Chpt #0061** *Call*: 217/544-6464, 32462 E CR 580 N, Mason City, IL 62664

**United Ostomy Assn Carbondale IL Chpt #0660** *Write*: 915 S Lake Dr, Du Quoin, IL 62832 *Call*: 618/542-2594

**United Ostomy Assn Champaign/Urbana IL Chpt #0217** Provides support to persons receiving physical, emotional and social Rehab following bladder or colon surgery. *Meetings*: Monthly. *Services*: Mutual aid, educational program or material, home or hospital visitation, newsletter. *Write*: 2594 County Rd, 2400 N Penfield, IL 61862 *Call*: 217/583-3261

**United Ostomy Assn Chicago IL Chpt #0063** *Write*: 1828G Wildberry Dr, Glenview, IL 60025 *Call*: 847/998-1515

**United Ostomy Assn Danville IL Chpt #0336** *Write*: 43 Schultz St, Danville, IL 61832 *Call*: 217/446-0981

**United Ostomy Assn DuPage IL Chpt #0375** *Write*: 325 Greenfield, Glen Ellyn, IL 60137 *Call*: 630/469-8185

**United Ostomy Assn Elgin IL Chpt #0306** *Write*: 513 Ridge Cir, Streamwood, IL 60107 *Call*: 630/837-3762

**United Ostomy Assn Galesburg IL Chpt #0427** *Write*: Rt 3, Box 295, Galesburg, IL 61401 *Call*: 309/343-7389

**United Ostomy Assn Illiana IL Chpt #0218** *Write*: 2625 Wallace Dr Flossmoor, IL *Call*:708/799-3342

**United Ostomy Assn, Illiana Ostomy Group** *Area Served: Cook-S and Will Counties* *Write*: 87 Candlegate Circle, Matteson, IL 60443 *Call*: 708/720-2265

**United Ostomy Assn Joliet IL Chpt #0064** *Write*: 247 Caterpillar Dr, #284, Joliet, IL 60436 *Call*: 815/729-9010

**United Ostomy Assn, Kankakee IL Chpt #0066** *Write*: 616 N River St, Bourbonnais, IL 60914 *Call*: 815/932-8603

**United Ostomy Assn, Kankakee Ostomy Assn, Inc** *Area Served: Kankakee and Will Counties* *Services*: Mutual aid, speakers bureau, written information, social activities, telephone support, professional service, referral to other services, educational program or material. *Write*: PO Box 1641, Kankakee, IL 60901 *Call*: 815/949-1551

**United Ostomy Assn, Lake County IL Chpt #0067** *Write*: 15 Crestland Rd, Highland Park IL 60061 *Call*: 847/362-4757

**United Ostomy Assn, Little Egypt IL Chpt #0626** *Write*: Rt 5, Box 230, Marion, IL 62959 *Call*: 618/964-1577

**United Ostomy Assn, Memorial Hospital of Carbondale** *Area Served: Jackson, Williamson and Perry Counties* *Write*: 404 W Main St, Carbondale, IL 62901 *Call*: 618/549-0721 5615

**United Ostomy Assn, N Suburb Chicago IL Chpt #0343** *Write*: 2441 Fir St, Glenview, IL 60025 *Call*: 847/7254-7453

**United Ostomy Assn, Peoria IL Chpt #0062** *Write*: 2929 N Bigelow, Peoria, IL 61604 *Call*: 309/688-9455

**United Ostomy Assn, Quincy IL Chpt #0479** *Write*: 604 S Main St, Palmyra, MO 63461 *Call*: 573/769-4655

**United Ostomy Assn, Rockford IL Chpt #0068** *Write*: 2520 Breckenridge Ln. Rockford, IL 61114 *Call*: 815/636-1814

**United Ostomy Assn, SE Chicago IL Chpt #0677** *Area Served: Cook County* *Write*: 9319 S Jeffery, Chicago, IL 60617

**United Ostomy Assn, Short Circuit IL Chpt #0069** *Write*: 1605 N Union St, Decatur, IL 62526 *Call*: 217/877-3232

**United Ostomy Assn, Sterling IL Chpt #0616** *Write*: 24869 Front St, Sterling, IL 61081 *Call*: 815/625-7971

**United Ostomy Assn, SW Suburb Chicago IL Chpt #0495** *Write*: 9202 S Pulaski Ave, Oak Lawn, IL 60453 *Call*: 708/423-5641

**United Ostomy Assn, W Suburb Cook County Co IL Chpt #0436** *Write*: 1442 F N Harlem, River Forest, IL 60305 *Call*: 708/771-3651

**United Ostomy Assn, Woodstock IL Sat #011** (Elgin Chapter) *Write*: 625 Stanford Dr, Marengo, IL 60152 *Call*: 815/568-7123

**United Ostomy Assn, Charleston-Mattoon-Effingham Ostomy Chapter #0363** *Area Served: Coles and Effingham Counties* Helps in the physical, emotional and social rehab of Ostomy patients thru mutual aid, information and understanding. *Meetings*: Monthly. *Services*: Mutual aid, educational program or material, written information, advocacy, newsletter, telephone support. *Write*: 3327 Moultrie, Mattoon, IL 61938 *Call*: 217/235-1552

## Ostomy-Child

**Pull-Thru Network United Ostomy Assn** *Area Served: National* Provides support for parents and children born with imperforate anus who have had or will have pull-through surgery and/or fecal incontinence. *Meetings*: Quarterly. *Services*: Mutual aid, educational program or material, written information, newsletter, referral to other services, telephone support, home or hospital visitation. *Write*: 1126 S Grant St, Wheaton, IL 60187 *Call*: 630/665-1268

# Paget's Disease

**Paget's Disease Foundation** *Area Served: National* *Write*: 165 Cadman Plaza E, Brooklyn, NY 11202

**Paget's Disease Foundation Paget's Disease Support and Resource Group** *Area Served: IL Services*: Mutual aid, written information, telephone support, referral to other services, educational program or material. *Write*: 1574 Anderson Ln, Buffalo Grove, IL 60089 *Call*: 708/634-3292

# Papillomatosis

**Lazar Foundation for Laryngeal Papillomatosis** *Area Served: National Write*: 84-D Broadway, Danville, NJ 07834 *Call*: 201/627-1243

# Parenteral, Enteral Nutrition

**Oley Foundation, Inc Albany Medical Center** *Area Served: National* Provides patient support, education, and research in the field of home parenteral or enteral nutrition. Network of regional patient volunteers available for local outreach and support. Newsletter mailed free of charge to all home nutrition support consumers andfamily members. Annual consumer/clinical conference also free to consumers and family members. *Services*: Mutual aid, educational program or material, telephone support, social activities, newsletter, written information. *Write*: A-23 Hun Memorial, Albany, NY 12208 *Call*: 518/262-5079

# Parkinson's Disease

**American Parkinson Disease Assn: Information and Referral Center** The information and referral center has listings of support groups throughout the state and the country. There is also a program for young-onset members. Provide educational materials and symposia, support groups, fund raising events, and volunteer opportunities. *Meetings*: See listings in newsletters or call 1-(800) 223-9776. *Write*: 2100 Pfingsten Rd, Glenview, IL 60025 *Call*: 847/657-5787

**American Parkinson's Disease Assn** *Area Served: Kane County Write*: 6 N Andover Ln, Geneva, IL 60134 *Call*: 630/232-9642

**American Parkinson's Disease Assn** *Area Served: Will and Grundy Counties Write*: 250 E Maple St, New Lenox, IL 60451 *Call*: 815/740-1100 7629

**American Parkinson's Disease Assn** *Area Served: Kane County* Provides information and referrals to Parkinson's patients and their families. *Meetings*: Monthly for patients and families. *Services*: Mutual aid, speakers bureau, written information, telephone support, referral to other services, educational program or material. *Write*: 6 N Andover Ln, Geneva, IL 60134 *Call*: 630/879-2627

**American Parkinson's Disease Assn** *Area Served: Lake County Write*: 434 Greentree Pkwy, Libertyville, IL 60048 *Call*: 847/367-0161

**American Parkinson's Disease Assn** *Area Served: National Write*: 60 Bay St, Ste 401, Staten Island, NY 10301 *Call*: 800/223-2732

**American Parkinson's Disease Assn Kewanee Public Hospitals** *Area Served: Stark, Henry and Bureau Counties Write*: 719 Elliott St, Kewanee, IL 61443 *Call*: 309/853-3361 3307

**American Parkinson's Disease Assn Parkinson's Disease Support Group** *Area Served: DuPage, Cook and Lake Counties Meetings*: Monthly for anyone with Parkinson's and anyone else interested. *Services*: Mutual aid, educational program or material. *Write*: 1801 35th St, Oak Brook, IL 60521 *Call*: 630/246-0302 *Fax*: 708/671-4248

**American Parkinson's Disease Assn Parkinson's Support Group of Greater Chicago** *Area Served: Cook-N and Lake Counties* Support groups for people with Parkinson's and their caregivers. *Meetings*: Weekly. *Services*: Mutual aid, educational program or material, social activities, newsletter, written information, professional service. *Write*: North Shore Senior Center, 7 Happ Rd, Northfield, IL 60093 *Call*: 847/446-8765

**American Parkinson's Disease Assn St Joseph Hospital** *Area Served: Cook County* Provides information and referrals to Parkinson's patients and their families. *Meetings*: Monthly for patients and families. *Services*: Mutual aid, speakers bureau, written information, telephone support, referral to other services, educational program or material. *Write*: 2900 N Lake Shore Dr, Chicago, IL 60657 *Call*: 773/769-1932

**Bounce Back Support Group Iroquois Memorial Hospital and Resident Home** *Area Served: Iroquois County Write*: 200 Fairman, Watseka, IL 60970 *Call*: 815/432-5841

**Central IL Parkinson's Disease Support Group Methodist Medical Center** *Area Served: Peoria County Write*: 221 NE Glen Oak, Peoria, IL 61636 *Call*: 309/682-3959

**LaGrange Parkinson's Disease Support Group South West Suburban Center on Aging** *Area Served: Cook County Write*: 111 W Harris, LaGrange, IL 60525 *Call*: 708/354-1323 *Fax*: 708/354-0282

**McHenry Kane Parkinson's Support Group** *Area Served: IL-NW* Mutual aid/support group to give information and support to Parkinson's disease families. Offers brochure information, social activities, and referrals to other groups, as needed. Members share coping skills for Parkinson's disease, show educational films and have guest speakers, doctors, therapies, etc. *Meetings*: Monthly for all interested. *Services*: Mutual aid, educational program or material, written information, social activities. *Write*: 111 Siesta Rd., Carpentersville, IL 60110 *Call*: 708/426-5346

**National Parkinson's Foundation** *Area Served: National* Research, grants, education, information, clinical services (L.A. and South Florida only). Call the 800 number for referral to 15 IL groups. *Services*: Written information. *Write*: 1501 NW 9th Ave, Miami, FL 33136 *Call*: 800/327-4545

**Parkinson Support Group Southwest Suburban Senior Center** *Area Served: Cook and DuPage Counties* Provide support and information to Parkinson patients and their caregivers. Provide information to those affected by the disease through monthly educational programs and other services which include peer support, group facilitators, and prearranged transportation. *Meetings*: 3rd Thursday of every month, from 1:30-3:00 pm at the senior center. *Write*: 111 W Harris, LaGrange, IL60525 *Call*: 708/354-9325 *Fax*: 708/354-9352

**Parkinson's Disease Education-Support Group McDonough District Hospital** *Area Served: IL* For people who are interested in learning more about Parkinson's disease and how to cope with its effects in their daily lives. *Meetings*: Monthly. *Services*: Mutual aid, written information, telephone support, professional service, referral to other services, advocacy. *Write*: 525 E Grant St, Macomb, IL 61455 *Call*: 309/833-4101 3483

**Parkinson's Disease Info Center IL Support Group** *Area Served: Macon County Write*: Fair Havens Christian Homes, 1790 S Fairview Ave, Decatur, IL 62521 *Call*: 217/429-2551

**Parkinson's Disease Support Group** *Area Served: Cook County Write*: 30748 S Stateline, Beecher, IL 60401 *Call*: 708/946-2106

**Parkinson's Disease Support Group First United Methodist Church** *Area Served: McLean County Write*: 211 N School, Normal, IL 61761 *Call*: 309/452-2096

**Parkinson's Disease Support Group Kewanee Hospital** *Area Served: Henry County* Mutual aid and referral; monthly meetings. *Write*: 719 Elliot St, Kewanee, IL 61443 *Call*: 309/853-3361 283

**Parkinson's Disease Support Group McDonough District Hospital Center for Wellness** *Area Served: McDonough County Write*: 525 E Grant St, Macomb, IL 61455 *Call*: 309/833-4101 3483

**Parkinson's Educational Group** *Area Served: Rock Island County Write*: 3456 34th Ave, Moline, IL 61265 *Call*: 309/797-1884

**Parkinson's Educational Program** *Area Served: National* Can give general and specific information. Can put caller in contact with another person who has the disease or has a member of the family with the disease, through direct phone or pen pal program. Physician referral program. Three known support groups in IL. *Services*: Mutual aid, written information, telephone support, referral to other services. *Write*: 3900 Birch St #105, Newport Beach, CA 92660 *Call*: 800/344-7872

**Parkinson's Educational Program Southern IL** *Area Served: Union and Jackson Counties* P.E.P.S.I. promotes understanding of Parkinson's Disease for

patient, family and friends through materials and monthly meetings. *Meetings*: Monthly. *Services*: Mutual aid, educational program or material, written information, speakers bureau, home or hospital visitation, newsletter. *Write*: 402 N Main St, Jonesboro, IL 62952
*Call*: 618/833-4952

**Parkinson's Exercise and Support Group Rush-Presbyterian-St Luke's Medical Center**
*Area Served: Cook County Write*: 710 S Paulina, Rm 421, Chicago, IL 60612 *Call*: 312/942-4703

**Parkinson's Self Help Group Pavilion Senior Center**
*Area Served: Cook County-NW* Offers support to Parkinsonians and their caregivers. *Services*: Mutual aid. *Write*: 199 N First St, Wheeling, IL 60090
*Call*: 847/459-2670

**Parkinson's Support Group** *Area Served: Winnebago County Write*: Rockford Memorial Hospital, 2400 N Rockton, Rockford, IL 61103 *Call*: 815/968-1919

**Parkinson's Support Group of Greater Chicago** *Area Served: Cook and Lake Counties* Provides mutual support, information and education for patients with Parkinson's Disease. Also offers a caregivers group and an exercise group. *Meetings*: Weekly but restricted to persons sharing the concern. *Services*: Mutual aid, advocacy, referral to other services, social activities, newsletter. *Write*: North Shore Senior Center, 7 Happ Rd, Northfield, IL 60093 *Call*: 847/446-8751

**Parkinson's Support Group St Elizabeth's Hospital-Belleville Area College** *Area Served: St Clair County Write*: 201 N Church St, Belleville, IL 62220 *Call*: 618/234-4410 33

**Parkinson's Support Group St. Margaret's Hospital**
Provide psycho social and emotional support. Resource informationavailable for education. Encouragement from facilitator and group members. referrals for other help. Education on Parkinson's disease. Monthly support group meetings: 1st Monday at 1:30 pm; English; no transportation; accessible. *Write*: 600 E 1st St, Spring Valley, IL 61362 *Call*: 815/664-1132 *Fax*: 815/664-1188

**PUBS-PEOPLE United By Parkinson's** *Area Served: Will, Cook and Kane Counties* Mutual aid and education. *Write*: Silver Cross Hospital, 1200 Maple Rd, Joliet, IL 60432 *Call*: 815/740-1100 7629

**South Suburban Parkinson Support Group**
*Area Served: Cook County-S* Provide support to Parkinsonians and their families and friends. Learn what the doctor doesn't have time to tell. Has speakers and social activities. *Meetings*: Monthly. *Services*: Mutual aid, educational program or material. *Write*: 3415 Vollmer Rd, Flossmoor, IL 60422 *Call*: 708/799-7531

**Under 60 Parkinson's Support Group Glenbrook Hospital** *Area Served: Cook County Write*: Divn of Neurology, 2100 Pfingsten Rd, Glenview, IL 60025-1301 *Call*: 847/657-5787 *Fax*: 847/657-5708

**United Parkinson Foundation** *Area Served: National* International, non-profit org. provides Parkinson's disease patients with the most updated information about their disorder, medications and therapies currently available, research progress, coping strategies, etc. Via quarterly-published newsletters andother printed materials. Research support. Services include materials, intn'l referral services available to local groups. *Meetings*: 8-12 symposiums per yr, throughout US, all free.
*Write*: 833 W Washington Blvd, Chicago, IL 60607
*Call*: 312/733-1893 *Email*: UPF_itf@msn.com

## Patient Rights

**IL Citizens for Better Care** *Area Served: IL* Nursing home advocacy group whose purpose is to assist consumers by providing information on nursing homes and assistance in handling complaints. Education seminars are also provided. *Meetings*: Vary for all interested. *Services*: Mutual aid, educational program or material, advocacy, telephone support, newsletter, written information.
*Write*: 220 S State St, Ste 800, Chicago, IL 60604
*Call*: 312/663-5120

## Perinatal Loss

**Renew Through Sharing Northwest Community Healthcare** Provides regional support program with two support groups for parents experiencing ectopic pregnancy, miscarriage, stillbirth, and newborn death. Program is based on national program renew through sharing- bereavement services. *Services*: One-on-one support to parent; parents grief support mtgs; monthly newsletter, annual walk to remember and subsequent pregnancy support group. *Meetings*: Parent support-4th Monday, monthly; pregnancy support-2nd Monday. *Write*: 800 W Central Rd, Arlington Heights, IL 60005-2392 *Call*: 847/618-5220

## Porphyria

**American Porphyria Foundation** *Area Served: National* *Write*: PO Box 27712, Houston, TX 77227
*Call*: 713/266-9617

# Post Polio Syndrome

**Central IL Polio Support Group Springfield Center for Independent Living** *Area Served: IL* Peer support group for post-polio survivors and interested persons. Provides information sharing, guest speakers and resource sharing in a small group setting. *Meetings*: Every other month for all interested. *Services*: Mutual aid. *Write*: 426 W Jefferson St, Springfield, IL 62704 *Call*: 217/523-2587

**International Polio Network** *Area Served: National* *Write*: 5100 Oakland Ave #206, St Louis, MO 63110 *Call*: 314/534-0475

**March of Dimes Birth Defects Foundation Greater IL Chapter** *Area Served: IL Write*: 4507 N Sterling, Ste 201, Peoria, IL 61615 *Call*: 309/682-3335

**Northwestern University Post-Polio Support Group** *Area Served: Chicago* Support and inform post-polio survivors. *Meetings*: Monthly. *Services*: Mutual aid. *Write*: 215 E Chestnut, #1601, Chicago, IL 60611 *Call*: 312/664-6071

**Polio Network of IL Post-Polio Support Group** *Area Served: Winnebago, Boone and DeKalb Counties* Share a common identity among members with emphasis on mutual aid through discussion and sharing of experiences. Group activities are often recreational activities with fees charged for event. Networking to insure latest information is shared. *Meetings*: For anyone interested. *Write*: 1040 N 2nd St, Rockford, IL 61107 *Call*: 815/968-7467

**Post-Polio Support Group Christ Hospital Chapter** *Area Served: Cook County* Offers support and information for post-polio patients and their families. *Services*: Mutual aid, social activities, referral to other services. *Write*: 4440 W 95th St, Oak Lawn, IL 60453 *Call*: 708/425-8000 5263

**Post-Polio Support Group Impact, Inc** *Area Served: Madison, Macoupin and Jersey Counties* Provides peer support for persons exhibiting the late effects of polio. *Services*: Mutual aid. *Write*: 2735 E Broadway, Alton, IL 62002 *Call*: 618/462-1411

**Post-Polio Support Group Methodist Medical Center** *Area Served: Peoria County Write*: PO Box 120462, Peoria, IL 61614 *Call*: 309/691-0494

**Post-Polio Support Group Passavant Area Hospital** *Area Served: Morgan County Write*: 1600 W Walnut, Jacksonville, IL 62650 *Call*: 217/245-9541 3594

**Post-Polio Support Group Springfield Center for Independent Living** *Area Served: Sangamon County* Support group for victims of post polio syndrome. Professional and peer support. *Meetings*: Monthly.

*Services*: Mutual aid, professional service. *Write*: 426 W Jefferson, Springfield, IL 62702 *Call*: 217/523-2587

**Quad Cities Polio Survivors Support Group** *Area Served: IL, IA* Educate and support polio survivors and those with post-polio syndrome. *Meetings*: Monthly for all interested. *Services*: Mutual aid, written information, social activities, referral to other services, educational program or material, advocacy. *Write*: 1613 12 St, Silvis, IL 61282 *Call*: 309/792-1116

**United Post Polio Survivors, Inc** *Area Served: Chicago* Peer support group for victims of post polio syndrome. Cross-disability and able-bodied persons also attend. *Meetings*: Monthly. *Services*: Mutual aid, educational program or material, advocacy. *Write*: PO Box 273, Itasca, IL 60143-0273 *Call*: 630/784-6332

# Postpartum Depression

**Beyond Baby Blues Northwest Community Hospital** *Area Served: Cook County* Postpartum depression support group (beyond baby blues) meet 3 Mondays per month. Please call 847/618-7433 for further information. *Write*: Post Partum Depression Svcs, 800 W Central Rd, Arlington Heights, IL 60005-2392 *Call*: 847/618-7433 *Fax*: 847/618-4239

**Bittersweet-Post Partum Depression Support Group Mother-Baby Unit** *Area Served: DuPage County Write*: 25 N Winfield, Winfield, IL 60190 *Call*: 630/682-1600 6459

**I'm Still Me (for New Mothers) Methodist Medical Center** *Area Served: IL Write*: 221 NE Glen Oak Ave, Peoria, IL 61636 *Call*: 309/671-2110

**Postpartum Depression Counseling Women's Health Advantage** *Area Served: Winnebago County Write*: 2350 Rockton, Rockford, IL 61103 *Call*: 815/961-6215

**Postpartum Depression Program EHS Good Samaritan Hospital** *Area Served: IL Write*: 3815 Highland Ave, Downers Grove, IL 60515 *Call*: 630/275-4436

**Postpartum Education for Parents** *Area Served: National* Increase parents' confidence in developing their own parenting techniques and enhance the parent-child relationship by teaching good parenting skills and fostering positive attitudes. Develop communications in the family and between people with similar concerns and to refer parents with special and/or medical concerns to professionals. *Services*: Mutual aid, educational program or material, home or hospital visitation, written information. *Write*: PO Box 6154, Santa Barbara, CA 93160 *Call*: 805/564-3888

# Prader Willi Syndrome

**Prader-Willi Syndrome Assn (USA)** *Area Served: National* *Write*: 1821 University Ave W, Ste N356, St Paul, MN 55104 *Call*: 800/926-4797

**IL Prader-Willi Group Prader-Will Syndrome Assn** *Area Served: IL* Assists parents whose children have been diagnosed with Prader-Willi syndrome. Offer support to parents from others having a P-W child. *Meetings*: 4 times a year, Chicago area, call for specific dates and times. *Write*: 8142 Chester, Niles, IL 60714-2304 *Call*: 847/825-3502

# Pregnancy

**Planned Parenthood Chicago Area** *Area Served: IL* *Write*: 14 E Jackson Blvd, 10th Floor, Chicago, IL 60604 *Call*: 312/427-2275

**The Facts About Unintended Pregnancies American College of Obstetricians and Gynecologists** *Area Served: National* *Write*: 409 12th St, SW, Washington, DC 20024-2588 *Call*: 800/468-3637

## Pregnancy-General

**Bradley Method of Natural Childbirth** *Area Served: Kane County* Comprehensive program of prenatal nutritional counseling, preparatory exercises, skills for labor, delivery post partum, and parenting. This is a family-centered approach to a safe, non-mechanized birth experience, whether in the hospital or out; caesarean preparation is included. Instruction book is free. *Meetings*: Weekly. *Services*: Mutual aid, written information, educational program or material. *Write*: 426 Kings Way, Aurora, IL 60506 *Call*: 630/897-6258

## Pregnancy-Cesarean

**Cesareans-Support, Education, and Concern, Inc C-Sec, Inc** *Area Served: National* *Write*: 22 Forest Rd, Framingham, MA 01701 *Call*: 708/490-0067

**International Cesarean Awareness Network, Inc** *Area Served:National* Help educate women and their families in cesarean prevention and support them in vaginal birth after cesarean (VBAC) through a speaker format and a lending library. Open to all people. *Meetings*: Monthly speakers, quarterly support. *Services*: Mutual aid, educational program or material, written information, advocacy, referral to other services, speakers bureau, referral to other services, telephone support, newsletter, book and video, guide to chapter development. *Write*: ICAN, 1304 Kingsgale Ave, Redondo Beach, CA 90278. *Call*: 310/542-6400 *Fax*: 310/542-5368

*Email*: icaninc@aol.com
*Web site*: www.childbirth.org/setion/ican.html

**Perinatal Support Network** *Area Served: Cook County* *Write*: Lutheran General Health System, 1775 Dempster St, Park Ridge, IL 60068 *Call*: 847/696-5991

**Vaginal Birth After Cesarean VBAC of IL** *Area Served: Cook, Will and Kankakee Counties* VBAC of IL is a support group working to meet the needs of cesarean couples planning a VBAC as well as those wanting cesarean prevention information. Meeting: Monthly. *Services*: Mutual aid, telephone support, written information, educational program or material, advocacy, referral to other services, speakers bureau. *Write*: 729 E 163rd St, South Holland, IL 60473 *Call*: 708/339-7523

**VBAC Support Group South Suburban Hospital** *Area Served: Cook County* *Write*: Marketing Dept, 17800 S Kedzie Ave, Hazel Crest, IL 60429 *Call*: 708/799-8000 3006 *Fax*: 708/799-4768

## Pregnancy-High Risk

**High Risk Moms, Inc** *Area Served: DuPage County* *Write*: PO Box 4013, Naperville, IL 60567 *Call*: 630/515-5453

**Kravitt Subsequent Pregnancy Support Group Support Center for Perinatal and Childhood Death** *Area Served: Cook County* Addresses the emotional issues for families as they contemplate or experience pregnancy after a pregnancy loss or infant death. *Meetings*: Monthly. *Services*: Mutual aid, referral to other services, written information, educational program or material, telephone support. *Write*: Evanston Hospital/Pediatrics, 2650 Ridge, Evanston, IL 60201 *Call*: 847/570-2882

**Parent and Child Education Society PACES** *Area Served: Cook County* *Write*: PO Box 213, 1920 Highland Ave, Ste 300, Lombard, IL 60148 *Call*: 630/910-8131

**Share Edward Hospital** *Area Served: DuPage and Will Counties* Support group for parents who have experienced a perinatal loss and are now pregnant. *Meetings*: Monthly for parents. *Services*: Mutual aid, educational program or material. *Write*: 801 S Washington, Naperville, IL 60566 *Call*: 630/527-3263 Answer Mach.

**The Group B Strep Assn** *Area Served: National* Educates about Group B streptococcus bacterial infections during pregnancy. Provides information, newsletter, referrals, support groups, advocacy, and social activities. *Write*: PO Box 16515, Chapel Hill, NC 27516 *Call*: 919/932-5344

**Parent-To-Parent Rush-Presbyterian-St Luke's Medical Center** *Area Served: Chicago-W* Assist families of patients in the special care nursery to obtain optimal psycho-social well-being; give support during this time of extreme stress. Group open to parents whose baby requires intensive care treatment. *Meetings*: Weekly. *Services*: Mutual aid, educational program or material, advocacy, telephone support, social activities, written information. *Write*: 7 Jones, Special Care Nursery, 1753 Congress Parkway, Chicago, IL 60612 *Call*: 312/942-5068

**Pediatric-ICN Family Support Group Central DuPage County Hospital** *Area Served: DuPage County* *Write*: 25 N Winfield Rd, Winfield, IL 60190 *Call*: 630/642-1600 6951

**Very Important Pregnancy Program Healthdyne Perinatal** *Services Area Served: IL Write*: Rockford Memorial Hospital, 2400 N Rockton Ave, Rockford, IL 61103 *Call*: 815/968-6861 5475

## Pregnancy-Teen

**Greater DuPage County Mym, Inc** *Area Served: DuPage, Cook and Kane Counties* Provide peer support groups for adolescent parents, both moms and dads. Deliver parenting education through groups. Home visits to teen parents; peer presented prevention program, support/education groups for teen mothers and fathers-facilitated by former teen parents. Weekly meetings; transportation costs can be covered, child care and meals provided at group meetings. *Write*: 739 Roosevelt Rd, Bldg 8, Ste 202, Glen Ellyn, IL 60137 *Call*: 630/790-8433 *Fax*: 630/790-8024

**Teen Pregnancy Silver Cross Hospital** *Area Served: Will, Grundy and Cook Counties* Provide prenatal education to the pregnant adolescent and her family, promote self-confidence, motivation and control throughout the pregnancy and post-partum period. *Meetings*: Weekly for girls 12-19 and their families. *Services*: Mutual aid, educational program or material, written information. *Write*: 1200 Maple Rd, Joliet, IL 60432 *Call*: 815/740-1100 7629

## Pregnancy-Unplanned

**Aid for Women The Success Institute** *Area Served: Lake and Cook Counties* *Call*: 847/948-7100

**Courage Program** *Area Served: Cook and Will Counties* *Write*: St Germaine's Church, 4240 W 98th St, Oak Lawn, IL 60453 *Call*: 708/636-5060

**Shawnee Crisis Pregnancy Centers** *Area Served: IL* *Write*: 215 W Main, Carbondale, IL 62901 *Call*: 618/549-2794

**Shawnee Crisis Pregnancy Centers** *Area Served: IL* *Write*: 807 W Main, Marion, IL 62959 *Call*: 618/997-2790

**Society for The Preservation of Human Dignity** *Area Served: Cook and Lake Counties Write*: 27 N Plum Grove, Palatine, IL 60067 *Call*: 847/359-4919

# Premenstrual Syndrome

**Light for Health** *Area Served: National* *Write*: 942 Twisted Oak Lane, Buffalo Grove, IL 60089 *Call*: 708/459-4492

**PMS Access Premenstrual Information and Referral** *Area Served: National* National information service offering free information on the causes, symptoms, and management of PMS. MD referral lists for PMS and menopause. Information packets on PMS and menopause and natural hormone replacement therapy (free). Support group lists for PMS and menopause. *Write*: PO Box 9326, Madison, WI 53715 *Call*: 800/222-4767 *Fax*:888/898-7412 *Email*: wha@womenshealth.com *Web site*: http://www.womenshealth.com

**PMS Center of IL** *Area Served: IL-NE* Support groups focuses on family relationships, education about PMS and home therapies, e.g. light therapy, diet, stress reduction, and acupressure. Also workshops and comprehensive individual evaluations covering menstrual medical, and genetic history. Treatments may include personalized diet modifications, nutritional supplements, stress reduction, exercise, progesterone, and/or bright light therapy. *Meetings*: Bimonthly, but restricted. *Write*: 942 Twisted Oak Lane, Buffalo Grove, IL 60089 *Call*: 708/520-3822

**PMS Support Group Women's Health Advantage** *Area Served: Winnebago County Write*: 2350 Rockton, Rockford, IL 61103 *Call*: 815/961-6215

# Progeria

**Progeria International Registry NY State Institute for Basic Research** *Area Served: National* Provide information and telephone support to health care providers and Progeria families. Progeria is an extremely rare genetic syndrome that affects children and causes the appearance of accelerated aging. *Services*: Mutual aid, educational program or material, telephone support, written information. *Write*: 1050 Forest Hill Rd, Staten Island, NY 10314 *Call*: 718/494-5363

# Prune Belly Syndrome

**Prune Belly Syndrome Network** *Area Served: National* Provides support for parents of children with Prune Belly Syndrome by sharing information. *Services*: Mutual aid, telephone support, written information. *Write*: 1005 E Carver Rd, Tempe, AZ 85284 *Call*: 602/838-9006

# Radiation

**National Assn of Radiation Survivors** *Area Served: National* Write: PO Box 278, Live Oak, CA 95953 *Call*: 800/798-5102

# Rare Disorders

**Mothers United for Moral Support MUMS** National support group for families who have a child with any disorder, delay or disability. Newsletters provide support, education, and information on resources available to families. Offers a matching service for rare disorders and matches families to national support groups specific to the disorder. *Services*: Mutual aid, written information, social activities, telephone support, referral to other services, newsletter. *Write*: 150 Custer Ct, Green Bay, WI 54301 *Call*: 414/336-5333

**National Org. for Rare Disorders, Inc NORD** *Area Served:* NORD is a unique federation of voluntary health org. dedicated to helping people with rare orphan diseasesand assisting the orgs. that serve them to provide education, advocacy, research, and service. Provides access to and information to assistance programs eligibility, physicians guide to rare diseases, research programs, and referral to sources of assistance, support and clinical trials. *Meetings*: Yearly patient/family confer. *Write*: PO Box 8923, New Fairfield, CT 06812-8923 *Call*: 203/746-6518 *Fax*: 203/746-6481 *Email*:orphan@nord-rdb.com *Web site*: www.NORD-RDB.com/~orphan

# Raynaud's Disease

**Raynaud's** *Area Served: Cook County* Write: PO Box 632, Park Ridge, IL 60068 *Call*: 847/622-6480

# Reflex Sympathetic Dystrophy Syndrome

**Reflex Sympathetic Dystrophy Syndrome Assn** *Area Served: National* Write: PO Box 821, Haddon Field, NJ 08033 *Call*: 609/795-8845

# Retardation

**American Assn on Mental Retardation** *Area Served: National* Publishes and distributes various kinds of academic works on mental retardation. Written information. *Write*: 1719 Kalorama Rd NW, Washington, DC 20009 *Call*: 800/424-3688

**Assn for Retardation Citizens for IL** *Area Served: IL* Write: 1820 Ridge Rd, Homewood, IL 60430 *Call*: 708/206-1930 *Fax*: 708/206-1171

**Assn for Retardation Citizens of IL ARC-Friendship Facilities** *Area Served: LaSalle County* Write: PO Box 219, Ottawa, IL 61350 *Call*: 815/434-0737

**Assn for Retardation Citizens of IL ARC Gateway Center** *Area Served: Bureau, Marshall and Putnam Counties* Advances thru all resources, the total well being, dignity and rights of all citizens who are mentally retarded and to foster the prevention of mental retardation. Program includes; early infant intervention, adult vocational program, adult residential services, family support, respite care, foster care, and recreational assistance. *Services*: Mutual aid, educational program or material, advocacy, telephone support, social activities, newsletter, written information. *Write*: 406 S Grosse Blvd, Princeton, IL 61356 *Call*: 815/875-4548

**Assn for Retarded Citizens of IL Abilities Plus Inc** *Area Served: Henry County* Write: 319 N Main St., Kewanee, IL 61443 *Call*: 309/852-4626

**Assn for Retarded Citizens of IL ARC Malcolm Eaton Enterprises** *Area Served: Stephenson County* Write: 570 Lamm Rd, Freeport, IL 61032 *Call*: 815/235-7181

**Assn for Retarded Citizens of IL ARC Rock Island County** *Area Served: Regional* Improve the quality of life of all persons with mentalretardation by providing a comprehensive range of programs and services and assuring the rights, worth and dignity of the persons it serves. *Services*: Provide professional service. *Write*: 4016 9$^{th}$ St, Rock Island, IL 61201 *Call*: 309/786-6474

**Assn for Retarded Citizens of IL** *Area Served: McHenry County* Two parent support groups. Mutual aid. *Write*: Pioneer Center of McHenry County, 4001 Dayton St, McHenry, IL 60050 *Call*: 815/344-1230

**Assn for Retarded Citizens of IL Coleman Tri-County Services ARC, IARF** *Area Served: Gallatin, White and Saline Counties* Write: Box 869, Harrisburg, IL 62946 *Call*: 618/252-0275

**Assn for Retarded Citizens of IL Coles County ARC** *Area Served: Regional* Write: PO Box 587, Charleston, IL 61920 *Call*: 217/345-7211

**Assn for Retarded Citizens of IL Marc Center** *Area Served: McLean County* Write: PO Box 3548, Bloomington, IL 61702 *Call*: 309/827-6272

**Assn for Retarded Citizens of IL Peoria County ARC** *Area Served: Peoria, Tazewell and Woodford Counties* Various interest groups meet at different times; membership meetings as a whole approximately 4 times per year for educational purposes. Parent-to-parent support group monthly; Down Syndrome group monthly. *Services*: Mutual aid, educational program or material. *Write*: PO Box 3418, Peoria, IL 61612 *Call*: 309/691-3800 *Fax*: 309/691-2058

**Assn for Retarded Citizens of IL Proviso ARC** *Area Served: Cook County* Support groups for parents and for people looking for employment. *Services*: Mutual aid. *Write*: 4100 Litt Dr, Hillside, IL 60162 *Call*: 708/547-3950

**Assn for Retarded Citizens of IL Springfield ARC** *Area Served: Sangamon and Menard Counties Write*: 232 Burns Lane St, Springfield, IL 62702 *Call*: 217/789-2560

**Assn for The Mentally Retarded Champaign County** *Area Served: Champaign County Write*: PO Box 92, Champaign, IL 61820 *Call*: 217/359-9204

**Assn for Retarded Citizens of IL ARC** *Area Served: Regional* No self-help groups. *Write*: Lawrence-Crawford Assn, RR 2, Sumner, IL 62466 *Call*: 618/947-2412

**Center for Enriched Living** *Area Served: Regional* Social center for mildly and moderately retarded children and young adults. We offer programs that are geared to the individual needs of our members and are available year round for afternoons and evenings plus weekend programs. Scholarships are available to members who are in need. Bus service available from several points. Meetings held weekly. Educational program or material social activities, newsletter, written information *Write*: 1321 Wilmot Rd, Deerfield, IL 60015 *Call*: 847/948-7001 *Fax*: 847/948-7721

**Good Time Gang Developmental Services Center** *Area Served: Champaign County Write*: 1304 W Bradley, Champaign, IL 61821 *Call*: 217/356-9176

**IL Special Olympics, Inc** *Area Served: IL* State Headquarters for Special Olympics providing sports training and athletic competition for children and adults with mental retardation. *Services*: Mutual aid, social activities, educational program or material, written information, newsletter, hotline, speakers bureau, referral to other services. *Write*: 605 E Willow, Normal, IL 61761 *Call*: 309/888-2551

**Iroquois Assn for Retarded Citizens** *Area Served: Iroquois County* Provide information and support for parents whose child is developmentally disabled. *Services*: Mutual aid. *Write*: 9th and Cemetery Rd, PO Box 338, Watseka, IL 60970 *Call*: 815/432-5288

**Parent Group for The Retarded Inc** *Area Served: IL* Provide recreational programs for the mentally and/or physically handicapped. *Services*: Social activities. *Write*: PO Box 764, Mattoon, IL 61938 *Call*: 217/895-2341

**Parent Support Group Gateway to Learning Special Ed and Training Center** *Area Served: Cook County Write*: 4925 N Lincoln Ave, Chicago, IL 60625 *Call*: 773/784-3200 *Fax*: 773/784-3299

## Rett Syndrome

**International Rett Syndrome Assn** *Area Served: National Write*: 9121 Piscataway Rd, Ste 2-B, Clinton, MD 20735 *Call*: 301/856-3334

**Resources for Retarded and Autistic Families** *Area Served: DuPage County Write*: 590 S York, Unit B, Elmhurst, IL 60126 *Call*: 630/279-2441

**Sequin Retarded Citizens Assoc, Inc Parent Group** *Area Served: Cook County* Help people who are widowed deal with the problems associated with this concern. *Meetings*: Held monthly for widows and widowers. *Services*: Mutual aid, social activities, referral to other services, speakers bureau, telephone support, home or hospital visitation. *Write*: 6223 W Ogden Ave, Berwyn, IL 60402 *Call*: 708/788-5777 *Fax*: 708/788-5784

## Reye's Syndrome

**National Reye's Syndrome Foundation Chicago Chapter** *Area Served: Cook County* Public awareness of Reye's Syndrome. Supports parents of victims of Reye's Syndrome. Raises money for research. *Services*: Educational program or material, mutual aid, referral to other services. *Write*: 4407 Shabbona, Lisle, IL 60532 *Call*: 630/420-8477

**National Reye's Syndrome Foundation** *Area Served: National Write*: 426 N Lewis St, PO Box 829, Bryan, OH 43506 *Call*: 800/233-7393

## Rubinstein Taybi Syndrome

**Rubinstein-Taybi Parent Contact Group** *Area Served: National Write*: PO Box 146, Smith Center, KS 66967 *Call*: 913/697-2984

## Sarcoidosis, Sarcoid

**Let's Breathe Sarcoidosis Support Group** *Area Served: LOCAL* Provides support, friendship and information to people with Sarcoidosis and their families. Provides newsletter, doctor referral, Sarcoidosis information and education on this disease. *Meetings*: 3rd Wednesday of the month at 7:00 pm at Rush North Shore Medical Center, 9600 Gross Point Rd, Skokie, IL. *Write*: 2225 Foster St,

Evanston, IL 60201-3354 *Call*: 847/328-9410
*Email*: BHARRIS354@AOL.COM

**National Sarcoidosis Resource Community (NSRC)
Support Groups** *Area Served: Illinois* Chapter of a
national network of people with Sarcoidosis. *Services*.
Self-help groups are central assistance for
themodifications required by this systemic illness
affecting many organs in the body. *Services*: Registry of
over 24,000 patients, physician and support group referral,
mutual aid, annual conference, newsletter, research, online
support. *Web site*:
www.geocities.com/HotSprings/Spa/3513/

**Bloomington-Normal Sarcoidosis Support Group
Sarcoidosis Research Institute SRI** Meet at Franklin
and Virginia Ave, Normal, IL 61761 *Contact*: Dr. Eddie
Glenn, 309/438-7884

**Champaign-Urbana Sarcoidosis Support Group
Sarcoidosis Research Institute SRI** Meet at 1400 W
Park, Urbana, IL 61801 *Contact*: Dr. Eddie Glenn,
309/438-7884

**Illinois Sarcoidosis Support Group, Chicago** PO Box
21334, Chicago IL 60621 *Contact*: Glenda Fulton,
312/288-2881

**Peoria Sarcoidosis Support Group Sarcoidosis
Research Institute SRI** Meet at 1137 W Lake Ave,
Peoria, IL 61790 *Contact*: Dr. Eddie Glenn, 309/438-7884

**Sarcoidosis Research Institute SRI** PO Box 733,
Normal, IL 61761 *Contact*: Dr. Eddie Glenn,
309/438-7884

**Springfield Sarcoidosis Support Group Sarcoidosis
Research Institute SRI** Meet place: 800 E Carpenter,
Springfield, IL 62769 *Contact*: Dr. Eddie Glenn,
309/438-7884

# Scleroderma

**Scleroderma Foundation of Greater Chicago** *Area
Served: IL, WI, IN* Assists scleroderma patients and their
families in understanding this disease, to help in locating
adequate medical assistance, to conduct public education
forums, to act as an information clearinghouse, to raise
funds for medical research and cure for scleroderma.
*Meetings*: Quarterly. *Services*: Mutual aid, educational
program or material, written information, referral to other
services, speakers bureau, referral to other services,
telephone support, newsletter. *Write*: 330 S Wells, #1318,
Chicago, IL 60606 *Call*: 312/922-3532

**United Scleroderma Foundation** *Area Served: National*
Pioneer in bringing new hope and knowledge to
scleroderma patients worldwide through public awareness
programs and the funding of scleroderma research.

Provides a variety of informational brochures and
furnishes physician and chapter referrals. No knownIL
chapters. *Write*: PO Box 399, Watsonville, CA 95077
*Call*: 800/722-4673

**United Scleroderma Foundation, Inc Windy City
Chapter** *Area Served: Rock Island County* Provides
support group and educational discussions. Warm and
friendly atmosphere for networking and gathering input of
fellow scleroderma patients. Meetings supply a great deal
of educational materials. *Write*: On 313 Cottonwood,
Wheaton, IL 60187 *Call*: 800/722-4673

# Scoliosis

**Scoliosis Research Society** *Area Served: National*
Offers informational materials that can be purchased.
Society is made up of orthopedic surgeons only. *Services*:
Written information. *Write*: 6300 N River Rd, Ste 727,
Rosemont, IL 60018 *Call*: 847/698-1627

# Sexually Transmitted Disease

**Citizens Alliance for Venereal Disease Awareness** *Area
Served: Chicago* Information services for venereal
disease. VD confidential hotline and literature is provided.
Also provides information about AIDS through the
Citizens AIDS Project. Currently developing an
educational module on the semantics of sexuality.
*Services*: Educational program or material newsletter,
written information. *Write*: PO Box 30915, Chicago, IL
60631 *Call*: 312/236-6339

**Sexually Transmitted Disease Program IL Department
of Public Health** *Area Served: IL Write*: 525 W
Jefferson, Springfield, IL 62761 *Call*: 800/252-8989

# Short Stature

**Human Growth Foundation** *Write*: 7777 Leesbury Pike,
Ste 2025, PO Box 3090, Falls Church, VA 22043
*Call*: 703/883-1773

**Little People of America, Inc** *Area Served: IL* LPA is
concerned with the short-statured person and his/her
family in terms of social, educational, medical,
employment and psychological aspects of living in the
average-sized world. *Meetings*: Monthly for short-statured
person, friends and family. *Services*: Mutual aid,
educational program or material, advocacy, referral to
other services, telephone support, social activities,
newsletter, written information. *Write*: 1616 N Kennicott,
Arlington Heights, IL 60004 *Call*: 708/253-1398

## Sickle Cell Disease

**Midwest Assn for Sickle Cell Anemia** *Area Served: Cook County* Thru community education, patient referral, genetic counseling, annual college scholarship awards, a summer camp program, patient grants and research grants, MASCA is dedicated to improving the quality of life for persons with sickle cell disease and raising community awareness. *Meetings*: Call County Health Department for locations. *Services*: Mutual aid, educational program or material, advocacy, referral to other services, telephone support, social activities, newsletter, written information. *Write*: 200 N Michigan Ave, Chicago, IL 60601 *Call*: 312/345-1100

**Parents of Children with Sickle Cell** *Area Served: Cook County Write*: The Children's Hospital, 2300 Children's Hospital, Chicago, IL 60614 *Call*: 773/880-4496 3700 *Fax*: 312/880-4798

**Sickle Cell Disease Assn of America, Inc** *Area Served: National Write*: 3345 Wilshire Blvd, Ste 1106, Los Angeles, CA 90010-1880 *Call*: 800/421-8435

**Sickle Cell Support Group Francis Nelson Health Center** *Area Served: Champaign County Write*: 1306 Carver Dr, Champaign, IL 61820 *Call*: 217/356-1558

## Sjogrens' Syndrome

**National Sjogrens Syndrome Assn** *Area Served: National* Provides emotional support and information for patients and professionals. Encourages research and offers support group meetings, conferences, phone support, newsletter, information and referrals. Assists in starting new groups. *Write*: 5815 N Black Canyon Hwy. #103, Phoenix, AZ 85015 *Call*: 602/433-9844 or 800/395-NSSA *Fax* 602/433-9838

**Sjogrens' Syndrome Foundation, Inc** *Area Served: National* Support groups and resource volunteers answer questions and offer guidance to those with Sjogrens' Syndrome. Informs the public about the disease. Newsletter, handbook, guidelines and chapter develoment, video, annual symposium. *Write*: 4817 Mohawk Rd, Rockford, IL 61107 *Call*: 516/933-6365 *Fax* 516-933-6368 *Email*: ssf@mail/idt.net *Web site*: www.sjogrens.com

**Sjogrens' Syndrome Foundation, Inc** *Area Served: Chicago Write*: 2246 Allegheny Dr, Naperville, IL 60565 *Call*: 630/369-4577

## Skin Disease

**American Academy of Dermatology** *Area Served: National* Offers continuing medical education of members, as well as public information and educational services and brochures on skin diseases. *Services*: Educational program or material referral to their services, written information. *Write*: 930 N Meacham Rd, PO Box 4014, Schaumburg, IL 60168-4014 *Call*: 847/330-0230 339

**Dystrophic Epidermolysis Bullosa Research Assn DEBRA of America** *Area Served: National* National voluntary health org. working to find acure for Epidermolysis Bullosa (EB), a debilitating skin disease, through research, education, advocacy, and providing support services to victims of EB and their families. No known IL chapters. *Services*: Educational program or material written information, advocacy, referral to other services, referral to other services, telephone support, newsletter. *Write*: 141 5$^{th}$ Ave, Ste 7-S, NY, NY 10010 *Call*: 212/995-2220

**National Psoriasis Foundation** *Area Served: National* National group to help people cope with psoriasis; educate the public about the condition; and support research. referral to self-help groups. *Services*: Telephone support, newsletter, written information, mutual aid, educational program or material. *Write*: 6600 SW 92$^{nd}$ Ave, Ste 300, Portland, OR 97223 *Call*: 503/244-7404

**National Vitiligo Foundation, Inc** *Area Served: National* Locate, inform and counsel Vitiligo patients and their families. Increase public awareness and concern for the Vitiligo patient. Support research to find a cure. No known IL group. *Services*: Mutual aid, educational program or material, written information, social activities, telephone support, referral to other services, newsletter. *Write*: PO Box 6337, Tyler, TX 75711 *Call*: 903/534-2925

## Sleep Disorders

**The Awake Network American Sleep Apnea Association** *Area Served: National* Provides education, support, and social interaction for persons with sleep apnea, their family and friends. *Write*: 2025 Pennsylvania Ave NW, Ste #905, Washington, DC 2006 *Call*: 202/293-3650 *Fax* 202/293-3656 emai:asaa@nicom.com *Web site*: http://www.uasaa.nicom.com

**Chicago Awake Network American Sleep Apnea Association** *Area Served: Chicago* Encourages support and improvement in medical care for persons with sleep disorder. *Write*: Family Stress and Pain Clinic, 30 N MichiganAve, Ste 1729, Chicago, IL 60602, *Call*: 773.935-3500 *Email*: stressrx@geocities.com

**Awake Support Group** *Area Served: Winnebago County* *Write*: Rockford Memorial Hospital, 2400 N Rockton Ave, Rockford, IL 61003 *Call*: 815/969-5595

**Nasal CPAP User's Group** *Area Served: Kane, Kendall and DeKalb Counties* Group of people with Obstructive Sleep Apnea Syndrome who use nasal CPAP during sleep to help them breathe. to discuss new trends in the treatment of sleepapnea, new equipment, etc., and to share common experiences. *Meetings*: Quarterly for people with Obstructive Sleep Apnea and their families. *Services*: Mutual aid, speakers bureau, written information, telephone support, newsletter. *Write*: Copley Memorial Hospital, 502 S Lincoln Ave, Aurora, IL 60505 *Call*: 630/844-1030 3314

**Sleep Disorders Support Group** *Area Served: Lake County* *Write*: Lake Forest Hospital 660 N Westmoreland Rd, Lake Forest, IL 60045 *Call*: 847/234-6189

# Sotos Syndrome

**Sotos Syndrome Support Group** *Area Served: National* *Write*: 1710 Braden Dr, Normal, IL 61761 *Call*: 309/452-0973

# Spasmodic Torticollis

**National Spasmodic Torticollis Assn, Inc** *Area Served: National* *Write*: PO Box 476, Elm Grove, WI 53122-0476 *Call*: 800/487-8385

**National Spasmodic Torticollis Assn, Inc Spasmodic Torticollis Support Group of IL** *Area Served: IL* *Write*: 2616 N Lehman Rd, Peoria, IL 61604 *Call*: 309/688-4627

# Speech Impairment

**American Speech-Language-Hearing Assn Consumer Information** *Area Served: National* Offers information on hearing and speech problems and distributes materials on pathologists and audiologists (certified by the American Speech-Language-Hearing Assn), hearing aids, and other topics related to hearing and speech. *Services*: Written information, educational program or material. *Write*: 10801 Rockville Pike, Rockville, MD 20852 *Call*: 800/638-8355

## Stuttering

**Fluency Group University of IL Speech and Hearing Clinic** *Area Served: Champaign County* *Write*: 901 S 6th St, Champaign, IL 61820 *Call*: 217/333-2230

**National Center for Stuttering Chicago Air Flow Group** *Area Served: National* *Write*: 200 E 33rd St, NY, NY 10016 *Call*: 800/221-2483

**National Stuttering Project** *Area Served: Cook and DuPage Counties* *Write*: 1044 S Waiola, LaGrange, IL 60525 *Call*: 708/354-0160

**National Stuttering Project** *Area Served: National* *Write*: 2151 Irving St, #208, San Francisco, CA 94122-1609 *Call*: 415/566-5324

**National Stuttering Project** *Area Served: National* Search for national stuttering project. Phone 847/548-8470 Days or 1-800/364-1677. *Write*: Lambs Farm, Libertyville, IL 60048 *Call*: 815/675-2511 *Email*: 200-0803@mcimail.com *Web site*: www.mankato.msus.edu/dept/comdis/kuster/stutter.html

**National Stuttering Project Chicago Stuttering Society** *Area Served: Local* Search for National Stuttering Project. 1-800/364-1677. *Write*: Ravenswood Hospital, 2312 W Irving Park Rd, Chicago, IL 60618 *Call*: 312/413-3278 *Email*:cdugan@uic.edu *Web site*: www.mankato.msus.ed u/dept/comdis/kuster/stutter.html

**National Stuttering Project Chicago Stuttering Society** *Area Served: IL* *Write*: 2136 W Agatite, Chicago, IL 60625 *Call*: 773/878-9719

**National Stuttering Project (NSP) Chicagoland** *Area Served: Local* Provides self-help support for people who stutter, family members and stuttering treatment professionals in the US. Offers information about treatment options. Offers advocacy, small group discussion and an opportunity to practice speaking in a non- threatening environment or stutter without fear of embarrassment. Offers education, regional and national conferences. *Meetings*: Monthly; 1-800/364-1677. *Write*: Wood Dale Library, Wood Dale, IL *Call*: 708/354-0160 *Email*: JAMcClure@aol.com *Web site*: www.mankato.msus.edu/dept/comd is/kuster/stutter.html

**National Stuttering Project University of IL** *Area Served: IL* *Write*: Fairchild Hall, #204, Normal, IL 61761 *Call*: 309/438-8643

**Self Help Group for Stutterers Oak Forest Hospital** *Area Served: Cook and Will Counties* Provides a supportive environment in which the members can feel free to stutter, can communicate about their stuttering and can gain valuable speaking experience. *Meetings*: Bi-monthly for persons with concern, families and friends. *Services*: Mutual aid. *Write*: 15900 S Cicero, Oak Forest, IL 60452 *Call*: 708/687-7200 3360

**Stutterers Support Group** *Area Served: IL* Provide self-help and guide people who stutter and their families. Treatment professionals available. Information, advocacy and Mutual support offered. *Meetings*: monthly, small-group discussions, expert speakers, and Regional workshops/national conferences. Call for time and dates. Provide information about treatment options. Local self-help groups are affiliated with the national stuttering project. *Write*: 9242 Gross Point Rd, #305, Skokie, IL 60077-1338 *Call*: 847/677-8280 *Email*: JAMcClure@aol.com

# Spina Bifida

**IL Spina Bifida Assn** *Area Served: IL* Non-profit org. interested in improving medical and social welfare of spina bifida patients. Offers information and educational programs, equipment loan scholarship fund, summer camp and family outreach. *Meetings*: Monthly for patient, family and friends. *Services*: Mutual aid, educational program or material, advocacy, referral to other services, social activities, newsletter, written information. *Write*: 4699 Auvergne, Ste 9, Lisle, IL 60532 *Call*: 630/960-2426

**Spina Bifida Assn of America** *Area Served: National* Provides information on spina bifida to new parents, support research into the cause of spina bifida, advocate in government and with legislators about the rights and potential of those with disabilities and spina bifida, support professional education of this birth defect. One chapter in IL. *Services*: Mutual aid, educational program or material, advocacy, referral to other services, social activities, newsletter, written information. *Write*: 4590 MacArthur Blvd Nw, Ste 250, Washington, DC 20007 *Call*: 800/621-3141

# Spinal Cord Injury (*See also* Paralysis)

**American Paralysis Assn Spinal Cord Injury Hotline** *Area Served: National* Provides information and referrals. *Write*: 2201 Argonne Dr, Baltimore, MD 21218 *Call*: 800/225-0292 *Web site*: www.apacure.com

**National Spinal Cord Injury Assn IL Chapter** *Area Served: IL* Addresses the needs of spinal cord injured persons through peer support on a one-to-one basis for disabled individuals and/or family members; education programs on disability related issues; professional education programs; prevention programs for students and other groups. 5 groups in Chicago area. *Meetings*: Monthly. *Services*: Mutual aid, educational program or material, advocacy, referral to other services, telephone support, referral to other services, newsletter, written information, speakers bureau. *Write*: 1032 S LaGrange Rd, LaGrange, IL 60525 *Call*: 708/352-6223

**National Spinal Cord Injury Hotline** *Area Served: National* Offers information and referral for spinal cord

injured persons and their families. 800/526-3436 (24 hrs for new injuries)

**Spinal Cord Family Support Group Northwestern Memorial Hospital** *Area Served: Cook County* Helps family/friends of people who have sustained a SCI recently (i.e., within 1 to 3 months) to cope with hospitalization and stress. Most patients are currently hospitalized on Northwestern's SCI Unit. The goals are education, support and problem solving. *Meetings*: Twice weekly for all interested. *Services*: Mutual aid, educational program or material. *Write*: Spinal Cord Injury Unit, Superior and Fairbanks Ct, Chicago, IL 60611 *Call*: 312/908-5170

**Spinal Cord Society** *Area Served: Madison County* *Write*: PO Box 304, Hamel, IL 62046 *Call*: 618/633-2568

**Spinal Cord Society** *Area Served: Montgomery County* Seeking cure, encouraging funding of research, legal advocacy. *Services*: Educational program or material advocacy, referral to other services, newsletter, written information. *Write*: RR 1, Litchfield, IL 62056 *Call*: 217/324-2045

**Spinal Cord Society Chicago Chapter** *Area Served: Chicago* Raises funds, increase awareness, and educate the public about spinal cord injuries and related problems. Our motto is cure, not care. *Services*: Educational program or material fundraising. *Write*: 6180 N Lemont, Chicago, IL 60646 *Call*: 773/777-4087

**Spinal Cord Support Group Marianjoy Rehab Hospital** *Area Served: DuPage County* *Write*: 26 W 171 Roosevelt Rd, PO Box 795, Wheaton, IL 60189 *Call*: 630/462-4217

# Spinal Muscular Atrophy

**Families of Spinal Muscular Atrophy** Offers families support and up-to-date information; to set up library of protocol for different stages of management; to raise money for research to reach goals of treatment, prevention and cure; to form a national registry and clearinghouse. *Services*: Referral to other services, telephone support, home or hospital visitation, newsletter, written information, MA. *Write*: PO Box 1465, Highland Park, IL 60035 *Call*: 847/367-7620

# Sports and Fitness

**ATHLETE NETWORK** *Area Served: National* Online community for student athletes. Prepares students and families for high school and college sports. Discusses the impact of recruitment, sports injuries, drugs, employment and life goals. *Call*: 773/481-8837 *Fax*: 773/481-8917 *Web site*: http//www.athletenetwork.com

**Women's Sports Foundation** *Area Served: National* Encourage communities to support and celebrate the participation and achievements of girls and women in sport and fitness. *Meetings*: Call for information. *Write*: Eisenhower Park, East Meadow, NY 11554 *Call*: 516/542-4700 *Fax*: 516/542-4716 *Email*:wosport@aol.com *Web site*: wwwlifetimetv.Com/WoSport

# Stroke

**AHA Stroke Connection American Heart Assn** *Area Served: National  Write*: 7272 Greenville Ave, Dallas, TX 75231 *Call*: 800/553-6321

**CGH Stroke Club CGH Medical Center**  Provide support group for those persons who have suffered a stroke and for their spouse or close family members. Speech and hearing services. Program and light refreshments. *Meetings*: 2nd Wednesday of each month, 3-4:30 pm,wheelchair accessible. *Write*: 100 E Lefevre, Sterling, IL 61081 *Call*: 815/625-0400 4490 *Fax*: 815/622-9605

**CHO Stroke Club Community Hospital of Ottawa** *Area Served: LaSalle County  Write*: 1100 E Norris Dr, Ottawa, IL 61350 *Call*: 815/433-3100 316

**Danville-Vermilion Stroke Survivor Support Group United Samaritan Medical Center** *Area Served: Vermilion  Write*: Rehab Dept, 812 N Logan Ave, Danville, IL 61832-3788 *Call*: 217/446-9209

**Forever Friends** *Area Served: Chicago  Write*: Hinsdale Hospital, B2 120 N Oak, Hinsdale, IL 60521 *Call*: 800/647-7227

**IL Valley Stroke Club St Mary's Hospital** *Area Served: IL*  Support for persons who have sustained a stroke and for their caregivers. *Meetings*: Monthly, except Jan and Feb. *Services*: Mutual aid, educational program or material, social activities. *Write*: 111 E Spring St, Streator, IL 61364 *Call*: 800/325-7699

**Joliet Stroke Club Our Lady of Angels Retirement Home** *Area Served: Will and Grundy Counties*  Brings together the disabled and their families for mutual aid, fellowship, and service to others. Objectives are to encourage socialization, the development of self-esteem and to provide resources for the newly disabled. *Meetings*: Monthly for patient and family. *Services*: Mutual aid, educational program or material, telephone support, social activities, newsletter, written information. *Write*: 2618 Caddy Lane, Joliet, IL 60435 *Call*: 815/725-1902

**North Side Stroke Club Thorek Hospital** *Area Served: Cook County*  Offers support, education and activities for stroke survivors and their caretakers. *Meetings*: Monthly. *Services*: Mutual aid, educational program or material.

*Write*: 850 W. Irving Park Rd., Chicago, IL 60613 *Call*: 773/975-6840

**Stroke-Cardiac Club Morrison Hospital** *Area Served: Whiteside County  Write*: 303 N Jackson Ave, Morrison, IL 61270 *Call*: 815/772-4003 292

**Stroke Caregiver Support Group Evanston Hospital** *Area Served: Cook County*  Provides support and professional guidance for people who have experienced stroke and for their families. Provides fellowship for those caring for stroke victims. *Services*: Mutual aid, referral to other services, social activities, newsletter. *Write*: 2650 Ridge, Evanston, IL 60201 *Call*: 847/570-2030

**Stroke Club**  *Area Served: Cook County  Write*: Lutheran General Health System, 1775 Dempster St, Park Ridge, IL 60068 *Call*: 847/696-6690

**Stroke Club Highland Park Hospital** *Area Served: Cook-N and Lake Counties*  Provides education, group support and socialization for persons with strokes and their families. *Services*: Mutual aid, educational program or material, speakers bureau, social activities, newsletter. *Write*: 718 Glenview Ave, Highland Park, IL 60035 *Call*: 847/432-8000 4088

**Stroke Club Loyola University Medical Center** *Area Served: Cook County Write*: 2160 1st Ave, Dept of Speech Pathology, Maywood, IL 60153 *Call*: 708/216-3775

**Stroke Club Ravenswood Hospital-Medical Center** *Area Served: IL*  For people who have had strokes and for their families. *Meetings*: Monthly. *Services*: Mutual aid. *Write*: 4550 N Winchester, Chicago, IL 60640 *Call*: 773/878-4300 7627

**Stroke Club Rush North Shore Medical Center** *Area Served: Cook and Lake Counties*  Support group for stroke survivors. The content of meetings varies: activities, lectures or open discussion. *Meetings*: Monthly. *Services*: Mutual aid. *Write*: 9600 Gross Point Rd, Skokie, IL 60076 *Call*: 847/933-6595

**Stroke Rehab Support Group SBLHC** *Area Served: Coles County  Write*: 1000 Health Care Dr, Mattoon, IL 61938 *Call*: 217/258-2392

**Stroke Support Group**  *Area Served: Cook County  Write*: Evanston Hospital 2650 Ridge Ave, Evanston, IL 60201 *Call*: 847/570-2135

**Stroke Support Group Life-Center for Independent Living** *Area Served: DeWitt, Ford and Livingston Counties  Write*: 1328 E Empire, Bloomington, IL 61701 *Call*: 309/663-5433

**Stroke Support Group Little Company of Mary Hospital** *Area Served: Cook-S*  Focuses on the rehab of health and function. *Meetings*: Monthly for all interested.

*Services*: Mutual aid, written information, educational program or material, social activities, referral to other services. *Write*: 2800 W 95ᵗʰ St, Evergreen Park, IL 60642 *Call*: 708/422-6200 5285

**Stroke Support Group Passavant Area Hospital**
*Area Served: Morgan County Write*: 1600 W Walnut, Jacksonville, IL 62650 *Call*: 217/245-9541 3594

**Stroke Support Group St Francis Medical Center**
*Area Served: IL Write*: 530 NE Glen Oak Ave, Peoria, IL 61637 *Call*: 309/655-6994

**Sauk Valley Stroke Club CGH Medical Center**
*Area Served: Regional* Offers support for speech and hearing Rehab following a stroke. *Write*: 100 E Lefevre Rd, Speech and Hearing Services, Sterling, IL 61081-1279 *Call*: 815/625-0400 4490 *Fax*: 815/622-9605

## Sturge Weber Syndrome

**The Sturge-Weber Foundation** *Area Served: National* *Write*: PO Box 460931, Aurora, CO 80046 *Call*: 800/627-5482

## Syringomyelia Chiari Malformation

**The American Syringomyelia Alliance Project, Inc**
**ASAP** *Area Served: National* Provides mutual aid through network and support program. Offers information through brochure, reports on Syringomyelia and Arnold Chiari, and video lectures. Yearly convention includes workshops and speakers; yearly walk-a-thon help with fund-raising. No known IL chapters. *Services*: Mutual aid, written information, social activities, telephone support, referral to other services, newsletter. *Write*: PO Box 1586, Longview, TX 75606-1586 *Call*: 903/236-7079

## Temporo Mandibular Joint Dysfunction

**Midwest TMJ Support Group Hinsdale Chapter** *Area Served: DuPage, Lake, Cook and Kane Counties* Provides support and education to persons with TMJ and related problems and to educate the public and health care providers thru free speakers on TMJ and its prevention, diagnosis and treatment. For all interested. Sponsored by Hinsdale Hospital Physical Therapy Dept. *Meetings*: Monthly. *Services*: Mutual aid, educational program or material. *Write*: 238 W St Charles Rd, Elmhurst, IL 60126 *Call*: 630/833-3992

**TMJ Support Group, Inc Jjamd Foundation, Inc**
*Area Served: National Write*: Forsyth's Research Institute, 140 Fenway, Boston, MA 02115 *Call*: 617/266-2550

## Thrombocytopenia

**Thrombocytopenia-Absent Radius Syndrome Assn**
**TARSA** *Area Served: National* Serves as a clearinghouse of information for parents of children with TAR syndrome, to act as a forum to share experiences, and to make immediate contact with parents newly confronted by the birth of a child with TAR syndrome. *Services*: Educational program or material advocacy, newsletter, written information, referral to other services. *Write*: 212 Sherwood Dr, RD 1, Linwood, NJ 08221-9745 *Call*: 609/927-0418

## Tourette Syndrome

**Tourette Syndrome Assn, Inc of IL** *Area Served: IL* Increase public and professional awareness, knowledge, acceptance, and understanding of Tourette Syndrome. Educate physicians, and other health service providers about symptoms and current treatment. Promote research seeking cause, control and cure, and provide supportive patient and family network. *Meetings*: Quarterly. *Services*: Mutual aid, educational program or material, written information, speakers bureau, telephone support, referral to other services, advocacy, hotline, newsletter. *Write*: 5102 Oakton St, #115, Skokie, IL 60077-3614 *Call*: 847/675-2121 *Fax*: 708/675-2147 *Email*: Tourette@ix.netcom.com *Web site*: http://tsa.ngh.harvard.edu

## Toxic Shock Syndrome

**Personal Products Consumer Response Center** *Area Served: National* Provides information on a wide range of women's health concerns including toxic shock syndrome. *Services*: Written information. *Write*: 199 Grandview Rd, Skillman, NJ 08558 *Call*: 800/526-3967

**Women's Med-Plus Center** *Area Served: National* *Write*: 173 E MacMillan St, Cincinnati, OH 46519 *Call*: 800/543-7225

## Treacher Collins Syndrome

**Treacher Collins Foundation** *Area Served: National* Support, inform and network families and individuals with TC syndrome and related conditions. Resource for information. Provide medical, educational and other service providers with information about TC syndrome.

Promote research. Provide networking, newsletter, brochures, library resource and referral. *Meetings*: As required-call. *Write*: PO Box 683, Norwich, VT 05055 *Call*: 802/649-3050

# Trisomy 18-13

**Support org. for Trisomy 18-13 and Related** *Write*: 1610 Douglas St, Joliet, IL 60435 *Call*: 815/744-5602

# Tuberous Sclerosis

**National Tuberous Sclerosis Assn** *Area Served: IL* Serves as a source of information, hope, and understanding to all persons affected by this genetic disease, while providing access to available services, treatment, and ongoing research. *Meetings*: Monthly. *Services*: Mutual aid,written information, newsletter, referral to other services. *Write*: 51A St Charles, Villa Park, IL 60181 *Call*: 630/279-7282 *Fax*: 708/279-7282

# Turner's Syndrome

**Turner's Syndrome Society** *Area Served: Chicago* Reach as many Turner's Syndrome individuals, their families, and interested professionals as possible with totally accurate and up-to-date information regarding this condition. *Services*: Mutual aid, speakers bureau, written information, social activities, telephone support, professional service, referral to other services, educational program or material, referral to other services, advocacy, home or hospital visitation, newsletter. *Write*: 6429 S Quincy, Willowbrook, IL 60521 *Call*: 630/654-2997 Answer Mach.

# Twin to Twin Transfusion Syndrome

**Twin to Twin Transfusion Syndrome (TTTS) Foundation** *Area Served: National Write*: 411 Longbeach Pkwy, Bay Village, OH 44140 *Call*: 216/899-8887

# Usher Syndrome

**Usher Syndrome Self-Help Network RP Foundation Fighting Blindness** *Area Served: National* Information network of individuals with Usher Syndrome and their families sharing similar experiences. *Services*: Telephone support, newsletter, written information. *Write*: 1401 Mt Royal Ave, 4th Fl, Baltimore, MD 21217 *Call*: 800/683-5555

# Vaccines

**National Vaccine Information Center Dissatisfied Parents Together** *Area Served: National* Help insure the use of the safest vaccines available; to inform the public about benefits/risks of vaccines; to monitor the government's compensation program; and support for vaccine injured families. *Meetings*: Quarterly. *Write*: 512 Maple Ave W #206, Vienna, VA 22180 *Call*: 703/938-3783

# Visual Impairment

## Visual Impairment-General

**American Council of The Blind** *Area Served: National* Promote the independence, dignity and well-being of blind and visually impaired people. Members are from all walks of life. ACB helps improve lifestyles through civil rights, employment, rehab services, safe and expanded transportation, travel and recreation, social security benefits, accessibility and more. ACB works in coalition with other disability groups. *Services*: Braille forum, large prints, information hotline. *Meetings*: Call. *Write*: 1155 15th St NW, Ste 720, Washington, DC 20005 *Call*: 800/424-8666 *Fax*: 202/467-5085 *Email*: ncrabb@access.digex.net *Web site*: WWW.ABC.ORG or BBS: (202)331-1058

**American Foundation for The Blind National Office** *Area Served: National* Provides information on conditions that lead to vision loss and blindness as well as information on services available to blind and visually impaired people. *Services*: Written information. *Write*: 15 W 16th St, NY, NY 10011 *Call*: 800/232-5463

**Blind Awareness** *Area Served: Chicago, Cook County* *Write*: 1337 N Monitor, Chicago, IL 60651 *Call*: 773/379-1434

**Deicke Center for Visual Rehab** *Area Served: DuPage, Kane and Will Counties* Helping to cope with a variety of vision impairments through self-help groups throughout DuPage County. Support for emotions, information and education. Also for family and friends of visually impaired. *Meeting*: Monthly. *Services*: Mutual aid, educational program or material, telephone support. *Write*: 219 E Cole Ave, Wheaton, IL 60187 *Call*: 800/637-1054 600

**Doubleday Large Print Home Library Doubleday and Co, Inc** *Area Served: National Write*: Member Services,

6550 E 30th St, PO Box 6325, Indianapolis, IN 46206-6325 *Call*: 800/688-4442

**Friendship Group of The Blind** *Area Served: DeKalb County Write*: 1626 Huntington Rd, DeKalb, IL 60115 *Call*: 815/758-1626

**Library Services-Blind and Physically Handicapped Library of Congress** *Area Served: National* National library service that provides braille and recorded books and magazines on free loan to anyone who cannot read standard print because of visual or physical disabilities. *Services*: Professional service, written information, referral to other services. *Write*: 1291 Taylor St N, Washington, DC 20542 *Call*: 800/424-8567

**Lighthouse National Center for Vision and Aging** *Area Served: National* National org. that provides information and resources on vision and aging to consumers, professionals and the business community. Services include a toll-free Information and Resource Unit, technical assistance and consultation, training, and the dissemination of research and training materials. Referrals to self-help groups for visually impaired older people. *Services*: Educational program or material written information, advocacy, referral to other services, newsletter. *Write*: 111 E 59th St, NY, NY 10022 *Call*: 800/334-5497

**Linc Inc, Blind and Visually Impaired** *Write*: 10 E Washington, Belleville, IL 62220 *Call*: 618/235-9988

**Looking Into Giving Help to The Sightless Deerfield Lions Club** *Area Served: Lake and Cook Counties* LIGHTS is a self-help group to help visually impaired individuals share ideas and learn with each other. *Meetings*: Monthly for all interested. *Services*: Mutual aid, educational program or material, written information, advocacy, referral to other services, speakers bureau, social activities, home or hospital visitation. *Write*: 824 Chestnut, #1, Deerfield, IL 60015 *Call*: 847/948-7440 Evening

**Loretto Support Group for Visually Impaired Women Deicke Center for Visual Rehab** *Area Served: DuPage and Kane Counties* Provides a warm atmosphere of support in which women confide feelings of loss, fears and needs. Promotes renewed self-image, independence and joy of life. Offers special social events. Guest speakers provide information on services and visual aids. Members develop a sense of family. *Meetings*: Monthly for visually impaired women. *Services*: Mutual aid. *Write*: 1600 Somerset Ln, Wheaton, IL 60187 *Call*: 630/653-4756

**Low Vision Support Group Community Health Center for Senior Adults** *Area Served: Cook County* Meets 1st and 3rd Fridays at 1:00 pm. Group's mission: mutual aid, social, mutual aid designed to help with adjusting to legal blindness. Group participates in social activities and provides tips, information, speakers on how to cope. The group is led by a trained medical social worker and co-led by a legally blind retired social worker. *Write*: Methodist Home, 1415 West Foster Ave, Chicago, IL 60640 *Call*: 773/769-5500 127

**Low Vision Support Group Danville Public Library** *Write*: 307 N Vermilion, Danville, IL *Call*: 217/442-4139

**Low Vision Support Group Deicke Center for Visual Rehab** *Area Served: DuPage, Will and Kane Counties* Provides support and education for low vision persons. *Meetings*: Monthly for all visually impaired, their family and friends. *Services*: Mutual aid. *Write*: 219 E Cole Ave, Wheaton, IL 60187 *Call*: 800/637-1054 600

**Low Vision Support Group for Senior Adults United Charities** *Area Served: Chicago-N* Provides support, education, socialization, sharing of concerns and coping skills with others experiencing vision loss from macular degeneration, cataracts, glaucoma, diabetes and other causes. *Meetings*: Twice monthly for people over 60 with vision loss. *Services*: Mutual aid, referral to other services, social activities. *Write*: 3445 N Central Ave, Chicago, IL 60634 *Call*: 773/282-9535

**Low Vision Support Group Lake County Forest-Lake County Bluff Senior Center** *Area Served: Lake County* Searchlight was formed to provide a support system for visually-impaired individuals that enables them to share concerns and problems as well as coping skills and effective life-style adjustments. *Meetings*: Every other month. *Services*: Mutual aid, referral to other services. *Write*: 400 E Illinois, Lake Forest, IL 60045 *Call*: 847/234-2209

**Low Vision Support Group Pace** *Area Served: Champaign, Piett, Vermilion and Douglas Counties Contact*: Champaign Family Service/Self-Help Center, 405 S State St, Champaign, IL 61820-5196 *Call*: 217/344-5433 or 217/352-0099

**Low Vision Support Group Smith Center** *Area Served: Cook County-N* Support for those who have vision disability but are not totally blind, for purpose of discussing feelings. Spouses are encouraged to come. *Meetings*: Bi-monthly. *Services*: Mutual aid, educational program or material, advocacy, telephone support, written information, social activities. *Write*: 5120 Galitz, Skokie, IL 60077 *Call*: 847/673-0500 207

**National Assn for Parents of The Visually Impaired** *Area Served: National* Provides help to parents to find information and resources for their blind and visually impaired children including those with additional disabilities. Provide leadership, support, and training to assist parents in helping children reach their potential. *Services*: Publications; conferences; updated legislation; fund-raising; coordination of services-federal, state, and local; and develop state and local orgs. *Meetings*: Please call for information. *Write*: PO Box 317, Watertown, MA 02272-0317 *Call*: 800/562-6265 *Fax*: 617/972-7444

**National RP Foundation Fighting Blindness** *Area Served: IL* Volunteer org. which provides information concerning Retinitis Pigmentosa (RP), Ushers Syndrome, Macular degeneration and other retinal diseases; helps patients cope with their condition; raises funds to finance research. *Meetings*: 5 times annually for anyone interested. *Services*: Referral to other services, telephone support, newsletter, written information. *Write*: 1011 S Waiola, LaGrange, IL 60525 *Call*: 708/354-8108

**National RP Foundation Fighting Blindness National Office** *Area Served: National* Volunteer org. which provides information concerning Retinitis Pigmentosa (RP), Ushers Syndrome, Macular degeneration and other retinal diseases; helps patients cope with their condition; raises funds to finance research. One IL affiliate. *Services*: Written information, mutual aid, educational program or material, referral to other services. *Write*: 1401 W Mount Royal Ave, 4th Fl, Baltimore, MD 21217 *Call*: 800/683-5555

**New Insights Support Group Central IL Sight Center** *Area Served: IL Write*: 117 E Washington, East Peoria, IL 61611 *Call*: 309/698-4001

**Peoria Area Blind People's Center** *Area Served: Peoria and Tazewell Counties Write*: 2905 W Garden St, Peoria, IL 61605 *Call*: 309/637-3693

**Quincy District Assn of The Blind** *Area Served: IL Write*: PO Box 85, Quincy, IL 62301 *Call*: 217/223-6923

**Recording for The Blind, Inc** *Area Served: National* Non-profit org. which records educational materials (books) for the print handicapped (those who can not use standard print due to physical, visual or perceptual handicap). Lenders must send in application and register; no charge for lending or recording books. *Services*: Written information. *Write*: 20 Roszel Rd, Princeton, NJ 08540 *Call*: 800/221-4792

**Sight-Loss Support Group St Elizabeth's Hospital-Belleville Area College** *Area Served: St Clair County Write*: 201 N Church St, Belleville, IL 62220 *Call*: 618/235-5302

**Sights Unlimited** *Area Served: Cook County* Gives opportunity to talk to others with similar problems. Teaches simple ways to cope in home situation. Informs about services available in community. Gives social outlet. Has speakers bureau if requested. *Meetings*: Monthly. *Services*: Mutual aid, speakers bureau, telephone support, referral to other services, advocacy, written information. *Write*: 2448 Walnut, Blue Island, IL 60406-0533 *Call*: 708/597-8901

**Textbooks and Consumer Publications Services for Blind and Handicapped** *Area Served: National* Free national library program of braille and recorded material for blind and physically handicapped persons. *Services*: Provide professional service. *Write*: Library of Congress, 1291 Taylor St, Washington, DC 20542 *Call*: 800/424-8567

**The Council of Families with Visual Impairment the American Council of The Blind** *Area Served: National Write*: 26616 River Rouge Dr, Dearborn Heights, MI 48127 *Call*: 313/561-4887

**The Foundation Fighting Blindness Chicago Area Affiliate** *Area Served: IL Write*: 1011 S Waiola, LaGrange, IL 60525 *Call*: 708/354-8108

**Variety Club West Suburban Special Recreation Assn** *Area Served: Cook County-W* Social program for adults with visual impairments. Participants assist in planning the activities which include weekly nights out for dining, theater, swimming, biking, dancing, and many other fun activities. *Meetings*: Weekly but restricted topersons sharing the concern. *Services*: Social activities. *Write*: 2915 Maple, Franklin Park, IL 60131 *Call*: 708/455-2100

**Vision Foundation, Inc** *Area Served: National* Self-help support org. for individuals coping with sight loss. Offers information and resources, help in establishing local support groups. No IL affiliates. *Services*: Educational program or material written information, newsletter, referral to other services.. *Write*: 818 Mt Auburn St, Watertown, MA 02172 *Call*: 617/926-4232

**Visions St Margaret's Hospital** *Area Served: LaSalle, Bureau and Putnam Counties* Provides psycho social and emotional support; resource information available for education; encouragement from facilitator and group members; referrals for other help. Serves blind and visually impaired persons and educates on the adjustment to vision loss and visual diseases. Support group meetings-twice monthly-1st and 3rd Thursday at 12:30 pm, in English, accessible, no transportation. *Write*: 600 E First St, Spring Valley, IL 61362 *Call*: 815/664-1132 *Fax*: 815/664-1188

**Visual Impairment Program West Suburban Special Recreation** Provide a professionally organized community based therapeutic recreation service for children and adults with visual impairments. Clubs include fitness walking, card clubs, nights on the town, museum tours, etc. Children who are blind can also become involved with our toy lending library and play intervention program. *Meetings*: Fitness class-once a week; craft class, bowling, and social clubs have varied schedules-call for specific dates and times. *Write*: 2915 Maple St, Franklin Park, IL 60131 *Call*: 847/455-2100 *Fax*: 847/455-2157

**Visually Impaired Motivators Village of Morton Grove** *Area Served: Cook County-N* Provides helpful information and supportive interaction that assists participants in adjusting to their impairment. Transportation can be arranged. *Meetings*: Monthly. *Services*: Mutual aid. *Write*: 6101 Capulina Ave, Morton Grove, IL 60053 *Call*: 847/965-4100 254

**Visually Impaired Seniors Regional Access and Mobilization Project (RAMP)** *Area Served: Winnebago County* Peer support and coping skills independent living classes for persons over 55 who are having problems with independent living because of a vision loss. *Meetings*: Monthly. *Services*: Mutual aid,written information, advocacy, referral to other services, home or hospital visitation, telephone support. *Write*: 1040 N. 2$^{nd}$ St, Rockford, IL 61107 *Call*: 815/968-7467

**Visually-Impaired Support Assn, Inc** *Area Served: Cook County -NW* Helps the newly blind and those facing blindness cope with the adjustment process through information, sharing and peer counseling. *Meetings*: Monthly. *Services*: Mutual aid, telephone support. *Write*: 593 A Edinburgh Lane, Prospect Heights, IL 60070 *Call*: 847/259-5352

**Visually-Impaired Support Group North Shore Senior Center** *Area Served: Cook and Lake Counties* Gathers together to exchange companionship, Mutual assistance and problem solving skills. The group emphasizes becoming aware of one's own problems and moving to do something about it with the members' support and encouragement. *Meetings*: Monthly. *Services*: Mutual aid, educational program or material, newsletter, written information, social activities. *Write*: 7 Happ Rd, Northfield, IL 60093 *Call*: 847/446-8751

**Visually Impaired Support Group Schaumburg Township** *Area Served: Cook County* Provides activities, programs, and a meeting place for visually impaired adults to meet and help themselves and each other. *Meetings*: Monthly. *Services*: Mutual aid, educational program or material, written information, advocacy, referral to other services, speakers bureau, telephone support, social activities, home or hospital visitation. *Write*: 25 IL Blvd, Hoffman Estates, IL 60194 *Call*: 708/884-0030

## Visual Impairment-Cataract And Glaucoma

**Cataract and Glaucoma Support Group Medical Arts Center** *Area Served: Lee Write*: 1620 Sauk Rd, Dixon, IL 61021 *Call*: 815/288-7711

**Cataract Support Group Gailey Eye Clinic** *Area Served: IL Write*: 1008 N Main, Bloomington, IL 61701 *Call*: 309/829-5311

**Central IL Sight Center** *Area Served: IL Write*: 117 E Washington, East Peoria, IL 61611 *Call*: 309/698-4001

# Williams Syndrome

**Williams Syndrome Assn** *Area Served: National Write*: PO Box 3297, Ballwin, MO 63022-3297 *Call*: 314/227-4411

**Williams Syndrome Assn IL State Chapter** *Area Served: IL* Parent support group for sharing of information, public and professional education, and advocating for and raising funds for research. *Services*: Mutual aid, educational program or material, advocacy, referral to other services, fundraising, written information, newsletter. *Write*: 218 S Park, Marissa, IL 62257 *Call*: 708/705-9814

# Wilson's Disease

**Wilson's Disease Assn** *Area Served: National* National group to promote and sponsor research regarding the cause, treatment, cure and prevention of Wilson's Disease and related disorders of copper metabolism; to promote public awareness for early diagnosis and treatment; to provide financial aid and moral support to individuals with the disease. No known IL chapters. *Services*: Educational program or material advocacy, referral to other services, telephone support, newsletter, written information, mutual aid, referral to other services, social activities. *Write*: PO Box 75324, Washington, DC 20013 *Call*: 703/636-3014

# Women's Health Resources

**Chicago Women's Health Center** *Area Served: Chicago* Provides the knowledge and tools for self-help health care for women. Teaches gynecological and breast self-examination; provides services such as PAP Smear, VD test, birth control, prenatal care, infertility checking, fertty awareness group. Provides group and individual mental health counseling. *Services*: Educational program or material written information, professional service. *Write*: 3435 N Sheffield, Chicago, IL 60657 *Call*: 312/935-6126

**Heart Support Group for Women** *Area Served: DuPage County Write*: Elmhurst Memorial Hospital, 200 Berteau Ave, Elmhurst, IL 60126 *Call*: 630/883-1400 4691

**Hope Clinic for Women** *Area Served: IL Write*: 1602 21$^{st}$ St, Granite City, IL 62040 *Call*: 800/844-3130

**National Black Women's Health Project** Empowers women through wellness; to address specifically the health concerns of black women in six areas: health education, advocacy, infant mortality, teen pregnancy, cervical cancer, and the emotional well-being of black women. *Meetings*: Twice a month but restricted to persons sharing the concern. *Services*: Mutual aid, educational program or material, written information, advocacy, social activities, newsletter. *Write*: 1237 Gordon St, SW, Atlanta, GA 30310 *Call*: 404/753-0916

# Justice

## Crime

### Crime-General

**Chimera Self-Defense for Women Chimera Educational Foundation** *Area Served: Chicago and Cook County Write*: 59 E Van Buren #714, Chicago, IL 60605 *Call*: 312/939-5341

**Citizens Against Crime** *Area Served: National Write*: PO Box 795-172 1022 S Greenville, Allen, TX 75002 *Call*: 214/390-7033

**IL Violent Crime Victims Clearinghouse IL Attorney General Office** *Area Served: IL* Gives information on financial assistance for crime victims in IL as well as referrals to professional and self-help programs within the caller's area. *Services*: written information, referral to other services. *Write*: 323 Main St, Peoria, IL 61602 *Call*: 800/228-3368

**Mothers Against Gangs** *Area Served: Evanston Write*: 1817 Church St, Evanston, IL 60201 *Call*: 847/332-2624

**Mothers Against Gangs** *Area Served: Kane, DuPage, Kendall and Will Counties* Provide a support group for mothers whose children have been killed or hurt by gang members, and mothers who are interested in opposing gangs in their neighborhood. Court advocacy, accompanying families to court, organized graffiti elimination, sibling loss group, parental stress workshop, individual and family counseling. *Meetings*: Monthly. *Services*: Mutual aid, educational program or material, fundraising, written information, advocacy, referral to other services, speakers bureau, referral to other services, telephone support, social activities. *Write*: 512 S Union, Aurora, IL 60505 *Call*: 630/898-8949

**National Assn for Crime Victims' Rights, Inc** *Area Served: National* Warns and educates potential crime victims of the hazards/experiences they will encounter if/when victimized. to teach avoidance of crime; to give the victim instant access to factual information concerning his rights, economic retribution and appeals or filing fees. Also provide direct referrals to self-help groups. *Services*: educational program or material advocacy, fundraising, telephone support, newsletter, written information, referral to other services. *Write*: PO Box 16161, Portland, OR 97216 *Call*: 503/252-9012

**National Org. for Victim Assistance** *Area Served: National* To be a national advocate for victim rights, and to strengthen local efforts to assist victims and witnesses. *Services*: Mutual aid, educational program or material, advocacy, telephone support, newsletter, written information. *Write*: PO Box 11000, Washington, DC 20008 *Call*: 202/232-6682

**Parents Against Gangs** *Area Served: Chicago* Grief support for parents and siblings. Homicide/violent crime program. Parenting classes. *Meetings*: Monthly. *Services*: Mutual aid. *Write*: 7419 N Winchester Ave, Chicago, IL 60626 *Call*: 773/761-8104

**Parents of Murdered Children Methodist Medical Center** *Area Served: IL Write*: 118 Glenview Ave, East Peoria, IL 61611 *Call*: 309/699-0216

### Crime-Ex Offenders

**Institute for Women Today Maria Shelter-Casa Notre Dame** *Area Served: Chicago, IL Write*: 7315 S Yale, Chicago, IL 60621 *Call*: 312/944-5350

**Jail Rehab Program** *Area Served: McHenry County* For individuals in County jail, on probation or parole. Counseling (drug/alcohol screening) for incarcerated individuals; liaison and referral sources afterward; psychological testing; offender assistance. for McHenry County residents only. *Services*: Mutual aid, educational program or material, advocacy, written information.. *Write*: 400 Russell, Woodstock, IL 60098 *Call*: 815/338-9199

**Safer Foundation** *Area Served: IL* Services for adult ex-offenders; job readiness; training and placement; basic literary skills for job simulated environments; intensive counseling, survival services (referral and follow-up services) to clients and families in the field and follow-up with employers who hire through us. *Services*: Mutual aid, educational program or material, telephone support, written information, professional service, referral to other services. *Write*: 571 W. Jackson, Chicago, IL 60661 *Call*: 312/922-2200

**Visible Voices** *Area Served: Cook, DuPage and Lake Counties Write*: 205 W Randolph, Ste 830, Chicago, IL 60606 *Call*: 312/332-5537

## Crime-Prevention

**South Suburban Ministers Fellowship** *Area Served: Cook County* *Write*: 14200 S Wood St, Dixmoor, IL 60426 *Call*: 312/596-1359

**Victim Assistance Lake County State's Attorney's Office** *Area Served: Lake County* To help the victim or witness of a crime to prepare for court appearances and will refer to counseling or social services as necessary. *Services*: provide professional service. *Write*: 18 N County St, 3$^{rd}$ Flr, Waukegan, IL 60085 *Call*: 847/360-6644

**Victim Services Evanston Police Department** *Area Served: Cook County* *Write*: 1454 Elmwood Ave, Evanston, IL 60204 *Call*: 847/866-5016

**Victim-Witness Assistance Program Cook County State's Attorney's Office** *Area Served: Cook County* *Write*: 2650 S California, 1$^{st}$ Fl, S Lobby, Chicago, IL 60608

# Legal Services

**Associated Divorce Consultants** *Area Served: Cook, DuPage and Lake Counties* *Write*: 801 Skokie Blvd, #217, Northbrook, IL 60062 *Call*: 847/564-9976

**Call A Lawyer Chicago Bar Assn** *Area Served: Chicago* Volunteer attorneys answering questions on civil and criminal matters; service open on 3$^{rd}$ Saturday of month from 9am to 12 noon. If an attorney is needed for further consultation with the client, caller will be asked to call back for referral during regular office hours Mon-Fri, 9am-4:30pm. *Services*: Telephone support, written information. *Write*: 321 S Plymouth Ct, Chicago, IL 60604 *Call*: 312/554-2001

**Center for Conflict Resolution** *Area Served: Chicago* Not-for-profit corporation offering Chicago-area residents free mediation services as an alternative means of dispute resolution. *Services*: advocacy, telephone support, written information. *Write*: 200 N Michigan, Ste 500, Chicago, IL 60601 *Call*: 312/372-6420

**Cook County Legal Assistance Foundation** *Area Served: Cook County -S* Legal help and counseling, court representation for persons of limited income. *Services*: written information, professional service, educational program or material, referral to other services. *Write*: 15325 S Page Ave, Harvey, IL 60426 *Call*: 708/339-5550

**DePaul Legal Clinic** *Area Served: Chicago* Handles civil cases only, no criminal cases. 3 supervising attorneys, large number of students. Flat fees charged for income eligible clients. *Services*: provide professional service. *Write*: 23 E Jackson, Chicago, IL 60604 *Call*: 312/341-8294

**Evanston Neighborhood Justice Center Evanston Human Relations** *Area Served: Evanston* Assists persons through mediation and conciliation with civil disputes as personal trained mediators, thereby needing no attorneys. Help persons to resolve landlord tenant, neighbor, employment, consumer merchant, and interpersonal disputes. Fosters self-help. *Services*: professional service, mutual aid, advocacy. *Write*: 2100 Ridge Ave, Evanston, IL 60204 *Call*: 847/866-2920 2485

**Free Legal Clinic Evanston YWCA** *Area Served: Cook County* Free monthly legal seminars on the first Wednesday of each month. Open to members and non-members, men and women. Professional legal advice on such topics as divorce family law, small businesses, tenant/landlord law, employment discrimination, and house buying. *Services*: Mutual aid, advocacy, written information, referral to other services.. *Write*: 1215 Church St, Evanston, IL 60201 *Call*: 847/864-8445

**Land of Lincoln Legal Assistance** *Area Served: Madison, Bond and Clinton Counties* *Write*: 413 E Broadway, Alton, IL 62002 *Call*: 800/642-5570

**Legal Aid Bureau United Charities** *Area Served: Cook County, Chicago* Legal Aid serves any Cook County resident whose income is below 125% of the federal poverty level. A special program is available for seniors 60 and over who have a legal problem and reside within the city of Chicago. *Services*: provide professional service. *Write*: 14 E Jackson, 15$^{th}$ Fl, Chicago, IL 60604 *Call*: 312/922-5625 4192

**Legal Assistance Foundation of Chicago** *Area Served: Chicago* *Write*: 343 S. Dearborn, Chicago, IL 60604 *Call*: 312/341-1070

**Legal Assistance Foundation of Chicago Englewood Office** *Area Served: Chicago-S* Provide legal assistance. No fee, but income determines eligibility. *Services*: provide professional service. *Write*: 852 W 63$^{rd}$ St, Chicago, IL 60621 *Call*: 773/651-3100

**Legal Assistance Foundation of Chicago** *Area Served: IL-N* *Write*: 975 N Main, Rockford, IL 61103 *Call*: 800/892-2985

**Legal Assistance** Provides legal assistance for low income citizens in civil matters. *Services*: provide professional service. *Write*: Highway 13 East, PO Box 424, Murphysboro, IL 62966 *Call*: 800/642-5335

**Prairie State Legal Services** *Area Served: DuPage County* Provides free (within eligibility requirements) civil legal services for low-income persons. *Services*: provide professional service. *Write*: 400 W Liberty Drive, Wheaton, IL 60187 *Call*: 630/690-2130

**Prairie State Legal Services** *Area Served: Aurora and Kane County Write*: 10 E State, Ste 102, St Charles, IL 60174 *Call*: 800/942-4612

**Prairie State Legal Services** *Area Served: LaSalle Bureau and Putnam Counties Write*: 613 LaSalle St, Ottawa, IL 61350 *Call*: 800/892-7888

**Prairie State Legal Services** *Area Served: Peoria, Marshall and Tazewell Counties* Free legal services for the poor. *Services*: provide professional service. *Write*: 414 Hamilton Blvd., #301, Peoria, IL 61602 *Call*: 800/322-2280

**Prairie State Legal Services** *Area Served: Rock Island and Whiteside Counties* Free legal services for the poor. *Services*: provide professional service. *Write*: 630 9th St, PO Box 4863, Rock Island, IL 61204-4863 *Call*: 800/322-9804

**Prairie State Legal Services** *Area Served: Kankakee and Kendall County Write*: 191 S Chicago St, Kankakee, IL 60901 *Call*: 800/346-2864

**Prairie State Legal Services Will County Legal Assistance Program** *Area Served: Will County* Provides legal services to the low income citizens Will County *Services*: provide professional service. *Write*: 16 W Van Buren, #204, Joliet, IL 60431 *Call*: 815/727-5123

**Pro Bono Advocates** *Area Served: Chicago, Cook County* Volunteer attorney program for free legal assistance to low-income residents. Also has reduced adjustable fee (RAF) program which provides legal services at low rates on a sliding scale. Service agency primarily concerned with victims of domestic violence. *Services*: provide

professional service. *Write*: 165 N Canal St, Chicago, IL 60661 *Call*: 312/906-8010

**Women's Law Assn Consultation and Referrals** *Area Served: Madison County* By appointment only on last Monday of month. *Services*: provide professional service. *Write*: YWCA 304 E Third St, Alton, IL 62002 *Call*: 618/465-7774

## Prisoners

**Friends Outside National Org.** *Area Served: National Write*: 3031 Tisch Way Ste 507, San Jose, CA 95128 *Call*: 408/985-8807

**Jewish Prisoners Assistance Foundation** *Area Served: IL* Help Jewish inmates monthly meetings with families, visitation to inmates while incarcerated; religious services to inmates. *Meetings*: Monthly for all interested. *Services*: Mutual aid, educational program or material, advocacy, telephone support, home or hospital visitation, newsletter, written information. *Write*: 3107 W. Devon, Chicago, IL 60659 *Call*: 773/262-2770

**Reach Prison Ministry** *Area Served: Macon County Write*: PO Box 1275, 3635 S Main St, Ste 525, Decatur, IL 62525 *Call*: 217/429-6250

## Racism

**Racism and Bigotry Anonymous** *Area Served: IL Write*: PO Box 29992, Chicago, IL 60627 *Call*: 708/677-4664 Answer Mach.

# Life Development

## Ethnic

**American Korean Service Center, Inc** *Area Served: Chicago Write*: 4150 N Sheridan Rd, Chicago, IL 60640

**American Lao Community** *Services Area Served: Chicago Write*: 4750 N Sheridan Rd, Chicago, IL 60640

**South East Asia Center** Provide educational and social services to the Southeast Asian refugee population in the Chicago area; encourage self-help measures as the means to survival, cultural orientation and societal participation; assist refugees with rights; and enhance the mutual understanding between Americans and southeast Asians. *Services*: Mutual aid, educational program or material, advocacy, telephone support, written information, professional service, speakers bureau, social activities, referral to other services, hotline, home or hospital

visitation, newsletter. *Write*: 1124 W Ainslie, Chicago, IL 60640 *Call*: 773/989-6927

## Self-Help

**Illinois Self-Help Coalition** Self-Help Clearing House serving Illinois Wright College South, 3400 N Austin Ave, Chicago, IL 60634 *Call*: 773/481-8837 *Fax*: 773/481-8917 *Web site*: http://www.selfhelp-Illinois.org

**Self-Help Center Family Services of Champaign County** Self-help Clearing House serving Central IL. *Write*: 405 S State St., Champaign, IL 61820 *Call*: 217/352-0099 *Web site*: http://www.prairienet.org/selfhelp/

## Single Persons

**East Peoria Christian Singles First Baptist Church of East Peoria** A non-denominational group for singles whether widowed, divorced or never married. Provides Christian fellowship and personal growth. *Meetings*: Monthly.*Services*: Mutual aid. *Write*: 600 E Washington St, East Peoria, IL 61611 *Call*: 309/699-1536

**Jewish Family and Community Services** *Area Served: Chicago Write*: 205 W Randolph, Ste 1100, Chicago, IL 60606 *Call*: 312/263-5523

**Single Adult Ministries First United Methodist Church** *Area Served: Peoria County Write*: 116 NE Perry, Peoria, IL 61603 *Call*: 309/673-3641

**Singles Celebrate Life First Baptist Church** *Area Served: Champaign County Write*: 202 W IL, Urbana, IL 61801 *Call*: 217/367-7016

# Loss

## Abortion

**Courage Program St. Germaine's Church** Assist callers through problematic pregnancies, help with the aftermath of a traumatic abortion, offer on-going support to single parents. *Meetings*: Monthly and weekly for specific concerns; open to callers and guests. *Services*: Mutual aid, educational program or material, advocacy, telephone support, home or hospital visitation, social activities, newsletter, written information, referral to other services, speakers bureau, hotline, professional service. *Write*: 4240 W 98th St, Oak Lawn, IL 60453 *Call*: 708/636-5060

**Crisis Pregnancy Services of DuPage County** *Area Served: DuPage County* Offers a support group with information and speakers on pregnancy, parenting and nutrition; group discussions to share experiences and concerns; assistance with childbirth preparation classes and acquisition of clothing, food, housing, employment and post-abortion counseling. Does not support the concept of legal abortion. *Services*: Mutual aid, educational program or material, telephone support, home or hospital visitation, written information. *Write*: 671 N. Cass, Westmont, IL 60559 *Call*: 630/455-0335 *Fax*: 630/789-0666

**Society for the Preservation of Human Dignity** *Area Served: Cook, Lake and DuPage Counties Write*: 37 N Plum Grove Rd, Palatine, IL 60067 *Call*: 847/359-4919 *Fax*: 708/359-4991

**Support Group for Prenatal Decisions Support Center for Perinatal and Childhood Death** *Area Served: Cook County* Group addresses the grief of having terminated a wanted pregnancy because of genetic or chromosomal abnormalities. *Meetings*: monthly for those who have lost a baby. *Services*: Mutual aid, referral to other services, educational program or material, telephone support,

written information. *Write*: Evanston Hospital/Pediatrics, 2650 Ridge, Evanston, IL 60201 *Call*: 847/570-2882

**WEBA-IL Women Exploited By Abortion** *Area Served: IL* One to one counseling by both peer and non-peer counselors with focus on helping women, men, orcouples come to grips with the emotional aftermath that can occur with abortion. Group directed by an independent board with Christian focus. All persons regardless of denomination are welcome to come. *Services*: Mutual aid, written information, referral to other services, speakers bureau, telephone support, newsletter. *Write*: PO Box 43292, Chicago, IL 60643 *Call*: 312/263-1175

**Women's Med-Plus Center** *Area Served: National Write*: 3219 Jefferson Ave N, Cincinnati, OH 45220 *Call*: 800/543-7225

## Adult Loss of Parent

**Adult Loss of Parent Group Rainbow Hospice, Inc** *Area Served: Cook, DuPage and Lake Counties* This is an 8-week group for adults who have had a parent die. The group uses expressive therapies, including music and art. It is a grief support group that uses a self-help model, but is professionally facilitated. Meets quarterly from 7:00-8:30 pm for 8 weeks. Dates to be announced. Registration is required, accessible by car, bus service limited (Pace). *Write*: Bereavement Center, 1550 N Northwest Hwy, Ste 220, Park Ridge, IL 60068-1427 *Call*: 847/699-3604 *Fax*: 847/699-2047

**Kaleidoscope Rainbows** *Area Served: IL* Support groups for young adults who have experienced the loss of a parent. 8 offices in IL *Services*: Mutual aid, educational program or material, written information, speakers bureau. *Write*: 1111 Tower Ln, Schaumburg, IL 60173 *Call*: 847/310-1880

# AIDS

**AIDS Loss Group Rainbow Hospice, Inc and Aids Pastoral Care Network** *Area Served: Cook and Lake Counties Write*: Bereavement Center, 1550 N Northwest Hwy, Ste 220, Park Ridge, IL 60068 *Call*: 847/699-3604

**Hospice Bereavement Support Group Rush Hospice Partners** *Area Served: Cook County Write*: 1035 Madison St, Oak Park, IL 60302 *Call*: 800/994-9494

# Bereavement

**Bereavement Support Group Community Nursing Service West Hospice** *Area Served: Cook County Write*: 1035 Madison St, Oak Park, IL 60302 *Call*: 708/386-9191 *Fax*: 708/386-7453

**Bereavement Support Group Covenant Hospice Care Program** *Area Served: Champaign County* Volunteers and professionals. Grief support groups open to all. *Services*: Mutual aid, educational program or material. *Write*: 1400 W Park, Urbana, IL 61801 *Call*: 217/337-2470

**Bereavement Support Group Grundy Community Hospice** *Area Served: Grundy County Write*: 1802 N Division, Ste 307, Morris, IL 60450 *Call*: 815/942-8525

**Bereavement Support Group Highland Park Hospital** *Area Served: Lake and Cook Counties Write*: 718 Glenview Ave, Highland Park, IL 60035 *Call*: 847/480-3858

**Bereavement Support Group Hospice of Lincolnland** *Area Served: IL* Bereavement support groups. *Services*: Mutual aid. *Write*: 75 Professional Plaza, Mattoon, IL 61938 *Call*: 217/234-4044

**Bereavement Support Group Little Company of Mary Hospital** *Area Served: Cook and Lake Counties Write*: 2800 W 95th St, Evergreen Park, IL 60642 *Call*: 708/422-6200 5480

**Bereavement Support Group Lutheran General Health System** *Area Served: Cook County Write*: Pastoral Counseling Center, 1610 Luther Ln, Park Ridge, IL 60068 *Call*: 847/518-1800 *Fax*: 708/323-9222

**Bereavement Support Group St. Margaret's Hospital** *Area Served: LaSalle County* Provide psycho-social and emotional support for bereaved. Resource information available for education, encouragement from facilitator and group members, referral for other help. Monthly support group meetings open to bereaved adults at any stage of grief recovery. *Meetings*: 2nd Tuesday of each month at 7:00 pm, in English, no transportation, accessible. *Write*: 600 E 1st St, Spring Valley, IL 61362 *Call*: 815/664-1132 *Fax*: 815/664-1188

**Bereavement Support Group St. Mary's Hospital** Informal group that provides help and comfort to and by persons who have experienced a loss. Members find relief in the knowledge that feelings and concerns are shared by others. *Meetings*: Monthly. *Services*: Mutual aid, written information, referral to other services, speakers bureau. *Write*: 111 E Spring St, Streator, IL 61364 *Call*: 800/325-7699

**Bereavement Support Group Star Hospice** *Area Served: Lake and McHenry Counties Write*: St Therese Medical Center, 2615 Washington St, Waukegan, IL 60085 *Call*: 847/360-2048

**Bereavement Support Groups DeKalb County Hospice** *Area Served: DeKalb County* Bereavement care focuses on the family. Support groups offer support to Hospice families and community members. *Services*: Mutual aid. *Write*: 615 N First St, DeKalb, IL 60115 *Call*: 815/756-3000

**Bereavement Support Groups DeKalb County Hospice** *Area Served: DeKalb County Write*: 615 N First St, DeKalb, IL 60115 *Call*: 815/756-3000

**Bereavement Support Groups United Medical Center** Adult and children's bereavement support groups to help those who are grieving the death of a loved one. *Meetings*: Twice a month. *Services*: Mutual aid, written information, social activities, telephone support, referral to other services, educational program or material. *Write*: Pastoral Care 501 10th Ave., Moline, IL 61265 *Call*: 309/757-2696

**Beyond Grief Support Group Saint James Hospital** *Area Served: Livingston, Grundy and Ford Counties* Gives support to persons who have experienced grief through the loss of a loved one and to give an avenue for expression of feelings and emotions for those experiencing grief. Group meets weekly. *Services*: Mutual aid. *Write*: 610 E Water St, Pontiac, IL 61764 *Call*: 815/842-2828 3322

**Center for Grief Recovery and Sibling Loss** *Area Served: Cook County* Purpose: Short-term, weekend, and ongoing recovery groups that provide support to adults who have lost a significant other (including, spouse, sibling, parent). Children, adolescent, individual, and family counseling is also available. *Meetings*: Monthly. *Services*: newsletter professional services/ referrals speakers bureau mutual aid self-help groups printed information public education/ phone support. Special access; mobility impair *Write*: 4513 N Ashland, Chicago, IL 60640 *Call*: 773/769-3928

**Center for Living with Dying** *Area Served: Cook and Will Counties* Purpose: Provides support to individuals, families and professionals dealing with the issues of loss, illness, grief, death, and dying. Also, to support any group experiencing trauma related to death or loss. *Meetings*: Weekly. *Services*: home visitation, member education, newsletter, speakers bureau, fund raising, printed information, public education, phone support. Special accessibility; mobility impaired. *Write*: 10300 W 131st St, Palos Park, IL 60464 *Call*: 708/923-1116 *Fax*: 708/923-6524

**Center for New Beginnings** Provide skilled, compassionate, emotional care for those facing life-altering transitions such as serious illness, death, divorce, and aging. Individual and group counseling provided by professionally trained and supervised volunteers. groups include: widows and widowers, grief program for children, and circle of cure (those affected by HIV/AIDS). *Meetings*: individual counseling as needed, 6-10 group sessions except circle of cure which is on-going. *Write*: 10300 W 131st St, Palos Park, IL 60464 *Call*: 708/923-1116 *Fax*: 708/923-6524

**Coping with Death and Dying Lakeview Mental Health Center** *Area Served: Cook County* Anyone who has experienced a loss of family member or friend by death is helped to experience their feelings. Facilitators and other group members provide support and insight. *Meetings*: Weekly. *Services*: Mutual aid. *Write*: 2847 N Clark St, Chicago, IL 60657 *Call*: 312/744-0167 *Fax*: 312/744-6215 *Email*: PC.RJL@WSHMC.ORG

**Erie Family Health Center** *Area Served: Chicago* *Write*: 1636 W Chicago, Chicago, IL 60622 *Call*: 312/666-3488 325 *Fax*: 312/666-5867

**General Grief Support Groups Hirsch Funeral Homes** *Area Served: Cook County Write*: 7151 W 183rd St, Tinley Park, IL 60477 *Call*: 708/755-9014 *Fax*: 708/755-9260

**Gold Star Families, Inc Chicago Police Department** *Area Served: Chicago Write*: PO Box 46514, Chicago, IL 60646-0514 *Call*: 773/631-1463

**Good Mourning: Children and Adolescent Grief Group Lutheran General Health System** *Area Served: Cook County Write*: 1775 Dempster St, Park Ridge, IL 60068 *Call*: 847/696-6395

**Good Mourning Edward Hospital** *Area Served: DuPage County* We believe that working through grief is most healthy when done with others. By helping people in grief find strength and independence we promote good health in body, mind, andspirit. *Meetings*: Weekly. *Services*: Mutual aid. *Write*: 801 S. Washington, Naperville, IL 60566 *Call*: 630/527-3564 3560 *Fax*: 708/527-3507

**Good Mourning Grief Support Group Edward Hospital** 9 year oldbereavement support group. We offer emotional support to persons who have experienced the death of a loved one. (Spouse, sister, brother, and other). Weekly support group meetings. Selected grief literature available. *Meetings*: every Thursday, Edward Hospital, room #1, 7:30-9 pm. *Write*: 801 S. Washington St.,

Naperville, IL 60566 *Call*: 630/527-3564 *Fax*: 630/527-3507

**Grief and Loss Support Group** *Area Served: Kankakee, Iroquois and Will Counties Write*: PO Box 2418 1900 W Court St, Kankakee, IL 60901 *Call*: 815/932-2421

**Grief and the Holidays Rainbow Hospice, Inc** *Area Served:* Cook and Lake Counties *Write*: Bereavement Center, 1550 N Northwest Hwy, Ste 220, Park Ridge, IL 60068 *Call*: 847/699-3604

**Grief Awareness St. Joseph Hospital** *Area Served: Kane County* Provides a supportive atmosphere for participants to share feelings, learn to accept feelings and understand the grieving process. *Meetings*: Monthly. *Services*: Mutual aid. *Write*: Pastoral Care Dept, 77 N. Airlite, Elgin, IL 60123 *Call*: 847/695-3200 5245 *Fax*: 708/931-5511

**Grief Hurts West Suburban Hospital Pastoral Care Division** *Area Served: Cook County* Awareness of the process of grief. A safe and accepting environment to share thoughts, feelings and awareness of the intensity and length of grief.*Meetings*: 7 weekly sessions, $28. for family members and friends. *Services*: Mutual aid/self-help groups. Special accessibility; mobility impaired. *Write*: Erie At Austin Blvd, Oak Park, IL 60302 *Call*: 708/383-6200 1430 *Fax*: 708/383-7410

**Grief Hurts West Suburban Hospital Medical Center** *Area Served: Cook County* Provides support group for those who have experienced the death of a loved one. *Services*: support and education. *Meetings*: 7 weekly sessions on Wednesday from 7:00-8:30 pm.(first group is free, second group is $35.00. Each group is seven sessions) *Write*: Erie At Austin, Oak Park, IL 60302 *Call*: 708/763-1430 *Fax*: 708/383-7410

**Grief Recovery Group** *Area Served: Ogle, Lee, Carroll and Jo Davies Counties Write*: 9802 W White Eagle Rd, Forreston, IL 61030 *Call*: 815/938-2242

**Grief Recovery Group Edward Hospital** *Area Served: DuPage County* Help members resolve their grief at the death of a loved one. *Services*: Mutual aid. *Write*: 801 S Washington, Naperville, IL 60566 *Call*: 630/355-0450 3564

**Grief Recovery Group Glen Oaks Medical Center** *Area Served: DuPage County* 5-week program to help manage personal loss, whether from death or divorce, with follow-up as needed. *Meetings*: Monthly. *Services*: Mutual aid. *Write*: 701 Winthrop Ave, Glendale Heights, IL 60139 *Call*: 630/858-9700 *Fax*: 708/790-6364

**Grief Recovery Group St Joseph Hospital** *Area Served: IL Write*: 77 N Airlite, Elgin, IL 60123 *Call*: 847/695-3200 5245

**Grief Recovery LaGrange Memorial Hospital**
*Area Served: IL Write*: 5101 S Willow Springs Rd, LaGrange, IL 60525 *Call*: 708/354-7070

**Grief Recovery Seminar Carle Foundation Hospital**
*Area Served: IL* A four-session series group touching the basic dynamics of the grief process and providing support (encouragement of sharing verbally) for members; this is a community service, open to all who have sustained the loss of a loved one by death. Information regarding the next series will be sent about2 weeks prior to the start of the series. *Services*: Mutual aid. *Write*: 611 W Park St, Urbana, IL 61801 *Call*: 217/383-3410

**Grief Recovery Support Group Hinsdale Hospital**
*Area Served: DuPage County* Support group for those who have lost a loved one (spouse, sibling, parent, friend). The 5-week series is repeated quarterly. *Services*: Mutual aid. *Write*: 120 N. Oak, Hinsdale, IL 60521 *Call*: 630/856-3920

**Grief Recovery Support Group** *Area Served: Peoria County Write*: Wilton Mortuary 2102 N Knoxville Ave, Peoria, IL 61604 *Call*: 309/688-2454

**Grief Recovery Support Group** *Area Served: Peoria* To allow grievers to gain information about the grief process and to share experiences with others who have lost a loved one. *Meetings*: Weekly for anyone interested. *Services*: Mutual aid, educational program or material, written information, speakers bureau. *Write*: 2101 N Knoxville, Peoria, IL 61603 *Call*: 309/688-2454

**Grief Support Group Bereavement Center** *Area Served: Cook County Write*: Rainbow Hospice 1775 Dempster St, Park Ridge, IL 60068 *Call*: 847/699-2000 *Fax*: 708/699-2047

**Grief Support Group Bromenn Lifecare Center**
*Area Served: McLean County Write*: 807 N Main, Bloomington, IL 61701 *Call*: 309/454-1400 5499

**Grief Support Group Covenant Medical Center**
*Area Served: Champaign County* Provides support and self-help for people who have lost a significant other. *Services*: Mutual aid. *Write*: 1400 W Park St, Urbana, IL 61801 *Call*: 217/337-2470

**Grief Support Group Erie Family Health Center** *Area Served: Cook County Write*: 1636 W Chicago, Chicago, IL 60622 *Call*: 312/666-3488

**Grief Support Group Kelley and Spalding Funeral Home** *Area Served: Lake County Write*: 1787 Deerfield Rd, Highland Park, IL 60035 *Call*: 847/831-4260 *Fax*: 708/945-5080

**Grief Support Group Kewanee Hospital** *Area Served: Henry County Write*: 719 Elliott St, Kewanee, IL 61443 *Call*: 309/853-3361 283

**Grief Support Group Lutheran General Health System**
*Area Served: Cook County Write*: Dept of Pastoral Care, 1775 Dempster St, Park Ridge, IL 60068 *Call*: 708/696-6395

**Grief Support Group Northtown-Rogers Park Health Center** *Area Served: Cook County Write*: 1607 W. Howard, Chicago, IL 60626 *Call*: 312/744-7617

**Grief Support Group Saint Elizabeth Hospital**
*Area Served: St. Clair and Madison Counties Write*: 211 S Third St, Belleville, IL 62221 *Call*: 618/234-2120 13423

**Grief Support Group Saint Mary Hospital** *Area Served: Adams County* Provides a loving, caring, supportive environment for adults who have experienced the loss of a loved one, enabling them to express and to share the sadness, loneliness, pain, and confusion. Meets twice a month. *Services*: Mutual aid. *Write*: 1415 Vermont St, Quincy, IL 62301-3119 *Call*: 217/223-8400 6824 *Fax*: 217/223-6896 *Email*: bayssy@quincy.edu

**Grief Support Group St Joseph's Hospital of Highland**
*Write*: 1515 Main St, Highland, IL 62249 *Call*: 618/654-7421

**Grief Support Group Vitas Innovative Hospice Care**
*Area Served: Cook and Will Counties Write*: 1055 W 175th St, Homewood, IL 60430 *Call*: 708/957-8777 *Fax*: 312/753-9816

**Grief to Hope Hospice of Northeastern IL Inc**
*Area Served: IL* A six-week grief support group; runs 4-6 times per year. *Services*: Mutual aid. *Write*: 410 S Hager, Barrington, IL 60010 *Call*: 847/381-5599

**Grieving and Coping Ingalls Memorial Hospice Ingalls Wellness Center** *Area Served: Cook County Write*: 29200 W 183rd St, Homewood, IL 60430 *Call*: 708/331-1360 or 708/331-0226

**Growing Through Grief Group Rush Hospice Partners**
*Area Served: Cook County Write*: 1035 Madison St., Oak Park, IL 60302 *Call*: 708/386-9191 521 *Fax*: 708/386-9933

**Healing Hearts of Rockford Memorial Hospital**
*Area Served: Winnebago and Boone Counties Write*: 2400 N Rockton Ave, Rockford, IL 61103 *Call*: 815/968-6861 5060

**Horizon Hospice** *Area Served: Cook County Write*: 833 W Chicago, Chicago, IL 60622 *Call*: 312/733-8900 *Fax*: 312/733-8952

**Hospice of Highland Park Hospital** Provide bereavement support for hospice families and community. *Services*: open group facilitated by LCSW-support for normal grief. *Meetings*: 1st and 3rd Tuesday on the month from 2-3:30 pm., in English. Held on the 2nd floor of hospital-social service counseling room. *Write*: 718 Glenview Ave,

Highland Park, IL 60035 *Call*: 847/480-3858
*Fax*: 847/480-3941

**Hospice of Northeastern IL, Inc(HNI)** *Area Served: Cook, Lake, DuPage and Boone Counties* Provides bereavement support to HNI families and the community who are grieving the death of a loved one. After support is offered through personal phone *Calls*, visits and letters. *Services*: support groups for adults, teens and children. Also offered is Camp Courage, a bereavement camp for kids. *Write*: 410 S Hager Ave, Barrington, IL 60010 *Call*: 847/381-5713 *Fax*: 708/381-5713

**Jewish Family and Community Service** Discussion groups for survivors of Nazi persecution. 50 years later services: groups *Meetings*: weekly, in English, bus, parking on St, *Call* for specific dates and times. *Write*: 2710 W. Devon, Chicago, IL 60659 *Call*: 773/274-1324 *Fax*: 773/508-0438

**Lake County Forest Hospital Hospice** *Area Served: Lake County* Both cancer and bereavement groups open to public. *Services*: Mutual aid. *Write*: 660 N Westmoreland Rd, Lake *County* Forest, IL 60045 *Call*: 847/234-5600 64446

**Life After Loss Carle Hospice** *Area Served: Champaign Count y Write*: 2011 Roundbarn Rd, Champaign, IL *Call*: 217/383-5151

**Life After Loss-Coping with The Holidays Rainbow Hospice, Inc** Adult support group for coping with the holidays after loss of an adult through death. The group uses poetry therapy techniques to explore positive alternatives for coping with the memories and feelings associated with the holidays. Offered annually before thanksgiving and going through the new year. Registration required. *Write*: 1550 N. Northwest Hwy SUITE 220, Park Ridge, IL 60068-1427 *Call*: 847/699-3604 *Fax*: 847/699-2047

**Live Today Saint Joseph Hospital** *Area Served: Clinton and Madison Counties Write*: 9515 Holy Cross Ln PO Box 99, Breese, IL 62230 *Call*: 618/526-4511 327

**Living After Loss: Holiday Group Rainbow Hospice, Inc** *Area Served: Cook and Lake Counties Write*: Bereavement Center 1550 N Northwest Hwy, Ste. 220, Park Ridge, IL 60068 *Call*: 847/699-3604

**Living: When A Loved One Has Died Little Company of Mary Hospital** *Area Served: Cook County* Gathers bereaved persons to help them understand their grief and to provide consistent support specific to their particular loss (spouse, parent, child, etc.) *Meetings*: fall/spring 4 weekly sessions followed by 4 monthly support groups. Group open to family and concerned persons. *Services*: Mutual aid, educational program or material, written information. *Write*: 2800 W. 95th St, Evergreen Park, IL 60642 *Call*: 708/422-6200 5480

**Loss and Grief Support Group Methodist Medical Center** *Area Served: Peoria County  Write*: Pastoral Care Department 221 NE Glen Oak, Peoria, IL 61636-0002 *Call*: 309/672-4172

**Loss and Grief Support Group United Samaritans Medical Center** *Area Served: Vermilion County  Write*: 812 N Logan Ave, Danville, IL 61832 *Call*: 217/431-4038

**Loss-Grief Group Ravenswood CMHC** *Area Served: IL Write*: 2312 W Irving Park Rd, Chicago, IL 60618 *Call*: 773/463-7000 1455

**New Beginnings Christ Hospital** *Area Served: Cook County* This is a support group to provide time for all those who are grieving the loss of a loved one, whether the loss is recent or whether there is unresolved grief of some duration. The group offers a new beginning. *Meetings*: Monthly for all interested. *Services*: Mutual aid, educational program or material, telephone support, referral to other services, information. *Write*: Dept. of Religion and Health 4440 W. 95th St, Oak Lawn, IL 60453 *Call*: 708/346-5175 *Fax*: 708/346-4445

**New Beginnings Good Samaritan Regional Health Center** *Area Served: Jefferson County* For anyone who has experienced a loss. *Meetings*: Monthly. *Services*: Mutual aid, educational program or material. *Write*: St Joanne Memorial Building 605 N 12$^{th}$ St, Mt. Vernon, IL 62864 *Call*: 618/242-4600 7444

**New Beginnings St Rathael** *Area Served: DuPage County Write*: 1215 Modaff Rd, Naperville, IL 60540

**New Identities Faith Church, UCC** *Area Served: Cook County Write*: 21302 Maple St, Matteson, IL 60443 *Call*: 708/755-1917

**Northtown-Rogers Park Health Center** *Area Served: Chicago Write*: 1607 W Howard, Chicago, IL 60626 *Call*: 312/744-7617 *Fax*: 312/744-1621

**People Needing People Hospice of Madison County** *Area Served: Madison County  Write*: St Elizabeth Medical Center 2100 Madison Ave, Granite City, IL 62040 *Call*: 618/789-3399

**Renewal Bereavement Support Group Decatur Memorial Hospital Office** *Area Served: IL Write*: 441 W Hay, Decatur, IL 62526 *Call*: 217/875-3755

**Rush Hospice Partners** *Area Served: Cook County* Bereavement support groups open to all interested. *Meetings*: Weekly. *Services*: Mutual aid. *Write*: 1035 Madison, Oak Park, IL 60302 *Call*: 708/386-9191

**The Compassionate Friends, Inc Chicago Chapter** *Area Served: Cook County Write*: 4312 N Avers, Chicago, IL 60618 *Call*: 312/666-3488

**Transitions From Grief VNA North Hospice**
*Area Served: Cook County Write*: 5215 Old Orchard Rd
1st Fl, Skokie, IL 60077 *Call*: 847/581-1717 6032

**Twinless Twins Support Group Intl.** *Area Served:
National Write*: 11220 St Joe Rd, Fort Wayne, IN 46835
*Call*: 219/627-5414

**Up with Life Wood River Hospice** *Area Served: Madison
County* Bereavement support open to the public. *Write*:
Wood River Township Hospital E Edwardsville Rd, Wood
River, IL 62095 *Call*: 618/254-3821 558

**VNA Hospice Visiting Nursing Assn North** Provide
grief support groups for adults experiencing the loss of a
loved one. Groups and programs offer support, hope,
encouragement and coping strategies. In-service
presentations to community and business org.s and holiday
programs. *Meetings*: daytime and evening groups
available. *Call* for specific times and dates. *Write*: 5215
Old Orchard Rd # 700, Skokie, IL 60077-1035
*Call*: 847/581-1717 *Fax*: 847/581-1919

**Whiteside County Hospice Bereavement Support
Group** *Area Served: Whiteside County Write*: PO Box
918, Rock Falls, IL 61071 *Call*: 815/626-9242
*Fax*: 815/626-7438

# Bereavement-Children

**Alliance of Perinatal Bereavement Facilitators Chicago
Region** *Area Served: Cook, Lake and DuPage Counties D
Write*: Rush-Maternal Child Nursing 805 JONES, 1653
Congress Pkwy, Chicago, IL 60612 *Call*: 312/942-5067

**Alliance of Perinatal Bereavement Support
Facilitators- Chicago Region** 10 year old Regional
network which serves the support programs of over 60
Chicago region hospitals. for coordinators of support
programs to network, identify common concerns and work
toward solutions within the area of perinatal death.
Quarterly meetings, quarterly newsletter, resource list of
Regional support groups and contact people, and annual
members workshop. *Meetings*: quarterly, rotating sites.
*Call* for specific times and dates. *Write*: Rush/Maternal
Child Nursing 1653 Congress Pkwy., Chicago, IL 60612
*Call*: 312/942-2298 *Fax*: 312/942-5615

**AMEND** *Area Served: Madison-W County* Aiding a
Mother and father Experiencing Neonatal Death
(AMEND). Peer grief counseling on a one-to-one basis for
moms and dads after a perinatal death; including
miscarriage. *Services*: Mutual aid, telephone support
*Write*: 2209 Gillis, Alton, IL 62002 *Call*: 618/466-7129

**Bereaved Parents St Joseph's Hospital Medical Center**
*Area Served: Will County Write*: 333 N Madison, Joliet, IL
60453 *Call*: 815/725-7133 3474

**Bereaved Parents, USA** *Area Served: National* Provides
support to parents and grandparents of children who have
died. *Services*: group meetings, quarterly national
newsletter, phone contacts, monthly chapter meetings
monthly chapter newsletters and national gatherings
(conferences) brochures. *Meetings*: monthly, call for
specific times and dates. *Write*: PO Box 95, Park Forest, IL
*Call*: 708/748-7672 *Fax*: 708/748-9184

**Care of Parents After Infant Death
Rush-Presbyterian-St. Lukes Medical Center**
*Area Served: Chicago* to support families experiencing a
pregnancy loss or infant death. to assist families through
the normal grieving process. to educate professionals about
the appropriate standards of care when caring for a family
experiencing this crisis. *Meetings* restricted to persons
sharing the concern. *Services*: Mutual aid, educational
program or material, written information, advocacy,
referral to other services, professional service, speakers
bureau, hotline, telephone support *Write*: 8 Jones
Maternal-Child Nursing 1653 Congress Parkway, Chicago,
IL 60612 *Call*: 312/942-5067

**Caring Connection Christ Hospital** *Area Served: Cook
County* Works with the bereaved parents in coping with
the trauma of the loss of a child. Discussion groups where
parents can listen, talk and share similar experiences so
that others may realize they are not alone. Trained
facilitators attend meetings. *Meetings*: 3rd Monday of each
month 7:30-9:00 pm. Located: harbor room in oak lawn.
*Call* 708)346-5175 for more information about caring
connection. *Write*: 4440 W 95th St, Oak Lawn, IL
60453-2600 *Call*: 708/346-1146 *Fax*: 708/346-4445

**Center for Loss In Multiple Birth, Inc CLIMB, Inc**
*Area Served: National* Support for parents who have
experienced the death of one or more of their twins, triplets
or higher multiples during pregnancy, infancy or
childhood. No known IL chapters. *Services*: telephone
support, newsletter, written information, educational
program or material, referral to other services, speakers
bureau. *Write*: PO Box 1064, Palmer, AK 99645
*Call*: 907/746-6123

**Coffee and Comfort** *Area Served: Cook County* Self-help
groups for parents who have had a child die. Periodic
meetings held for siblings. *Meetings*: Monthly with
daycare available. *Services*: Mutual aid, written
information, referral to other services, speakers bureau.
*Write*: 7500 W Sycamore Dr, Orland Park, IL 60462
*Call*: 708/460-1392

**The Compassionate Friends, Inc** *Area Served: Macon
County Write*: Box 4644, Decatur, IL 62525
*Call*: 217/429-1794

**The Compassionate Friends, Inc Bloomington-Normal
Chapter** *Area Served: McLean County Write*: PO Box
788, Bloomington, IL 61702-0788 *Call*: 309/454-7000

**The Compassionate Friends, Inc Chicago Chapter**
*Area Served: Cook County* A self-help org. offering friendship and understanding to bereaved parents and siblings. to support and aid parents in the positive resolution of the grief experienced and to foster the physical and emotional health. *Meetings*: Monthly. Spanish language and information is available. 30 chapters in IL. *Services*: Mutual aid, educational program or material, telephone support, newsletter, written information. *Write*: 4312 N Avers, Chicago, IL 60618-3696 *Call*: 773/463-7106

**The Compassionate Friends, Inc Chicago Loop Chapter** *Area Served: Cook County Write*: 1130 S Michigan Ave. #4105, Chicago, IL 60605 *Call*: 312/939-4289

**The Compassionate Firends, Inc Decatur Area Chapter** *Area Served: Clinton County Write*: C/O Luv Realty 345 West Prairie, Ste 9, Decatur, IL 62522 *Call*: 217/428-7600

**The Compassionate Friends, Inc Elgin Area Chapter** *Area Served: Kane County Write*: 799 S McLean, Elgin, IL 60121 *Call*: 847/337-6924

**The Compassionate Friends, Inc Fox Valley Chapter** *Area Served: Kane County Write*: 221 S 5th St, St Charles, IL 60174 *Call*: 708/377-6399

**The Compassionate Friends, Inc Galesburg Area Chapter** *Area Served: Knox, Fulton and Henry Counties Write*: PO Box 1261, Galesburg, IL 61401 *Call*: 309/342-5994

**The Compassionate Friends, Inc Hoopeston Chapter** *Area Served: Vermilion County Write*: 38851 N 1650 E Rd, Hoopeston, IL 60942 *Call*: 217/283-5309

**The Compassionate Friends, Inc IL and National Office** *Area Served: National* Provide family support and community education through grief-related resources to help the bereaved reach physical and emotional health. *Services*: referrals to local chapters, develop and distribute resources (audio, videos, books, etc). Publish newsletter, coordinate Regional and national conferences and provide training and educational materials to chapter leaders and community professionals. *Meetings*: varies per chapter-*Call* for time/date/location. *Write*: PO Box 3696, Oak Brook, IL 60522-3696 *Call*: 630/990-0010 *Fax*: 630/990-0246 *Email*: T2HT72A@prodigy.com *Web site*: http://pages.prodigy.com/CA/lycg97a/lycg97tcf.html

**The Compassionate Friends, Inc Northwest Suburban Chapter** *Area Served: Cook County Write*: 307 N Northwest Hwy, Park Ridge, IL 60068 *Call*: 847/692-3092

**The Compassionate Friends, Inc Pana Area Chapter** *Area Served: Christian County Write*: 814 Holly, Pana, IL 62557 *Call*: 217/562-2704

**The Compassionate Friends, Inc Pekin Memorial Hospital** *Area Served: Peoria County Write*: Social Service Department 600 S 13TH ST, Pekin, IL 61554 *Call*: 309/352-4570

**The Compassionate Friends, Inc Quad City Area Chapter** *Area Served: Rock Island County Write*: Messiah Lutheran Church 9196 N High St, Port Byron, IL 61275 *Call*: 309/523-2287

**The Compassionate Friends, Inc Springfield Chapter** *Area Served: Sangamon Christian and Scott Counties Write*: PO Box 914, Springfield, IL 62705 *Call*: 217/789-0816

**The Compassionate Friends, Inc St Elizabeth's Hospital** *Area Served: Madison and St. Clair Counties Write*: 211 S 3rd St, Belleville, IL 62222 *Call*: 618/234-2120 1091

**The Compassionate Friends, Inc St Clair County Chapter** *Area Served: St Clair County Write*: 308 W Second, O=Fallon, IL 62269 *Call*: 618/632-7234

**The Compassionate Friends, Inc St John's Church** *Area Served: Whiteside, Lee, Bureau and Ogle Counties Write*: PO Box 396, Sterling, IL 61081 *Call*: 815/438-5713

**The Compassionate Friends, Inc West Suburban Chapter** *Area Served: DuPage County Write*: PO Box 703, Hinsdale, IL 60521 *Call*: 630/990-0010

**The Compassionate Friends, Inc Will County Chapter** *Area Served: Will County Write*: 26945 S Kankakee St, Manhattan, IL 60442 *Call*: 815/478-3597

**The Compassionate Friends St Elizabeth's Hospital** *Area Served: St. Clair and Madison Counties M Write*: 211 S Third St, Belleville, IL 62222-0694 *Call*: 618/234-2120 1342

**East Central IL SIDS Foundation** *Area Served: Champaign County Write*: 914 W Hill St, Champaign, IL 61821 *Call*: 217/359-7880

**Empty Cradle Support Group for Parents Mahomet Lutheran Church** *Area Served: Champaign, Piatt, DeWitt and Vermillion Counties Write*: PO Box 703 410 E Andover, #2, Mahomet, IL 61853 *Call*: 217/586-5936

**Grieving Parents Support Network** *Area Served: McLean County* A self-help group for bereaved parents. *Services*: Mutual aid, educational program or material, referral to other services, Home or Hospital visitation, hotline.*Write*: 1419 Chadwick Dr, Normal, IL 61761 *Call*: 309/454-7000

**Healing Our Lost Dreams Lutheran General Health System** *Area Served: Cook County Write*: Pastoral Counseling Center 1610 Luther Ln, Park Ridge, IL 60068 *Call*: 847/696-6395 *Fax*: 708/823-9222

**Heart to Heart Hoffman Estates Medical Center**
*Area Served: Cook County, DuPage County Write*: 1555
N Barrington Rd, Hoffman Estates, IL 60194
*Call*: 708/490-6957 *Fax*: 708/490-6948

**Hour-Helping Ourselves Understand and Renew
Columbus Hospital** *Area Served:IL Write*:2550 N
Lakeview, Chicago, IL 60614 *Call*: 773/883-6443

**I Lost A Child Memorial Hospital** *Area Served: IL*
*Write*: 404 W Main St, Carbondale, IL 62901
*Call*: 618/549-0721 5200

**Kravitt Perinatal Loss Support Group Support Center
for Perinatal and Childhood Death** *Area Served: Cook,
Lake and DuPage Counties Write*: Evanston Hospital
2650 Ridge, Evanston, IL 60201 *Call*: 847/570-2882

**Little Angels Parents Support Group United
Samaritans Medical Center** *Area Served: Vermillion,
Edgar and Iroquois Counties Write*: 812 N Logan Ave,
Danville, IL 1832 *Call*: 217/443-5283

**Living with The Loss of A Child St Joseph Medical
Center** *Area Served: McLean County Write*: Dept of
Pastoral Care 2200 E Washington, Bloomington, IL 61701
*Call*: 309/662-3311 1060

**Loss of Child Bereavement Support Group**
*Area Served: DuPage County Write*: Elmhurst
Presbyterian Church 367 SPRING RD, Elmhurst, IL 60126
*Call*: 630/987-1177

**Loving Memories Highland Park Hospital** *Area Served:
Lake County Write*: 718 Glenview Ave OB Dept, Highland
Park, IL 60035 *Call*: 847/480-3711 *Fax*: 708/480-3944

**Miscarriage and Stillbirth Support Group MISS**
*Area Served: Lake, Cook and DuPage Counties* To help
women and their spouses with the grief of their loss, to let
them know there are other women who have gone thru this
also and understand. Also to help the woman with the
choice of another pregnancy. *Meetings*: as needed.
*Services*: Mutual aid, educational program or material,
telephone support, Home or Hospital visitation, written
information. *Write*: 458 Chesterfield Lane, Vernon Hills,
IL 60061 *Call*: 847/816-8633

**National Share Office St. Elizabeth's Hospital**
SHARE--through mutual help groups, provides a caring,
supportive atmosphere where members can share their
experiences, thoughts and feelings. parents learn there that
the deeply-felt long-lasting feelings they are having are
normal. Support groups, telephone support, information,
speakers and newsletters. *Meetings*: 2nd Thursday,
monthly at 7:30 PM. *Write*: Pastoral Care 211 South Third
St, Belleville, IL 62222 *Call*: 618/234-2120 1091

**Open Arms Swedish Covenant Hospital** *Area Served:
Chicago* Provides support and understanding for parents

who have lost a child through miscarriage, stillbirth or
infant death, by sharing with other parents and the
resources of support personnel. *Meetings*: bimonthly for
bereaved parents. *Services*: Mutual aid, written
information, referral to other services, telephone support,
newsletter. *Write*: 5145 N. California, Chicago, IL 60625
*Call*: 773/989-3834 *Fax*: 312/275-2433

**Parent Bereavement Group United Samaritans
Medical Center** *Area Served: Vermilion County Write*:
812 N Logan Ave, Danville, IL 61832 *Call*: 217/443-5283

**Parents Communicating Hope Palos Community
Hospital** *Area Served: Cook and Will Counties* Provides
information and emotional support to parents and family
members who have experienced a miscarriage, stillbirth or
newborn death. Mutual aid, self-help groups, public
education, special accessibility and mobility impaired.
*Meetings*: last Monday of every month, 7:30-9 pm,
conference room B. *Write*: 12251 S. 80th Ave, Palos
Heights, IL 60463 *Call*: 708/923-4840 *Fax*: 708/923-4849

**Parents Living with Loss Bromenn Healthcare and St
Joseph's Medical Center** *Area Served: McLean County*
Offers Mutual help for parents who have lost a child.
Professionals are present to serve as facilitators and to
keep group safe. *Meetings*: Monthly. *Services*: Mutual aid.
*Write*: Virginia At Franklin, Normal, IL 61761
*Call*: 309/454-1400 5499

**Parents Who Have Lost A Child** *Area Served: Cook and
Lake Counties* To discuss the various problems confronted
by parents who have lost a child. The group is
interreligious and interracial and provides an opportunity
for parents to confront their loss in a supportive and open
atmosphere. *Meetings*: Monthly. *Services*: Mutual aid.
*Write*: PO Box 409, Glencoe, IL 60022
*Call*: 847/729-9034 *Fax*: 312/743-3057

**Perinatal Grief Support Central DuPage County
Hospital** *Area Served: DuPage County Write*: Behaviorial
Health *Services* 25 N Winfield, Winfield, IL 60190
*Call*: 630/682-1660 6951 *Fax*: 708/682-1707

**Perinatal Bereavement Support Group St Joseph
Medical Center** *Area Served: Will, Grundy and Kankakee
Counties* For grieving parents who have suffered the loss
of a child through miscarriage,stillbirth, neonatal death or
death after birth. *Meetings*: Monthly. *Services*: Mutual aid,
written information, referral to other services. *Write*: 333
N Madison St, Joliet, IL 60435 *Call*: 815/741-7535 3391

**Perinatal Loss Support Group Northwestern Memorial
Hospital** *Area Served: Cook County Write*: Women's
Health Department 333 E Superior, Chicago, IL 60611
*Call*: 312/908-9971

**Renew Through Sharing Central DuPage County
Hospital** *Area Served: DuPage County Write*: Maternal

Child Department 25 N Winfield Rd, Winfield, IL 60190
*Call*: 630/682-1600 6427 *Fax*: 708/682-1707

**Renew Through Sharing Lake County Forest Hospital**
*Area Served: Lake County Write*: 660 N Westmoreland
Rd, Lake *County* Forest, IL 60045 *Call*: 847/234-6161

**Renew Through Sharing Northwest Community**
**Hospital** *Area Served: Cook County* Help the caregiver
better understand the feelings and needs of the person they
are caring for. Develop a greater awareness of their own
needs and responses to their situation. *Meetings*: Twice
monthly. *Services*: Mutual aid, referral to other services.
*Write*: 800 W Central Rd, Arlington Heights, IL 60005
*Call*: 708/259-1000 5163 *Fax*: 708/590-6332

**Renew Through Sharing** *Area Served: Stephenson*
*County Write*: 1045 W Stephenson, Freeport, IL 61032
*Call*: 815/235-0244

**RTS Bereavement Support Group Good Shepherd**
**Hospital** *Area Served: Lake County Write*: 450 W Hwy
22, Barrington, IL 60010 *Call*: 847/381-9600 5453
*Fax*: 708/842-4453

**Share Good Samaritan Regional Health Center**
*Area Served: Jefferson County Write*: 605 N 12th, Mt.
Vernon, IL 62864 *Call*: 618/242-4600 7444

**Share Memorial Hospital** *Area Served: Hancock County*
*Write*: PO Box 160, Carthage, IL 62321-0160
*Call*: 217/357-3131 2292

**Share Pregnancy and Infant Loss Support, Inc Heart of**
**IL Share** *Area Served: Peoria, Tazewell, Woodford and*
*Marshall Counties* This is a support group for parents who
have experienced loss through miscarriage, stillbirth, or
early infant death. The goal of this group is to share
experiences, give and receive emotional support, and
resolve grief. Yearly memorial service. *Meetings*: Monthly
for parents. *Services*: Mutual aid, speakers bureau, written
information, professional service, referral to other services,
educational program or material, newsletter, advocacy.
*Write*: St Francis Medical Center 530 NE Glen Oak,
Peoria, IL 61637 *Call*: 309/655-2090

**Share Pregnancy and Infant Loss Support, Inc Heart of**
**IL Center** *Area Served: Peoria Write*: Methodist Medical
Center 211 NE Glen Oak, Peoria, IL 61636
*Call*: 309/672-4850

**Share CGH Medical Center** *Area Served: Whiteside, Lee*
*and Ogle Counties Write*: 100 E Lefevre Rd, Sterling, IL
61081 *Call*: 815/625-0400 5504

**Share Sharing Parents** *Area Served: Madison and St.*
*Clair Counties Write*: Anderson Hospital Route 162 and
159, Maryville, IL 62062 *Call*: 618/288-5711 466

**Share Edward Hospital** *Area Served: DuPage, Will and*
*Kendall Counties Write*: 801 S Washington, Naperville, IL
60566 *Call*: 630/527-3263

**Share Passavant Hospital** *Area Served: Morgan, Scott*
*and Pike Counties Write*: 1600 W Walnut St, Jacksonville,
IL 62650 *Call*: 217/245-9541

**Share St Francis Hospital** *Area Served: Monroe and*
*Macoupin Counties Write*: 1215 E Union Ave, Litchfield,
IL 62056 *Call*: 217/324-2191 543

**Share Schuyler Counseling and Health** *Services Area*
*Served: Schuyler County Write*: 127 S Liberty, Rushville,
IL 62681 *Call*: 217/323-1610

**Share St Mary's Hospital** *Area Served: Macon, Moultrie*
*and Shelby Counties Write*: 1800 E Lake Shore Dr,
Decatur, IL 62521-3883 *Call*: 217/464-2966 2592

**Share - Pregnancy and Infant Loss Support, Inc C/O**
**Blessing Hospital** Provide, on a monthly basis, a safe
place with facilitator to work through the loss of a child
(neo-natal through adult). provide speakers for specified
issues or topics on request of attendees. serve 300 families.
*Services*: resource library, quarterly newsletter, one-on-one
crisis intervention and group interaction and support.
*Meetings*: 2nd Thursday of each month at 7:30pm, 2nd
floor of Blessing Hospital-11th St. campus, accessible,
private area. *Write*: PO Box 7005, Quincy, IL 62305
*Call*: 217/223-8400 6821 *Fax*: 217/223-6891

**Share Blessing Hospital** *Area Served: Adams County*
*Write*: 1005 Broadway, Quincy, IL 62301
*Call*: 217/223-5811 1405

**Share Good Samaritan Hospital** *Area Served: IL*
*Write*: 3815 Highland Ave, Downers Grove, IL 60515
*Call*: 630/275-1520 1520

**Share St Elizabeth's Hospital** *Area Served: St. Clair and*
*Madison Counties Write*: 211 S Third St, Belleville, IL
62222-0694 *Call*: 618/234-2120 1293

**Share Sarah Bush Lincoln Health Center** *Area Served:*
*Coles, Cumberland and Shelby Counties Write*: social
Service Department 1000 Health Care Dr, Mattoon, IL
61938 *Call*: 217/348-2392

**Share Good Samaritan Hospital** *Area Served: DuPage*
*County Write*: 3815 Highland Ave, Downers Grove, IL
60515 *Call*: 630/963-5900 3400

**Share Loyola Hospital** *Area Served: Cook County Write*:
Pastoral Care Department 2160 S. First Ave, Maywood, IL
60153 *Call*: 708/216-9056 *Fax*: 708/216-8773

**Share Covenant Medical Center** *Area Served:*
*Champaign County Write*: 1400 W Park, Urbana, IL 61801
*Call*: 217/337-2229

**Share St Anthony's Memorial Hospital** *Area Served: Effingham, Clay, Jasper and Shelby Counties Write*: 503 N Maple St, Effingham, IL 62401 *Call*: 217/868-5757

**SIDS Alliance** *Area Served: National* Emotional support for families of sudden infant death syndrome. *Write*: 1314 Bedford Ave #210, Baltimore, MD 21208 *Call*: 800/221-7437 *Fax*: 410/653-8709

**Silver Cross Support Group Silver Cross Hospital Newborn Nursery** *Area Served: Will County Write*: 1200 Maple Rd, Joliet, IL 60432 *Call*: 815/740-1100

**Still Missed Pregnancy Loss Support Program** *Area Served: DuPage, Cook and Will Counties* Support program designed to help families cope with the grief associated with the loss of a baby from miscarriage, ectopic pregnancy, stillbirth or neonatal death. *Services*: monthly support group meetings, lending library, annual memorial remembrance service, telephone support available. *Meetings*: 2nd Monday of each month from 7:30-9:00 pm, in English, free parking adjacent to building. *Write*: Hinsdale Hospital 120 N. Oak, Hinsdale, IL 60521-3829 *Call*: 630/856-4497

**Support Group for Bereaved Parents Evanston Hospital** *Area Served: IL* Support group for parents who have experienced pregnancy loss, infant and childhood death. *Meetings*: Monthly for bereaved parents. *Write*: 2650 Ridge, Evanston, IL 60201 *Call*: 847/570-2882 *Fax*: 708/570-0231

**A Support Group for Parents Who Have Lost a Child Our Lady of The Wayside Church** *Area Served: Cook County Write*: 432 W Park, Arlington Heights, IL 60005 *Call*: 708/253-5353

**Surviving Our Loss Soul** *Area Served: Livingston and LaSalle Counties* Support for persons who have lost a child through miscarriage, stillbirth, SIDS or a child at any age. *Meetings*: Four times a year. *Services*: Mutual aid, writteninformation, referral to other services, professional service. *Write*: St. Mary's Hospital 111 E Spring St, Streator, IL 61364 *Call*: 800/325-7699

**Together In The Loss of A Child Prentice Hospital** *Area Served: Cook County* Support group for bereaved parents who have experienced a miscarriage or early infant death or stillbirth. *Meetings*: Monthly for parents, spouses and friends. *Services*: Mutual aid, educational program or material, telephone support, newsletter, written information. *Write*: 333 Superior St, Chicago, IL 60611 *Call*: 312/908-9971

**Touch EHS Bethany Hospital** *Area Served: Cook County Write*: 3435 W Van Buren, Chicago, IL 60624 *Call*: 773/854-3592

# Bereavement-Murder

**Families of Homicide Victims Support Group Victims Service Agency** *Area Served: New York* Provides peer support and telephone reassurance for parents and siblings of homicide victims. Acts as a model for other groups in the New York area as well as nationwide. *Services*: Mutual aid, telephone support *Write*: 210 Joralemen St., Brooklyn, NY 11201 *Call*: 718/834-6688

**Parents of Murdered Children** *Area Served: Cook County* To help people understand what effect murder has on those left behind, and to assist others who are going through the criminal justice system. *Meetings*: monthly. *Services*: written information, telephone support, MA/educational program or material. *Write*: 8946 Beck, Hometown, IL 60456 *Call*: 708/862-4241

**Parents of Murdered Children** *Area Served: National Write*: 100 East 8th St, B-41, Cincinnati, OH 45202 *Call*: 513/721-5683

**Victim Witness Assistance Unit Cook County** *Area Served: Cook County* State's Attorney Office Provide emotional support to families and friends of homicide victims. *Services*: 8 support groups; for adults, adolescents (age 13-20), children (ages 4-12); facilitated by a licenced therapist. Court accompaniment; crisis intervention; victim compensation assistance; information and referral. *Meetings*: monthly-*Call* for dates and times; all locations are accessible, Spanish. *Write*: 2650 S. California, Lobby, Chicago, IL 60608 *Call*: 773/890-7200 *Fax*:773/890-2838 *Web site*: HTTP://WWW.STAT ESAttorney.org.

# Bereavement-Spouse

**Alpha Share Group Saint Anthony Medical Center** *Area Served: Winnebago, Boone and Ogle Write*: 5666 E State St, Rockford, IL 61108 *Call*: 815/395-5064

**Alpha St Anthony Medical Center** *Area Served: Winnebago County Write*: 5666 E State St, Rockford, IL 61108 *Call*: 815/395-5064

**Begin Again Northwest Community Hospital** *Area Served: Cook County Write*: 800 W Central Rd, Arlington Heights, IL 60005 *Call*: 708/259-3463

**Beginning Again Lutheran Community Services for The Aged** *Area Served: Cook County* To provide support for community residents who have lost a loved one, through death. *Meetings*: Bi-monthly but restricted to persons who have lost a loved one. *Services*: Mutual aid, written information. *Write*: Park Place Senior Center 306 W Park Place, Arlington Heights, IL 60005-4699 *Call*: 708/253-3710 3385 *Fax*: 708/253-1427

**Bereavement Classes Jewish Family and Community** *Services Area Served: Lake County* An 8 week series for individuals who are adjusting to living alone as a result of the death of a spouse. Group will explore and exchange ideas about coping and managing. This series may be offered several times per year and/or develop into an ongoing group. *Meetings*: Weekly. *Services*: Mutual aid, educational program or material, written information. *Write*: 1250 Radcliffe Rd, #206, Buffalo Grove, IL 60089 *Call*: 708/392-8820

**Christian Single Helpmate Groups, Inc** *Area Served: Cook County* Provides a safe and supportive Christian atmosphere for those who have experienced the loss of a love. The support is given through discussion that is led by a peer. *Meetings*: Open to any single person who has experienced the loss of their love through death, divorce, or separation. Professionals welcome. *Meetings*: Weekly. *Services*: Mutual aid, written information, social activities. *Write*: 14700 S 94th Ave, Orland Park, IL 60462 *Call*: 708/349-0431

**Christian Single Helpmate Groups, Inc North IL Dist Lutheran Church-Missouri Synod** *Area Served: IL* *Write*: 6418 Bradley, Woodridge, IL 60517 *Call*: 630/969-0679

**Coping with The Death of A Spouse North Center - United Charities** *Area Served: Cook County* Assists widowed persons over the age of 50 who have been widowed less than 2 years. Addresses a wide range of social, psychological, economic, legal and family issues/problems. Series of meetings runs consecutively for 6or 8 weeks and is open to person with concern. Series presented twice during the year -- in the spring and in the fall. Mutual aid, educational program or material, referral to other services, Home or Hospital visitation, speakers bureau *Write*: 3445 N. Central Ave, Chicago, IL 60634-4420 *Call*: 773/282-9535 *Fax*: 312/282-6698

**Horizons Community** *Services Area Served: Cook County Write*: 961 W Montana, Chicago, IL 60614 *Call*: 773/929-4357

**Morning's Light Alexian Brothers Medical Center** *Area Served: Cook and DuPage Counties* Provides widowed persons the opportunity to express feelings of grief, deal with all stages of grief and learn about the process of grieving and healing. The goal is to help individuals heal, grow and move ahead with their lives. *Meetings*: Twice a month. *Services*: Mutual aid. *Write*: 800 Biesterfield Rd., Elk Grove Village, IL 60007-3397 *Call*: 708/806-7267

**NAIM Conference** *Area Served: Cook, Lake and DuPage Counties* Helps the widowed begin a new way of life spiritually and emotionally. *Meetings*: Monthly. *Services*: Mutual aid, written information, referral to other services, social activities, newsletter. *Write*: 721 N LaSalle, Chicago, IL 60610 *Call*: 312/944-1286

**NAIM Conference Downers Grove Chapter** *Area Served: DuPage County Write*: Divine Savior Parish 6700 Main St, Downers Grove, IL 60516 *Call*: 630/969-1532

**New Horizons Support Group (Widows-Widowers) McDonough District Hospital Hospice** *Area Served: IL* *Write*: 525 E Grant St, Macomb, IL 61455 *Call*: 309/833-4101 3065

**Open Door Social Mount Prospect Senior Center** *Area Served: Cook County Write*: 50 S Emerson St, Mt Prospect, IL 60056 *Call*: 708/870-5680

**Parenting Alone-Widows and Widowers Jewish Family and Community Service** *Area Served: Cook County Write*: 205 W Randolph Ste 1100, Chicago, IL 60606 *Call*: 312/263-5523

**Society of Military Widows Chapter #3** *Area Served: National* Assists survivors of career military men including men killed on duty. to provide companionship, counsel, and practical help. No known IL chapter. *Services*: Mutual aid, advocacy, newsletter, written information. *Write*: 14802 Bothell Way NE #201, Seattle, WA 98155 *Call*: 206/364-8241

**Solitaires** *Area Served: Boone and Winnebago Counties* to help people who are widowed deal with the problems associated with this concern. *Meetings*: held monthly for widows and widowers. *Services*: Mutual aid, social activities, referral to other services, speakers bureau, telephone support, home or Hospital visitation. *Write*: 222 E Jackson, Belvedere, IL 61008 *Call*: 815/547-6061

**Spouse Survivors Parents of Murdered Children** *Area Served: National* We are a self-help group with social functions and a victims rights group. *Meetings* are for persons whose spouses were murdered. No known IL chapters. *Services*: Mutual aid, educational program or material, written information, speakers bureau, fundraising, social activities, newsletter. *Write*: 888 Newbridge Rd, North Bellmore, NY 11710 *Call*: 516/783-8837

**Support Groups for Widows/Widowers Center for Family Ministry** *Area Served: Will County* Provides referrals to support programs for widowed people in a 7-*County* area. Also offers peer support group facilitator training twice a year. *Services*: referral to other services, newsletter, educational program or material. *Write*: Diocese of Joliet 402 S. Independence Blvd., Romeoville, IL 60441 *Call*: 815/838-5334

**Theos** *Area Served: Christian County* THEOS (They Help Each Other Spiritually) is an international network of individuals which help widowed people face their grief and let them see there is life after the loss of their spouse.

*Meetings*: 1st Thursday of each month at 1:30 p.m., car pool if needed, elevator in presbyterian church. *Write*: 1219 Lawrence Ave., Taylorville, IL 62568-1223 *Call*: 217/824-3841

**Theos Blake Lambe Funeral Home** *Area Served: Cook County* Mini-seminars and ongoing support for widows/widowers. *Meetings*: Monthly in Chicago and Lombard. *Services*: Mutual aid, educational program or material. *Write*: 4727 W 103rd, Oak Lawn, IL 60453 *Call*: 708/361-0500 *Fax*: 708/636-1281

**Theos Institute for Living** *Area Served: IL Write*: 690 Oak St, Winnetka, IL 60093 *Call*: 847/446-6955 *Fax*: 708/551-5413

**Theos Path Crisis Center** *Area Served: McLean County Write*: 13 Grandview Dr, Normal, IL 61761 *Call*: 309/827-4005

**Theos Wheaton Bible Church** *Area Served: DuPage County* THEOS (They Help Each Other Spiritually) is an international, interdenominational network of individuals, groups and programs through which recently widowed men and women assist each other to heal and become whole. *Meetings*: Monthly but restricted to persons sharing the concern. *Services*: Mutual aid, written information, referral to other services, speakers bureau, social activities. *Write*: Main and Franklin, Wheaton, IL 60187 *Call*: 630/260-1600

**Why Me Lord? Self-Help Group Rariden Senior Services** *Area Served: Macon County Write*: 109 Tiffany Terrace, Decatur, IL 62526-2178 *Call*: 217/875-1665

**Widow and Widower Support Group Silver Cross Hospital** *Area Served: Will County Write*: 1200 Maple Rd, Joliet, IL 60432 *Call*: 815/740-1100 7602

**Widowed-Next Step Group Rainbow Hospice, Inc** *Area Served: Cook DuPage and Lake Counties* Provides grief support for people who have been widowed a year or longer and are dealing with life transitions. It is facilitated by one of our widowed persons service volunteers who is also widowed. Each month there is a specific focus for the group. Open-ended group-no need to preregister for the group. *Meetings*: 4th Tuesday of the month, 7:00-8:30 pm. (Follows a self-help model and is facilitated by someone who is widowed.) *Write*: Bereavement Center 1550 N Northwest Hwy, Ste 220, Park Ridge, IL 60068-1427 *Call*: 847/699-3604 *Fax*: 847/699-3604

**Widowed Outreach Network Condell Memorial Hospital** *Area Served: Lake County* A group of men and women to aid the widowed and newly bereaved bridge the gap from initial shock and grief to recovery. *Meetings*: Monthly, restricted to widowed persons. *Services*: Mutual aid, telephone support, social activities, written information, newsletter. *Write*: 900 Garfield Ave, Libertyville, IL 60048 *Call*: 847/566-4519

**Widowed Persons Service AARP** *Area Served: Jackson County Write*: 1211 W College, Carbondale, IL 62901 *Call*: 618/867-3118

**Widowed Persons Service AARP** *Area Served: DuPage and Cook Counties Write*: 25 N Bruner St, Hinsdale, IL 60521 *Call*: 630/323-6837

**Widowed Persons Service AARP** *Area Served: Kane County Write*: New England Congregational Ch 406 W Galena Blvd, Aurora, IL 60506 *Call*: 630/896-4790

**Widowers, Widows, & Young Widows Group Hospice of the North Shore** *Area Served: Cook County* North Shore Hospice sponsors three groups: 1) for widowers with child-rearing responsibilities; 2) for widows who have lost a spouse in the last 12 months; and 3) for young widows. *Meetings*: Bi-monthly. *Services*: Mutual aid. *Write*: 2821 Central St, Evanston, IL 60201 *Call*: 847/467-7423

**Widows & Widowers: Building A New Life Jewish Family & Community Service** *Area Served: Cook County Write*: 205 W Randolph Ste 1100, Chicago, IL 60606 *Call*: 312/263-5523

**Widows and Widowers Learning to Live Alone** Jewish Family and Community Service *Area Served:* Cook and Lake Counties *Write*: Niles District Office 5050 Church St, Skokie, IL 60077 *Call*: 847/675-0390

**Widows and Widowers Rainbow Hospice** *Area Served: Cook County* Provides one-to-one and telephone outreach to the newly widowed. WPS volunteers are people who themselves are widowed and have gone through a special training program. This is a self-help model that is co-sponsored by Rainbow Hospice, Inc, Lutheran General Hospital, Ballard a health care residence, and AARP. Monthly brunch and dinner for the widowed. *Meetings*: see calendar or *Call*. Registration required. *Write*: 1515 N Northwest Hgwy, Park Ridge, IL 60068-1427 *Call*: 847/699-3605 *Fax*: 847/699-2047

**Widows Or Widowers and Co Hirsch Memorial Chapel** *Area Served: IL* A support group for the grieving widow or widower who has dependent children. Children participate in their own discussion group. *Meetings*: Monthly. *Services*: Mutual aid. *Write*: 7151 W 183rd St, Tinley Park, IL 60477 *Call*: 708/755-9014

**Widows Or Widowers St Michael Church** *Area Served: Cook County* We are a support group (almost 450 members) who offer social, psychological and religious support in a non-denominational setting. *Meetings*: Monthly for all interested. *Services*: Mutual aid, educational program or material, social activities. *Write*: 14327 S Highland, Orland Park, IL 60462 *Call*: 708/349-0903

**Widow Support Group Rainbow Hospice, Inc**
*Area Served: Cook, DuPage and Lake Counties* Provides an on-going grief support group for persons who are widowed. It follows a self-help model, but is professionally facilitated. (Founded in 1976)*Meetings*: 2nd and 4th Tuesdays from 7-8:30 p.m. *Write*: bereavement center 1550 n Northwest hwy, Ste 220, Park Ridge, IL 60068-1427 *Call*: 847/699-3604 *Fax*: 847/699-3604

**Young Widows and Widowers Jewish Family and Community Service** *Area Served: Cook County Write*: 205 W Randolph Ste 1100, Chicago, IL 60606 *Call*: 312/263-5523

**Young Widows Support Group Geneva Lutheran Church** *Area Served: Kane County Write*: 301 S Third St, Geneva, IL 60134 *Call*: 630/232-0165

**Younger Widowed Support Group Rainbow Hospice, Inc** *Area Served: Cook, DuPage and Lake Counties* Provides on-going grief support for younger widowed persons. It follows a self-help model, but is professionally facilitated. *Services*: sitter service available during the time of this group-must *Call* ahead to reserve. *Meetings*: 1st and 3rd Tuesdays at 7-8:30 p.m.. At the bereavement center. Registration taken when someone comes to the group. *Write*: Bereavement Center 1550 N Northwest Hwy, Ste 220, Park Ridge, IL 60068-1427 *Call*: 847/699-3604 *Fax*: 847/699-2047

# Bereavement-Suicide

**American Assn of Suicidology** *Area Served: National* to assist and encourage suicide survivor activities by maintaining information on survivors self-help groups. Makes referrals to ten groups in il. Provides information, newsletter, education, and fund raising. *Write*: 2459 S. Ash, Denver, CO 80222 *Call*: 303/692-0985

**Bereaved Parents and Survivors of Suicide**
*Area Served: Winnebago County* Membership is intended for bereaved parents and survivors of suicide who need support. *Meetings*: Monthly. *Services*: Mutual aid, educational program or material. *Write*: 2205 Primrose, Rockford, IL 61108 *Call*: 815/399/6124

**Call for Help, Inc Suicide and Crisis Program** Provides 24-hour telephone service in areas of crisis and suicide intervention, psychiatric related problems with information and referral. *Services*: telephone support, written information, referral to other services. *Write*: 9400 Lebanon Rd, Edgemont, IL 62203 *Call*: 618/397-0975

**Listening, Sharing, Caring** *Area Served: Macon County* LSC brings together people who share in the common tragic experience of having lost a loved one by suicide. Through a Mutual sharing of thoughts and feelings each person feels more accepted and less alone, and acquires the confidence to resume and rebuild their lives again.

*Services*: support group, materials, bibliographies and pamphlets. *Meetings*: 4th Monday of each month at 7 p.m. At Grace United Methodist Church. *Write*: Grace United Methodist Church 901 N Main St, Decatur, IL 62521-1027 *Call*: 217/767-2268

**Loving Outreach to Survivors of Suicide Loss**
*Area Served:* Cook and Lake Counties We provide a place where survivors share their feelings in the aftermath of a suicide. Veteran members offer healing hope to the newly grieving survivor. Separate survivor groups for special relationships: spouse; parent; sibling; and for children 6-11 years who have lost a parent. *Meetings*: 8-week sessions-4 times a year for newly-bereaved. *Services*: MA/educational program or material, written information, referral to other services, professional service, speakers bureau, telephone support, newsletter. *Write*: Catholic Charities 126 N. Des Plaines, Chicago, IL 60661-2357 *Call*: 312/655-7283

**Ray of Hope Inc** *Area Served: National* Provides mutual support groups for persons coping with bereavement after suicide of a loved one. Offers consultations, presentations, and workshops. Also offers booklets, cassettes and educational video entitled Survivorship After Suicide. No known IL groups. *Services*: Mutual aid, educational program or material, telephone support, written information.*Write*: PO Box 2323, Iowa City, IA 52244 *Call*: 319/337-9890

**Survivors of Suicide** *Area Served: Kane County* SOS provides a safe environment in which survivors can explore their feelings of grief and anger and feel a common bond with others who have been there. *Meetings* are for the whole family. *Services*: Mutual aid, educational program or material, telephone support, Home or Hospital visitation, newsletter, written information. *Write*: 206 S. Fordham, Aurora, IL 60506 *Call*: 630/897-5531

**Survivors of Suicide Call for Help, Inc** *Area Served: South IL* to support survivors during their unique grief process and return them to normal functioning as soon as possible. *Meetings*: Monthly. Mutual aid. National org.. *Write*: 9400 Lebanon Rd, Edgemont, IL 62203 *Call*: 618/397-0963

**Survivors of Suicide** *Area Served: Lee and Ogle Counties Write*: KSB Hospital 403 East First St, Dixon, IL 61021 *Call*: 815/288-5331 276

**Survivors of Suicide Support Group Central IL Task Force/Self Destructive Behaviors** *Area Served: Peoria County* Support group for anyone grieving a suicidal death. People have the opportunity to work through their grief within the context of an understanding and supportive group of peers. *Meetings*: Twice monthly on the 1st and 3rd Tuesday of each month from 7-8:30 PM. *Write*: 5407 N. University St., Peoria, IL 61614 *Call*: 309/697-3342

**The Samaritans Safe Place** *Area Served: National*
*Write*: 500 Commonwealth Ave, Boston, MA 02215
*Call*: 617/247-0220

**Youth Suicide National Center** *Area Served: National*
to establish a clearinghouse of information on youth
suicide and its prevention. *Services*: Educational program
or material, referral to other services, telephone support,
written information. *Write*: 445 Virginia Ave, San Mateo,
CA 94402 *Call*: 415/342-5755

## Bereavement-Youth

**Community Bereavement Support Group SaintTherese
Medical Center** *Area Served: Lake County* Support group
for children, grades kindergarten through 5th and grades
6th- 8th, to help deal with the loss of a loved one. In
addition,a concurrent parents' meeting is also offered.
*Meetings*: monthly. *Services*: Mutual aid, educational
program or material. *Write*: 2615 W. Washington St,
Waukegan, IL 60085 *Call*: 847/360-2259

**Good Mourning Grief Support Group Lutheran
General Children's Medical Center** *Area Served: Cook,
Lake and McHenry Counties* Provides a place for bereaved
children (5 to 11) and teens (12 to 19) who have
experienced the death of a parent or sibling to support one
another. Activities are planned for the children. *Meetings*:
Twice a month for teens and monthly for children but
restricted to persons sharing the concern. *Services*: Mutual
aid, social activities. *Write*: 1775 Dempster St, Park Ridge,
IL 60068 *Call*: 847/696-6395

**Heartlight Children's Memorial Hospital** *Area Served:
Cook County* Center For grieving children and families
provides group support in a caring and accepting
environment and promotes the natural healing process for
children and families who have experienced the death of a
loved one. Evenings begin with supper and are followed
by concurrent support groups for parents during the
children's meeting. *Meetings*: Every other week. Mutual
aid. *Write*: 2300 Children's Plaza Box 130, Chicago, IL
60614 *Call*: 773/880-3383

**Kids Time St Elizabeth's Hospital** *Area Served: St. Clair
and Madison Counties M Write*: 211 S Third St, Belleville,
IL 62222-0694 *Call*: 618/234-2120 1091

**Luz Del Corazon Bereavement Group for Children The
Children's Hospital** *Area Served: Cook County*
*Write*: 2300 Children's Plaza #130, Chicago, IL 60614
*Call*: 773/880-4214

**New Mourning Program Evanston Hospital**
*Area Served: Cook and Lake Counties.* Helps schools and
community groups become a base of support when a child,
parent, or teacher dies. *Services*: speakers bureau. *Write*:
Dept of Pediatrics 2650 Ridge, 2WH, Evanston, IL 60201
*Call*: 847/570-2882

**Ongoing Teen Bereavement Support Group the
Hospice of Northeastern IL, Inc** *Area Served: Cook
County Write*: 410 S Hager Ave, Barrington, IL 60010
*Call*: 847/381-5599

**Rainbows** *Area Served: IL* A support group program for
children who have experienced the loss of a parent either
through death or divorce. 675 Rainbow groups in IL.
*Services*: Mutual aid, educational program or material,
written information, speakers bureau. *Write*: 1111 Tower
Lane, Schaumburg, IL 60173 *Call*: 847/310-1880 *Fax*:
708/310-0120 *Email* rainbowshdqtrs@worldnet.att.net
*Web site*: http://www.rainbows.org

**Rainbows Woodland Hospital** *Area Served: Cook
County Write*: 1650 Moon Lake *County* Blvd, Hoffman
Estates, IL 60194 *Call*: 800/342-0469 6538

**Rainbows** *Area Served: IL* Provides support groups for
children who have suffered the loss of a parent through
death or divorce. The program is divided into 2 six-week
sessions, usually meeting weekly. Serves 7 counties.
*Services*: Mutual aid, written information, referral to other
services. *Write*: Center for Family Ministry 402 S
Independence Blvd, Romeoville, IL 60441
*Call*: 815/838-5334

**Rainbows for All Children** *Area Served: Cook County*
*Write*: 2650 Ridge Ave, Evanston, IL 60201
*Call*: 847/570-2030

**Teen Age Grief (TAG) St Elizabeth's Hospital**
*Area Served: St. Clair and Madison Counties Write*: 211 S
Third St, Belleville, IL 62222-1915
*Call*: 618/235-8315 *Fax*: 618/234-4391
*Email*: seacampe.VAX.LCLS.LIB.IL.US
*Web site*: WWW.APCI.NET/~ste

**Youth In Grief Hospice of The North Shore**
*Area Served: Cook County* A support group for young
people who have experienced the death of a loved one
within the last twelve months. The focus is on
understanding normal bereavement. *Meetings*: Bi-monthly.
*Services*: Mutual aid, speakers bureau. *Write*: 2821 Central
St, Evanston, IL 60201 *Call*: 847/467-7423

# Mental Health & Wellness

## Advocacy

**The Write Thing Mental Health Assn of Evanston**
Provide consumers, family members, professionals, and others with up-to-date legislative information on mental health care issues and concerns to make advocacy efforts easier by providing ready-to-sign-and-send letters, address lists, and telephone numbers. *Meetings*: 2nd Monday, monthly from 7:30 TO8:30 PM. *Write*: 2120 Lincoln St, Evanston, IL 60201 *Call*: 847/675-5261 *Fax*: 847/869-4710 *Email*: caprecover@enteract.com

## Anxiety

**Agoraphobics In Motion** *Area Served: Cook and DuPage Counties* To be able to function without being dependent on other people. Also, to reach out to people who are housebound. Uses a 12 Step program and the ten tools of recovery. Interested persons are requested to *Write* for information and referral to a group nearest them: enclose a SASE Eight IL chapters. *Meetings*: Weekly to persons with concern. *Services*: Mutual aid. *Write*: PO Box 42606, Chicago, IL 60642 *Call*: 708/246-7013

**Alliance for the Mentally Ill AMI of Greater Chicago** *Area Served: Chicago, Cook County Write*: 833 N Orleans, 2nd Floor, Chicago, IL 60610 *Call*: 312/642-3338

**Anxiety Control Techniques** *Area Served: Cook County-S, Will County-N* A self-help group for persons with anxiety and panic attacks to support one another in overcoming their fears. Other issues addressed are relaxation, breathing, codependency, assertiveness and positive thinking. *Meetings*: Weekly. *Services*: Mutual aid, social activities. *Write*: PO Box 566, Tinley Park, IL 60477 *Call*: 708/614-9016

**Anxiety Mutual-Help Group** *Area Served: Cook-NW* A peer-led support group to assist those experiencing anxiety and panic attacks, and phobias. *Meetings*: Weekly but restricted to persons sharing the concern. *Services*: Mutual aid, referral to other services, speakers bureau. *Call*: 708/359-9546

**Anxiety, Panic Attack and Agoraphobic Support Group** *Area Served: DuPage County Write*: Central DuPage *County* Hospital 25 N Winfield Rd, Winfield, IL 60190 *Call*: 708/682-1600 2009

**Clarendon Hills Self Help Support Group** *Area Served: Cook and DuPage County Write*: 819 Franklin St, Westmont, IL 60559 *Call*: 630/789-8412

**DuPage County Area Phobia Support Group CPC** *Area Served: Lake County* Support meetings for family, friends, or consumers who are faced with understanding chronic mental illness. Offers free group counseling, education meetings, and advocacy to improve care for mentally ill. *Services*: Mutual aid, educational program or material, written information, advocacy, referral to other services, speakers bureau, referral to other services, telephone support, newsletter, hotline. *Write*: 2025 W. Washington St., Waukegan, IL 60085 *Call*: 847/234-8383

**Portage-Cragin Relative Support Group Lutheran Social Services** *Area Served: Chicago* Support and educational group for relatives and friends of chronically mentally ill. *Meetings*: Monthly. *Services*: Mutual aid. *Write*: 4840 W Byron St, Chicago, IL 60641 *Call*: 773/282-7800 237

**Reach for Serenity** *Area Served: Cook-S* Self-help group for family members or close friends of people with emotional illness. to help guide people through what we went through in learning to cope with these emotionally disturbed persons. Uses modified 12-step program. Primarily phone support. *Meetings*: As needed. *Services*: Mutual aid, telephone support *Write*: 9704 S. 50th Court, Oak Lawn, IL 60453 *Call*: 708/422-4929

**REACH-Reassurance to Each Southwest Alliance for the Mentally Ill** *Area Served: Cook-S* REACH is a 12-step self-help group that provides support for the family members. Makes information available to educate people about mental illness. Offers a social outlet for the people who feel an emotional and physical commitment to the mentally ill. *Meetings*: Weekly for family and friends. *Services*: Mutual aid, educational program or material, advocacy, telephone support, social activities, newsletter, written information. *Write*: PO Box 23, Oak Lawn, IL 60454 *Call*: 708/425-0925

**Sibling-Adult Children of Mentally Ill Support Grp National SAC Network** *Area Served: Cook County, IL-NE* to recognize and build on the special needs, interests and contributions of siblings and adult children of the mentally ill. to provide siblings and adult children with support, education and resources that enhance their lives. *Services*: Mutual aid. *Write*: Ami-Greater Chicago 833 N. Orleans St., Chicago, IL 60610 *Call*: 312/642-3338

**Thresholds Family Support Group Thresholds**
*Area Served: Cook County* Group led by two social workers with focus on both psycho-education and support. *Meetings*: Weekly for family members of individuals with mental illness. *Services*: Mutual aid, social activities, referral to other services, advocacy. *Write*: 2700 N. Lakeview, Chicago, IL 60614 *Call*: 773/281-3800 2490

# Clutter

**Clutters Anonymous** *Area Served: National Write*: PO Box 25884, Santa Ana, CA 92799 *Call*: 714/494-0694

**Messies Anonymous** *Area Served: National* To improve the lives of disorganized people by providing peer encouragement to control house and life. *Call* for IL contacts. *Services*: Mutual aid, educational program or material. *Write*: 5025 SW 114th Ave, Miami, FL 33165 *Call*: 305/271-8404

# Cults

**Commission on Cults and Missionaries Maynard Bernstein Resource Center on Cults** *Area Served: National Write*: 6505 Wilshire Blvd, Los Angeles, CA 90048 *Call*: 213/852-1234

**Cult Awareness Network** *Area Served: National* National non-profit corporation founded to educate the public about the harmful effects of mind control as used by the destructive cults. CAN is a network of volunteers in 32 states. CAN confines its concern to unethical or illegal practices, including coercive persuasion andmind control. CAN passes no judgement on doctrine or beliefs. *Services*: Mutual aid, educational program or material, fundraising, referral to other services, telephone support, newsletter, written information. *Write*: 2421 W. Pratt, Ste 1173, Chicago, IL 60645 *Call*: 773/267-7777 *Fax*: 08/382-8974

**Cult Awareness Network IL Affiliate** *Area Served: IL Write*: PO Box 193, Lake *County* Bluff, IL 60044 *Call*: 847/528-4401

**International Cult Education Program** *Area Served: National Write*: PO Box 1232 Gracie Station, NY, NY 10028

**Spiritual Counterfeits Project** *Area Served: National Write*: PO Box 4308, Berkeley, CA 94704

# Depression

**Depression Group** *Area Served: Lake County, Cook County Write*: Highland Park Hospital 718 Glenview Ave, Highland Park, IL 60035 *Call*: 847/480-3710

**Depressive-Manic Depressive Support Group**
*Area Served: Kane, DuPage, Kendall County Write*: Mercy Center 1325 N Highland Ave, Aurora, IL 60506 *Call*: 630/653-3560

**Depressive-Manic Depressive Assn** *Area Served: IL-NE Write*: PO Box 59637, Chicago, IL 60659 *Call*: 773/774-5100

**Light for Health** *Area Served: National Write*: 942 Twisted Oak Lane, Buffalo Grove, IL 60089 *Call*: 708/459-4455

**National Depressive and Manic Depressive Assn NDMDA of Hinsdale** *Area Served: DuPage, Cook and Will Counties Write*: Box 535, Hinsdale, IL 60521 *Call*: 630/789-7450

**National Depressive and Manic Depressive Assn Alexian Brothers Medical Center** *Area Served: Cook-NW* Group support for people who are depressed or manic depressive and their families and/or concerned others. *Meetings*: Monthly. *Services*: Mutual aid, educational program or material, written information, advocacy,speakers bureau, telephone support, newsletter, social activities. *Write*: Niehoff Pavilion 800 W. Biesterfield, Elk Grove Village, IL 60007 *Call*: 708/437-5500 4678

**National Depressive and Manic Depressive Assn (NDMDA)** *Area Served: IL, National* Educates patients, professionals, and the public concerning the nature of depressive and manic-depressive illnesses as a medical disease; to foster self-help for patients and families; to eliminate discrimination and stigma; to improve the availability and quality of help and support; and to advocate for research toward the elimination of these illnesses. 17 self-help groups meeting in IL. *Services*: Mutual aid, educational program or material, written information, advocacy, speakers bureau, telephone support, newsletter, social activities. *Write*: 730 N. Franklin, Ste 501, Chicago, IL 60610 *Call*: 312/642-0049

**National Depressive and Manic Depressive Assn North Shore Chapter** *Area Served: Lake County Write*: 2218 Rolling Ridge, Lindenhurst, IL 60046 *Call*: 847/356-4390

**National Depressive and Manic Depressive Assn NDMDA Support Group** *Area Served: McLean County* Provides information, fellowship, and moral support to those who have been diagnosed as having these illnesses and to their support people. to educate the public by making it known that these illnesses are the result of a biochemical imbalance in the brain. to provide referral information on treatment and supportive services. *Meetings*: Twice monthly for patients and families. *Services*: Mutual aid, speakers bureau, written information, social activities, telephone support, referral to other services, educational program or material, newsletter. *Write*: PO Box 5126, Bloomington, IL 61702

**North Shore Depressive Assn** *Area Served: Lake County* to provide a system of family support groups to assist patients and family members affected by depression and manic depression. Our group meets once a month and is open to family and friends, general public and professionals. *Services*: Mutual aid, written information, educational program or material, advocacy, referral to other services, speakers bureau, referral to other services, hotline, telephone support, newsletter. *Write*: 38540 Burr Oak Lane, Wadsworth, IL 60083 *Call*: 847/356-4390

# Emotional Problems

**Recovery Inc** *Area Served: National and Illinois* A member managed community mental health org. that offers a self-help method of will training. The Recovery method is a system of techniques for controlling temperamental behavior and changing attitudes toward nervous symptoms of anxiety,depression and fears. Groups are led by well-trained lay leaders. Referral to more than 30 group meetings in Illinois. *Meetings*: Please *Call*. *Services*: Mutual aid, telephone support, newsletter. *Write*: 802 N Dearborn St. Chicago, IL 60610. *Call*: 312/337-5661,  *Fax*: 312/337-5756, *Web site* http://www.ed.psy.edu/~recovery.<BR>

**Grow USA** *Area Served: Illinois.* A member run mental health org. fostering maturity and personal growth. Referral to more than 100 Illinois group meetings. *Services*: Rehab, friendship, self-activation, Mutual help and leadership development. *Write*: 2403 W Springfield Ave, Champaign, IL 61821. *Call* 217/352-6089.<BR>

# Family

**Alliance for the Mentally Ill AMI of South Suburbs** *Area Served: Cook-S, Will County Write*: PO Box 275, Olympia Fields, IL 60461 *Call*: 708/798-0434

# Men's Issues

**MAN: Men's Anger Network** *Area Served: Cook County Write*: 1525 E 53rd St, Ste 630, Chicago, IL 60615 *Call*: 312/955-4234

**Oakton Community College Men's Program** Provide support group for those men interested in meeting to talk with other men about anything at all, such as job relocation, career change, relational concerns and parenting. No experience needed. *Meetings*: every Wednesday evening from 7:30-10:00 pm, room 2429. *Write*: 1600 Golf Rd, Des Plaines, IL 60016 *Call*: 847/635-1874

# Mental Illness

**The Thursday Evening Club** *Area Served: DuPage County* Provides social therapy for persons who have been suffering from mental illness. Members relearn social skills and are encouraged to accept as much responsibility as possible for the club. The club offers friendship and fun and adds quality to the lives of often lonely people. Volunteers help with activities. *Meetings*: Weekly for patient and family. *Services*: telephone support, social activities. *Write*: 22 W 210 Stanton Rd, Glen Ellyn, IL 60137 *Call*: 630/469-2185 Answer Machine

**IL Department of Mental Health Developmental Disabilities** *Area Served: IL* General information line/referrals to mental health agencies. Provides funding for qualified community mental health agencies that submit proposals. *Services*: written information, referral to other services, fundraising. *Write*: 100 W. Randolph, Ste 6-400, Chicago, IL 60601 *Call*: 312/814-4964 *Fax*: 312/814-4832

# Obsessive Compulsive Disorder

**OC Foundation, Inc** *Area Served: National* Early intervention in controlling and finding a cure for obsessive compulsive disorders and improving quality of life. *Write*: PO Box 70, Milford, CT 06460 *Call*: 203/878.5669, 203/874.3843 voice message *Fax*: 203/874-2826 *Email*: jphs28a@prodigy.com *Web site*: http://pages.prodigy.com/alwillen.ocf.html

**Obsessive Compulsive Disorders Support Group Horizons Center for Counseling Services** *Area Served: McHenry, Kane and DuPage Counties* to serve persons suffering with obsessive-compulsive and related disorders. Provides discussion, support, education. *Services*: Mutual aid, referral to other services, newsletter. *Write*: 970 S McHenry Blvd, Crystal Lake, IL 60014 *Call*: 800/765-9999 815 *Fax*: 815/455-3951

**Obsessive Compulsive Support Group Rush-Presbyterian-St Luke's Medical Center** *Area Served: IL Write*: Psychiatry 955 Professional Building, Chicago, IL 60612 *Call*: 312/942-5375 *Fax*: 312/942-3113

**Obsessive Compulsive Foundation of Metro Chicago** *Area Served: Chicago Write*: 2300 Lincoln Park West, Chicago, IL 60614 *Call*: 773/880-2035 Answer Mach.

**OCD Foundation, Inc Chicago Area Obsessive Compulsive Disorder Group** *Area Served: DuPage, McHenry, Kane County* to support persons suffering with OCD and their families. Works to provide a positive environment and outlook through education, information and sharing experiences. *Meetings*: Restricted to persons sharing the concern. *Services*: Mutual aid, educational program or material, written information, advocacy, referral to other services, professional service, speakers bureau, telephone support, social activities, newsletter.*Write*: 507 Thom Hill, Carol Stream, IL 60188 *Call*: 630/690-3030

**Northwest Suburban Obsessive-Compulsive** *Area Served: Cook County Write*: 951 Plum Grove Rd, Ste C, Schaumburg, IL 60173 *Call*: 847/605-0453

# Personal Growth

**Growth Seminars** *Area Served: Cook County, Will County Write*: 9357 S Winchester Ave, Chicago, IL 60620 *Call*: 773/779-6311

**National Assn to Advance Fat Acceptance** *Area Served: IL* Seeks to promote and increase the happiness and well-being of fat people, their self-acceptance, self-confidence and dignity; to promote tolerance within society towards fat people as well as a clear understanding that fat people are no different than thin people. *Meetings*: Monthly for all interested. *Services*: Mutual aid, educational program or material, advocacy, telephone support, social activities, newsletter, written information, referral to other services, speakers bureau, fundraising. *Write*: PO Box 11418, Chicago, IL 60611 *Call*: 800/442-1214

**The Think Group PMA Seminar** *Area Served: Chicago* Develop ability to understand and reason; organize daily goals efficiently; discover how attitude changes one's daily performance; develop solid value judgements; learn how a Positive Mental Attitude can help increase productivity in one's job and social life; discover secrets to what makes one successful and happy. *Meetings*: Weekly. *Services*: Mutual aid, educational program or material. *Write*: 3104 W. Palmer Square, Chicago, IL 60647 *Call*: 773/276-6603 *Fax*: 312/276-3974

# T'ai Chi

**Chicago Area T'ai Chi and Illinois Self-Help Coalition** *Area Served: Regional* To develop and provide T'ai Chi programs within self-help groups and wellness programs. This ancient Chinese Martial Art thought to affect vitality actually improves flexibility and balance. Provides training and education for group leaders and develops programs within self-help groups for specific populations such as HIV+, cancer, aging, chronic illness and mental health. *Write*: Wright College South 3400 N Austin Ave, Chicago, IL 60634 *Call*: 773/481-8837 *Fax*: 773/481-8903 *Email*: DIPeace@aol.com

# Schizophrenia

**Schizophrenics Anonymous Mental Health Assn In DuPage County** *Area Served: DuPage County* to help restore dignity and a sense of purpose for persons who are working for or recovery from schizophrenia or related disorders. to offer fellowship, positive support and companionship; to improve our attitudes about our live and our illness; to provide members with the latest information; and to encourage members to take positive Steps toward recovery. *Meetings*: Weekly. *Services*: Mutual aid, written information, social activities, telephone support, newsletter. *Call*: 708/627-9550 Answer Machine

# Self-Injury

**Self Abuse Finally Ends (SAFE)** *Area Served: IL-NE* to give support to women who have a compulsion to harm themselves through self-inflicted injuries. to give them an opportunity to express themselves and share their feelings and experiences with others who have similar histories. *Meetings*: Weekly for persons with concern. *Services*: Mutual aid, educational program or material, referral to other services, fundraising, telephone support, social activities, newsletter, written information. *Write*: PO Box 267810, Chicago, IL 60626 *Call*: 773/722-3113

# Stress

## Stress-Farmers

**Farm Resource Center** *Area Served: IL* Provides financial information and referral as well as referrals to counselors, mental health agencies, ministers, etc., for stress, alcoholism, drug abuse, marital difficulties, physical abuse, suicide, etc. *Services*: written information, referral to other services. *Write*: PO Box 87, Mound City, IL 62963 *Call*: 800/851-4719

## Stress-Physicians

**IL State Medical Society** *Area Served: IL* for individual physicians, family, friends or colleagues concerned about physician or medical student at risk for alcoholism, drug abuse or any other cause of physical or mental impairment. Provides referrals, advocacy, monitoring, interventions, general counseling, and advice. No treatment. *Services*: educational program or material advocacy, telephone support, written information, referral to other services. *Write*: 20 N. Michigan Ave, Ste 700, Chicago, IL 60602 *Call*: 312/580-2499

# Stress-Police

**International Law Enforcement Stress Assn**
*Area Served: National* Unites police, criminal justice agencies and other concerned org.s and individuals in coping with the problem of law enforcement stress. *Services*: Mutual aid, educational program or material, telephone support, Home or Hospital visitation, referral to other services. *Write*: 5485 David Blvd, Port Charlotte, FL 33981 *Call*: 813/697-8863

# Stress-Truck Drivers

**Loved Ones and Drivers Support (LOADS)**
*Area Served: IL Write*: 270 Londonderry Ct, Plover, WI 54467 *Call*: 715/345-9952

# Stress-Veterans

**Agent Orange Class Assistance Program Universal Family Connection** *Area Served: Cook County* Readjustment counseling for Vietnam Veterans and their families. *Services*: provide professional service. *Write*: 7949 S. Western Ave, Chicago, IL 60620 *Call*: 773/445-0448

**Citizen Soldier Atom, Inc** *Area Served: National Write*: 175 5th Ave Ste 808, NY, NY 10010 *Call*: 212/777-3470

**Disabled American Veterans #8** *Area Served: IL Write*: Box 4084, Urbana, IL 61801 *Call*: 217/367-5053

**Paralyzed Veterans of America Regional Office** *Area Served: IL* to help paralyzed veterans and patients through support meetings and activities. Regional office handles all government claims for housing, education, employment, etc. *Meetings*: Monthly for members. *Services*: Mutual aid, educational program or material, fundraising, advocacy, referral to other services, telephone support, social activities, newsletter, written information. *Write*: 536 S. Clark St, #400, Chicago, IL 60605 *Call*: 312/663-1872

**Paralyzed Veterans of America Vaughan Chapter** *Area Served: IL* A chapter of a 50 year old veterans' advocacy org.. Provides information on veteran's issues such as American disability act, disability and veteran's resources, social activities, peer counseling, and fund-raising. Publishes a newsletter. Offers transportation. Board meets 1st Thursday of the month. *Write*: 901 W. Jackson Ste 205, Chicago, IL 60607 *Call*: 312/226-2650 *Fax*: 312/226-8598

**Readjustment Counseling Program Oak Park Vet Center** *Area Served: Cook-W, DuPage and Kane Counties* Offers support groups for combat veterans and for wives of veterans. *Meetings*: Weekly. *Services*: Mutual aid, written information, referral to other services, professional service. *Write*: 155 S. Oak Park Ave, Oak Park, IL 60302 *Call*: 708/383-3225

**Vet Center #407** *Area Served: Cook, Kankakee and Will Counties* Readjustment counseling for veterans. Offers counseling (individual, marital, employment, vocational), information and referral, assistance in filing for disability benefits. Prime concern is the post-discharge effect of war-related issues. Many offer support groups dealing with post traumatic stress and groups for veterans' partners. *Services*: Mutual aid, educational program or material, telephone support, written information, referral to other services, professional service. *Write*: 1600 Halsted St, Chicago Heights, IL 60411 *Call*: 708/754-0340

**Vet Center #421** *Area Served: IL Write*: 624 S Fourth St, Springfield, IL 62703 *Call*: 217/492-4955

**Vet Center** *Area Served: Peoria County Write*: 3310 N Prospect Rd, Peoria, IL 61603 *Call*: 309/671-7300

**Vet Center** *Area Served: St. Clair, Madison and Monroe Counties Write*: 1269 N 89th St Ste 1, East St Louis, IL 62203 *Call*: 618/397-6602

**Vet Center Chicago-Northside** *Area Served: Chicago-NORTH* Readjustment counseling for Vietnam Veterans. Provides rap groups. *Services* include individual counseling, marital counseling, vocational counseling, information and referral. Prime concern is war-related issues and how they have affected life since discharge. *Services*: Mutual aid, educational program or material, telephone support, written information, professional service. *Write*: 565 Howard St, Chicago, IL 60202 *Call*: 708/332-1019

**Vetwork The Stone Church** *Area Served: IL-NE* A group of combat veterans offering a counseling alternative to other VA vet centers. Members provide referrals, direction and a listening ear to those interested. *Meetings*: Weekly. *Services*: referral to other services, Mutual aid, speakers bureau, hotline, newsletter. *Write*: 6330 West 127th St, Palos Heights, IL 60463 *Call*: 708/389-8644

**Vietnam Veterans Rap Group** *Area Served: McHenry, Lake and Kane Counties* Helps Vietnam Veterans adjust to everyday living and overcome problems directly and indirectly related to their service. Offers individual, family, and marital counseling. *Meetings*: Weekly for veterans. *Services*: Mutual aid, educational program or material, advocacy, newsletter, professional service. *Write*: 327 Vine St, Woodstock, IL 60098 *Call*: 815/334-0411

**Vietnow** *Area Served: DeKalb County Write*: PO Box 421, DeKalb, IL 60115 *Call*: 815/895-2358

**Vietnow DuPage County Chapter** *Area Served: DuPage County* to unite fraternally those who served in the US Armed Forces during the Vietnam Era. to educate and promote public awarenessof the difficulties in readjustment encountered by the Vietnam veteran, the Vietnam era veteran, and their families. *Services*: Mutual aid, educational program or material, social activities.

*Write*: PO Box 629, Lisle, IL 60532 *Call*: 630/393-6161 Answer Mach.

**Vietnow Freeport Chapter** *Area Served: Stephenson County Write*: PO Box 323, Freeport, IL 61032 *Call*: 815/235-8669

**Vietnow Illiana Chapter** *Area Served: IL Write*: PO Box 302, Danville, IL 61834-0302 *Call*: 217/382-5530

**Vietnow Lake County Chapter** *Area Served: Lake County Write*: PO Box 8995, Waukegan, IL 60079 *Call*: 847/336-6411

**Vietnow McHenry County Chapter** *Area Served: McHenry County Write*: PO Box 825, Woodstock, IL 60098 *Call*: 815/344-8387

**Vietnow Rock River Valley Chapter** *Write*: PO Box 1, Nachusa, IL 61057 *Call*: 815/288-5872

**Vietnow Rockford Chapter** *Area Served: Winnebago County* Veterans helping other veterans and their families. *Services*: Mutual aid, educational program or material, advocacy, telephone support, social activities, written information. *Write*: 1835 Broadway, East Wing, Rockford, IL 61104 *Call*: 815/395-8484

**Vietnow Tri-County Chapter** *Area Served:Kendall, Kane and LaSalle Counties Meetings*: Monthly. *Services*: Mutual aid. *Write*: 1382 Sandwich Dr, Sandwich, IL 60548 *Call*: 815/498-9103

# Women's Issues

**National Org. for Women Chicago Chapter** *Area Served: Chicago Write*: 53 W Jackson, Ste 924, Chicago, IL 60604 *Call*: 312/922-0025

**National Org. for Women IL NOW** *Area Served: IL* Elevating the status and rights of women. Focus on issues around women's equality include protecting women's access to reproductive healthcare inclusive of abortion service, civil rights lesbians/gays/people of color and people with disabilities, stopping violence against women/girls. Chapters host open-to-the-public monthly topics. Focus is on changing the legal and societal basis for women's oppression. *Meetings*: *Call* for dates, accessible *Write*: 522 E Monroe St Ste 501, Springfield, IL 62701 *Call*: 217/528-2077 *Fax*: 217/528-2078 *Email*: acyunczy@ix.netcom.com *Web site*: http://www.netimage.com/ilnow

**Self-Empowering Woman Support Group Passavant Area Hospital** *Area Served: Morgan County* *Write*: 1600 W Walnut, Jacksonville, IL 62650 *Call*: 217/245-9541 3594

**Self-Esteem for Women Southwest Women Working Together** *Area Served: Chicago Write*: 3201 W 63rd St, Chicago, IL 60629 *Call*: 773/582-0550

**Special Services Center Belleville Area College** *Area Served: IL Write*: 2500 Carlyle Rd, Belleville, IL 62221 *Call*: 618/235-2700 368

**Thursday Nite Women's Self Esteem Group** *Area Served: Cook County-NW Write*: 500 W Touhy, #41a, Des Plaines, IL 60018 *Call*: 847/298-3889

**Women for Women Program Kimmel Leadership Center** *Area Served: Madison County Write*: Southern IL University, Edwardsville, IL 62026 *Call*: 618/398-2511

**Women In Transition** *Area Served: Cook County Write*: Northwestern Memorial Hospital 333 E Superior, Chicago, IL 60611 *Call*: 312/908-8400

**Women's Center Lewis and Clark Community College** *Area Served: Madison County Write*: 5800 Godfrey Rd, Godfrey, IL 62035 *Call*: 618/466-3411 4152

**Women's Connection Jewish Family and Community Service** *Area Served: Cook County Write*: 205 W Randolph St, Ste 1100, Chicago, IL 60606 *Call*: 312/263-5523

# Youth at Risk

**Aunt Martha's Youth Service Center** *Area Served: Cook, Will and Kankakee Counties* Community based comprehensive youth service helping youth and families. 24-hour crisis intervention. *Services*: professional service. *Write*: 4343 Lincoln Highway, #340, Matteson, IL 60443 *Call*: 708/747-2701

**Latino Youth** *Area Served: Cook County* Provides various services for youth: an alternative high school, counseling mentors, GED, vocational training, temporary housing for runaways (10-18 years of age, up to 21 days), support groups and other services. *Meetings*: Weekly. *Services*: Mutual aid, educational program or material, social activities, professional service. *Write*: 2200 S. Marshall Blvd., Chicago, IL 60623 *Call*: 773/277-0400

**In-House Prevention Program FNHC** *Area Served: Champaign County Write*: 1306 N Carver Dr, Champaign County, IL 61820 *Call*: 217/359-0109

**Kidsrights** *Area Served: National Write*: 10100 Park Cedar Dr, Charlotte, NC 28210 *Call*: 800/892-5437

**Male Project Planned Parenthood** *Area Served: Champaign County Write*: 1102 Bloomington Rd, Champaign, IL 61821 *Call*: 217/359-3418

**Youth Empowerment Services Value Groups Youth Service Bureau** *Area Served: McHenry County* to provide education and support in a peer support to people aged 10-22. Groups have a wide range of concerns: prevention of pregnancy, abuse, substances, drop-out and truancy. Value Group meetings open to people not involved in Youth Empowerment *Services. Meetings*: Weekly. *Services*: Mutual aid, referral to other services, professional service, social activities, written information. *Write*: 101 S. Jefferson, Woodstock, IL 60098 *Call*: 815/338-7360

**Youth Outreach Program Evanston Police Department** *Area Served: Cook County-N* Police-based social service program which provides supervision, informal counseling and psychological services to youth with social, behavioral and adjustment problems. Motivates by education and recreation. *Services*: Mutual aid, educational program or material, social activities. *Write*: 1454 Elmwood Ave, Evanston, IL 60201 *Call*: 847/866-5015

# Sexuality & Gender

## Bisexuality

**Bi-Net Chicago The Lesbian and Gay Community Center** *Area Served: Cook County Write*: 2863 N Clark, Chicago, IL 60657 *Call*: 773/275-0186

**Bisexuality Coalition Student Assn** *Area Served: DeKalb County Write*: Rm 256a, Homes Student Center NIU, DeKalb, IL 60115 *Call*: 815/753-0584

**Review** *Area Served: National* Support system for bi and gay married men trying to find workable, and acceptable, solutions to our individual life situations. to help end the isolation and offer discussion on a wide variety of possible approaches to the challenges that face us. *Meetings*: monthly, - *Call* for times and dates. *Write*: PO Box 7406, Villa Park, IL 60181-7406 *Call*: 630/620-6946 *Email*: UMANGUY@AOL.COM

## Gay and Lesbian

### Gay and Lesbian-General

**Evangelicals Concerned Chicago Region** *Area Served: Cook, DuPage and Kane Counties* Provides support and guidance in the integration of faith with homosexuality. Offers Bible studies, seminars, discussion groups, social events, quarterly newsletter, educational materials, consultation/education with local churches, referrals. *Meetings*: Monthly. *Services*: Mutual aid, educational program or material, social activities, written information, referral to other services. *Write*: PO Box 4861, Aurora, IL 60507 *Call*: 630/896-3018

**Kindred Hearts Women's Center Wheadon Church** 13 year old org.; volunteer run; groups and social activities for women, most of whom are lesbian. We provide asafe space to meet, support in countering homophobia and related issues. Support groups for coming out of marriages; bi-sexual rap groups; lesbians after 40; and make the most

out of life groups. *Meetings*: groups are 6-8 weeks; English only; *Call* for specific dates and times. Friday nite social group meets twice monthly. Not accessible. *Write*: 2214 Ridge, Evanston, IL 60201 *Call*: 847/604-0913

**Fox Valley Gay Assn** *Area Served: Kane, Cook and McHenry Counties* Support and social events for gays and lesbians in the Fox Valley. *Services*: Mutual aid, social activities. *Write*: PO Box 393, Elgin, IL 60121 *Call*: 847/392-6882

**Girth and Mirth** *Area Served: IL* Social club for big and gay men, to help with their self-image and to counteract societal stereotypes. Local chapter of affiliated Big Men's Clubs, a national org.. *Meetings*: Bi-weekly for all interested. *Services*: educational program or material advocacy, social activities, newsletter, hotline, referral to other services, speakers bureau. *Write*: PO Box 14384, Chicago, IL 60614 *Call*: 773/776-9223

**Homosexuals Anonymous Fellowship Services HAFS** *Area Served: National* to offer a Christian fellowship for men and women who have chosen to help each other to live free from homosexuality. Two chapters in IL. *Services*: Mutual aid, newsletter, written information, educational program or material, referral to other services, speakers bureau, telephone support *Write*: PO Box 7881, Reading, PA 19603 *Call*: 215/376-1146

**Horizons Community Services, Inc** *Area Served: Chicago and Cook County* Offers gay and lesbian switchboard for information and referral; peer counseling program; speakers service--co-ed teams; youth group with adult advisors; gay parents group; legal services; AIDS/HIV services program; self-help/support non-therapeutic groups on gay and lesbian related issues; anti-violence project. *Meetings*: Weekly. *Services*: Mutual aid, educational program or material, advocacy. *Write*: 961 W. Montana, Chicago, IL 60614 *Call*: 773/929-4357

**Kinheart Women's Center** *Area Served: Cook County-N* Women's org. which is based upon a feminist framework and provides counseling, support groups of various kinds and seminars on sexuality and homophobia. *Meetings*: Weekly for lesbian, bi-sexual, and heterosexual women. *Services*: Mutual aid, educational program or material, telephone support, social activities, newsletter. *Write*: 2214 Ridge, Evanston, IL 60201 *Call*: 847/491-1103

**Les-Bi-Gay People with Disabilities social Support Group/Fox River Valley** *Area Served: Kankakee and Kendall Counties Write*: Center for Independent Living 730 W Chicago Ave, Elgin, IL 60123 *Call*: 847/695-5818

**Lutherans Concerned Educational program or material, North America Lutherans Concerned-Chicago** *Area Served: Chicago and Cook County* Primary focus is working to change the Lutheran churches in metro Chicago so as to better meet the needs of gay men/lesbians. *Meetings*: Monthly for all interested. *Write*: PO Box 10197 Ft. Dearborn Station, Chicago, IL 60610 *Call*: 773/342-1647 Answer Mach.

**Spectrum University of IL** *Area Served: Champaign County* Self-help groups for lesbians, gays and bisexuals. *Services*: Mutual aid, educational program or material, written information, referral to other services, speakers bureau, telephone support, social activities, newsletter. *Write*: 280 IL Union, M B#91 1401 W. Green St., Urbana, IL 61801 *Call*: 217/333-1187

**University of Chicago Gay and Lesbian Alliance** *Area Served: Chicago* Provide support for the lesbian and gay community in Hyde Park. *Meetings*: Weekly, including a coming-out group. *Services*: Mutual aid. *Write*: 1212 East 59th St, Chicago, IL 60637 *Call*: 773/702-9734 Answer Mach.

**West Suburban Gay Assn** *Area Served: DuPage, Cook and Kane Counties* Primarily a social org.; hotline and information on activities can be gained from above phone number. *Meetings*: Several special events per month. *Services*: telephone support, social activities, newsletter. *Write*: PO Box 161, Glen Ellyn, IL 60138 *Call*: 630/790-9742

## Gay and Lesbian-Family and Friends

**Families, and Friends of Lesbians and Gays** *Area Served: National* Promotes the health and well-being of gay, lesbian and bisexual persons. for parents family and friends. *Services*: support and education, publications, and resources. *Meetings*: sometimes once a month-depends on the affiliate. *Call* for dates and times and locations nearest you. *Write*: 1101 14th St NW, Ste 1030, Washington, DC 20005 *Call*: 202/638-4200 *Fax*: 202/638-0243 *Email*: INFO@PFLAG.ORG *Web site*: HTTP://WWW.PFLAG.ORG

**Parents, Families, & Friends of Lesbian & Gays PFLAG Chicago/Southside** *Write*: 1709-1/2 East 87th Ste. 138, Chicago, IL 60617

**Parents, Families, and Friends of Lesbians and Gay PFLAG** North Suburban *Write*:, Glenview, IL 60025

**Parents, Families, and Friends of Lesbians and Gay PFLAG Moline** *Write*: 3732 40th St, Moline, IL 61265 *Call*: 309/797-7986

**Parents, Families, and Friends of Lesbians and Gay PFLAG Carbondale** *Area Served: SOUTH IL Write*: 505 Orchard Drive, Carbondale, IL 62901 *Call*: 618/457-5479

**Parents, Families, and Friends of Lesbians and Gay PFLAG Chicago** *Write*: PO Box 11023, Chicago, IL 60611-0023 *Call*: 773/472-3079

**Parents and Friends of Lesbians and Gays PFLAG Springfield** Support group for parents and friends of gays and lesbians. speakers bureau, hotline. Contact persons who share concern, but no active meetings. *Services*: Mutual aid, educational program or material, newsletter, written information. *Write*:, Springfield, IL 62708 *Call*: 217/753-2214

**Parents, Families, and Friends of Lesbians and Gay PFLAG Chicago/West Suburban** *Write*: PO Box 105, Downers Grove, IL 60517 *Call*: 630/968-9060

**Parents, Families, and Friends of Lesbians and Gay PFLAG Bloomington** *Area Served: Central IL Write*: PO Box 615, Bloomington, IL 61702-0615

**Parents, Families, Friends of Lesbians and Gays PFLAG Streamwood** *Write*: 713 Wildwood Lane, Streamwood, IL 60107-2049 *Call*: 630/968-9060

**Parents, Families, Friends of Lesbians and Gays PFLAG St. Louis** *Write*: 114 Westridge, Collinsville, IL 62234 *Call*: 314/821-3524 *Email*: Rgrif@aol.com

**Parents, Family and Friends of Lesbians and Gays** *Area Served: Chicago Write*: PO Box 11023, Chicago, IL 60611 *Call*: 773/472-3079 Answer Mach.

## Gay and Lesbian-Youth

**Pride Youth Support Program** *Area Served: Cook County, Lake County Write*: 1779 Maple St, Northfield, IL 60093 *Call*: 847/441-9880

**Oak Park Youth Drop-In Center Oak Park Lesbian and Gay Assn** *Area Served: Chicago* The Oak Park Center provides a safe place for gay, lesbian, or other youth to discuss their concerns and explore questions relating to their sexuality. Two adult advisors are present at all times. *Meetings* are unstructured but sometimes include a program or movie and discussion afterward. *Meetings*: Weekly *Services*: Mutual aid, social activities, educational program or material. *Write*: PO Box 0784, Oak Park, IL 60303 *Call*: 708/216-9723

# Gender Issues

**American Educational Gender Information** *Services* **AEGIS** *Area Served: National* Provides a variety of services for helping professionals and individuals with gender issues. Provide free information and referrals; the journal *Chrysalis* and a variety of other materials; the national transgender library and archive; support groups; workshops and seminars; extensive database of helping professionals and published works on gender issues, support for family members. *Meetings: Call* for information. *Write*: PO Box 33724, Decatur, GA 30033-0724 *Call*: 770/939-0244 *Fax*: 770/939-1770 *Email*: aegis@mindspring.com *Web site*: http://www.renorg/rafil/aegis.html

**Sex Information and Education Council of The Us SIECUS** *Area Served: National* SIECUS affirms that sexuality is a natural and healthy part of living and advocates the right of individuals to make responsible sexual choices. SIECUS develops, collects, and disseminates information and promotes education About sexuality. Library services available. *Meetings*: none *Write*: 130 W 42nd St Ste 350, NY, NY 10036 *Call*: 212/819-9770 *Email*: siecus@siecus.org *Web site*: http://www.siecus.org

**Society for The Second Self Tri Ess** *Area Served: National Write*: PO Box 194, Tulare, CA 93275 *Call*: 209/688-9246

**International Foundation for Gender Education** *Area Served: National* Maintains a list of over 200 support org.s and services world-wide for male and female cross-dressers and transsexuals. Publishes a journal *Call*ed TV/TS Tapestry. *Services*: Mutual aid, written info, newsletter. *Write*: PO Box 367, Wayland, MA 01778 *Call*: 617/894-8340

# Violence

## Child Abuse

**Assault and Abuse Services of Stephenson County** *Area Served: Stephenson County* Community outreach services, including case management and counseling, for families in need of assistance as referred by The Department of Children and Family Services *Services*: (DCFS) *Write*: 7 Stephenson *County* St, Ste 211, Freeport, IL 61032 *Call*: 815/232-7200

**Child Abuse Prevention Services Parental Stress Services** *Area Served: Chicago Write*: 600 S Federal St Ste 205, Chicago, IL 60605 *Call*: 312/427-1161 *Fax*: 312/427-3038

**Child Abuse Hotline IL Department of Children and Family Services** *Area Served: IL* Toll-free hotline to report child abuse and neglect in IL. Investigations of reported abuse begin within 24 hours. *Services*: written information, referral to other services. *Write*: 406 East Monroe, Springfield, IL 62701 *Call*: 800/252-2873 *Fax*: 217/785-3473

**Children's Home and Aid Society IL Parents Anonymous** *Area Served: IL Write*: 125 S Wacker Dr, 14th Flor, Chicago, IL 60606 *Call*: 312/424-0200 *Fax*: 312/424-6800

**National Committee to Prevent Child Abuse** *Area Served: National* Prevents child abuse in all its forms. Three chapters in IL. *Services*: referral to other services, newsletter, written information, educational program or material, advocacy. *Write*: 332 S. Michigan Ave. Ste. 1600, Chicago, IL 60604 *Call*: 312/663-3520 110 *Fax*: 312/939-8962

**National Child Abuse Hotline Childhelp USA** *Area Served: National* . Provides information and makes referrals to counseling and local support groups, such as Parents Anonymous. Provides professional crisis counseling by trained staff holding a minimum of a Master's degree. *Services*: written information, referral to other services. *Write*: 6463 Independence Ave, Woodland Hills, CA 91367*Call*: 800/422-4453

**Parental Stress Group Erie Family Health Center** *Area Served: Chicago-N* Helps parents (or child care providers) to deal with stress related to children's discipline, behavioral problems and school relatedproblems. English or Spanish. *Meetings*: Weekly for parents and children. *Services*: Mutual aid, educational program or material, telephone support, written information, hotline. *Write*: 1656 W. Chicago Ave, Chicago, IL 60622 *Call*: 312/666-3488 *Fax*: 312/666-5867

**Parents Anonymous of IL Children's Home and Aid Society of IL** *Area Served: IL* Self-help org. committed to the treatment and prevention of child abuse through peer-led, professionally-facilitated weekly support meetings (not 12-step) and children's groups. Provides state and local training, information, materials, consultation and chapter development through several child welfare agencies. Members learn parenting skills and to handle their stress and anger. Other than referral, *Call*

312/424-6822 *Write*: 125 S Wacker Dr Ste 1400, Chicago, IL 60606 *Call*: 800/443-4376 *Fax*: 312/424-6800

**Parents Anonymous** *Area Served: National.* A national self-help org. committed to child abuse treatment and prevention through peer-led, professionally-facilitated self-help groups. The il chapter has over 70 groups. Also provides advocacy, materials, training, consultation and assists in chapter development. See il chapter list or search by city, County, or zip. *Write*: 675 W Foothill Blve, #220, Claremont, CA 91711-3416 *Call*: 909/621-6184; *Fax* 909/625-6304; *Email*: ParentsAnon@msn.com; *Web site*: http://www.parentsanonymous-natl.org

# Elder Abuse

**Senior Strength** *Area Served: IL-Central.* 12-week series for survivors of elder abuse. *Meetings*: Weekly. *Services*: Mutual aid. *Write*: 1225 N North St, Peoria, IL 61606 *Call*: 800/559-7233 or 309/637-3905

# Domestic Violence

## Domestic Violence-General

**A Safe Place** *Area Served: Cook, Lake and McHenry Counties.* Shelter serving battered women and their children, offering a comprehensive program of services including two support groups, one on domestic violence, the other on parenting and cultural awareness. Children's group formed as needed. *Meetings*: Weekly, open to any battered woman and her children. *Services*: Mutual aid, educational program or material, written information, advocacy, referral to other services, speakers bureau, hotline, newsletter. *Write*: PO Box 1067, Waukegan, IL 60079 *Call*: 847/249-4450

## Domestic Violence-Female Victims

**Abused Women's Support Group Family Rescue Shelter** *Area Served: IL Write*: PO Box 17528, Chicago, IL 60617 *Call*: 773/375-8400

**Alternatives to Domestic Violence** *Area Served: LaSalle, Livingston and Marshall Counties* For abused adults and their children providing education, Mutual aid and support, and a safe environment. *Services*: Mutual aid, educational program or material. *Write*: PO Box 593, Streator, IL 61354 *Call*: 800/892-3375

**Anna Bixby Women's Center Saline County** *Area Served: Saline-S County Write*: 213 S. Shaw, Harrisburg, IL 62946 *Call*: 618/252-8380

**Battered Women's Support Group Turning Point, Inc** *Area Served: McHenry County* Provides opportunity for women to meet others in similar circumstances; to grow and change thru the support of others. *Meetings*: Weekly for battered women. *Services*: Mutual aid, educational program or material. *Write*: PO Box 723, Woodstock, IL 60098 *Call*: 815/338-8081

**Battered Women's Support Group Travelers and Immigrants Aid Women's Program** *Area Served: Cook County* Ongoing support and sharing groups for battered women. *Services*: Mutual aid, educational program or material, advocacy, referral to other services, speakers bureau, telephone support *Write*: 1950 W. Pershing Rd, Chicago, IL 60609 *Call*: 773/847-4417

**Battered Women's Support Group Community Crisis Center** *Area Served: Kane and Cook-NW Counties* Provides an informal atmosphere where abused women can come together to be heard, understood and accepted. to help them learn about the dynamics of domestic violence. to clarify all of their alternatives. to support them in developing a plan of action based upon their own choice. *Meetings*: Weekly. *Services*: Mutual aid, educational program or material, advocacy, telephone support, written information, professional service, hotline. *Write*: PO Box 1390, Elgin, IL 60121 *Call*: 847/697-2380

**Center for Prevention of Abuse Peoria County** *Area Served: Tazewell, Woodford and Fulton Counties Write*: PO Box 3172, Peoria, IL 61612 *Call*: 309/691-0551

**Chicago Abused Women Coalition Greenhouse Shelter** *Area Served: Cook County* Shelter for battered women and their children. Provides emergency temporary shelter, individual and group counseling, a 24-hour hotline, referrals, advocacy, food, transportation, medical care, children's programming, and housing. *Meetings*: weekly for resident and non-resident women. *Write*: PO Box 477916, Chicago, IL 60647-7916 *Call*: 773/278-4566

**Coalition Against Domestic Violence Coles County** *Area Served: Coles County Write*: PO Box 732, Charleston, IL 61920 *Call*: 217/348-5931

**Domestic Violence Support Group Peoria County Center for Prevention of Abuse** *Area Served: Peoria, Tazewell and Woodford Counties Write*: PO Box 3855, Peoria, IL 61612 *Call*: 800/559-7233

**Domestic Violence Support Group Mujeres Latinas En Accion** *Area Served: Cook, Lake and DuPage Counties* Offers an opportunity for battered women to meet within a group in order to give and receive support, discuss fears and feelings, gain new trust and control over their lives. Group is conducted in Spanish. *Meetings*: Weekly for any women who has been a victim of domestic violence. *Services*: Mutual aid, educational program or material, referral to other services, advocacy, telephone support, professional service, written information, social activities, hotline. *Write*: 1823 W. 17th St, Chicago, IL 60608 *Call*: 312/226-1544

**Domestic Violence Support Groups South Suburban Family Shelter, Inc** *Area Served: Cook County -S and Will County* Gives immediate safety to a woman and her children if she is in a life-threatening situation. Four on-going support groups. to give her support, information, and encouragement to work at her own decisions for herself, to take control of her life and to inform her of the options available. *Meetings*: Weekly for any victim of domestic violence. *Services*: Mutual aid, educational program or material, advocacy. *Write*: PO Box 937, Homewood, IL 60430 *Call*: 708/335-4125

**Dove Domestic Violence Program Macon County Dove Inc** *Area Served: Macon, DeWitt, Shelby and Moultrie Counties Write*: 788 E Clay, Decatur, IL 62521 *Call*: 217/423-0960 *Email*: lrfamily@lincolnnet.net

**Evanston Shelter for Battered Women Evanston-North Shore YWCA** *Area Served: Cook-N* Support groups for battered women based on a self-help model, designed to facilitate support and information sharing. Also offers: 24-hour crisis hotline, individual and group counseling for women and children (residential and walk-in), legal advocacy, systems advocacy, and community outreach and education. *Meetings*: Weekly for battered women. *Services*: Mutual aid, educational program or material, advocacy, telephone support, social activities, newsletter. *Write*: P.O.Box 5164, Evanston, IL 60204-5164 *Call*: 847/864-8780

**Family Options** *Area Served: Chicago Write*: 3214 W 63rd St, Chicago, IL 60629 *Call*: 773/436-2400

**Family Shelter Service** *Area Served: DuPage County* Offers domestic violence support groups for adults and children (run concurrently) in English and Spanish. *Meetings*: Weekly open to any woman and her children who are victims of domestic violence. *Services*: Mutual aid, educational program or material, advocacy, telephone support, newsletter, written information, professional service. *Write*: PO Box 3404, Glen Ellyn, IL 60138 *Call*: 630/469-5650 *Fax*: 630/260-0284

**Freedom House Domestic Violence Shelter Bureau County** *Area Served: Bureau, Henry and Marshall Counties Write*: PO Box 544, Princeton, IL 61356 *Call*: 815/875-8233

**Friends Helping Others Support Group Henry County** *Area Served: Henry County Write*: 719 Elliot St., Kewanee, IL 61443 *Call*: 309/853-3361 283

**Friends of Battered Women and Their Children** *Area Served: Chicago Write*: PO Box 5185, Evanston, IL 60204 *Call*: 800/603-4357 *Fax*: 312/274-6508

**Fulton County Women's Crisis Service Fulton County** *Area Served: Fulton and Mason Counties Write*: 700 E Oak St.#203, Canton, IL 61520 *Call*: 309/647-7487

**Groundwork Will County** *Area Served: Will and Grundy Counties* Serves victims of domestic abuse. Emergency shelter and support group. *Meetings*: Three times a week for all who share the concern. *Services*: Mutualaid, educational program or material, hotline, advocacy. *Write*: 1550 Plainfield Rd., Joliet, IL 60434 *Call*: 815/729-1228

**Harbor House Kankakee County** *Area Served: Kankakee and Iroquois Counties Write*: PO Box 1824, Kankakee, IL 60901 *Call*: 815/932-5814

**Help Offer Protective Environment Ogle County HOPE** *Area Served: Ogle and Lee Counties* The purpose of HOPE is to help victims of domestic violence. We offer 24-hour crisis hotline, temporary shelter, counseling, support groups, legal advocacy, and public education. *Meetings*: Monthly. *Services*: Mutual aid, educational program or material, written information, advocacy, telephone support, social activities, newsletter. *Write*: PO Box 131, Rochelle, IL 61068 *Call*: 815/562-4323

**IL Coalition Against Domestic Violence Women's Crisis Center** *Area Served: Morgan, Scott and Greene Counties Write*: 446 E State St., Jacksonville, IL 62650 *Call*: 217/243-4357

**IL Coalition Against Domestic Violence Mutual Ground, Inc** *Area Served: Kane and Kendall Counties* Comprehensive services for victims of domestic violence, including support groups for women and concurrently, for children. *Meetings*: Weekly for women and their children who are victims of domestic violence. *Services*: Mutual aid, educational program or material, advocacy, newsletter, written information, telephone support, hotline, speakers bureau, professional service, referral to other services, *Write*: PO Box 843, Aurora, IL 60507 *Call*: 630/897-8383

**IL Coalition Against Domestic Violence Quad County Coalition Against Domestic Violence** *Area Served: McDonough, Hancock and Henry Counties* Comprehensive services for victims of domestic violence, including support groups for women and concurrently, for children. *Meetings*: Weekly for women and their children who are victims of domestic violence. *Services*: Mutual aid. *Write*: PO Box 175, Macomb, IL 61455 *Call*: 309/837-5555

**IL Coalition Against Domestic Violence Physical and Emotional Abuse Recovery League** *Area Served: Whiteside County* Provides advocacy, support and counseling for adults and children who are victims of domestic violence. A shelter for battered women. *Meetings*: Weekly and open to all sharing the concern. *Write*: 412 First Ave., Sterling, IL 61081 *Call*: 815/625-0343

**IL Coalition Against Domestic Violence Stopping Woman Abuse Now (Swan)** *Area Served: Richland and*

*Clay Counties* Shelter for domestic violence victims and homeless women. Support groups formed as needed in areas of parenting, domestic violence, personal growth. *Meetings*: Weekly, and open to all interested women. *Services*: Mutual aid. *Write*: Box 176 1114 S. West St., Olney, IL 62450 *Call*: 618/392-3556

**Lifespan** *Area Served: Cook County and Chicago.* Lifespan is committed to the cessation of abuse. We empower women to become self-sufficient and violent-free. We provide services to well women in crisis. Self esteem group for women; support group for children. *Meetings*: Weekly. *Services*: Mutual aid, educational program or material, advocacy, telephone support, newsletter, written information, hotline, speakers bureau, professional service. *Write*: PO Box 445, Des Plaines, IL 60016 *Call*: 847/824-4454

**Neopolitan Lighthouse** *Area Served: Chicago* Provides comprehensive services in a safe, supportive place, for battered women and their children. *Services*: Mutual aid, educational program or material, professional service. *Write*: PO Box 24709, Chicago, IL 60624 *Call*: 773/638-0228 *Fax*: 312/638-0323

**Oasis Women's Center** *Area Served: Madison, Calhoun and Jersey Counties* Comprehensive services for battered and abused women and their children, including support group. referrals, educational information, emergency food and clothing, arrangements for emergency medical care. *Meetings*: Weekly. *Services*: Mutual aid, educational program or material, advocacy, telephone support *Write*: 111 Market, Alton, IL 62002 *Call*: 618/465-1978

**Parenting Group A Woman's Place** *Area Served: Champaign County Write*: 505 W. Green St, Urbana, IL 61801 *Call*: 217/384-4462

**People Against Violent Environments (PAVE)** *Area Served: Marshall, Jefferson and Clay Counties Write*: PO Box 342, Centralia, IL 62801 *Call*: 618/533-7233

**Quanada** *Area Served: Adams, Brown and Hancock Counties Write*: 2707 Maine, Quincy, IL 62301 *Call*: 217/222-0069

**Rainbow House** *Area Served: Chicago* A temporary residential shelter for battered women and children. Provides shelter for periods up to one month. Group and individual counseling, information and referral, advocacy with social service agencies, police, etc. as needed. Off-site support group available weekly. *Services*: Mutual aid, educational program or material, advocacy, telephone support, newsletter, written information. *Write*: PO Box 29019, Chicago, IL 60629 *Call*: 773/762-6611, 773/521-5501 *FAX* 773/521-4866

**Safe Passage** *Area Served: DeKalb County Write*: PO Box 621, DeKalb, IL 60115 *Call*: 815/756-5228

**Sarah's Inn** *Area Served: Cook County -W* Individual counseling, group support, 24hr. hotline, Legal advocacy and emergency shelter for victims of domestic violence. Support groups provide a safe place for abused women to share their stories and learn about the dynamics of domestic violence. *Meetings*: Four times a week for any battered woman. *Services*: Mutual aid, educational program or material, advocacy, telephone support, newsletter, written information, referral to other services, hotline, professional service. *Write*: PO Box 1435, Oak Park, IL 60403 *Call*: 708/386-4225

**Sojourn Women's Center** *Area Served: Sangamon, Menard and Logan Counties* Battered women's support services. Education, hotline, and support groups. *Write*: PO Box 4626, Springfield, IL 62708 *Call*: 217/544-2484

**South Suburban Family Shelter, Inc** South Suburbs of Chicago Provides comprehensive services to victims of domestic violence and their families. 24 hr. Hotline 708)335-3028, emergency shelter, transitional housing, group and individual counseling for adult victims/child victims/witnesses, court advocacy, Hospital advocacy, parenting classes, dating/domestic violence prevention, public education, professional training, abuser treatment *Meetings*: *Call* for information. *Write*: PO Box 937, Homewood, IL 60430 *Call*: 708/335-4125 *Fax*: 708/335-7660

**Southwest Women Working Together** *Area Served: Cook County* Provides individual and group counseling for women and children. Offers groups for incest self-esteem, divorced and separated. Offers advocacy, referrals, phone support. Accessible. Weekly meetings *Write*: 4051 W 63rd St, Chicago, IL 60629 *Call*: 773/582-0550 *Fax*: 773/582-9669

**Support Group for Battered Women Travelers and Immigrants Aid - Women's Program** *Area Served: Chicago* To be a support resource for isolated women who share the same concern. *Meetings*: Weekly, in a 10-week series. *Services*: Mutual aid. *Write*: 1950 W. Pershing Rd., Chicago, IL 60609 *Call*: 773/847-5602 *Fax*: 312/847-4942

**Support Group for Battered Women Crisis Center for South Suburbia** *Area Served: Cook County -S* Provides emotional support and educational information. Provides an informal atmosphere where abused women can be reassured that they can be heard, and understood and accepted. Other groups and resources available concerning: parenting, assertiveness, and growth group. *Meetings* restricted to those who have completed intake. *Services*: Mutual aid, educational program or material. *Write*: 7700 Tumber Dr, Tinley Park, IL 60477 *Call*: 708/429-7255

**Talk T.U.F.F., Inc** *Area Served: Cook County* Helps people experiencing domestic violence. Members discuss their experiences and share safe methods to end abuse. *Write*: PO Box 578760, Chicago, IL 60657

**Voices Domestic Violence Program Freeport YWCA** *Area Served: Stephenson County Write*: 641 W. Stephenson *County* St., Freeport, IL 61032 *Call*: 815/235-1641

**Women's Center** *Area Served: Jackson, Williamson and Franklin Counties Write*: 405 W. Mill St., Carbondale, IL 62901 *Call*: 618/529-2324

**Women's Crisis Center of Metro East, Inc** *Area Served: St. Clair and Madison Counties Write*: PO Box 8217, Belleville, IL 62222 *Call*: 618/235-0893

**Working Against Violent Environments Phase Inc** *Area Served: Winnebago County Write*: 319 S Church St., Rockford, IL 61101 *Call*: 815/962-6102

## Domestic Violence-Women and Children Victims

**ADV Children's Group** *Area Served: LaSalle, Livingston and Marshall Counties Write*: PO Box 593, Streator, IL 61364 *Call*: 800/893-3375

**Children Living with Domestic Violence Turning Point, Inc** *Area Served: McHenry County* Program for pre-school thru high school children living in homes of battered women. Teaches positive conflict resolution skills to help coping with home situation. Gives a forum for safe discussion. *Meetings*: Weekly for children. *Services*: Mutual aid, educational program or material. *Write*: PO Box 723, Woodstock, IL 60098 *Call*: 815/338-8081

**Starting Point Prayer Group, Inc.** *Area Served: Warren, Henderson and Knox Counties* to help people help themselves. We are a spiritually based homeless shelter domestic violence. Membership is open to persons with chemical dependency and domestic abuse and their families and friends. *Services*: social activities, newsletter, referral to other services. *Write*: 205 South 1st St PO Box 314, Monmouth, IL 61462 *Call*: 309/734-7812

**YWCA Women's Shelter** *Area Served: Vermilion and Iroquois Counties Write*: 201 N. Hazel, Danville, IL 61832 *Call*: 217/443-5566

# Incest

## Incest-Family

**ILLINOIS False Memory Syndrome Society** *Area Served: IL Write*: PO Box 3332, Joliet, IL 60434 *Call*: 708/980-7693 *Fax*: 708/980-9633

**Parents United** *Area Served: National* Professionally-guided self-help for recovery from child sex abuse. Separate groups for children and adults abused as children. Three IL groups. *Services*: Mutual aid. *Write*: 232 E Gish Rd, San Jose, CA 95112 *Call*: 408/453-7611

**Parents United Lutheran social Service of IL** *Area Served: Peoria County* Helps families cope with child sexual abuse. *Meetings*: Weekly. *Services*: MA/telephone support, social activities, newsletter, written information. *Write*: 610 Abington, Peoria, IL 61603 *Call*: 309/671-0300

**Parents United IL Department of Children and Family Services** *Area Served: Williamson County* Parents United is a self-help group of individuals andfamilies who have experienced child sexual abuse. Purpose is to prevent child abuse and to assist families who have experienced this problem. Groups for offenders and non-offending spouses weekly. *Services*: Mutual aid, telephone support, social activities, newsletter, written information. *Write*: 2309 W. Main, Marion, IL 62959 *Call*: 618/993-8639

**Parents United Institute for Human Resources** *Area Served: Livingston County Write*: PO Box 768, Pontiac, IL 61764 *Call*: 815/844-6109

## Incest-Survivor

**Grand Recovery** *Area Served: Cook County Write*: 264 W 162nd St, South Holland, IL 60473 *Call*: 708/333-1857

**Incest Survivors Anonymous (ISA)** *Area Served: National* . Adapts the 12 Step model of AA to incest. Members discuss current needs, feelings, and problems. The goal is to work and live the principles of is a 12 Steps and traditions. No perpetrators. *Meetings*: weekly. *Services*: self-help groups, education and support. Contact national for il groups. *Write*: PO Box 17245, Long Beach, CA 90807-7245 *Call*: 310/428-5599

**Incest Survivors Anonymous** *Area Served: National* Carries the message to the incest survivor who still suffers, by borrowing the 12-steps of A.A. which are adapted to incest, by encouraging and understanding other incest survivors, and by welcoming and giving comfort. Members discuss personal needs, feelings and present day problems whose patterns originated in childhood. No perpetrators. *Meetings*: Weekly. *Services*: Mutual aid, educational program or material. *Write*: World Service Office PO Box 17245, Long Beach, CA 90805-0613 *Call*: 310/428-5599

**Incest Survivors** *Area Served: DuPage County* Referral to groups in DuPage *County Services*: referral to other services. *Write*: 5726 Primrose, Lisle, IL 60532 *Call*: 630/960-5320

**Incest Survivors Support Group YWCA** *Area Served: Cook County* Sexual assault, incest, and divorce. *Meetings*: Weekly, for screened individuals. *Services*: Mutual aid, educational program or material, written information, newsletter, hotline, speakers bureau, advocacy, referral to other services, social activities, referral to other agencies, provides professional service. *Write*: 4343 W. Lincoln Hgwy Ste 210, Matteson, IL 60443 *Call*: 708/748-6600 *Fax*: 708/748-6606

**Mars Station Computer Bulletin Board** *Area Served: National* Offers information and support to all sexual abuse survivors, their families and friends. Also has a nationwide listing of treatment providers, both public and private. *Services*: written information, referral to other services. *Write*: 602 Winona Ct, Silver Springs, MD 20902-0038 *Call*: 301/649-5458

**Survivors of Incest Anonymous World Service Office, Inc** *Area Served: National* A 12-step, self-help recovery program modeled after Alcoholics Anonymous. We define incest very broadly. No fees/dues. Provide support groups, literature (29 pieces=$25.25), pen pals, bulletins ($15.00 yrly), speakers, and information on starting local SIA groups. *Meetings*: varies, send a self-addressed, stamped, envelope to our mailing address. *Write*: PO Box 21817, Baltimore, MD 21222-6817 *Call*: 410/282-3400 *Fax*: 410/282-3400

## Incest-Youth

**Adolescent Survivors of Sexual Abuse Support Group Northwest Community Hospital** *Area Served: Cook County* Provides emotional support and opportunity to share ideas and feelings and to learn to cope with the trauma. *Meetings*: Weekly in six-week cycles. *Services*: Mutual aid. *Write*: 800 W. Central Rd. Youth *Services*, Arlington Heights, IL 60005 *Call*: 708/259-1000 5211 *Fax*: 708/506-4377

**Child Sexual Abuse Program Loop YWCA** *Area Served: Cook County* to provide individual and group therapy for child, offending and non-offending spouse; referral program, educational and informational materials and legal advocacy when needed. *Services*: Mutual aid, educational program or material, advocacy, referral to other services, telephone support, written information. *Write*: 180 N. Wabash, Chicago, IL 60601 *Call*: 312/372-4105 275 *Fax*: 312/372-4673

**Daughters and Sons United LaSalle County Youth Service Bureau, Inc** *Area Served: LaSalle County* Support group for sexually abused children and teens aged 12 to 18 years. *Services*: Mutual aid. *Write*: 827 Columbus St, Ottawa, IL 61350 *Call*: 815/433-3953

**Mutual Ground, Inc** *Area Served: Kane and Kendall Counties* A 24 hour crisis intervention at hospitals, police stations, etc.; individual and group counseling for victims of rape or incest and their family and friends; information about medical and legal procedures; social service referrals; children's therapy; and self-help groups. Residents of Kane and Kendall counties only. *Services*: Mutual aid, educational program or material, advocacy, telephone support, newsletter, written information, professional service. *Write*: PO Box 843, Aurora, IL 60507 *Call*: 630/897-8383 *Fax*: 708/897-8439

**Rockford Sexual Assault Counseling, Inc** *Area Served: NW IL* Provides counseling and support services for teen victims of sexual assault and abuse and their families, to assist them in understanding and coping with physical, medical, emotional and legalproblems associated with the crime. Offers prevention and education programs as well as survivors' group. *Services*: Mutual aid, speakers bureau, written information, telephone support, professional service, educational program or material, advocacy, hotline, referral to other services. *Write*: 202 W. State St, Ste 514, Rockford, IL 61101 *Call*: 815/964-4044

**Safe LaSalle County Youth Service Bureau, Inc** *Area Served: Cook County* Support group for sexually abused children, aged 6-12, facilitated by professionals. The group meets weekly for 6 weeks. *Services*: Mutual aid. *Write*: 827 Columbus St, Ottawa, IL 61350 *Call*: 815/433-3953

**Youth Education Class A Woman's Place** *Area Served: Champaign, Douglas and Piatt Counties* *Write*: 505 W Green St, Urbana, IL 61801 *Call*: 217/384-4462

# Male Offenders

**Abuser Groups Harbor House** *Area Served: Cook County* Support groups for men who are abusive. *Services*: Mutual aid. *Write*: PO Box 1824, Kankakee, IL 60901 *Call*: 815/932-5814

**Batterers Anonymous** *Area Served: National* to provide social contact and Mutual support to men who batter. Members establish buddy system to help each other through crises. A manual is available which explains how to start a group. *Meetings* are open; primarily focus on men who batter women; some meetings welcome women who batter men. *Services*: Mutual aid, educational program or material, telephone support, written information. *Write*: 8485 Tamarind, Ste D, Fontana, CA 92335 *Call*: 909/355-1100

**Batterers Support Group Community Crisis Center** *Area Served: Cook - NW Suburban*. Offer support and encouragement to search out positive alternatives to the abusive behavior these men exhibit toward women; cope with abuse issues, develop skills for handling stress, learn to interrelate more effectively with the women in their lives. *Meetings*: weekly. *Services*: Mutual aid, educational program or material, telephone support, written

information. *Write*: PO Box 1390, Elgin, IL 60121
*Call*: 847/697-2380  *Fax*: 708/742-4182

**Men Overcoming Violence Lakeview Lutheran
Church** *Area Served: Cook County*  MOV acts to create a
dialogue through which we will be able to change. We
support and challenge one another to solve our problem of
violence. to be involved in this kind of change *Call* MOV
and become a participant in activitieswhich lead to ending
violence. *Meetings*: Weekly. *Services*: Mutual aid,
educational program or material, telephone support,
written information. *Write*: 835 W. Addison, Chicago, IL
60657 *Call*: 773/327-0036  *Fax*: 312/327-0800

**Men's Alternative to Women Abuse Group Turning
Point** *Area Served: McHenry County*  For men who have
been abusive to women in their intimate relationships.
Primary goal is to stop the violent behavior, but also to
help develop positive skills in response to feelings of
anger. We also have a therapy group. *Meetings*: Weekly.
*Services*: Mutual aid, educational program or material,
professional service. *Write*: PO Box 723, Woodstock, IL
60098 *Call*: 813/338-8081

**New Directions** *Area Served: Whiteside County  Write*:
208 Brink Circle, Sterling, IL 61081 *Call*: 815/625-5552

**Program for Men Who Batter Crisis Center for South
Suburbia** *Area Served: Cook County*  Group is primarily
focused to stop abusive behavior and learn new coping
mechanisms to deal with anger and stress in a non-violent
manner. A male and female therapist facilitate this
structured group. *Meetings*: Weekly. *Services*: educational
program or material written information. *Write*: 7700
Timber Dr., Tinley Park, IL 60447 *Call*: 708/429-7233
*Fax*: 708/429-7293

**Violence Anonymous** *Write*: PO Box 70022, San Diego,
CA 92167 *Call*: 619/270-3684

# Male Survivors

**Male Survivors of Abuse Ravenswood CMHC** *Area
Served: IL*  Group members gain support through sharing
experiences, feelings and ways to cope. Leaders are peers
trained to facilitate a format that provides safety and
support for group members. *Meetings*: Six weeks groups
but restricted to persons sharing the concern. *Services*:
Mutual aid. *Write*: 2312 W. Irving Park Rd, Chicago, IL
60618 *Call*: 773/463-7000 1455  *Fax*: 312/463-8938

# Prevention (General)

**The Center for Prevention of Abuse** *Area Served: IL*
*Write*: PO Box 3172, Peoria, IL 61612 *Call*: 800/559-7233

# Sexual Abuse

## Sexual Abuse-General

**Center of Support for Parents of Adult Sex Offenders**
Provide support and resources to parents of adult sex
offenders at any time in the process of discovery of
offenses. We offer a support group in the bay area;
resources to help offender get treatment; and consultation
to establish new support groups. *Meetings*-every other
month in bay area. Primary goal beyond support for
families is to educate public about what will end abuse of
children. *Write*: PO Box 460126, San Francisco, CA
94146 *Call*: 415/826-3081 Ans. Machine

**Families of Sex Offenders Anonymous** Support group
for family and friends of sex offenders to try to understand
what happened, support them and find treatment. No
known IL groups. *Services*: written information, telephone
support, referral to other services. *Write*: 152 W Walk,
West Haven, CT 06516 *Call*: 203/931-0015

## Sexual Abuse-Offenders

**Molesters Anonymous The MAN Program**
*Area Served: National*  To provide a model Rehab program
for child molesters; provides a Buddy System and a
behavioral strategy for eliminating sexually abusive
behavior. A book on how to start a Molesters Anonymous
group is available for $12.95. No known IL chapter.
*Services*: Mutual aid, educational program or material,
telephone support, written information. *Write*: 8485
Tamarind Ave, Ste D, Fontana, CA 92335
*Call*: 909/355-1100

## Sexual Abuse-Spouses of Offenders

**Spouses/Partners of Survivors of Incest Ravenswood
CMHC** *Area Served: Cook County*  Group members gain
support through sharing experiences, feelings and ways to
cope. Leaders are peers trained to facilitate format that
provides safety and support for group members. *Meetings*:
Six week introductory as well as on-going group,
restricted to persons sharing the concern. *Services*: Mutual
aid. *Write*: 2312 W. Irving Park Rd, Chicago, IL 60618
*Call*: 773/463-7000 1455

**Spouses of Sex Offenders LaSalle County Youth
Service Bureau, Inc** *Area Served: LaSalle, Bureau and
Marshall Counties*  Mutual Aid Support group for spouses
of sex offenders. *Services*: Mutual aid. *Write*: 827
Columbus St, Ottawa, IL 61350 *Call*: 815/433-3953

## Sexual Abuse-Survivor

**Christians United Against Child Sexual Abuse**
*Area Served: DuPage and Cook Counties.*  For adult

survivors of childhood sexual abuse. to educate and support survivors of sexual abuse as well as their support persons and the community. *Meetings*: Monthly. *Services*: Mutual aid, educational program or material, written information, advocacy, referral to other services, professional service, speakers bureau, telephone support, social activities, newsletter. *Write*: C/O Phyl Froehle 722 East St, Lemont, IL 60439 *Call*: 630/257-8755

**Safe Place Naperville Church of The Brethren**
*Area Served: IL* For adult survivors of childhood sexual abuse to educate and support survivors of sexual abuse as well as their support persons and the community. *Meetings*: Monthly. *Services*: Mutual aid, educational program or material, written information, advocacy, referral to other services, professional service, speakers bureau, telephone support, social activities, newsletter. *Write*: 1020 W. Jefferson, Naperville, IL 60540 *Call*: 630/719-9427

**The Brady St 12-Step Family Group St. Paul Lutheran Church** *Area Served: Scott County* 12 Step-based program of recovery and support for adult survivors of sexual abuse. *Meetings*: Weekly. *Services*: Mutual aid, speakers bureau, written information, telephone support, referral to other services. *Write*: 2136 Brady St, Davenport, IA 52803 *Call*: 319/326-3547

**Women Incest Survivors Groups Ravenswood MHC**
*Area Served: IL* A continuing group of women dealing with the effects incest has had on their lives. *Meetings*: Weekly. *Services*: Mutual aid. *Write*: 2312 W. Irving Park Rd, Chicago, IL 60618 *Call*: 773/463-7000 1455 *Fax*: 312/463-8938

## Sexual Abuse-Youth

**Juvenile Sex Offenders Program LaSalle County Youth Service Bureau, Inc** Support group, facilitated by professionals, for sex offenders under the age of 18. *Services*: Mutual aid. *Write*: 827 Columbus St, Ottawa, IL 61350 *Call*: 815/433-3953

# Sexual Assault

**Chimera, Inc, Self-Defense for Women Chimera Education Foundation** *Area Served: National* *Write*: 59 E Van Buren St #714, Chicago, IL 60605 *Call*: 312/939-5341

**DuPage County Women Against Rape YWCA/DuPage**
*Area Served: DuPage County* An org. of women dedicated to lessening the trauma of rape and sexual assault for its survivors and their families; to aiding in the transition from victim to survivor and educating the public on the issues of rape. DWAR is the volunteer arm of the YWCA-DuPage. *Meetings*: Monthly. *Services*: Mutual

aid, educational program or material, advocacy, telephone support, written information. *Write*: 739 Roosevelt, #8-210, Glen Ellyn, IL 60137 *Call*: 630/790-6600

**Growing Strong Sexual Abuse Assault Support Group**
*Area Served: Macon and Piatt Counties* *Write*: 151 E Decatur, Decatur, IL 62521 *Call*: 217/428-0770

**IL Coalition Against Sexual Assault** *Area Served: IL* Administrative headquarters for the thirty sexual assault survivor care centers in IL. Advocates for survivors and promotes legislation related to sexual assault. *Services*: written information, professional service, referral to other services, educational program or material, newsletter. *Write*: 123 S 7th St Ste 500, Springfield, IL 62701 *Call*: 217/753-4117

**IL Coalition Against Sexual Assault Growing Strong**
*Area Served: Moultrie, Piatt and DeWitt Counties* *Write*: Sexual Assault Center 151 E Decatur, Decatur, IL 62521 *Call*: 217/428-0770

**IL Coalition Against Sexual Assault Lake** *County* **Council Against Sexual Assault** *Area Served: Lake and McHenry Counties* *Write*: 1 Greenleaf, Ste E, Gurnee, IL 60031 *Call*: 847/872-7799 *Fax*: 708/244-6380

**IL Coalition Against Sexual Assault Sexual Assault Victim's Care Unit** *Area Served: St. Clair County* *Write*: 9400 Lebanon Rd, East St Louis, IL 62201 *Call*: 618/397-0975

**IL Coalition Against Sexual Assault Rape Victim Service Program** *Area Served: IL-NE Write*: 5710 N Broadway, Chicago, IL 60660 *Call*: 773/334-8608 *Fax*: 312/728-6517

**IL Coalition Against Sexual Assault Mutual Ground, Inc** *Area Served: Kane and Kendall Counties* Offers 24-hour crisis intervention at hospitals, police stations, individual and group counseling for victims of rape or incest and their families and friends, information about medical examination and legal procedures, referral to social service agencies, children's therapy program. for residents of Kane and Kendall counties only. *Services*: Mutual aid, educational program or material, advocacy, telephone support, newsletter, written information. *Write*: PO Box 843, Aurora, IL 60507 *Call*: 630/897-8383

**IL Coalition Against Sexual Assault YWCA Sexual Assault Program** *Area Served: Whiteside and Lee Counties* *Write*: 412 First Ave, Sterling, IL 61081 *Call*: 815/625-0333

**IL Coalition Against Sexual Assault Volunteers of America** *Area Served: St. Clair County* *Write*: 4700 S State St Ste #2, East St Louis, IL 62205 *Call*: 618/271-9833

**IL Coalition Against Sexual Assault Sexual Assault and Family Emergency Corporation** *Area Served: Bond, Fayette and Marion Counties* SAFE provides support services for victims of sexual assault and abuse, including a support group for adult survivors of incest. *Meetings*: Weekly. *Services*: Mutual aid, telephone support, professional service, referral to other services, educational program or material, advocacy, hotline. *Write*: PO Box 192, Vandalia, IL 62471 *Call*: 618/283-1414

**IL Coalition Against Sexual Assault Sexual Assault Crisis Service** *Area Served: Vermilion County* *Write*: YWCA 201 N Hazel, Danville, IL 61832 *Call*: 217/443-5566

**IL Coalition Against Sexual Assault Quad City Rape-Sexual Assault Counseling Program** *Area Served: Rock Island County* *Write*: Family Resources, Inc 115 W 6TH ST, Davenport, IA 52803 *Call*: 309/797-1777

**IL Coalition Against Sexual Assault Community Mental Health Council Victim** *Services Area Served: Chicago-S Services*: advocacy, telephone support, speakers bureau, referral to other services, educational program or material, hotline. *Write*: 8704 S. Constance St, Chicago, IL 60617 *Call*: 773/734-4033 *Fax*: 312/734-5994

**IL Coalition Against Sexual Assault Rape Crisis Center of Midcentral IL** *Area Served: IL Write*: PO Box 995, Bloomington, IL 61702 *Call*: 309/827-4005

**IL Coalition Against Sexual Assault Rape Action Committee of The Women's Center** *Area Served: Jackson, Williamson and Franklin Counties Write*: 406 W Mill, Carbondale, IL 62901 *Call*: 618/529-2324

**IL Coalition Against Sexual Assault Quanada-Sapis** *Area Served: Adams, Schuyler and Piett Counties* These groups have similar goals: to provide confidential crisis intervention, counseling, and support services for victims and their families to assist them in understanding and coping with the physical, medical, emotional and legal problems associated with crime. Mostly staffed by trained volunteers and some professionals. Some offer weekly professionally-led support groups for adult survivors of sexual abuse or incest. *Services*: Mutual aid, educational program or material, professional service. *Write*: 510 Maine St, Quincy, IL 62301 *Call*: 217/222-3069

**New Directions** *Area Served: Whiteside County Write*: First Presbyterian Church 410 2nd Ave, Sterling, IL 61081 *Call*: 309/659-7122

**Northwest Action Against Rape** *Area Served: Cook County* to assist sexual assault victims and their families and friends. to provide community education, counseling and advocacy. Separate groups for adult and adolescent sexual assault victims: adult groups run for 12 weeks (twice yearly); adolescent groups run for 8 weeks (one to two times yearly). Half-day workshops for significant others offered quarterly. *Services*: Mutual aid, educational program or material, professional service, speakers bureau, written information, hotline, advocacy, referral to other services.. *Write*: 415 W Golf Rd, Arlington Heights, IL 60005 *Call*: 847/806-6526 *Fax*: 847/806-6526

**Rape and Sexual Abuse Care Center SIU** *Area Served: Madison, Jersey and Macoupin Counties Write*: Box 1154, Edwardsville, IL 62026 *Call*: 618/692-2197

**Rape Crisis Services A Women's Fund, Inc** *Area Served: Champaign, Douglas and Piatt Counties Write*: 1304 E MainSt, Urbana, IL 61801 *Call*: 217/384-4444 *Fax* 217/384-4462

**Rape Crisis Services Victims of Incest Can Emerge Survivors** *Area Served: National Write*: 505 W Green St, Urbana, IL 61801 *Call*: 217/384-4462

**Rape-Sexual Assault Counseling Program Family Resources, Inc** *Area Served: Rock Island, Scott (Iowa) and Henry Counties Write*: 115 W 6th St, Davenport, IA 52803 *Call*: 309/797-1777

**Rape Victim Advocates** *Area Served: Chicago* Helps rape victims by providing counseling, support and pertinent information in Hospital emergency rooms as well as maintaining contact with victims through the post-rape period of adjustment. Servicing hospitals in Chicago, volunteers are on *Call* 24 hours a day, 365 days a year. Offers support to both female and male victims. *Services*: speakers bureau, telephone support, referral to other services, educational program or material, advocacy, newsletter. *Write*: 222 S. Morgan, Ste 2C, Chicago, IL 60607 *Call*: 312/733-6954

**Rape Victim Counselor Program Mt. Sinai Hospital** *Area Served: Chicago* Designed to help the rape victim from the moment she enters the emergency room at Mt. Sinai Hospital. Employees of the Hospital go through 16 hours of training to provide one to one support to these women, with two follow-up *Calls* made after release from the Hospital. referrals to counseling programs for future ongoing support. *Services*: (advocacy, telephone support, written information. *Write*: California At 15th, Chicago, IL 60608 *Call*: 773/650-6912

**Rockford Sexual Assault Counseling, Inc** *Area Served: Winnebago, Boon and Ogle Counties* Provides counseling and support services for teen and adult victims and families of sexual assault and abuse to assist them in understanding and coping with physical, medical, emotional and legal problems associated with the crime. Prevention and education programs as well as survivor's group available. *Services*: Mutual aid, speakers bureau, written information, telephone support, professional service, educational program or material, advocacy, hotline, referral to other services.. *Write*: 202 W. State St, Ste 302, Rockford, IL 61101 *Call*: 815/964-2995

**Sexual Assault-Abuse Service Ben Gordon Center**
*Area Served: DeKalb County* *Write*: 12 Health *Services* Dr, DeKalb, IL 60115 *Call*: 815/756-4875

**Sexual Assault Support Group Growing Strong Sexual Assault Center** *Area Served: Macon County* *Write*: 151 E Decatur, Decatur, IL 62521 *Call*: 217/428-0770

**Sexual Assault Survivors Support Group Community Crisis Center, Inc** *Area Served: Kane, Cook and McHenry Counties* Support group for survivors of non-familial sexual assault. Provides support throughthe process of healing after the trauma of sexual assault. *Services*: Mutual aid. *Write*: PO Box 1390, Elgin, IL 60121 *Call*: 847/697-2380

**Support for Victims of Sexual Assault Southwest Women Working Together** *Area Served: Chicago-C* Help victims to deal with feelings such as guilt, anger, fear or shame. Opportunity to share feelings with others who have had this experience. *Meetings*: Weekly for twenty weeks. *Services*: Mutual aid, educational program or material, referral to other services, professional service. *Write*: 4051 W. 63rd St, Chicago, IL 60629 *Call*: 773/528-0550

**Support Group for Sexual Assault Survivors YWCA of Metropolitan Chicago** *Area Served: Cook County-S* Assists and support victims of sexual assault and incest. Groups meet on a weekly basis. Groups limited to per-screened participants. A 24-hour crisis line is available. Ten free sessions then sliding scale cost. *Services*: telephone support. *Write*: South Suburban District 4343 W. Lincoln Highway, Matteson, IL 60443 *Call*: 708/748-6600

**Support Groups for Victims of Rape Ravenswood CMHC** *Area Served: IL* Group members gain support through sharing experiences, feelings, and ways to cope. Leaders are peer trained to facilitate a format that provides safety and support for group members. *Meetings*: Six week groups but restricted to persons sharingthe concern. *Services*: Mutual aid. *Write*: 2312 W Irving Park Rd, Chicago, IL 60618 *Call*: 773/463-7000 1455

**Survivors Network of Those Abused By Priests SNAP** *Area Served: IL* *Write*: 8025 S Honore, Chicago, IL 60620 *Call*: 773/483-1059

**The Rape and Sexual Abuse Care Center Southern IL University** *Area Served: IL* *Write*: Campus Box 1154, Edwardsville, IL 62025 *Call*: 618/692-2197

**Women Survivors of Sexual Abuse (WSSA)** *Area Served: Cook County* *Write*: First Presbyterian Church 1427 Chicago Ave, Evanston, IL 60201 *Call*: 847/864-1472

**Women's Services - Rape Program Loop YWCA** *Area Served: Chicago* Support groups for women who have been sexually assaulted to come together to share issues important to each member, such as: trust, intimacy and sexuality issues; support networks; dealing with friends and family;life style disruption; feelings of anger and fear. Pre-screening required for groups. *Meetings*: Weekly. *Services*: Mutual aid, educational program or material, advocacy, telephone support, written information. *Write*: 180 N. Wabash, Chicago, IL 60601 *Call*: 312/372-4105

# Index of Illinois Self-Help Groups

## A

# C

# N

---

# O

# P

# U

# V

# Self-Help at Wright College
# Center for Lifelong Learning

3400 North Austin Avenue
Chicago, Illinois 60634
Phone: 773/481-8800
www.ccc.edu/wright/home.htm

The administration at Wright College has created a caring environment that connects people to resources. Because self-help and learning are so closely linked, the College's Center for Lifelong Learning at Wright College supports the Illinois Self-Help Coalition as a community outreach. The College also incorporates self-help into part of its continuing education programs.

Other Wright College outreach and continuing education programs may be of interest to *Insiders' Guide* readers:

WRIGHT MAINTAINS A CAREER CENTER where testing and counseling are provided. Most career training programs include modules to help students brush up on essential writing and math skills and business communications. Students are also taught how to balance personal and work goals.

THE CENTER FOR LIFELONG LEARNING offers career training in the fields of allied health, business, computers, and human services. When students complete career programs—which can last a few weeks or months—they receive certificates signifying that they are prepared for specific employment.

CAREER TRAINING provides training for people who need to learn new job skills because the increase in technology in the workplace has rendered their current skills obsolete. This includes people seeking career advancement, those entering the work force for the first time, and those returning to work after a long absence.

THE ADULT LEARNING SKILLS PROGRAMS offers educational experiences to suit the needs of adult learners, especially those who have not completed their formal education.